Use

p 145
154
158 mimicry not enough
for empathy

191 "Everyday aes.
206 lang. trying to keep
up w conscious exp.

207 percept. & emo.
outstrip outstrip capacity
of lang. to render them.

209 what can't be
described, can be
pointed at

210 Cleanth Brooks
material work of art.
itself

Film, Art, and the Third Culture

Film, Art, and the Third Culture

A Naturalized Aesthetics of Film

Murray Smith

OXFORD

UNIVERSITY PRESS

OXFORD
UNIVERSITY PRESS

Great Clarendon Street, Oxford, OX2 6DP,
United Kingdom

Oxford University Press is a department of the University of Oxford.
It furthers the University's objective of excellence in research, scholarship,
and education by publishing worldwide. Oxford is a registered trade mark of
Oxford University Press in the UK and in certain other countries

First Edition published in 2017
Impression: 1

Published in the United States of America by Oxford University Press
198 Madison Avenue, New York, NY 10016, United States of America

British Library Cataloguing in Publication Data
Data available

Library of Congress Control Number: 2016954539

ISBN 978-0-19-879064-8

Printed in Great Britain by
Clays Ltd, St Ives plc

For Miri, finally

Contents

Part I. Building the Third Culture

Part II. Science and Sentiment

Acknowledgements

In November 2015, the Royal Institute of Philosophy Annual Debate pitched James Ladyman and Raymond Tallis against one another in relation to the motion, 'Human Nature is Better Understood through Science than through Philosophical and Artistic Reflection'; two years earlier, Steven Pinker and Leon Wieseltier had exchanged fire in the pages of *The New Republic* over Pinker's defence of scientific approaches to cultural phenomena, in his essay 'Science is Not your Enemy'. These are but two of the recent episodes in the long-standing drama initiated (in recent times, at least) by C. P. Snow's essay 'The Two Cultures', which appeared in its first version in October 1956, triggering a debate that has since then been staged and restaged in print, in public debate, and in the classroom on myriad occasions. Across the sixty-year span between the publication of Snow's essay and the drafting of these acknowledgements, Snow's argument has been praised, celebrated, scorned, debunked, deconstructed, rebuffed, and rehabilitated; the issue that Snow raised—the nature, history, and future of the relationship between the sciences, and the arts and humanities—has drifted in and out of fashion. But Snow's intervention has never been left alone for long, and that is in large part because the question he addressed is one that has been with us for centuries (as the epigraph from Spinoza demonstrates) and remains a vexed matter. *Film, Art, and the Third Culture* is an attempt to demonstrate how and why the debate persists—if not always under the banner of the 'two cultures'—in relation to the arts and culture in general, and film in particular.

The book has been a long time in the making, so inevitably there are many individuals, groups, and institutions that I need to thank; and it gives me great pleasure to do so. The University of Kent has been my base of operations now for almost a quarter-century. The School of Art's commitment to regular research leave has been indispensable, while a Leverhulme Research Fellowship in 2005–6 enabled me to begin work on what eventually took shape as *Film, Art, and the Third Culture*. I thank the Leverhulme Trust for supporting the kind of exploratory, risk-laden research that tends not to fare well with the more conservative decision-making dynamics of other funding bodies. On a personal level, I thank my colleagues at Kent for the congenial atmosphere in which we pursue the core business of teaching and research in the face of the vicissitudes of higher education in the UK, and the endless stream of new—good, bad, and ugly—institutional imperatives. In particular, I thank my colleagues in Film, past and present—Clio Barnard, Lavinia Brydon, Jinhee Choi, Maurizio Cinquegrani, Elizabeth Cowie, Mattias Frey, Katie Grant, Frances Guerin, Lawrence Jackson, Tamar Jeffers-McDonald, Andrew Klevan, Virginia Pitts, Cecilia Sayad, Peter Stanfield, Sarah Turner, Aylish Wood—for maintaining the space and diversity in which I can exercise my philosophical and psychological interests; and I thank my colleagues in other parts of the School of Arts, including Paul Allain, Helen Brooks, Martin Hammer, Nickie Shaughnessy, and Robert Shaughnessy, for encouraging those interests. Gillian Lodge deserves special mention for superlative, sanity-saving REF support. Elsewhere at Kent, the Philosophy Reading Group, run by Sean Sayers for more than fifteen years now and engaging with a wide range of philosophers—though Kant and Hegel are never far from sight—has been a source of insight and inspiration, as have Jon Williamson's 'reasoning and evidence' reading groups with their emphasis on the philosophy of science. Over the years, Sean, Jon, Simon Kirchin, David Corfield, Julia Tanney, Alan Thomas, Edward Harcourt, Richard Norman, Tony Skillen, the late Laurence Goldstein, the late Frank Cioffi, Edward Greenwood, David Ellis, Graeme Forbes, Ruth Hibbert, Matt Wittingham, Veli-Pekka Parkkinen, and Michael Wilde have all contributed to my philosophical education.

My co-conspirators in the Aesthetics Research Centre (ARC)—Margrethe Bruun Vaage, Ben Curry, Jonathan Friday, Hans Maes, Michael Newall—however, deserve a special shout-out for their collaboration and company. (Time for a trip to *The Sportsman*?) Now more than a decade old, ARC has created a unique space in which philosophical aesthetics and the study of the individual arts may join debate in a genuinely interdisciplinary manner. That debate has been sustained in part by my doctoral supervisees over this period: Dan Barratt, Gary Bettinson, Angelo Cioffi, Sérgio Dias Branco, Mick Grierson, Neil McCartney, Ted Nannicelli, Ivan Nunes, Alaina Schempp, Sabina Sitoianu, Paul Taberham, Aaron Taylor, Matt Thorpe, and Dominic Topp. Along with my undergraduate and MA students, they have delighted, instructed, and occasionally tortured me as I sought to wrestle the book into shape.

Friends and colleagues beyond Kent have been no less important to the gestation and maturation of the project. Paisley Livingston and Carl Plantinga read the manuscript in its entirety on behalf of Oxford; special thanks to them for their patient, detailed, and thoughtful feedback, which certainly has made the book much better and saved me from many embarrassments. Sherri Irvin and Elisabeth Schellekens provided insightful comments on the manuscript in the context of a panel readdressing the question first posed by George Dickie, 'Is psychology relevant to aesthetics?'; I would certainly have acted on these comments had time in the production process allowed. These generous folk cannot, of course, be blamed for the many other failings that doubtless remain. Patrick Hughes and John Smith graciously permitted me to draw on their work. At Oxford, Peter Momtchiloff waited patiently for the manuscript to reach maturity, and has offered expert guidance throughout the process (as well as some amazing music). I thank Peter and the team at Oxford—Matthias Butler, Clement Raj, Jane Robson, Susan Smyth, Carrie Hickman, and Rio Ruskin-Tompkins—for their support, enthusiasm, and attention to detail. Emre Caglayan helped dig me out of the pit of bibliographic despair, and Ryan Doran spared me the hardship of producing the index for the book. I thank them both for their diligent and exacting work.

Further afield, the Society for Cognitive Studies of the Moving Image has been fundamental to the consolidation of 'cognitive film theory', and more generally to supporting a philosophically sophisticated, naturalistic approach to film. Founded in 1995 by Joe and Barbara Anderson, SCSMI is now approaching the twentieth anniversary of its first formal gathering, which took in Lawrence, Kansas, in 1997. The atmosphere of friendly but rigorous criticism within SCSMI has been essential to the development of this work, and I thank my many friends in the organization for their feedback over the years, in particular Todd Berliner, James Cutting, Dirk Eitzen, Jens Eder, Kathrin Fahlenbrach, András Kovács, Birger Langkaer, Steve Prince, Johannes Riis, Sheena Rogers, Jeff Smith, Tim Smith, Ed Tan, and Pia Tikka. Behind SCSMI stands the Film department at the University of Wisconsin-Madison, home to the Andersons in the 1970s, my home from 1985 to 1991, and a place that exercised a decisive and enduring influence on my approach to film, to art, and research in general. One channel through which I continue to feel the force of the 'Wisconsin Project' is through the Filmies email list, which keeps me in touch with members of that community across the generations. Commander-in-Chief David Bordwell continues to set the standard for the rest of us: I thank David for his support, leadership, and inspiration.

Right alongside SCSMI stand the British Society of Aesthetics and the American Society for Aesthetics, communities in which I have learned much and made many friendships; here I must mention Catharine Abell, Paloma Atencia-Linares, Caroline Auty, Tom Baker, Noël Carroll, Diarmuid Costello, Greg Currie, David Davies, Simon Fokt, Cynthia Freeland, Stacie Friend, Berys Gaut, Andy Hamilton, Mathew Kieran, Sam Liao, Jerry Levinson, Dom Lopes, Aaron Meskin, James McGuigan, Shelby Moser, Bence Nanay, Jenefer Robinson, Nola Semczyszyn, Kate Thomson-Jones, Ken Walton, Tom Wartenberg, and Dawn Wilson. My thanks to Noll Brinck-mann for her support and for translating several pieces by me; and to Torben Grodal in Copenhagen, Vinzenz Hediger and Martin Seel in Frankfurt, Héctor Pérez and Fernando Canet in Valencia, Julian Hanich in Groningen, Michael Smith in Princeton, and Ophelia Deroy, Vittorio Gallese, and Barry Smith at the Institute of Philosophy in London for their support and (in some cases multiple) generous invitations.

Last but certainly not least, I thank the awkward squad of friends who escape or transcend the various groups mentioned above: Richard Allen, Sam Bailey, Steffen Borge, Howard Bowman, Abi Cooper, James Dean, Eric Edgar, Anna Edgar-Chan, Cecily Fahey, Doug Farland, David Herd, Charlie Keil, Ron Radano, Laurence Skillern, Richard Tacey, Greg Taylor, and Malcolm Turvey. Thanks to my sister Fiona, my brother Nigel, and my sister-in-law Noriko Manabe for their support, and diverting visits in Nottingham and Princeton. Vivian Song, Ricardo Pou, and my nieces Claudia, Ceci, and Josie have been unfailingly generous hosts during summer stints in Katonah. My parents, Jan and Richard, have been a rock of support throughout. Above all, I thank my wife Miri Song—to whom I dedicate this book—and our sons Charlie and Theo, for inspiring me, and for putting up with me.

I have drawn on a number of previously published essays in composing this work, though in every case these earlier pieces have been substantially revised, and the act of fusing them into a cohesive whole has, I hope, transformed and enriched each individual part. I thank the editors of the following publications for their feedback on them, and the publishers for permission to use material from them: 'Triangulating Aesthetic Experience', in Arthur P. Shimamura and Stephen E. Palmer (eds), *Aesthetic Science: Connecting Minds, Brains, and Experience* (New York: Oxford University Press, 2012); 'The Pit of Naturalism: Neuroscience and the Naturalized Aesthetics of Film', in Ted Nannicelli and Paul Taberham (eds), *Cognitive Media Theory* (New York: Routledge, 2013); 'Consciousness', in Paisley Livingston and Carl Plantinga (eds), *The Routledge Companion to Philosophy and Film* (New York: Routledge, 2010); 'Wer hat Angst vor Charles Darwin? Die Filmkunst im Zeitalter der Evolution', in Matthias Brütsch et al. (eds), *Emotionalität und Film* (Marburg: Schüren, 2005); 'What Difference does it Make? Science, Sentiment, and Film', *Projections*, 2/1 (2008); 'Empathy, Expansionism, and the Extended Mind', in Amy Coplan and Peter Goldie (eds), *Empathy: Philosophical and Psychological Perspectives* (Oxford: Oxford University Press, 2011); and 'Feeling Prufish', *Midwest Studies in Philosophy*, 34 (2010).

Thanks are also due to the publishers who have provided permission to use the various epigraph quotes that appear in the volume:

Introduction: C. P. Snow, 'The Two Cultures: A Second Look' (1963), in *The Two Cultures* (Cambridge: Cambridge University Press, 1998), 70–1.

Chapter 1: Wilfrid Sellars, 'Philosophy and the Scientific Image of Man', in Robert Colodny (ed.), *Frontiers of Science and Philosophy*, (Pittsburgh, PA: University of Pittsburgh Press, 1962), 37. Kendall Walton, 'Aesthetics: What? Why? And Wherefore?', *Journal of Aesthetics and Art Criticism*, 65/2 (Spring 2007): 150.

Chapter 2: Charles Darwin, *Charles Darwin's Notebooks, 1836–1844: Geology, Transmutation of Species, Metaphysical Enquiries*, ed. Paul H. Barrett, Peter J. Gautrey, Sandra Herbert, David Kohn, and Sydney Smith (Cambridge: Cambridge University Press, 1987), Notebook N, p. 564. Isaac Newton, quoted in Gary Marcus, *Kluge: The Haphazard Construction of the Human Mind* (London: Faber, 2008), 144.

Chapter 3: Jerry Fodor, 'Diary', *London Review of Books*, 21/19 (30 Sept. 1999), 69, <http://www.lrb.co.uk/v21/n19/jerry-fodor/diary>. David Freedberg and Vittorio Gallese, 'Motion, Emotion and Empathy in Esthetic Experience', *Trends in Cognitive Sciences*, 11/5 (2007): 197.

Chapter 4: René Descartes, 'Second Meditation', in *Discourse on Method and the Meditations*, translated and introduced by F. E. Sutcliffe (Harmondsworth: Penguin, 1968), 103.

Chapter 4 and the Conclusion: William James, *The Principles of Psychology*, i (New York: Dover Publications, 1950), 239, 449.

Chapter 5: Charles Darwin, *The Expression of the Emotions in Man and Animals*, 3rd edn (London: HarperCollins, 1998), 234. Ingmar Bergman, quoted in William Wolf, 'Face to Face with Ingmar Bergman', *New York Magazine* 13/42 (27 Oct. 1980), 38.

Chapter 6: Stephen Jay Gould, 'Biological Potentiality vs. Biological Determinism', in *Ever since Darwin: Reflections in Natural History* (Harmondsworth: Pelican, 1980), 251. Richard Dawkins, *The Selfish Gene* (Oxford: Oxford University Press, 1976), 215.

Chapter 7: Nick Hornby, *Fever Pitch: A Fan's Life* (London: Victor Gollancz, 1992), 11–12. Billy Cox (Jimi Hendrix's main bass player following the break-up of the Jimi Hendrix Experience) is quoted in Tom Wheeler, *The Stratocaster Chronicles* (Milwaukee: Hal Leonard, 2004), 137.

Chapter 8: Michael Baxandall, *Patterns of Intention: On the Historical Explanation of Pictures* (New Haven: Yale University Press, 1985), 12. Ronald de Sousa, *The Rationality of Emotion* (Cambridge, MA: MIT Press, 1987), 184.

Canterbury, July 2016

List of Figures

Most writers on the emotions and on human conduct seem to be treating rather of matters outside nature than of natural phenomena following nature's general laws. They appear to conceive man to be situated in nature as a kingdom within a kingdom: for they believe that he disturbs rather than follows nature's order, that he has absolute control over his actions, and that he is determined solely by himself. However, my argument is this. Nothing comes to pass in nature, which can be set down to a flaw therein; for nature is always the same, and everywhere one and the same in her efficacy and power of action; that is, nature's laws and ordinances, whereby all things come to pass and change from one form to another, are everywhere and always the same; so that there should be one and the same method of understanding the nature of all things whatsoever, namely, through nature's universal laws and rules.

Baruch Spinoza, *Ethics*, part 3, 'On the Origin and Nature of the Emotions' (1677)

Introduction

It is probably too early to speak of a third culture already in existence. But I am now convinced that this is coming.

C. P. Snow

Sixty years ago, in 1956, C. P. Snow first advanced in public his ideas concerning the 'two cultures'—the schism that he perceived between scientists and advocates of 'traditional culture'—in an essay published in *The New Statesman*.[1] Snow's intervention, delivered as the Rede Lecture in Cambridge in 1959, and further amplified in a revised and extended version published in 1963, became the focus of an often heated debate that continued through the 1960s, and—as I will argue—continues to resonate today. Indeed few debates over the past half-century have been quite as vituperative or as enduring: although discussion of the two cultures ceded the headlines to other intellectual controversies in the 1970s, the underlying issues have never gone away, and the debate repeatedly resurfaces, whether in reflections on the original exchanges or in the guise of new but closely related controversies (consider the 'Science Wars' of the 1990s, or the arguments today over the legitimacy of evolutionary psychology and neuroscience). Notwithstanding the view expressed by many that Snow paints an oversimplified picture of the relationship between the arts and humanities and the sciences, his essay is routinely revisited.[2] At a minimum, Snow hit a raw nerve, and one that still pulsates.[3]

None of this should really surprise us, as the 'two cultures' debate was not really new in anything but name and local colour. The issues at stake were the focus of the German *Methodenstreit* debates of the late nineteenth century and early twentieth centuries, on the methodology of the natural and human sciences.[4] As Wilhelm Dilthey—one of the most significant contributors to these debates—recognized, the underlying dispute is one that can be traced back through Western philosophy, arising ultimately from the third of the 'antinomies' identified by Kant: humans are at once creatures inhabiting the world of causality (as revealed by the natural sciences), and rational agents able to understand, theorize, and manipulate the causal world (as investigated by philosophy and the human sciences).[5] So if the issues were so long-standing, what was all the fuss about?

Snow decried what he saw as a widening gulf between the 'culture' of scientists and that of 'literary intellectuals' (usually understood as code for the arts and humanities as a whole).[6] In a much-quoted passage he complained of an ignorance of and contempt for scientific knowledge among humanists:

A good many times I have been present at gatherings of people who, by the standards of the traditional culture, are thought highly educated and who have with considerable gusto been expressing their incredulity at the illiteracy of scientists. Once or twice I have been provoked and have asked the company how many of them could describe the Second Law of Thermodynamics. The response was cold: it was also negative. Yet I was asking something which is the scientific equivalent of: *Have you read a work of Shakespeare's?*[7]

Thus Snow identifies a kind of philistinism towards science, as both a living body of knowledge and method and a major part of our intellectual inheritance, through these asymmetrical expectations regarding what would later come to be called 'cultural literacy'.

In the revised and extended essay of 1963, Snow envisaged a 'third culture' in which the rift would be healed and a unified intellectual culture might flourish. Another parallel with German philosophical debate is striking here: one might compare Snow's ambition with the unified vision of science pursued by the philosophers of science associated (in different ways) with the Vienna Circle, including Otto Neurath, Carl Hempel, and F. A. Hayek.[8] There is something importantly right and valuable about this ambition: an academic system in which disciplines are not only highly specialized but 'siloed', occupying separate spheres with firm boundaries and little communication across them, is not an ideal intellectual culture. The contrasting project of integration is surely to be applauded. But such integration could mean many things and take many forms. We need to step back here and consider the various ways in which the relationship between the natural sciences and the arts and humanities might be conceived. How have the two cultures been positioned in relation to one another, philosophically speaking?

Broadly speaking, we can distinguish four different answers to this question. The first two answers are types of *naturalism*, where that term is used to pick out scientifically oriented approaches to investigating and understanding the world (a topic that I pursue in more detail in Chapter 1). The first of these two naturalistic positions is sometimes described as *replacement naturalism*. On this view, the human sciences are simply a sub-domain of science more generally; over time, the study of human behaviour will simply be subsumed by the methods of the natural sciences. The eliminativism of Paul and Patricia Churchland (who hold that our ordinary or 'folk' psychological theories are subject to 'elimination' by the findings of neuroscience), and the more aggressive varieties of sociobiology (where our ordinary understanding of the diversity of human motivation is apt to be reduced to the dispositions forged by natural and sexual selection), would count as examples of such replacement naturalism.[9] Also relevant here is the adoption of Snow's 'third culture' expression by John Brockman. While Snow's third culture is one in which humanists and scientists are 'on speaking terms', Brockman adopts the phrase to refer to, and advocate in favour of, a situation in which 'literary intellectuals' are by-passed by scientists who communicate 'directly with the general public'.[10]

Replacement naturalism's cousin, *cooperative naturalism*, has a very different temper.[11] Here the goal is a genuinely integrative one, where the knowledge and methods of the natural sciences come to *complement* rather than replace or eliminate those of the human sciences. Steven Pinker crisply articulates such a cooperative perspective in arguing that 'the promise of science is to enrich and diversify the intellectual tools of humanistic scholarship, not to obliterate them...there can be no replacement for the varieties of close reading, thick description, and deep immersion that erudite scholars can apply to individual works'. Pinker immediately follows this passage with a cooperative plea: 'But must these be the only paths to understanding?'[12]

Standing in contrast to these varieties of naturalism is *autonomism*, the view that the study of human behaviour must proceed by quite distinct methods from those fit for the physical and (non-human) animal world. Dilthey's (epic but still incomplete) *Introduction to the Human Sciences* is one of the most ambitious attempts to defend autonomism; F. R. Leavis's response to Snow, delivered as the Richmond Lecture at Downing College in 1962, is one of its most cantankerous manifestations.[13] The fourth and final position takes autononism as its groundplan, but freely avails itself of morsels of scientific insight in a highly selective and inconsistent manner, appropriating scientific findings to bolster arguments and interpretations which otherwise have no systematic relationship with scientific knowledge or methods. More or less rigorous autononism, along with such freewheeling *cherry-picking*, as I shall label it, between them represent the orthodoxy, the mode of operation for the majority of researchers working in the humanities. And while cherry-picking might seem to resemble, at first glance, cooperative naturalism, it is in fact a false friend, more interested in the magpie theft of isolated scientific discoveries for the purposes of decorating non- or anti-scientific speculations than in combining the methods and insights of the human and natural sciences. Such superficial and often disingenuous ventures are quarantined from rather than integrated with our scientific understanding of the world.

Towards a Naturalized Aesthetics of Film

This brief overview of the history and prehistory of the two cultures debate sets the scene for the current project. The ambition of *Film, Art, and the Third Culture* is to outline and put into practice a *naturalized aesthetics of film*—an approach that, while fully acknowledging the diversity of artistic forms and their cultural contexts, sees film art as a manifestation of a cluster of deeply entrenched, basic human capacities, and thus treats it as a phenomenon which is likely to be illuminated by various types of scientific as well as traditional humanistic research. In this way, the book offers an account of film art that embraces the goal of a third culture, conceived in terms of the nonreductive, cooperative naturalism just described. Such an approach integrates methods and knowledge drawn from across the humanities, the social and the natural sciences, and contrasts with work rooted in the world of the two cultures—work based on the assumption that the humanities and the sciences embody radically distinct and (for the most part) separate, even incommensurable, enterprises. The vast bulk of research into film and art has been, and today still is, conducted in the spirit of the two cultures, even where reference is made to scientific knowledge. In this work, my aim is to lay the groundwork for, and exemplify, a genuinely and systematically 'third cultural' approach to the study of film in particular, and art in general.

It is important to stress that the position I advocate is not one according to which the traditional methods and principles of the humanities—close critical analysis and evaluation, introspective reflection, qualitative research, conceptual analysis, historical narration—should be supplanted by a battery of scientific techniques, from statistical tables to brain scans, evolutionary trees, and genetic maps. The vision is rather one of an integrated research culture, in which the questions posed determine what methods are brought into play, without the traditional barriers between disciplines and the worlds of science, engineering, the arts, and the humanities intervening.

It is also important to underline that within this framework the influence between the human and natural sciences runs in both directions: just as questions once thought the exclusive property of the humanities may be illuminated by scientific methods, so may scientific insights be prefigured, sharpened, and more deeply understood—in terms of their relations with human interests and values—by examining them as cultural phenomena, that is, as objects of humanistic enquiry. How does this work? Sometimes the influence of the human on the natural sciences is felt in the recognition that some phenomena are unavoidably hybrid in nature. In the world of medical research, for example, we see the identification of 'culture-bound' syndromes, such as the condition of *latah* ('jumpiness') touched on in Chapter 3, which appears to be a distinctive cultural elaboration of the universal physiological startle response.[14] In a more general sense, when scientific methods are brought to bear on cultural and artistic phenomena, scholars in the humanities are typically best placed to identify the problems that need addressing, pose the questions to be explored, and clarify the concepts through which the questions are articulated and on the basis of which empirical investigation should proceed.[15] In his study of expression, Mitchell Green argues that humanists interested in

emotion, communication, human nature, or even the arts, ignore at their peril developments in such fields as evolutionary biology, experimental psychology, and even neuroscience. At the same time, such developments don't by themselves answer the humanist's questions. Rather, we need a framework in which we can pursue clear and precise inquiry about how, for instance, the evolution of a trait makes a difference for its communicative function; about how the *mirror*

behaviour of this or that cluster of neurons should be thought relevant to my ability to 'feel' someone else's pain; about how the sensory organs known as ampullae of Lorenzini found in sharks could pertain to the nature of consciousness as it is studied by philosophers.[16]

Researchers from the human sciences in this way possess expertise that is essential to the interdisciplinary ethos of the third culture. Green also notes the way in which, historically, philosophers have often identified and theorized phenomena that are as a result made conceptually visible and tractable for empirical researchers. Green himself mentions Paul Grice's foundational work on pragmatics ('concocted apparently in his armchair'); psychologist Michael Tomasello also credits Grice with the discovery of 'the fundamentally cooperative structure of human communication'. Neuroscientist Vittorio Gallese acknowledges Maurice Merleau-Ponty's ideas concerning the embodied nature of perception as the basis of his own theory of 'embodied simulation' (and has pursued substantial collaborations with philosophers, as well as art historians and film scholars); Richard Wollheim, who engaged in a sustained fashion with empirical researchers in the traditions of both psychoanalysis and perceptual psychology, also deserves recognition for his prescient ideas regarding 'the embodied eye'.[17] Through such contributions humanists play a critical role in the early stages of research. They play an equally important role in the concluding phases of research, helping to interpret empirical findings and data. Moreover, it is within the humanities that the work of evaluation—moral, political, aesthetic—is and must be undertaken; for science must bracket questions pertaining to these types of value in order to function as science.

value

Scientific ideas and technologies may also feed back into the cultural sphere as materials, tools, and themes for artistic projects and practices. From the delights of Heston Blumenthal's 'molecular gastronomy', to the digital sampling and sequencing pervasive in contemporary music, to the very technology of cinema, the arts routinely adapt scientific discoveries and technological innovations to aesthetic ends. In all these ways, phenomena that begin in the lab end up passing through the looking glass of the arts.

Art, Aesthetics, and Film

The subtitle of this study describes it as a naturalized aesthetics of film. Some might object that it would be more aptly described as a naturalized philosophy of the art of the moving image. That's quite a mouthful, and one good reason to go with the more economical title. But there are other, non-aesthetic, reasons for sticking with the subtitle as it is, which are worth reviewing here. What rides on referring to 'aesthetics' rather than the 'philosophy of art'? And of speaking of 'film' in place of 'the moving image'?

Aesthetics is commonly used as a general term for that domain of philosophy dealing with (our experience of) beauty, the sublime, and related phenomena in the natural world and in the arts. That apparently innocuous formulation passes over a mass of controversies, beginning with the question of whether it is right to bind the study of beauty in nature so closely with the study of the arts. Aesthetics is riven by internal debates and disagreements about how the discipline should be conceived, labelled, and subdivided, and where its boundaries lie. Although I occasionally allude to these debates, I make no claim to address them systematically in this work. Rather I assume the loose, flexible, and widely adopted characterization I give above as a backdrop, while gradually fleshing out a naturalistic conception of art, taking film as my primary example, thereby offering one perspective on the relationship between aesthetic experience, art, and nature.

Many philosophers insist on distinguishing 'aesthetics' from the 'philosophy of art', broadly for two reasons. First, not all aesthetic experiences are driven by works of art; natural phenomena, and a wide array of everyday objects and events, may prompt and serve as objects of aesthetic appreciation. Relatedly, we often appraise the aesthetic dimension of objects and artefacts whose principal function is non-aesthetic, just as I appraised the subtitle of this book a few lines above. And second, not all works of art are dominated by aesthetic characteristics or pursue an aesthetic agenda, so to speak; sometimes cognitive or moral properties play a more important role, and some artworks and movements are avowedly 'anti-aesthetic'. Marcel Duch-amp's *Fountain* (1917) is arguably one such work. According to Arthur Danto we misconceive Duchamp's readymade if we think of it as a statement about the unrecognized elegance of the urinal; Duchamp himself said of the work, 'The danger to be avoided lies in aesthetic delectation.'[18] For theorists such as Danto and Noël Carroll, the close identification of art with the aesthetic in Kant's *Critique of Judgement* deflects us from appreciating the much more variable relationship between the two phenomena.[19] Aesthetics is thus neither identical with art nor subsumed by art, but neither does it subsume art; aesthetics and art are rather best regarded as overlapping categories.

Advocates of the 'aesthetic theory of art', however, answer these points with another pair of observations: in most artistic traditions, the aesthetic dimensions of artworks play a central role; and when we look for sustained, complex, and enduring aesthetic experiences, we typically look in the direction of artworks. This point may have particular force in the case of film. Although the art of film came into being on the back of modern industrial technology, and continues to develop through its relationship with subsequent technological inventions (synchronous sound, 3D, and digital cinematography, for example), most traditions of filmmaking seek to engage us aesthetically: through the moving, horrific, suspenseful, surprising, or funny stories that they tell, realized through visually compelling camerawork and aurally striking sound design. The particular aesthetic character of films varies enormously of course, from the flamboyant to the subtle, minimal to maximal, classical to modernist, and so on. But at least within the traditions of narrative filmmaking very few films disdain aesthetic demands. There is a historical irony here then: for all its entanglement with modern technology, from the standpoint of contemporary

avant-garde practice and cutting edge theory, the centrality of aesthetic values in
most filmmaking may make film a decidedly 'backward-looking' art form. There are
significant conceptual and 'anti-aesthetic' films and filmmakers—Duchamp himself
made one such film, *Anémic Cinéma,* in 1926—but while these trends became central
to the institutions of the art world over the course of the twentieth century, they
remain marginal in the world of film.

I should stress that my primary goal is to articulate and defend some principles
and strategies underlying a naturalized aesthetics of film, many of which carry over to
other art forms and the aesthetic domain more generally. But I do not pretend to
furnish an exhaustive, naturalistic theory of art and the aesthetic here, if such a
thing is achievable. While I sign up to the adage attributed to D'Arcy Wentworth
Thompson to the effect that 'everything is the way it is because it got that way'—that
there is a (true) story to be told regarding the emergence of aesthetics and art—it is
not part of my ambition to offer an evolutionary history or theory of these domains
as a whole. The more modest challenge of outlining a naturalized aesthetics of film is
big enough. For the most part I attempt to meet this challenge in 'piecemeal' fashion,
that is, by tackling specific problems or aspects of film aesthetics while drawing on a
naturalistic methodology. There are, though, three recurrent and related motifs that
give overall shape to the position I outline here. The first of these motifs is my
attention to aesthetic *experience.* If most works of (film) art are characterized by
aesthetic properties, what sort of experience do they give rise to? And do such
experiences have a special character that marks them off from regular experiences?
The second and third motifs provide the beginnings of an answer to these questions.
The second motif is the idea that aesthetic experience is distinguished from ordinary
experience by a particular kind of self-consciousness; a fully fledged aesthetic experience, I say, is one that we *savour* rather than simply have. We reflect on aesthetic
experiences as we have them, and in retrospect; and such reflection is not merely a
contingent feature of aesthetic experiences, but a core aspect of them.[20] The third
motif is the claim that many aesthetic experiences involve an *expansion* of ordinary
experience—they arise, that is, from the pushing or pulling of ordinary perception
and cognition out of their comfort zones and customary functioning. Putting the
second and third motifs together, we have the proposal that aesthetic experience
arises when our perceptual, affective, and cognitive capacities are engaged in a way
that goes beyond their normal functioning, and that such engagement prompts us to
savour and reflect upon the resultant experiences. Moreover, to forge a further
connection with my argument earlier, artworks are the primary prompts for such
expansive and self-conscious experiences. As I put it in Chapter 4, elaborating on an
expression we owe to filmmaker Stan Brakhage, the vocation of art is to offer us an
adventure in perception and cognition.

What of the 'moving image'? In English, at least, many expressions have served to
refer to the new medium introduced to the world by the Lumière brothers in late
1895: the cinematograph, the photoplay, film, the motion picture, and the movies.

Although 'film' is the most compact term and the default choice in many contexts—there are many 'film studies' departments, but not many 'cinema studies' departments; we refer to film theory, the philosophy of film, and the film industry—in many ways it is the least felicitous of these designations. Why so? The word 'film' derives from the strip of photosensitive material onto which shots were recorded and then edited, and from which edited works were projected, in the predigital era. Initially made of acetate, the film industry switched to the less hazardous celluloid ('safety film') in the 1930s. 'Tape'—as in 'videotape'—marked a further departure: while there is still a strip of material onto which information is recorded, the mechanism of recording is now electronic rather than photochemical. Digital movie making embodies a further notable change at this level of description, for now a computer hard drive takes the place of the film strip, and digital encoding takes over as the mechanism of recording. The word 'film' will soon become entirely detached from its causal origin for most users, as photochemical photography and filmmaking become at best archaic technologies, like woodcarving.

Through all of these changes, however, we can pick out a stable functional kind: what Edison invented, and what runs through all of the changes just enumerated, is a *picture that moves*. Often that moving picture will be a 'live action' recording of actors in sets or locations, but it might be an animation. Sound too is important here; from the outset, motion pictures have been accompanied by music and other forms of sound. For almost ninety years, the *talkie*—the motion picture with synchronous sound and a musical score—has been the centre of gravity for the film and television industries worldwide. In this way, film resembles another functional kind that also came into being around the turn of the twentieth century: the car. Just as cars serve as 'self-propelled vehicles' whether powered by petrol, diesel, electric, biofuels, hydrogen, or a variety of other actual and possible fuels, so a variety of technologies can produce moving pictures with sonic accompaniment. And *that* is the primary target of the naturalized aesthetics I seek to articulate here. The word 'film' just happens to be the most elegant, and widely used, term to point to this durable and indefinitely flexible art form.

Things to Come

Film, Art, and the Third Culture falls into two parts. Part I, Building the Third Culture, is comprised of four chapters that focus on establishing the underlying principles of a naturalized approach to (film) aesthetics. In Part II, Science and Sentiment, the emphasis shifts to a series of case studies over four chapters, all bearing on the nature and role of emotion in the arts, and film art in particular. The focus on emotion is prefigured in Part I by preliminary discussion of the topic; similarly, argument concerning the underlying principles and questions arising in a naturalized approach to aesthetics continues throughout Part II. Thus, while the emphasis shifts, there is a high degree of continuity across the two parts of the book.

Another strategy that unifies the work as a whole is its comparative approach to artworks. I examine a wide range of works from disparate traditions across the whole spectrum and history of film art, encompassing emphatically classical and radically experimental works, from Howard Hawks and Alfred Hitchcock to Jean-Luc Godard and John Smith. I also discuss filmmaking in relation to other artistic practices and forms, from painting and photography through to literature and music. This comparative approach is integrally tied to the third cultural perspective of the book, in three ways. First, since I treat art here as a manifestation of basic human capacities serving fundamental needs, one expects to see significant similarities of form and function across disparate cultural and historical settings; these similarities are what allow us to identify an object or a practice as a candidate for aesthetic or artistic appreciation in the first place. Second, comparison at the same time pushes us to attend to the cultural as well as the biological dimensions of art, bringing into relief contrasting as well as shared features, thereby acting as an important counterbalance to the confirmation bias which might lead us to look exclusively at evidence in favour of a biologically grounded, universalist view of art. Similarity and difference are two sides of the same coin; comparison makes salient the variation in the aesthetic possibilities mined by different traditions of filmmaking. By ranging as widely across time and place as the relatively short history of the motion picture permits, and extending this timeframe by incorporating discussion of practices with much longer histories, the cross-cultural ambition of the third cultural perspective can be tested. Third, attention to older art forms is also motivated by the 'synthetic' character of filmmaking, which emerged through a process of dialogue with—as much as differentiation from—the stage, literature, the graphic arts, and music. The basic principle of comparison—the idea that one can gain insight into an object or process by juxtaposing it with distinct but related objects and processes—thereby courses through the book in a multitude of ways.

Part I commences with a chapter which frames the study as a whole, 'Aesthetics Naturalized'. Here I provide an exposition of recent and historical debates bearing on the idea of a naturalized approach to aesthetics—including those concerning philosophical naturalism in general, scientific knowledge and method, conceptual analysis and theory construction as philosophical approaches, explanation and understanding, the nature of artistic cognition, intention and causality, the personal and subpersonal aspects of mind. Through an exploration of these issues I set out what I take to be the underlying principles of a naturalized aesthetics, its virtues and vices. Aesthetics, I argue, is neither methodologically nor substantively insulated from the sciences, nor should it be. Aesthetics is distinct but not detached from the social and natural sciences, and indeed other human sciences, whose methods and accumulated wisdom are often relevant to research in aesthetics. I advance two related strategies for realizing a naturalistic aesthetics: *theory construction* and *thick explanation*. If the former can be thought of as an alternative (or successor) to conceptual analysis, the latter might be regarded as a complement to the 'thick description' theorized by Gilbert Ryle and further developed by Clifford Geertz.

Along with a defence of the basic credo of a naturalized aesthetics, Chapter 1 initiates discussion of a number of basic themes through which the approach is manifested concretely. These themes, which weave their way through the rest of the volume, include:

- attention to *evolutionary theory* and *neuroscience*, as sources of ideas and constraints on the plausibility of aesthetic and cultural theories—foundations of a *biocultural* approach to human behaviour seeking to identify the interplay between biological capacities and the cultural elaborations of those capacities, contrasting with the 'culturalism' that prevails in the humanities today;
- attention to the *subpersonal* as well as the personal level of human cognition and behaviour, as part of a commitment to the 'multi-levelled' explanation of aesthetic and artistic phenomena, and a recognition of degrees of explanatory adequacy;
- exploration of the *qualified integrity* and *bounded rationality* of human cognition;

- suspicion of 'linguaform' theory, and an insistence upon the significance of *emotional, sensory, and motor experience*—of the *embodied* nature of human cognition in general, along with language, in the shaping of aesthetic and artistic phenomena;
- and last but not least, an exploration of the contribution that might be made by the sciences to the most elusive quarry of all, *consciousness* itself, and in particular the various forms of consciousness that enter into our experience of artworks.

Along the way, I explore work by artist Patrick Hughes and filmmakers M. Night Shyamalan, Steven Spielberg, Lars von Trier, Ernie Gehr, Frederick Wiseman, and Chantal Ackerman. I conclude Chapter 1 by insisting upon the differences between making, appreciating, and explaining art, underlining that it is principally in relation to explanation that we can expect that knowledge and methods drawn from the sciences will make a significant contribution to the study of film art.

With a preliminary understanding of philosophical naturalism in general and naturalized aesthetics in particular in place, alongside an appreciation of the historical background to the contemporary debate, in Chapter 2 I turn my attention to a central concept within aesthetics and examine the methods and types of evidence at our disposal when we seek to investigate and understand *aesthetic experience*. The concept of aesthetic experience has recently undergone a revival of interest, with one focus of debate on the question of whether the value of an artwork reduces to the value of the experience that it affords. Here I address a different question: given the centrality of aesthetic experience to many accounts of art, what methods are available for the analysis and explanation of this experience? In particular, is aesthetic experience amenable to any kind of scientific investigation? Or is the experiential dimension of art exactly that fundamental dimension of it which lies beyond the purview of science?

Rather than accepting the orthodox, affirmative answer to this last question, I argue that we need to pause and examine three levels of analysis, and their respective forms of evidence, that come into play when we seek to understand any aspect of mind: the phenomenological (that is, how we experience things), the psychological, and the neural. Once we understand that each of these levels plays a role in the investigation of mental phenomena, and have some understanding of how the three levels interrelate, we see that scientific methodology does have a role to play in the investigation of aesthetic experience. Developing a metaphor briefly alluded to by Owen Flanagan, I argue that this method of *triangulating* phenomenological, psychological, and neural evidence has much to offer, and support this claim through case studies on *suspense* and *empathy*, along with commentary on *colour, auditory*, and *facial perception* in the context of film spectatorship. In exploring these phenomena in the light of triangulation, I discuss films by Godard, Spielberg, Stan Brakhage, Paul Sharits, Wim Wenders, Alexander Sokurov, Mike Figgis, Béla Tarr, James Cameron, and Johnnie To.

Discussion of these phenomena also serves to deepen the discussion of three of the characteristic 'themes' of naturalized aesthetics introduced in Chapter 1: the *embodied* nature of cognition; the *qualified integrity* of human rationality, constrained as it is by the contingencies of its embodiment, bounded by the limitations of time and energy, and always embedded ('situated') in particular circumstances; and the focus on *subpersonal mechanisms*—as well as personal level explanation— that the scientific study of aesthetic experience drives us towards. The binding together of the personal and subpersonal levels is one route to thick explanation. While noting in this way the significant role that attention to the subpersonal level can play in our understanding of the mind, I also offer a warning against *neural behaviourism*—the all-too-prevalent idea that neuroscientific methods are sufficient for an understanding of the mind; that brain activity speaks for itself. On the contrary, I argue that evidence from the brain is 'mute' until it is triangulated with other kinds of evidence.

Chapter 3 sustains this focus on the subpersonal, by developing the model of triangulation introduced in Chapter 2 and by exploring in greater detail the potential of neuroscience to illuminate our understanding of art, aesthetics, and film. In effect, in this chapter I test Gabrielle Starr's claim 'that understanding the neural underpinnings of aesthetic experience—not just the experience of beauty or wonderment, but the other pleasures and displeasures of the arts and the natural world—can reshape our understanding of aesthetics and the arts'.[21] At the outset of the chapter I describe a number of emerging areas of practice and research, including *neurocinema* (cinema employing the tools of neuroscience to enhance or modify the cinematic experience); *neurocinematic studies* (the study of film using the methods and tools of neuroscience); and *neuroaesthetics* (the wider, and more established, study of art and the aesthetic in the light of neuroscience). I review each of these trends in the light of debates in philosophy of mind on the pertinence of neural evidence to questions about mental phenomena, where perspectives range from strong scepticism regarding the relevance and value of neural evidence (Jerry Fodor, Raymond Tallis) to a rather uncritical and undiscriminating embrace of all things neural ('cheerleading' for the brain, as Colin McGinn puts it).[22] I argue that the picture is more complicated than is suggested by either of these perspectives, but in doing so I maintain that, used carefully, neuroscientific (and related) methods certainly have the potential to add to our understanding of film art. Indeed, they may have done so already, through the first wave of neuroscientific studies conducted specifically on film, including work by Uri Hasson, Tim Smith, Talma Hendler and Gal Raz, Pia Tikka, Art Shimamura, and Vittorio Gallese and Michele Guerra.[23] Beyond these neuroscientific projects specifically devoted to film, I also argue that existing and ongoing neuroscientific research into various psychological capacities sheds light on aspects of our experience of film. Here I focus on the *startle response* and *mirror responses* in particular, developing the exploration of film suspense in Chapter 2 by showing how these two psychological phenomena play a role in the generation of suspense, and how attention to the neural mechanisms underpinning them refines our understanding of the process as a whole. I analyse works directed by Jacques Tourneur, Kurosawa Akira, Jon Favreau, and Danny Boyle in the context of these ideas.

Chapter 4 further develops the model of 'triangulation' by shifting focus to the 'phenomenological' or experiential level, and mining various traditions of research for their relevance to the model. I begin with a review of basic concepts—including *attention, consciousness, self-consciousness, the unconscious,* and *the 'cognitive'* or *'adaptive' unconscious*—while also surveying the fate of the idea of the conscious mind, and research on it, during the heyday(s) of psychoanalysis and psychological behaviourism. I complement this survey of the history of the idea of consciousness in philosophical and psychological terms with a discussion of the representation of various types of conscious state in films. Once again in line with the comparative approach already sketched, here I draw on a range of films from different traditions, including works by Brakhage, Miguel Gomes, Ozu Yasujirō, Michelangelo Antonioni, Errol Morris, Sergei Parajanov, Ridley Scott, and Trần Anh Hùng.

Chapter 4 culminates with a detailed consideration of the arguments around *qualia*: qualitative properties of perceptual and other psychological states, like the tartness of a Granny Smith, the queasiness of seasickness, or—to take a less generic example, memorialized in the title of one of Ozu's films—the flavour of green tea over rice. I pay particular attention to the debate triggered by Frank Jackson's seminal essay 'Epiphenomenal Qualia', in which qualia are exemplified by the 'hurtfulness of pains, the itchiness of itches, pangs of jealousy, or ... the characteristic experience of tasting a lemon, smelling a rose, hearing a loud noise or seeing the sky'.[24] In this essay, Jackson argues that our qualitative experience of, for example, colour

perception cannot be reduced to knowledge of its physical underpinnings; in the
famous thought experiment contained within the essay, Mary (the brilliant but
sheltered colour scientist) learns something new when she first *experiences* red,
even though she knew already all there was to know about the optics and neurophysiology of the perception of red. In other words, Jackson's argument spotlights a
problem for physicalist accounts of the mind and mounts a defence of dualism, and
to that extent undermines a naturalistic approach to the mind in general, and to
aesthetic experience in particular. If Jackson's arguments in this paper hold, then the
prognosis for the model of triangulation elaborated in Chapter 2, and the neuros-
cientifically informed projects discussed in Chapter 3, would not be bright. But there
are many reasons to doubt the force of Jackson's thought experiment, and the
intuitions it pumps—as Jackson himself has recognized in later reflections on his
original paper, in which he presents himself as a staunch advocate of philosophical
naturalism in general. The critical issue, as Jackson argued in his 1982 paper, is
whether and how we can find a place for qualia within a naturalistic description of
the world. If we can, what are the implications for arguments about the distinctive
kind of knowledge that art can deliver? Through the arguments of Jackson, then, this
concluding section of chapter 4—and of Part I as a whole—traces an arc that moves
away from and then returns to the naturalistic programme.

In Part II the focus of the book shifts to a series of case studies on the representation, expression, and experience of emotions in the context of art and film; case
studies which seek to implement, test, and refine the principles of naturalized
aesthetics advanced in Part I. Chapter 5 returns to the discussion of evolutionary
theory and psychology, one of the key contemporary influences on and resources for
a naturalized aesthetics. Here I explore what evolutionary theorists have to say about
two matters of particular importance for film art: fiction and emotion. After a general
discussion of these two phenomena, I focus more closely on the vital role of facial
expression in films (thereby developing further the theme of embodied cognition
introduced in Chapters 1 and 2). I seek to connect central questions in the history of
film theory—questions concerning the universal comprehensibility of cinematic
depiction, for example, and the role of context in our understanding of emotional
expressions, raised by the famous 'Kuleshov effect'—with the science of emotion.
Does an evolutionary perspective on emotion suggest particular answers to these
questions—and if so, what answers? Once again the comparative method comes to
the fore here, as I examine the use of facial expression in disparate national and
regional filmmaking traditions (including Britain, the US, France, Hong Kong, and
Japan, through films by Hawks, Hitchcock, Spielberg, Boyle, Carl Theodor Dreyer,
Georges Franju, Sergio Leone, Kitano Takeshi, and Wong Kar-wai). I argue that
alongside the Kuleshov effect we need to recognize a related 'Kuleshov fallacy',
involving the idea that the meaning of individual shots is entirely determined
by the context established by editing, and that the content of individual shots
(including the expressive behaviours depicted by them) plays no significant role in

their interpretation. I also pursue a comparative analysis of the representation and expression of emotion in motion pictures, and in the still forms of painting and photography, exploring the way in which the presence or absence of motion shapes the depiction of emotion.

I conclude the chapter with a discussion of *affective mimicry*—the transmission of emotional states through involuntary mimicry of facial (and vocal) expressions. This discussion builds on the exploration of the neural mirror system in Chapter 3 (and points forward to the culminating discussion of empathy in Chapter 7), but the emphasis here is on the explanatory 'depth' that reference to scientific theories of emotion can bring to humanistic discussions. Picking up on the idea of 'thick explanation' introduced in Chapter 1, I argue that not all explanations are equal; some are narrow and lack the fuller explanatory adequacy of other explanations, even as they offer some degree of explanation. I argue that an account of emotion in film informed by insights from psychology, neuroscience, and evolutionary theory allows for the articulation of 'thicker', more robust explanations than would be possible without reference to the findings and models of these fields.

Chapter 6 sustains the attention to emotion, through the introduction of further specific concepts and issues, including mood, emotion episodes, and a comparison of cognitive and non-cognitive accounts of emotion. In this chapter I also tackle the problem of *modernism*. Much of the research in cognitive film theory (film theory informed by research in the cognitive sciences) and naturalized aesthetics has taken 'classical' filmmaking, and the techniques associated with such filmmaking, as its object of study. And one line of criticism of such research is that it *can only* illuminate such traditional, mainstream practices. Through a case study on Edgar Reitz's *Heimat* (1984, 1992, and 2004) which sustains the attention to modernist and avant-garde works dealt with in earlier chapters—including films by Brakhage, Kitano, Kar-wai, and Robert Bresson—I aim to show how a naturalistic approach can shed light on experimental as well as orthodox works. Perhaps it is also worth emphasizing that the focus on *Heimat*—financed by and broadcast on television, but directed by a feature filmmaker, and the subject of special cinema screenings—is indicative of the inclusive conception of 'film' underpinning the current work, encompassing moving image works made with a variety of different technologies and exhibited in different contexts.

This case study also returns the argument to the question of the 'universality' of filmic representation, initially broached in Chapter 5. Before the advent of the 'talkies', the vision of cinema as a universal 'language' was premised on the primarily pictorial character of film, with language restricted to the relatively modest role of intertitles. The introduction of dialogue in the late 1920s fatally undermined what-ever validity that argument may have had during the 'silent' era; and yet film remains an international business and art form, as both the continued prominence of Hollywood worldwide, and the emergence of the category of 'world cinema', testify. In thinking about the ability of films to travel across and between cultures, we are led to think not only about language, but the role of local knowledge, the cultural norms specific to particular societies, and the degree of variation we find in the scope of cultural assumptions and norms. The upshot is a more complex answer to the question of universality than either the one favoured by the silent 'universalists' or the contemporary culturalist view (which emphasizes the differences and even 'incommensurability' among works emerging from distinct cultures). On the basis of this discussion, I distinguish between the dominant culturalist paradigm and the alternative biocultural perspective on art and culture, defending the latter and showing how it meshes with a naturalistic philosophical stance.

Chapter 7 examines empathy as a particular kind of emotional state. In taking up *Ch 7* this subject, I resume and develop the discussion of mirror responses in Chapters 2, 3, and 5, placing these generally low-level, involuntary responses in relation to the higher order imaginative process typically conjured up by the term 'empathy'. This provides another excellent example of the integration of the personal and subpersonal levels within naturalistic explanations of aesthetic experience, while at the same time showing how the unity, coherence, and self-transparency of the mind is notably qualified on this account. I examine arguments concerning the functions and value of empathy, distinguishing what I term 'mindfeeling' from the more widely recognized 'mindreading' role performed by empathy, as well as debates around the conditions apt to trigger empathy. Here I also conjoin recent debates on empathy with the debate on the *extended mind*—the idea that mental processes cannot be narrowly located 'just north of the neck' but critically depend upon the body, and the social and material environments in which agents act; that the mind is 'neither brain nor ghost', but rather a 'behavioral field' arising from the interaction of brain, body, and world.[25] Empathy, ① I propose, is amplified in both scope and intensity by the institutions and practices of representational art—by storytelling and depiction in general, and filmmaking in particular. I explore this thesis through commentary on films by Hitchcock, Julio Médem, and Paul Greengrass.

I elaborate further on the augmentation of human cognition by the exploitation of the physical and social environment, and the more general interdependence of mind and world, through the evolutionary concept of *niche construction*—a concept that recognizes that species adapt their environments as well as adapting to them. This is a critical juncture in the overall argument of the book, stitching together concepts from film and art theory (empathy), evolutionary theory (niche construction), and neuroscience (mirror neurons), thereby furnishing another instance of the method of triangulation in action. It is also an important opportunity to emphasize that, no matter how important the grey matter is, attention to the brain—and to the deliverances of neuroscience—will never be sufficient alone for an understanding of art and the mind. The 'inward' direction of research on the mind exemplified by neuroscience is often contrasted with the 'outward' direction of embodied and extended theories of mind, as if the two tendencies are mutually exclusive; on the view advanced here, however, they are complementary. Triangulating psychological,

① *behavioral field arising from interaction of brain, body, world* phenomenological, and neural evidence is in this way very different to what we might term 'neurofundamentalism'—the brain as the Key to All Mythologies.

Chapter 8 both continues the series of case studies on emotion that comprise Part II, while simultaneously acting as the culmination to the main argument of the work as a whole—that our capacity to understand and explain art, aesthetics, and film is enhanced rather than vitiated by venturing beyond the humanities, and by appealing to the knowledge and the methods of the sciences; and that one important way of putting into practice such a naturalistic, or third cultural, approach to film involves the triangulation of insights from phenomenology, psychology, and neuroscience. I return to this central argument by considering at the outset of the chapter the types of emotion that have been the focus of work in aesthetics and research on film. On the whole, the emotions at stake have been 'garden-variety' emotions—states like the fear and disgust elicited by horror films, or the sadness evoked by melodramas. While accepting the explanatory power of much of this research, I note the tension between the generic nature of these emotions, and the very specific emotional qualia elicited by each individual work. Behind this tension, and echoing it, lie the contrasting goals of scientific research on the one hand, and artistic expression and appreciation on the other: while science aims at generalities, classically in the form of laws, works of art aim at the particular—the particular combination of sights, sounds, and ideas embodied by works which (in successful cases) compel sustained attention and reflection. From the point of view of science, any particular instance of redness is as good as any other, insofar as the instance conforms to the relevant laws (of light and of human neurophysiology); but from the point of view of art, the red we find in any given work is peculiar to it, and not something that we could swap with the red of another work without cost. An important challenge to the scientifically informed, naturalistic approach represented by the book as a whole, then, is the *particularity* of art—a feature which seems to set it at odds with the scientific project. How can this challenge be met?

Naturalized aesthetics should not be understood as a science, if by that we mean a discipline whose only goal is the formulation of laws and generalizations covering a given domain, even as it is informed and constrained by knowledge drawn from the sciences. I argue that a naturalized aesthetics does not preclude recognition of the particularity of artworks, or the special qualia that each work prompts; on the contrary, it provides us with tools for identifying and describing just these features. With respect to emotions, these tools include Paul Ekman's concept of *blending*, which refers to the combination and interaction of emotions, thereby moving us a step away from garden-variety and towards more 'exotic' emotions, including those which are peculiar to individual works. I also note how the tools of cognitive science help us to appreciate the perceptual complexity of art and film, a complexity often obscured by the stress on language in the semiotic tradition—an emphasis which flattens the important perceptual and experiential contrasts at play across the appreciation of literary, depictive, and musical art forms. Such work enables us to recognize the *multimodal nature of film perception*, involving not only the interplay of sight and sound, but also the indirect triggering of touch and balance, and perhaps even pain, taste, and smell.

Returning to an issue I first introduce in Chapter 1, I also consider here research from the cognitive sciences that may help to refine and demystify the idea that an artwork may prompt in us experiences that are 'ineffable' or beyond paraphrase. Drawing on the work of music psychologists, Diana Raffman has shown how, in perceiving notes, we may be able to discern but not memorize very subtle variations in pitch. Such *nuance ineffability* may carry over to other sense modalities, and explain why direct acquaintance with an artwork is irreplaceable, and why our experience of an artwork always exceeds our powers of description. Moreover, it is the very elusiveness of the qualia elicited by artworks that motivates the creative efforts of art critics and theorists to capture and evoke them through metaphor, neologism, and other expressive devices. In this way, concepts and insights drawn from the cognitive sciences help us understand a host of central features of the art world. I examine these various themes in Chapter 8 in relation to films by Neil Jordan, Anna Boden and Ryan Fleck, and Iain Forsyth and Jane Pollard.

Film, Art, and the Third Culture is, I hope, distinctive in a number of ways—in its combination of philosophy, film theory, and criticism; in its attention not only to film, but to the other arts, ancient and modern, high and low, and to aesthetic experience in general; and in its interest in ethics, metaphysics, philosophy of science, philosophy of mind, and cognitive science alongside aesthetics. Many works claim interdisciplinarity, but I strive to offer here a variety that is wider ranging, more robust, and subjected to critical reflection to an unusual degree. 'Naturalism' too has become a buzzword, but the term is often used loosely and admits a range of interpretations; the naturalized aesthetics I defend in the pages that follow is a moderately strong, though not reductive, variety, explicitly and clearly set forth as such. Critics of naturalized aesthetics fear that it undercuts and devalues our experience of art, 'explaining it away' by tying it to ulterior motivations like survival, reproduction, and status, but the point rather is to show how our understanding and appreciation of film, art, and aesthetic experience is heightened when we set it within this most ambitious and demanding of research programmes.

PART I
Building the Third Culture

PART I

Building the Data Culture

1

Aesthetics Naturalized

The aim of philosophy, abstractly formulated, is to understand how things in the broadest possible sense of the term hang together in the broadest possible sense of the term. Under 'things in the broadest possible sense' I include such radically different items as not only 'cabbages and kings', but numbers and duties, possibilities and finger snaps, aesthetic experience and death.

Wilfrid Sellars

We philosophers, aestheticians included, do spend much of our lives lolling around in armchairs. Many have urged us to pay attention to empirical psychology and cognitive science, as well as less formal empirical observations. There has not been enough discussion, especially among aestheticians, of how and why we should, however.

Kendall Walton

Mention the word 'naturalism' to people in the arts and humanities, and most of them will take you to be referring to an artistic style—Emile Zola and Theodore Dreiser in the novel, Gerhard Hauptmann in theatre, Erich von Stroheim, or in more recent times the Dardennes brothers, in film. Philosophers, especially those working within the analytic tradition, will take you to mean something very different.[1] For them, 'naturalism' names a philosophical stance, a stance described by one commentator as the 'the current orthodoxy within Anglo-American philosophy, an outlook that shapes the way philosophers understand the mission and problems of philosophy',[2] and by another, in still stronger and more wide-reaching terms, as the 'most forceful metaphilosophical trend of the twentieth century'.[3] And yet this philosophical approach has only recently assumed prominence in philosophical aesthetics, and is virtually unknown in film and art theory, at least under this description.[4] Moreover, while naturalism has been riding high on the philosophical charts for some time now, not everyone appreciates its rhythms and harmonies, and some say that its compositional principles are slack, vague, or incoherent. So an exploration of philosophical naturalism, as a candidate methodology for the theorization of film in particular and art more generally, is long overdue.

As early as 1922, the American philosopher Roy Wood Sellars could declare: 'we are all naturalists now!'[5] As this pronouncement implies, the idea of 'naturalism' as a philosophical stance has been debated for a century or more; indeed Philip Kitcher

argues that modern philosophy, prior to Frege, 'was distinguished ... by its willing-
ness to draw on the ideas of the emerging sciences, to cull concepts from ventures in
psychology and physics, later still to find inspiration in Darwin'.[6] Broadly speaking,
philosophical naturalism may be defined as a commitment to the pursuit of philosophical questions in the light of the knowledge and methods of the sciences, or more
particularly, as the name suggests, the natural sciences (though how one defines and
decides what is to count as a natural science turns out to be a surprisingly complex
matter). To approach some phenomenon naturalistically is to seek to place and
explain it within the natural order, while the rational-empirical methods of
science—framing hypotheses, seeking evidence, considering alternative hypotheses
and countervailing evidence—are, on this view, our best bet in realizing this aim.
When Andy Clark asks, at the outset of his *Mindware*, 'What are beliefs, thoughts,
and reasons, and how do they take their place among the other things that make up
the natural world?' and answers that question by exploring various research programmes in cognitive science, he is undertaking an exercise in naturalistic philosophy. Similarly, Fred Dretske articulates a naturalistic perspective when he states that
'[b]y conceiving of mental facts ... as part of the natural order, as manifestations of
overall biological and developmental design, one can see where intentionality comes
from and why'.[7] In this way Dretske and Clark each advocate a naturalistic approach
to the mind.

In the most basic terms, such an approach insists that psychology can and should
be conducted as a science. That philosophy of mind is intimately related to scientific
psychology should come as no surprise: one of the leading journals of analytic
philosophy, *Mind*, began in 1876 as 'a quarterly review of psychology and philosophy' (and remained so until 1972). Writing specifically on the subject of visual
representation, Richard Wollheim urges us to recognize 'that there are many philosophical questions that cannot be answered unless we know the relevant psychology,
and there are many psychological questions whose answers await the relevant
philosophy'.[8] Thus if visual representation is defined in part by the capacity to see
three-dimensional spaces within two-dimensional configurations, empirical psychological investigation of that capacity is necessary to understand it properly. Wollheim
thereby argues that philosophy (of mind) and psychology are interdependent.

Typically naturalism in the sense at stake here is held to have two aspects: a
substantive (metaphysical) commitment to the study of all phenomena, including
human behaviour, as a part of the physically constituted, biologically evolved world;
and a methodological commitment to the methods and standards of the natural
sciences.[9] A decisive moment in the history of philosophical naturalism came in the
early 1950s with the publication of W. V. O. Quine's 'Two Dogmas of Empiricism',
followed by his 'Epistemology Naturalized' in 1969.[10] In these papers, Quine argued
in favour of the continuity of philosophy with science, and against the notion of 'first
philosophy'—philosophy as a practice standing prior to, and in some sense above or
wholly separate from, empirical investigation. Quine thus resists the idea that the job

of philosophy is exclusively to maintain the highways and byways of the a priori, while the sciences take care of the a posteriori.

Within the domain of aesthetics, Kendall Walton has furnished an account of philosophical method along similar lines. 'What philosophers do', writes Walton, 'is pretty much what scientists do after the data are in: organizing the data in a perspicuous manner, devising conceptual structures, constructing theories, to clarify and explain the data.'[11] *Theory construction*—as Walton labels philosophical activity conceived in this way—is not unique to scientists or philosophers, but something rooted in the basic human effort to understand the world. Philosophers are, however, specialists in that aspect of theory construction which works with and alongside the gathering of data through observation and experiment. In this respect, at least, Walton concedes that there is something at least '*quasi*-a priori' about philosophy:

The theories philosophers construct are empirical in the sense that they are based on and aim to explain empirical data, but constructing them once the data are in requires no additional empirical investigation. Deciding which of several competing theories best explains a given body of data, or a body of possible or hypothetical data . . . would seem to be about as a priori a task as there is.[12]

Walton's treatment of ordinary language concepts is also Quinean in character. Walton's prominent arguments on the 'transparent' nature of photography do not involve the clarification and defence of the everyday notion of 'seeing', but rather a *revision* of that ordinary notion—sharpened to serve the purposes of a theory of photography more effectively than is possible for the unreformed folk concept. Both folk and specialist theories (Walton opens 'Transparent Pictures' with a quotation from André Bazin[13]) claim that there is something distinctive about photography, something that marks it off from other types of depiction. But they do not succeed in giving us precise and plausible accounts of this distinctive quality. Walton's act of theory construction proceeds by seeking to specify what it is, if anything, that observing an object in a photograph shares with observing it either directly, or in a mirror, or through a telescope—irrespective of whether this shared quality is one that is captured by the current, everyday English concept of 'seeing'. We could just as well, says Walton, express the 'transparency claim' by saying 'that we *perceive, schmee*, or *perschmeive*, or whatever, things through photographs and in the other ways, but not through paintings and drawings'.[14] Walton thereby engages in a process of what Quine terms 'paraphrase', whereby we work from everyday concepts but seek to formulate reformed or alternative concepts—which nonetheless perform the most important functions of the original everyday concepts.[15]

The naturalistic stance has gained ground in the humanities more generally over the past two decades, through cognitive film theory, literary cognitivism, and literary Darwinism. In philosophical aesthetics, a naturalistic stance has made itself felt through a number of overlapping strands of enquiry. Many aestheticians, like their peers in philosophy of mind and psychology, have put themselves into dialogue with the cognitive sciences, drawing upon psychological research on perception, imagination, and emotion. Some have pushed on into the further fields of evolutionary theory and neuroscience, while others have aligned themselves specifically with the field of experimental philosophy ('XPhi'), where the substance and role of 'intuitions' in everyday thought and philosophical argument are subjected to empirical as well as conceptual investigation.[16]

Sometimes the impression is given that all of this is brand new. But there have been earlier naturalistic interventions within aesthetics: essays were published on this topic in the *Journal of Aesthetics and Art Criticism* by David Fenner and Douglas Dempster in the early 1990s, and Dempster notes the naturalistic atmosphere prevailing at the time of the founding of the American Society for Aesthetics in 1942, evident in the work of one its earliest presidents, Thomas Munro. Similarly, the founder of the British Society of Aesthetics, Herbert Read, articulated a biological account of the origins of art.[17] The contemporary work in philosophical aesthetics and art theory cited here, moreover, has often taken inspiration from parallel work in fields such as anthropology, including Ellen Dissanayake's influential account of aesthetic activity as the 'making special' of everyday activities.[18]

It is important to recognize that the appeals to and the uses made of science in this body of research are quite diverse; naturalism comes in different varieties and strengths. Thus, as we saw in the Introduction, one can distinguish between *replacement* naturalism and *cooperative* or *integrative* naturalism, both of which contrast decisively with *cherry-picking*—the selective and ad hoc appeal to science. Another important distinction we need to note in this regard is one that I have already noted in passing: that between scientific *knowledge* and *method*. The first task of the naturalistic aesthetician is 'simply' to synthesize, make explicit, and show the relevance to aesthetics of the scientific knowledge that is already, if provisionally, 'out there'. The famous passage from Wilfrid Sellars quoted at the outset of this chapter has a decidedly naturalistic flavour insofar as it ascribes to philosophy a synthetic ambition: the goal of philosophy is 'to understand how things in the broadest possible sense of the term hang together', and notably aesthetic experience appears (just prior to death) on Sellars's diverse list of things to be put in order.[19] To grasp what this involves requires, among other things, further exploration of the relationship between scientific knowledge and method.

Naturalism, Knowledge, and Method

To take a philosophically naturalistic stance on some phenomenon is to aim to make sense of it in the context of the knowledge and methods of the sciences. Although obviously connected, scientific knowledge and scientific methods are not identical. Most of the scientifically derived knowledge that we have about the world we possess by virtue of testimony—that is, through formal and informal learning about historical and contemporary scientific research on the world. Chances are, I don't know about the elliptical orbits of the planets because I've made the observations and done the calculations myself. And when I take aspirin, confident in the knowledge that it will ease my aching head, it's not that I've conducted rigorous double-blind studies on the pain-relieving effects of the drug. But I have good reason to believe that others have, and my experience of taking the drug and witnessing its effects on others consolidates my confidence in received scientific wisdom. Once a scientific theory becomes widely accepted and institutionalized—as in the case of the germ theory of disease, for example, or scientific medicine more generally—the knowledge embedded within the theory becomes largely detached from the methods that enabled its discovery. While my action is guided by medical *knowledge*, then, my action—as a lay person—is not guided by scientific *method*, but by ordinary practical reasoning.

That doesn't make the knowledge we possess beyond doubt, but again it is likely to be new scientific study that shifts our assumptions. To this extent, we cannot take the motto of the Royal Society—*nullius in verba*, or 'take no one's word for it'—at face value; we rely on what we take to be authoritative testimony, including scientific testimony, all the time, and it is hard to imagine a world in which we didn't. As Jason Bourne and many other amnesiac protagonists discover with particular force, we would lack knowledge of even our own names and birthdates were we to avoid reliance on testimony. *Radical* epistemic autonomy—as symbolized by the Royal Society motto—seems neither possible nor desirable.

A more modest conception of epistemic autonomy, however, holds that while we can take—indeed we have to take—the word of others all the time, we can and should also investigate for ourselves the putative truths which come to us via testimony. We routinely accept things on the basis of testimony, but our acceptance is or ought always to be provisional; depending on time, resources, and our interests, we should probe things for ourselves. And that process delivers an enhanced version of the knowledge gained by testimony, characterized by an appreciation of the grounds, reasoning behind, or evidence for some claim, rather than just the claim itself. Our knowledge, we might say, is thickened and made more robust by such scrutiny of testimony. So naturalism does not involve a commitment to some impossible-to-meet standard for what counts as knowledge. Naturalism is consistent with a reliabilist approach to knowledge and its justification (the idea that we have knowledge and our beliefs are justified to the extent that we have gained them through reliable processes) and with fallibilism (sceptical alertness to the fallibility of any given claim).

So we are awash in scientifically derived knowledge of the world, on which we rely even as we (ideally) retain a variable degree of scepticism towards it. The naturalist embraces both parts of this equation. The naturalist, however, will also be alert to the ways in which not only scientific knowledge, but scientific methods—broadly construed—might be used to refine and deepen our knowledge of some phenomenon. I speak of scientific methods because, although we can characterize 'the scientific method' in very abstract terms, there is considerable variation in the particular methods used by different disciplines we regard as scientific. Laboratory sciences, such as chemistry or molecular biology, are able to conduct controlled experiments; sciences like palaeontology and geology rely instead on amassing data from the environment and examining the record of natural history.[20] Many social sciences recognize a distinction between 'nomothetic' and 'idiographic' methods—focusing on, respectively, generalization and particularity (a point to which I'll return, in relation to the ideas of Clifford Geertz). This variation in the specific methods adopted by different sciences will be important in thinking about the reach of naturalism across the social sciences and the humanities.

Notwithstanding the distinction between knowledge and method, and the tighter relationship between scientific knowledge and practical reasoning than between scientific method and such ordinary reasoning, the seed for this openness to scientific method lies in ordinary experience—for my experience with aspirin is nothing other than a kind of informal, ongoing experiment on the drug. In this sense, at least, there is nothing 'unnatural' about the nature of science. As Sellars argued, 'what we call the scientific enterprise is the flowering of a dimension of discourse which already exists in what historians call the "prescientific stage"'.[21]

From Conceptual Analysis to Theory Construction: Three Cases

In a passage which resonates with these considerations, Edouard Machery writes that 'philosophy is the pursuit of empirical knowledge by (typically, though not exclusively) conceptual means: philosophy is in the business of examining, criticizing, reforming the findings, theories, methods developed by scientists and of grasping the implications of sciences for our understanding of the world and our place in it'.[22] With its emphasis on the empirical—'philosophy is the pursuit of empirical knowledge'—and its casting of the conceptual as a means to empirical discovery, however, Machery's characterization of philosophy and philosophical method is strikingly different to the orthodox vision of analytic philosophy. Machery here describes what has emerged, at least for naturalistic philosophers, as the successor to the 'conceptual analysis' that is conventionally, if inaccurately, held to be the central method of analytic philosophy.[23] This alternative understanding of the *telos* and method of philosophy is often termed 'theory construction' (or 'theory building'), as we've seen in the case of Walton.[24] In order to grasp what theory construction is, it will be helpful to see how it contrasts with the party line, aka, conceptual analysis.

Conceptual analysis aims to clarify or elucidate the individual concepts, or the conceptual frameworks, by which we understand the world. According to the traditional account we do this by seeking the necessary and sufficient conditions that define a concept; according to the influential Wittgensteinian alternative, we look for the typical features that characterize a concept. On either view, conceptual analysis is said to contrast with empirical research on the world, which is concerned with describing and explaining the phenomena—physical, chemical, biological, psychological, social—of the world itself. Empirical researchers necessarily depend on the concepts by and through which we understand the world; but they are not generally engaged in reflection upon those concepts.

To borrow an example from Noël Carroll: say the topic under consideration is pornography.[25] The philosopher is interested in the concept 'pornography', in terms of the features of an object or act that make it fall under that concept, or the relationship between pornography and other concepts, whether neighbouring (such as the obscene and the erotic) or contrasting (the chaste, the discreet, the subtle). The empirical researcher, by contrast, deploys that concept in exploring pornography in the world, by observation or experiment. Accordingly, philosophy should remain at some remove from work in the empirical sciences, concerning itself with conceptual clarification prior to and over and above the interpretation of empirical data. As Gilbert Ryle bluntly states, 'questions of fact... are not the province of philosophy'; or as Peter Hacker puts it, the business of philosophy is to discriminate sense from nonsense, which he considers quite distinct from and antecedent to the separation of facts from falsehoods.[26] Speaking from within philosophical aesthetics, George Dickie articulated a similar position: 'There is much confusion in the talk about works of art and in talk about talk about works of art, but it is confusion, not lack of information'.[27]

On this view, conceptual analysis may guide empirical research but will likely be consistent with a range of outcomes on the empirical level. From this perspective, philosophical aesthetics is largely, if not wholly, autonomous from the sciences; and to the extent that it trades with empirical research, goods move in only one direction—aesthetics sets the terms (the conceptual framework) within which empirical research must operate. Empirical research has little or no capacity to reshape the landscape of aesthetic explanation. Commenting in this spirit on neuroscience in particular, for example, Greg Currie expresses doubt that such research has the capacity to 'reorganize... the space of aesthetic reasons'.[28]

Even in this compressed description, there is much that is right about this picture. That is why it has come to be an orthodoxy and why it is hard to dislodge. But for all that, it is at best a flawed and incomplete picture. A grain of truth is heavily watered by tradition, and grows into a forest of entrenched assumption, making it difficult for other truths to find any light. The web of belief and received wisdom can make revising our assumptions and theories hard work.

To begin this process of revision, consider the fact that the empirical researcher will often be confronted with objects and events whose status as 'pornographic' may not be obvious. *Nymphomaniac* (Lars von Trier, 2013) is certainly thematically connected with pornography, but does its aspiration to artistic status remove it from the sphere of pornography? Questions like this will force the sociologist or cultural historian back on to their assumptions regarding pornography; they will be compelled, in other words, to do at least some informal conceptual analysis. Meanwhile, across campus in the philosophy building, our philosopher inevitably finds herself contemplating particular examples of what she takes to be pornographic phenomena, as she tries to figure out the necessary and sufficient conditions, or at least the typical features, of pornography. Perhaps she even does a bit of online research to find out what others seem to regard as pornographic, or to scrutinize candidate pornographic objects in order to come up with as precise and accurate a definition or characterization of pornography as possible. (XPhi philosophers embrace and extend such informal empirical research, arguing that it is so critical to philosophy that it cannot be left to expert 'intuition' or anecdote.) So there is at least a bit of trafficking across the conceptual–empirical border going on. But perhaps this leaves the basic division of labour intact. The distinct, ultimate goals of the philosopher and the empirical researcher still seem to be in place.[29]

Perhaps. Theory construction—conceived as the naturalistic philosopher's alternative to conceptual analysis—emphasizes this interplay between conceptual and empirical work, and the movement of traffic in both directions. Conceptual clarification does not simply precede and guide empirical research; there is feedback from the empirical domain to the conceptual sphere. In his theory of emotion, Paul Griffiths argues that concepts should be regarded as provisional 'schemas' rather than fixed and final entities, the stereotypes and extension of which may be revised in the light of new empirical discoveries; Walton similarly argues that we should regard our current concept of 'imagination' as a 'placeholder for a notion yet to be fully clarified'.[30] While some schematic concepts turn out to be robust (that which is wet and potable usually turns out to be H_2O), others require revision (barnacles turn out to be crustaceans, though they were not initially categorized as such) or elimination (the Aristotelian category of 'superlunary' objects; the medical condition 'hysteroid depression'). (Notably, Griffiths goes onto argue that 'emotion' itself, conceived as a single, unified category, should be eliminated; Derek Matravers has advanced the equally provocative thesis that the concept of 'imagination' should be put out to pasture.[31]) Conceptual analysis may sharpen our grasp of the current stereotype and extension of a concept, but in divorcing itself from the empirical process such analysis cannot recognize the dynamic nature of our understanding of the world and the ways in which this is reflected in conceptual change. Turning his attention to emotions in particular and complaining of the 'poverty of conceptual analysis', Griffiths argues that '[a]ll conceptual analysis will reveal is the current stereotype of [for example] fear. To insist that all and only the things that fit this stereotype are examples of the kind is simply to stand in the way of clarifying the concept. It is exactly akin to insisting that whales are fish because people called them so.'[32]

Theory construction in this way is closely related to Quine's original recommendations for a 'naturalized epistemology', in its emphasis on the revisability of our concepts in the light of empirical investigation. Quine held that *no* aspects of our conceptualization of the world—even the most seemingly abstract and purely formal, logical relations—are immune from potential revision in the light of empirical discovery. Quine's view is controversial, but a more moderate version of theory construction simply that holds that a great many of our concepts are subject to revision in this way. Not all of our conceptual schemes are perfectly sealed echo chambers or 'prison houses', as paradigm shifts in our understanding of the world demonstrate: empirical discovery played a critical role in releasing us from a Ptolemaic conception of the universe, for example, and from the assumption that Earth is flat.[33] Similarly, in the context of the cognitive sciences, Jaegwon Kim argues that 'research results at the level of [neural] realizers [of mental functions] may lead to the reshaping of the higher-level mental concepts in various ways'.[34] We no longer take reference to the humours seriously as a scientific account of the mind; but we do now countenance once seemingly inconceivable phenomena such as 'blindsight' (visual perception in the absence of conscious awareness; the neologism itself is evidence of conceptual revision and reorganization).[35] Things are eliminated from and added to our theories; the stereotypes and extensions of concepts that survive are sometimes revised (as the extension of 'sight' is widened here to accommodate unconscious instances).

On a more modest scale our aesthetic concepts and the 'space of aesthetic reasons' might, in small or more dramatic ways, be 'reorganized' by insights from the empirical sciences. And that is why aesthetics, or at least a branch of it, cannot and should not remain too far removed from the sciences. Even where answers at an abstract, conceptual level are consistent with several specific, empirical explanations, it is still a matter of interest to know which are in fact realized. For the naturalistic philosopher, philosophy should be concerned not only with possibility, but with actuality as well. As Currie himself puts it:

> to be told the conditions that make it possible to do something...is not yet to be told how we actually do it, for actuality is a much narrower condition than possibility. Indeed, mere assurance of possibility can itself be no solution to a problem about what we humans, with our contingent mental makeup, do or don't do; many things that are logically possible cannot be done *by us*.[36]

In sum, whatever knowledge and capacities come preloaded in human beings, the human mind is heavily furnished by engagement with the world, and a dialogue between empirical and conceptual methods is needed to illuminate such a mind.

Let us consider some examples of theory construction in action, in the context of aesthetics, beginning with Diana Raffman's arguments concerning 'nuance ineffability' in our experience of music.[37] 'Ineffability' in general refers to those aspects of experience that may elude linguistic representation, or indeed any form of expression, description, or representation. Art has long been held up as a primary location or source of ineffable experience (and valued for this reason). Nonetheless, the nature of ineffable experience, indeed its very existence, are matters of dispute; a concept referring to the 'inexpressible' is vulnerable to being dismissed as an obscure notion sustained only by the more mystical trends in modern art theory and practice. Raffman's argument, however, specifies the notion of ineffability more precisely, and does so by drawing on the empirical work of auditory and music psychologists. What this research shows is that human listeners have a capacity to *hear* fine differences—nuances—in pitch and timbre, which they cannot *remember*. And since these nuances elude memory, they are not easily codified linguistically or represented in any other systematic way. Thus listeners are in the position of being able to perceive features of music that rapidly fall out of memory, that they cannot notate with any precision, and which come alive to them only in the act of hearing. In the terminology used by Michael Martin in relation to visual perception, our discriminative capacities outreach our identificatory capacities.[38]

So here we have a case where knowledge from a cluster of scientific disciplines (a) provides evidence for and thereby gives credibility to a phenomenon whose existence has been disputed, (b) specifies the nature of that phenomenon, or at least a subtype of the phenomenon, and (c) explains what features of our cognitive architecture give rise to the phenomenon. Call these the *existence, ontological,* and *psychological* implications of this body of scientific knowledge. Through these implications, the abstract, conceptual problem of the ineffable, as traditionally debated within aesthetics, is thereby given shape, made tractable, and detailed in an unprecedented way. It is in this sense that traffic flows from the empirical to the conceptual domain as well as vice versa. The problem of ineffability is opened up to argument, refinement, and challenge by counterexample. Moreover, specifying an actual, particular type of ineffability does not foreclose debate on other types of ineffability—types that may bear on other sense modalities, or on non-sensory aspects of experience, for example. In this way, the empirical evidence that Raffman draws upon may also have relevance for ineffability in the visual and literary arts. Indeed, by giving credibility to one form of ineffability, we have new reason to take seriously arguments concerning other possible types of ineffability.

Alongside Raffman's empirical-cum-conceptual exploration of ineffability we may place two comparable efforts to rehabilitate and enrich particular aesthetic concepts in the spirit of theory construction: Jenefer Robinson's exploration of 'aesthetic distance' and Bence Nanay's account of 'aesthetic attention'.[39] Robinson argues that Edward Bullough's notion of 'aesthetic distance'—once highly influential but now widely regarded as outmoded, and dismissed by Dickie as a 'myth'—can be cashed out in terms of psychologist Richard Lazarus's theory of emotional *coping.*[40] Lazarus's theory concerns the strategies we have for coping with aversive emotions such as fear, disgust, and grief. Coping strategies may be externally 'problem-directed' (taking the form of attempts to improve the situation) or internally directed (in the form of attempts to recast our thoughts and feelings about the situation). Thus, in the case of Bullough's example of being caught in fog at sea, '[i]n appreciating the fog aesthetically I am *coping* with the situation by focusing on a non-threatening aspect of it', namely its 'milky whiteness'.[41] This is an internally directed solution insofar as it acts on our apprehension of the situation—attending to a particular aspect of it—rather than acting on the situation itself.

Robinson argues that the formal aspects of works of art enable us, in a parallel fashion, to cope with the aversive emotions prompted by certain works and genres of art. The pity and fear elicited by a tragedy are made bearable—indeed, made available for appreciative contemplation—by virtue of the formal qualities of the work, such as its narrative structure and dramatic language; Robinson writes specifically of the strategies of *avoidance* and *intellectualization* (and we might add *aestheticization* to this list). The coping facilitated by the formal properties of artworks is at once internally directed (in that it involves a transformation of our emotional experience) and externally directed (in that it is an object of perception, namely the artwork itself, that enables this transformation).

We thus have the following dialectic: Bullough posits the concept 'aesthetic distance' which aims to capture a distinctive feature of aesthetic experience (a concept strongly reminiscent of earlier concepts, including Kant's notion of 'disinterest'); Dickie argues that the concept fails to refer to a real psychological process, and is in this sense a 'myth'; Robinson responds that 'aesthetic distance' may be understood as a type of emotional coping, where it is attention to the form (of a work of art, or a natural phenomenon) that plays the critical role. As in the case of ineffability, here knowledge from scientific research on emotion (a) lends credence to the existence of a disputed aesthetic phenomenon, (b) provides an account of the nature of the phenomenon, by relating it to a well-understood (or at least better understood) aspect of our psychology, and (c) suggests how the type of affective experience characteristic of our engagement with works of art fits into our cognitive architecture as a whole. The same trio of existence, ontological, and psychological implications that we encountered in relation to ineffability are made salient. (We will see these implications again in relation to later examples, including the investigation of empathy in the light of mirror neuron research in Chapters 2, 3, and 7.) If Robinson succeeds in rehabilitating the concept of 'aesthetic distance' through this argument, then it is partly by virtue of Lazarus's empirically driven theory of emotion and emotional coping.

Bence Nanay's recent account of 'aesthetic attention' occupies adjacent territory. As with Robinson, Nanay's conceptual starting point is the idea that the type of attention at work in our aesthetic appreciation of art and nature is in some way special, that is, qualitatively different from ordinary attention; alongside Bullough's notion of aesthetic distance, Nanay points to the Russian Formalist notion of 'defamiliarization' as one important historical attempt to delineate this special kind of attention. (I pick up on defamiliarization in Chapter 4.) Nanay's empirical move— that is, the gesture equivalent to Raffman's appeal to psychoacoustics and Robinson's drafting of the theory of emotional coping—is to draw upon the empirical findings of perceptual psychologists. In particular, Nanay draws upon the distinction between *focused* and *distributed* attention—that is, between narrowing our attention onto a particular object within the visual field available to us, on the one hand, or allowing our attention to graze across a wider set of specific targets of attention within that field, on the other. Specifically, Nanay proposes that the elusive, special quality of aesthetic attention—or one aspect or type of such attention, at any rate—may be understood as a distinctive combination of these two types of attention. Aesthetic attention on this account is characterized as focused in relation to the aesthetic *object* as a whole, but distributed in relation to the object's *properties*.[42] As in the case of aesthetic distance, the strategy is to explicate the concept that we begin with—the concept available from ordinary experience, folk theory, or prior specialist theory—in relation to and using the resources of relevant empirical research. In this way, the space of aesthetic reason is indeed reorganized in virtue of empirical discoveries.

Nanay's thesis is a general one about aesthetic attention, one concerned to show what makes such attention distinctive in structure and phenomenology. It is evident how the design of a movie theatre enables such attention: the dimming of the lights and soundproofing of the space facilitate our attention on the aesthetic object (the movie, rather than the architectural décor), leaving the design of the film itself to move and shape our attention across the levels of visual and sonic form, narrative, character, theme, and symbolism—that is, in Nanay's terms, the different sorts of property comprising an artwork. Note, however, that this dialectic between focused and distributed attention may be structured in much more specific ways: Nanay concludes his study with a suggestive analysis of a number of films by Abbas Kiarostami, including *Mosāfer/The Traveller* (1974), *Ta'm-e gīlās/A Taste of Cherry* (1993), and *Bād mā rā khāhad bord/The Wind Will Carry Us* (1999), showing how they create a dynamic between the main body of the film, governed by an emotionally charged, empathic form of attention strongly focused on the protagonist, and a coda in which such focused attention gives way to a much more distributed form of attention to the multitude of other objects (and properties of objects) surrounding the protagonist.[43]

From Explanation to Understanding (and Back Again)

Theory construction goes hand in hand with an emphasis on explanation. According to one tradition of thought, explanation in turn goes hand in hand with understanding; Michael Strevens holds that 'scientific understanding [is] that state produced, and only produced, by grasping a true explanation'.[44] I frequently use the term 'understanding' in just this sense, across this work; and where I use the term without further qualification, this is the sense of 'understanding' that I intend. The explanatory focus of naturalism, however, is commonly contrasted with the aim of facilitating 'understanding' (*Verstehen*) defined as a distinct method characteristic of the interpretative disciplines typical of the humanities. And according to another tradition of thought, empathy (the focus of Chapter 7) is the primary route to such understanding. But is there a clean and simple distinction between explanation, and understanding in this latter sense—between the domain of causal interaction and explanation, and the domain of meaning and interpretation? Certainly this is the view of many theorists of the human sciences. 'We explain nature', wrote Wilhelm Dilthey, 'but we understand mental life'.[45] The cultural anthropologist Clifford Geertz articulated a similar creed: 'Believing, with Max Weber, that man is an animal suspended in webs of significance he himself has spun, I take culture to be those webs, and the analysis of it to be therefore not an experimental science in search of law but an interpretive one in search of meaning.'[46] Even theorists who query the obsession with interpretation in the humanities nevertheless often assume the same underlying distinction; thus David Bordwell argues that

Scholars often resist the cognitive approach to art because they're reluctant to mount causal or functional explanations. Instead of asking how films work or how spectators understand films, many scholars prefer to offer interpretive commentary on films. Even what's called film theory is largely a mixture of received doctrines, highly selective evidence, and more or less free association. Which is to say that many humanists treat doing film theory as a sort of abstract version of doing film criticism. They don't embrace the practices of rational inquiry, which include assessing a wide body of evidence, seeking out counterexamples, and showing how a line of argument is more adequate than its rivals.[47]

Two factors are important here in complicating this picture. The first concerns the place of meaning in the biological world. We think of meaning prototypically in human contexts—from the local and immediate meanings conveyed by language, gesture, and facial expression, to the larger-scale meanings embodied in paintings, novels, and films, for example. And many theories of art put meaning in the limelight: in the domain of philosophical aesthetics, consider Arthur Danto's argument that art is defined by meaning and embodiment, summarized in his appropriation of Hegel's characterization of art as 'the sensuous embodiment of the idea'. Meaning is nevertheless also rife in the non-human world. Neither dogs nor dolphins write novels, but like all other animals, they signal to and communicate with one another, through bodily and facial expression, movement, and chemical emission. And—keeping the other side of the equation in mind—humans are hardly exempt from chemical signalling: witness the thriving deodorant and perfume industries. The radio announcer puts in Ernst Lubitsch's *Trouble in Paradise* (1932) makes the point well: 'Remember, it doesn't matter what you say, it doesn't matter how you look, it's how you smell!' As with bodily expression, chemical communication is at once naturally grounded and culturally elaborated.

Humans have vastly extended the means by which meaning can be created and communicated, through all manner of social institutions (religion, fiction) and physical structures acting as vehicles of symbolic meaning, from clothing and bodily decoration to architectural monuments (though even here we find analogues in the non-human world: consider the vividly decorated nests of the bower bird). In fact the human exploitation of the external environment reaches well beyond the communication of meaning, enhancing many types of cognition. Clark argues that 'the sketchpad is not just a convenience for the artist, nor simply a kind of external memory or durable medium for the storage of particular ideas. Instead, the iterated process of externalizing and reperceiving is integral to the process of artistic cognition itself.'[48] In the context of filmmaking, we see this process of externalized cognition at many points in the process of production, from the literal sketching involved in storyboarding, to the cycle of revision-and-reperception that constitutes editing. Filmmakers do not arrive at editing decisions 'in the head' alone, but through a reiterated process of trial edits which are then viewed for their qualities and effectiveness. Such 'environmental looping', as Clark describes it, is a key aspect of the larger theory of the 'extended mind' (considered at length in Chapter 7).

The point here is not to put human and non-human meaning into some kind of competition, but merely to insist that meaning per se is not the unique possession of the human kingdom, and that such meaning must have evolved from the non-human animal world in the first place, as Darwin demonstrates in relation to emotion in his *The Expression of the Emotions in Man and Animals*. (Chapter 5 explores emotional expression in film in the light of Darwin's study.) *Meaning is a perfectly natural phenomenon.* The fact that specific meanings can only be had in particular contexts, and in the human case those contexts will inevitably involve culturally specific factors, in no way undermines the natural origins and character of meaning.

For all of these reasons, Paul Grice's decision to label the kind of meaning generated by humans in conversation—arguably the paradigm for all human meaning—as 'non-natural' meaning is, at least from the perspective of philosophical naturalism, an unhappy and misleading choice.[49] Grice posits a distinction between 'natural' meaning (where meaning arises from a simple causal relationship: smoke means fire; dark clouds mean rain) and the 'non-natural' meaning created in human conversation, where intentions play a critical mediating role between the meaningful entity (the utterance) and the meaning that is created through it and taken from it.[50] A speaker intends to convey a certain meaning through an utterance, and the speaker's interlocutor interprets the utterance as a vehicle of the speaker's intention; figuring out the meaning of a speech act is a kind of reverse engineering. The intended meaning may be simple or complex, subtle or brazen, and the relationship between the intended meaning and the utterance may be direct or ironic. But we can nevertheless trace the lineage and form of human conversational exchanges back to the communicative exchanges of species lacking language.[51] And as I will argue, the presence of intention does not straightforwardly place a phenomenon outside the domain of causality. Finally, labelling something 'non-natural' implies that it is not amenable to empirical or scientific study, which would put in doubt the scientific credentials of linguistics. Are we to believe that linguistics has discovered nothing about the nature and origins of language? There are strong reasons, then, for resisting Grice's characterization of conversational meaning as 'non-natural', even as we can recognize that there is a distinction to be made between purely causal meanings, and those mediated by animal (including human) intentions.

Certainly the complexity of meaning, and the capacity for abstract and recursive layers of meaning, is greater within than outwith the sphere of human behaviour; *symbolic* representation and meaning in particular might well be distinctively human.[52] To take a specific example: many non-human animals are capable of *deception*—of sending false or misleading information, of false signalling. Mark Rowlands discusses such deceptive behaviour among apes and dogs (contrasting it with the absence, on his account, of such behaviour among wolves).[53] We can probably also attribute the capacity *to lie* to some species other than humans (unless we stipulate that lying must involve language). But *perjury* is a uniquely human form of deception—or at least a form of deception restricted to beings with the conceptual resources enabled by language, as well as institutions of law. Nonetheless, it is clear how perjury developed from, and depends conceptually on, simpler forms of deception; and it is clear that all of these forms of deception count as kinds of meaning. So meaning cannot be restricted to that 'kingdom within a kingdom', the human world; here we have one of those threads that make apparently disparate phenomena 'hang together', to recall Sellars's famous expression. This point is given emphasis in 'teleosemantic' theories of the mind, such as Dretske's alluded to earlier, which theorize beliefs and other mental contents in terms of evolved, biological purposes.[54]

We also find such elaborations of basic deception in the sphere of art and aesthetic experience. Consider, for example, the notions of *misdirection* and *dramatic illusion*. Misdirection describes the artistic strategy of channelling the perceiver's attention in a particular direction so that she fails to notice some other critical detail. (Misdirection is thus closely related to feigning, feinting, dummying, and sports-specific moves such as the 'counter trey' in American football; it is also central to the practice of theatrical magic.[55]) The perceiver is led to make a wrong inference, or form an expectation which will then be defeated—all in the name of creating surprise, suspense, or some other aesthetic effect. At the shot-to-shot level, continuity editing works in just this way, timing edits so that our attention is drawn to movements, expressions, and gestures in the diegesis rather than the cuts; not for nothing is such editing often said to be 'invisible'. At the level of the sequence, in Chapter 3 I examine the 'threat scene' pioneered by producer Val Lewton, in which we are led to expect an intrusion into the frame from one direction—perhaps by virtue of a character glancing in that direction—only for the intrusion to come from a different direction, or to fail to materialize at all.

A more intricate example of misdirection, working at the level of the narrative as a whole, occurs in *The Sixth Sense* (M. Night Shyamalan, 1999). Roughly midway through the film, the young protagonist (Haley Joel Osment), staring intently at Malcolm Crowe (Bruce Willis), tells him that he sees dead people—in effect waving the solution to the film's central enigma under the spectator's nose, for though he does not recognize it himself, Malcolm himself is dead. The narrative framing of the scene, however, misdirects us: multiple earlier (and subsequent) cues support the assumption that Malcolm is alive and well, so the chances are that we will be blind to the narrative twist quite literally staring us in the face.[56] We will encounter many further examples of misdirection across the present study; in particular, in Chapters 5, 6, and 8 we will see how social deception and aesthetic misdirection come together in the dramatic exploitation of the 'social smile' and other expressive ruses.

Dramatic illusion, meanwhile, refers to the idea that, when we engage fully with a film or stage play, we come to believe in the reality of the represented events (or in more complex formulations, we 'suspend our disbelief', or 'disavow' our knowledge that we are perceiving a representation). The notion has played a particularly important role in film theory.[57] The plausibility of any particular account of dramatic (or specifically cinematic) illusion is less important here than the fact that, like misdirection, the concept represents a development of basic deception, specific to the domain of the arts.

Taking stock: all of this suggests, first, that the conventional dichotomy between (scientific) explanation and (humanistic) interpretation is inadequate; and second, that meaning and interpretation can be treated naturalistically. What is more, at least one type of interpretation *is a form of explanation*. In aiming to establish the meaning intended by the author of a work, *intentionalist* interpretations have the structure of an explanation. When Paisley Livingston argues that the right interpretation of *Day of Wrath* (Carl Theodor Dreyer, 1943) involves us concluding that Anne (Lisbeth Movin) is not a witch but an ordinary woman, his case rests on a combination of filmic and contextual evidence that Dreyer shaped the film in such a way that we would eventually alight upon this conclusion, having (also by design) undergone various hesitations along the way. Thus, on Livingston's view, when a viewer of the film interprets it in this way, this outcome is explained by Dreyer's intentions as they are embodied in the design of the film.[58] And ironically, Gricean-inspired accounts of (so-called) 'non-natural' meaning, including those advanced by Livingston and Currie, are integral to the most compelling models of intentionalist interpretation.[59] In the next section, we will see how this square gets circled.

What of other types of interpretation? Anti-intentionalist interpretations that pay no special heed to the intentions of authors can also be approached from a naturalistic perspective, albeit in a different way. Such interpretations are in effect appropriations, actions that seek to create meaning from works regardless of the intentions of those who made them, and can thus be explained as further acts of meaning creation, returning us to the natural grounding of meaning and communication. Anti-intentionalist interpretations are in this sense forward- rather than backward-looking; they are interested in what sense *can be* made of a work, rather than what meaning it *was designed* to convey. Thus, even anti-intentionalist interpretations, which strive not to be intentional explanations, can nonetheless be explained. Bordwell's *Making Meaning* advances a naturalistic theory of interpretation, deeply informed by cognitive science, which encompasses both intentionalist and anti-intentionalist interpretation. The spread of ideas and meaning irrespective of intention has been theorized by memetics, and by Dan Sperber's related 'epidemiological' theory of cultural transmission (in a book not coincidentally titled *Explaining*

Culture).[60] All in all, then, there is ample reason for doubting a neat and clean separation between explanation and humanistic understanding, and for recognizing the capacity of naturalism to encompass interpretation in many of its guises.

Perceptualism and Expansionism

This same body of naturalistic theory of interpretation also addresses another potential problem faced by naturalized aesthetics. Roger Rothman and Ian Verstegen discuss what they call 'perceptualism'—a focus on the perceptual level of our experience and appreciation of art, and 'a commitment to the analysis of art from the perspective of perceptual psychology'.[61] Appeals to science are all very well, the hermeneutic theorist might say, so long as we are only interested in the low-level, perceptual features of paintings and photos and movies. Vision scientists can tell us about edge detection and contrast effects, while their colleagues in the psychoacoustics lab can tell us about the McGurk, ventriloquist, and illusory flash effects.[62] But they can't lay a glove on more complex meanings—the higher-order implications of works bearing on existential, moral, or political questions. The Gricean-inspired research programme on communicative action, however, which extends the focus on conversational meaning in Grice's original model to the larger scale and more indirect forms of communication at play in the arts, answers this worry by showing how naturalists are not fixated on or restricted to the basic perceptual comprehension of works.

Naturalists might also retort to the charge of perceptualism with two more observations. First, they can point out that low-level features of works—those lying beneath the radar of conscious attention—nevertheless play a critical role in allowing us to categorize works properly, and that such categorization materially affects the nature of our appreciation. We can identify with a high degree of reliability the genre of a piece of music—whether it is a piece of jazz, country music, or heavy metal—based on a very brief fragment; and that identification will shape our expectations and our response.[63] The same considerations apply to our apprehension of films.[64] Second, naturalists can also underline that experiencing and appreciating artworks does not involve a simple one-way escalator, from early vision to purely conceptual activity; rather it draws us into a cycle of perception, emotion, cognition, and reflection. As we watch a film, for example, our embodied minds are always encountering new images and sounds, even as we formulate higher-order interpretations which relate what we are currently seeing and hearing with what we have already perceived, and in general work on processing the film at a more abstract level.

Moreover, the character of many of the perceptual experiences generated by films and other artworks will often be quite unlike ordinary perceptual experience—not because of some ghostly or 'non-natural' sphere into which such experience propels us, but because artworks by design push and pull our perception in ways that happen rarely and only accidentally (if at all) in ordinary experience. The precisely engineered, undulating wave patterns of Bridget Riley's Op Art paintings do not turn up in nature, any more than do the mosaic surfaces of Impressionism or the precisely rendered forms of realism. Even when motivated by realism, pictorial invention invariably delivers new forms of visual experience, rather than merely staging illusions of familiar experience; witness the phenomenon of 3D cinema. Dominic Lopes labels this tendency of artworks to push our embodied minds into new territory *expansionism*: in our engagement with works of art, our 'capacities are frequently extended in quite new directions, operating in ways not seen outside artistic contexts'.[65] In just this spirit, Rothman and Verstegen argue that Rudolf Arnheim's analysis of Cubism allows us to appreciate 'one of Picasso and Braque's most signal pictorial achievements: to have extended our experience of visual resemblance to the point where it seems almost to vanish entirely'.[66] The notion of expansionism plays a particularly important role in the naturalized aesthetics being developed here, then, in that it shows that philosophical naturalism has no special tie with artistic realism.

The forms that such 'expansion' of ordinary perceptual experience can take are very diverse—indeed indefinitely various. Tonality is one significant area of technique in this respect: virtually any tonal scheme—colour or monochromatic, with whatever nuances of contrast and saturation—will depart from our ordinary visual experience; Chapter 2 picks up on this aspect of film style. Framing and shot-scale can deprive us of cues pertaining to the size of depicted objects, allowing us to see visual details in panoramic splendour (Figure 1.1). Lens choice is similarly fundamental. Telephoto and zoom lenses warp standard perspective relations, compressing spatial planes and making parallel lines appear to converge in the

Figure 1.1 In John Smith's *Dad's Stick* (2012), an extreme close-up transforms a functional object—a stick used to mix house paint—into a panoramic colour field.

foreground rather than the distance. The 'contrazoom', pioneered by Alfred Hitchcock in *Vertigo* (1958) and now widely used to express disorientation or shock,
contorts ordinary visual experience by keeping shot-scale (more or less) constant
while perspective relations shift around a central figure (Figures 1.2a–1.2d).

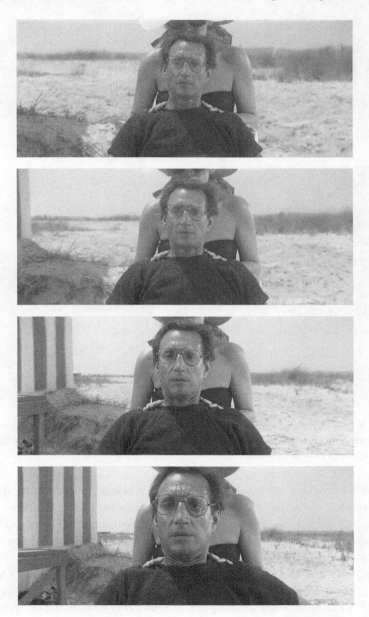

Figures 1.2a–1.2d The contrazoom in *Jaws* (Steven Speilberg, 1975).

Figure 1.3 Digitally distorted space in *Antichrist* (Lars von Trier, 2009).

Figure 1.4 Space as represented by the SuperView setting in GoPro cameras: the central area of the frame remains in standard, linear perspective, while the zones to each side of the image map the space in curvilinear fashion.

Digital film introduces still other possibilities in a whole range of contexts, from the erratic 'ripples' disturbing the visual space of Lars von Trier's *Antichrist* (2009) (Figure 1.3),[67] to the 'SuperView' option on GoPro cameras (Figure 1.4), which keeps the central area of the frame in standard perspective while the areas to each side are stretched in the manner of a wide-angle lens.

Staying with lens effects but moving away from narrative film, in *Serene Velocity* (1970), Ernie Gehr makes varied perspective relations 'pop in and out at us rhythmically',[68] while in *Saturday Morning* (1978), Dan Curry bamboozles our perceptual assumptions about scale, vantage point, and sound source, defamiliarizing the most humdrum activities. A kindred focus on perspective and perceptual experience is evident in the work of artist Patrick Hughes, who has developed a system of 'reverspective', an optical illusion in which those parts of a three-dimensional representation closest to the viewer appear to be the furthest away (Figures 1.5a–1.5b). The illusion only snaps into place once we place ourselves within a narrowly defined angle in front of the representation; our experience of approaching and withdrawing from Hughes's reverspective works involves a moment of dramatic

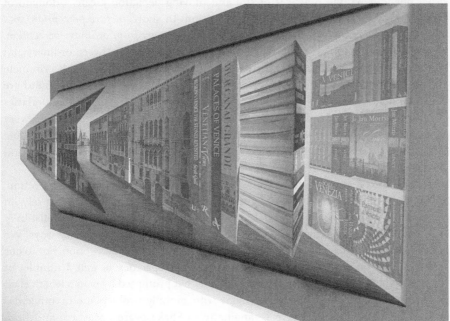

Figures 1.5a–1.5b *The Books of Venice* (2013), a 'reverspective' composition by Patrick Hughes.

visual transformation, as we move into and out of the physical zone in which the illusion takes hold.

In commenting on such play with visual perspective in film, Bordwell rejects a model of depiction in film based narrowly on the optical principles of linear perspective, as laid out by Leon Battista Alberti in *De Pictura* (1439-41). Bordwell notes the ways in which staging, composition, and choice of lens length can transform linear perspective: 'The Renaissance masters of perspective knew that the mechanical projection of light was something quite apart from the perceptual experience of the picture.'[69] Lopes makes a parallel observation about pictorial depiction, arguing that

there is no reason why pictorial designs must be projections on to an imaginary interposed plane, or why pictures must represent their subjects as having combinations of properties that they could be seen to have from some viewpoint. That is to say, there is no reason why the dimensions of variation over which pictures' contents and subjects are recognizable should be circumscribed by the rules of optics.[70]

Arguably, *seeing-in* itself is the basic form of expansion here. Wollheim defines 'seeing-in' as our capacity to see, in a non-illusionary fashion, three-dimensional spaces and objects in two-dimensional surfaces, contrasting such 'seeing-in' with ordinary 'face-to-face' seeing.[71] Although seeing-in is a natural perceptual capacity, evident in our ability to see faces and figures in clouds and other naturally occurring visual phenomena, the practices of still and moving depiction create a domain of experience quite distinct from face-to-face vision. In short, *picture perception, and motion picture perception, are phenomenologically distinct from ordinary perception.* A parallel argument might be made regarding the relationship between ordinary and musical sounds: while we have the capacity in our ordinary audition to discriminate pitches, rhythms, and timbres, in the domain of music these aspects of sound are shaped and stretched to expand our auditory experience far beyond the boundaries of ordinary audition. In this way, the notion of expansion points towards a very general thesis about the role of aesthetic experience in the arts, as well as illuminating specific artistic styles (like Cubism) and techniques (such as lens effects in film and photography).

Here we also rejoin the discussion of 'aesthetic distance' and 'aesthetic attention' initiated above: whatever is special about aesthetic experience, it need not rely on invocations of 'spirit' or mythical states of mind, but can be explained naturalistically in terms of the redeployment of our ordinary capacities in extraordinary ways. We need only add that the process of expansion applies not only to perception, but to our entire suite of perceptual, cognitive, and emotional capacities as well. Examples of cognitive or emotional expansion might include that prompted by works which elicit our sympathetic or empathic engagement with morally problematic or otherwise unusual or unattractive characters, ranging from Shakespeare's Macbeth and Lear, Milton's Lucifer, Goncharov's Oblomov, Dostoevsky's Underground Man, and Michel

Houllebecq's Michel Renault, right up to the gallery of contemporary televisual antiheroes, including Tony Soprano, Walter White, and Ray Donovan.[72] Or, moving in a different direction, there are works which sustain our attention on ordinary, even banal, activities and routines, inviting us to see them afresh and re-evaluate them: consider, for example, Frederick Wiseman's documentaries on institutional life, from *High School* (1968) to *National Gallery* (2014), or Chantal Ackerman's *Jeanne Dielman, 23 quai du Commerce, 1080 Bruxelles* (1975). The expansive effects of art, we might say, defamiliarize our perceptual, cognitive, and/or emotional experience of these phenomena. (I revisit the relationship between expansionism and defamiliarization in Chapter 4, and develop the idea of expansionism specifically in relation to empathy in Chapter 7.)

From Causes to Reasons (and Back Again)

I claimed above that two factors complicate the received wisdom that the sciences pursue explanation, while the humanities aim for understanding. If the first challenges the putative divide between the human world and (the rest of) the biological world, the second queries the equally entrenched idea that there is an ontological (and thus epistemological) gulf between the human world—the space of reason, agency, and intention—and the causal, physical world. Note that this is no minor difference of emphasis, if the arguments of the preceding section are on the right tracks; for this new divide is not then between the human and the physical worlds, but between the animal world as a whole—all those parts of the biosphere possessing some level of mental function—and the domain of the narrowly physical. Conceived in dichotomous, 'two-cultural' terms, in this new schism biology sits with the humanities on one side of the dividing line, with physics on the other.

What considerations support such a picture? Consider the relationship between movement and action. Actions are not mere physical movements, but movements animated by intentions, and intentions in turn are motivated by reasons—we have reasons to act in some ways but not in others. My leg swinging towards the football counts as an action because I intend to kick the football, and I have reason to do that because I'm participating in a football game, the ball has come to me, and I see an opportunity to pass it to a well-positioned teammate. By contrast, if another player strikes my ulnar nerve—otherwise known as my funny bone—in an accidental collision, and my arm lurches in response to the sharp tingling sensation so caused, the movement of my arm is unintended and no reasons can be marshalled to explain it. Many infer from this orthodox picture that conceiving of the world in causal terms on the one hand, and in rational terms on the other, are radically different and incommensurable enterprises.

There are at least two reasons for resisting this conclusion. First, agency and intention do not always coincide. Some of our actions are, in the terminology of Brian O'Shaughnessy, *sub-intentional*. 'We fidget, we drum our fingers idly on the table, roll our tongues around our mouths, tap a foot to an imagined rhythm. These are all actions, but done with no purpose and without the direction of intention.'[73] In such cases, intention never enters the picture; we return to this topic later in the chapter. In another type of case, agency on the one hand, and reasoning and intention on the other, may come apart in a way that reveals the role of causality in human affairs in a different way. When I intend to kick the ball away from my team's goal but miscue and send the ball neatly past my own goalkeeper, I have scored an own goal even though I didn't intend to. That is, I have been the cause of a goal for my opponents, even though I had every reason to avoid this and indeed intended to avoid this outcome. Had I not attempted to clear the ball, the goal would not have been scored—or at least, *this* goal would not have been scored; it is possible that a goal of a different character, with a different explanation, might have obtained.

The world is replete with such unintended byproducts of intended action—with accidents. Such events happen and can be explained, but not in terms of agents having reasons for actions. Unintended byproducts by definition happen 'behind the backs' of agents. Donald Davidson elaborates this idea through what he calls (after Joel Feinberg) the 'accordion effect': 'an agent causes what his actions cause, even if some of the effects of the action were unintended'.[74] This principle is recognized in the law: witness the recent case of the French schoolteacher held responsible (and charged with manslaughter) for the deaths of the teenagers he led onto a closed piste, doubtless intending only to make the children happy. Turning to the photographic arts, consider Henri Cartier-Bresson's *Cardinal Pacelli, Montmartre, Paris* (1938). In shooting this photograph, Cartier-Bresson caused 'the man in the upper left, with the unfortunate mustache, [to] be shown as looking away from the Cardinal' even if Cartier-Bresson had no intention to capture this particular detail photographically (and could not have anticipated just this detail at the moment he depressed the shutter).[75] In film and photography, perhaps above all other arts, *intentional agency, unintended agency,* and *pure causality* are keenly intertwined. A dualist metaphysics that drives a wedge between causal and rational explanation makes an unhappy dance partner for such art forms.

2.   The second reason for doubting the idea that the 'space of reasons' is radically separate from the space of causal interaction and explanation is that *intentional action is a form of causality.* Or as Davidson puts it: rational explanation 'is a species of ordinary causal explanation'—one that adds to simple causal interactions many complexities, but a form of causal explanation nonetheless.[76] When I intend to wash up, then—assuming that I am more competent with the dishes than with a ball at my feet—the dishes end up cleaner. My intention to clean the dishes is part of the causal chain that leads from the state of affairs in which the dishes are smeared with the remains of chili con carne to the state of affairs in which the dishes sit imperfectly rinsed in the drying rack. Had I not acted successfully on my intention to clean the dishes, the dishes would not be clean (or else some other explanation would be required—most

likely another intentional-causal explanation, since a tsunami or flash flood is unlikely to have washed through the house).

To apply this line of thinking to an artistic case, consider the following counter-factual: 'if John had not seen the film intended by Jane to elicit experience *, John would not have experienced * by seeing Jane's film'. Since Jane has intended, among other things, to startle her audience with some loud, unexpected sounds, John's experience is constituted at least in part by certain physical, bodily responses. Thus, the explanation of John's embodied experience requires reference to Jane's intention; intention, action, and physical cause and effect are bound up within the same explanation. It is in this sense that the language of intention and reason is commensurate with the language of causality; and some theorists readily recognize this. Michael Baxandall, for example, states that 'one of a number of unforced and . . . unavoidable ways in which we think of pictures is as products of purposeful activity, and therefore caused'.[77]

Summarizing the picture I outline here: intentional agency is a form of agency, and agency is form of causality. Non-human animals share the capacity for reasoned, intentional agency with humans to different degrees, dependent on the cognitive resources of each particular species. We may add that narratives (at least of the canonical variety) put intentional agency at their centre. Narratives represent agents performing actions and pursuing goals (in *Hamlet* (1599–1602), Claudius murders his brother, Hamlet's father; Hamlet wants to kill his uncle, and intends to stab him through the curtain) but in a dynamic relationship with unintended acts (Hamlet stabs Polonius though he doesn't intend to) and brute physical causes (cold weather shrouds Elsinore at the beginning of the play; Claudius claims that Hamlet's father dies of natural causes). In Juan Antonio Bayona's *Lo imposible/The Impossible* (2012), the tsunami destroys the standing intentions of the characters at the outset, and the film details their efforts to pursue new goals through intended actions, some of which have unintended consequences. Narratives attempting to represent the agency and reasoning of various non-human species do exist,[78] but much more commonly, animal agents are 'personified', that is, represented as if they possessed the full complement of human cognitive attributes.

Beneath and Beyond Intention: In the Realm of the Subpersonal

We noted above O'Shaughnessy's identification of sub-intentional actions, those behavioural tics which manifest themselves without intentional directedness. But there are bigger game living on this terrain than those drumming fingers and rolling tongues. Here we need to take stock of a variety of ideas concerning phenomena lying beyond intention and outside consciousness. The most significant of these ideas, as we shall see, is the distinction between the *personal* and the *subpersonal*. How do these ideas bear upon our experience of cinema and the other arts, and the explanation of such experience?

We engage with films as spectators. But just what kind of an entity is a 'spectator'? The pretheoretical answer is that a spectator is a *person*—that is to say, a more or less coherent, continuous, goal-oriented, conscious individual human agent, possessed of certain rational and reflective capacities—in Locke's words, a 'thinking intelligent Being, that has reason and reflection, and can consider it self as it self'.[79] On the basis of possession of such capacities, we ascribe certain rights and duties to persons. A spectator is such a being engaged in a certain kind of activity; an activity that is at once cognitive (it involves making sense of and experiencing films) and social (typically we watch and discuss films with others, at least in the cinema), these two dimensions coming together in what psychologists term 'joint attention', the shared focus of two or more individuals on a single object. Joint attention emerges early in development, and in its mature form—most infants mastering the skill to this level by the age of fourteen months—involves not merely shared gazing at a single object of attention, but mutual awareness of shared gaze. Agents jointly attending to an object are, in effect, attending to both the object and to each other's attention to the object, as is manifest in the glances of the agents alternating between the object itself and each other.[80]

However, in contrast to the case of joint attention, much of the perceptual and cognitive work that we undertake when we make sense of and interact with a film happens at the level of the 'cognitive unconscious'—rapidly and automatically, beneath the level of conscious intention, with little reflection or self-consciousness, or what Robinson in her theory of emotion terms 'secondary appraisal' (Chapter 6 explores Robinson's account of emotion in some detail).[81] When we see spaces and characters in the two-dimensional surface of the screen, and when we see figures in motion, we have little or no control over the processes that give rise to such experience. In these cases, we see (or have the experience of seeing) things— volumetric figures in motion—that are not literally there.

In parallel fashion, we also sometimes *fail* to see particular features that *are* present in the cinematic visual array, such as certain types of cut and camera movement, as suggested in the notion of 'invisible editing'. Editing in this mode exploits the phenomenon of 'change blindness' (to which we return in Chapters 2 and 4), that is, the 'gappy' nature of human perception (allowing us to see how our perceptual capacities have limitations and characteristic ways of malfunctioning which can be ludically exploited). Moving up a level from such basic perception, when we recognize a character (that is, discriminate a character as an individual) or when we attribute thoughts and emotions to characters, we usually just do it, so to speak. Getting an explanatory grip on how all this happens involves a journey into the realm of the *subpersonal*.[82]

Our personhood—our capacity to act as a conscious, goal-oriented intentional being—supervenes on a host of *subpersonal* capacities, that is, lower-level processing capacities that allow us to represent, deliberate on, and act in and on the world. These subpersonal capacities depend upon a variety of mechanisms, including the saccadic movement of our eyes, our distinct visual systems supporting action and object recognition,[83] the startle response, the systems governing breathing, digestion, and the cycle of waking and sleep, the 'affect programmes' associated with the basic emotions, mirror neurons, and so on and on. Such subpersonal mechanisms, that form the focus of research in physiology, psychophysiology, and neuroscience, can be identified as specific, individual systems to the extent that their functioning can be impaired while other mechanisms, even closely related ones, remain intact.

Let me take the circadian ('body') clock as an example of a subpersonal mechanism. The body clock regulates the cycle of waking and sleeping, and it does so beneath conscious intention. That is, we find ourselves getting tired or wakeful; but we can't simply decide to be wakeful or tired, as insomniacs especially know all too well. You can intervene—act intentionally—on your body, by taking drugs or setting up your environment in a particular way or undertaking certain activities, which are likely to make you feel tired or wakeful. But you can't just will or intend to be wakeful or tired.

The phenomenon of jet lag is particularly instructive in this regard. When we suffer jet leg, our body clock falls out of alignment with the temporal orientation of our location. In such a context, while at the level of conscious intention we know full well where we are within the cycle of the day, our body clock tells us something very different. Similarly, when I'm seasick, my visual sense of orientation remains intact even as my vestibular system signals trouble. And when I experience the Müller-Lyer illusion, my visual system tells me that one line is longer than the other, even as another part of my mind, benefiting from the input of a ruler, tells me that the lines are of the same length. Thus, talk of (parts of) my body having its (their) own mind is perfectly cogent, if metaphorical. These examples show how subpersonal mechanisms, while normally acting in concert to enable coherent agency, can function with some degree of autonomy and pull in different directions. The vision of the mind 'as an assortment of subagencies'[84] comes home to roost here. Taken individually these mechanisms are relatively dumb, or at least limited in function; they are 'subpersonal' precisely in the sense that, in isolation, none of them instantiates personhood. In unison, however, they afford the kind of reflective and flexible agency that characterizes fully fledged personhood.

Hacker and his co-author Maxwell Bennett would doubtless count talk of our body clock telling us things an instance of the 'mereological fallacy'—that is, the ascription of psychological predicates ('knows', 'feels', 'senses', and so forth) to the brain, or any other part of the body, rather than the person as a whole; a form of ascription which they regard as nonsensical, if taken literally.[85] Notably, however, they allow that such ascriptions may function metaphorically. This is a significant concession if we assume that metaphors have cognitive value, that is, if we hold that metaphors are able to aid our understanding of the world. So what's the score here?

Bennett and Hacker clearly believe that metaphors can be misleading, especially when they are not recognized for what they are and lead to mistaken inferences.[86] If metaphors can be epistemically defective, however, it follows that they can be epistemically effective, helping us to understand certain matters in ways closed to non-figurative language. They certainly help themselves to metaphors when it suits them. Of Colin Blakemore's talk of 'neural maps', they say: 'These alleged metaphorical uses are so many banana skins in the pathway of their user.'[87] As they themselves demonstrate in their discussion of Blakemore, metaphors can be more or less apt, illuminating or obscuring crucial features of the target of the metaphor. Bennett and Hacker must hold that metaphors possess this kind of cognitive power, else it would be odd that they worry so much about unacknowledged metaphor. Rather than arguing that metaphor plays no legitimate role in science or philosophy, their claim seems to be the more modest one that metaphors must be used with care, assessed for their aptness, and not confused with literal uses of language (and that these norms are not carefully enough observed in neuroscience and neurophilosophy). So it seems that, even on their view, we can ask whether a metaphor is apt and justified.

In the case at hand, saying that there are circumstances in which the body clock 'believes' and 'tells' us that it is a different time of day than it actually is in the time zone we inhabit gives us a description and an explanation of the distinctive embodied state of mind known as 'jet lag'. The metaphor is neither merely ornamental (it is doing real cognitive work, giving us an understanding of jet lag, and also pointing us towards the larger truth concerning our cognitive constitution as an imperfectly integrated assemblage of sub-systems), nor nonsensical (it is a widespread and easily grasped metaphor; speakers who say that their body clock is 'telling them' to get some sleep are not taken to be implying that their body clock has the power of speech, any more than Hacker and Bennett are taken to be suggesting that metaphors are a type of fruit). Disallowing such idioms would certainly lead to a degradation of our understanding of the mind.[88]

The pull between our subpersonal responses and our overall personal judgement is very evident in some of the most basic perceptual responses which make cinema possible. For example, we see depth and movement in cinematic images even as we know the screen is flat and that the underlying film strip is comprised of a succession of still images. Similarly, when we see films with surreal sound–image combinations— say the deep voice of a grown man synched with the speech movements of a child, or the blasts of a tuba synched with pulls on a cow's udder—we know consciously that the sound and image were created separately and that the object we see does not and cannot have made the sound we hear, but we cannot stop ourselves perceiving a single unified sound–image event. The same is true for the phenomenon of sonic 'ventriloquism': the sounds of characters speaking emanates from speakers some distance from the points on the screen where the characters' mouths are visually represented, and yet we experience the characters as speaking entities in a perceptually unified fashion. Even when we are shown the placement of speakers, the sounds are successfully 'thrown' from the speakers and caught by those parts of the image to which they belong.[89]

So a naturalistic approach to film spectatorship requires that we do not stop with the experience and explanatory concepts related to the level of personhood (beliefs, desires, intentions, feelings), but urges that we thicken our account by engaging with the subpersonal mechanisms underpinning personhood. Attention to the subpersonal level allows us to explain such basic, constitutive features of cinema as seeing depth and motion, and integrating sound and image, about which analysis at the personal level has little to say. As the argument develops, we will see in more detail the payoff that comes from this effort to expand our explanatory toolkit. But it is important to register two other points first.

First, one might wonder whether there is a conflict between the relatively disunified picture of human agency arising from attention to subpersonal mechanisms on the one hand, and intentionalist explanation on the other hand. For such explanations might seem to depend upon a robust and unified conception of agency: agents—at least artistic agents—know what they are doing and seek to realize their aims in the way they design their works. In fact intentionalist explanations need not be so demanding or so blunt. We've already seen that intended actions lead as much to unintended as to intended outcomes. We often need to attribute multiple, complex intentions to artistic agents; similarly, we often need to recognize the coexistence of conflicting intentions in collaboratively made artworks like films. Writing of the dimension of 'control' that is integral to intentionalist accounts of authorship, Livingston writes that 'the relevant sense of control is compatible with the spontaneous and non-deliberative elements of artistic production ... "control" here is not to be confused with some ideal of deliberate self-control'.[90] Moreover, whatever degree of disunity and lack of self-knowledge that recognition of the subpersonal brings into play, agency requires a norm of moderately tight integration of the subpersonal components, as is suggested by Michael Smith's 'coherence constraint' (too much incoherence among the mental states of a person undermines agency).[91] So in fact the requirements of intentional explanation, and the implications of subpersonal mental architecture, are not incompatible.

The second point we need to take on board at this juncture takes us back to 'perceptualism' (that is, the theoretical emphasis on the perceptual aspect of art appreciation). In this section we have explored the idea that a naturalistic stance drives us 'downwards', from the personal to the subpersonal level. It might look as if any movement in the other direction—from the personal to the interpersonal—is going to take us away from naturalism and towards autonomism. But that may not be right. Proponents of the 'extended mind', and of 'situated' and 'distributed' cognition, contend that cognition may not be 'brainbound', but rather distributed across multiple agents or in other ways be dependent on the environment beyond the individual 'biological skin-bag'.[92] More modestly, as we've already noted, cognitive and developmental psychologists regard 'joint attention' as an important capacity, one that grounds the possibility for the larger 'community of minds' in which much of human thought and action comes to fruition. Even understanding your own feelings and states of mind is not a strictly private affair, but one that involves you in dialogue with your fellows. As Owen Flanagan puts it:

I can say how I think things seem for you, sometimes before you see that this is how they seem to you. Sometimes you will even treat my account of how things seem for you as authoritative. 'You're right, I just don't feel the same way about him anymore'. Saying how things seem is a project involving intersubjective give-and-take...Getting clear on the phenomenology is not an essentially private enterprise. Good phenomenology is group phenomenology.[93]

In short, any plausible science of the mind—and any naturalistic account of the mind—will need to accommodate the interpersonal, social dimension of human cognition. It cannot remain fixated on the low-level perceptual or cognitive capacities of individual agents.

By the same token, human sociality cannot be treated as forbidden territory for naturalism, any more than it is an impediment for the naturalistic study of other social animals. A comparative, ethological perspective on human behaviour—that is, an approach that looks at humans as one animal species among the multitude of other species—sheds further light on the naturalistic stance. Not so long ago, it was regarded as a philosophical error to attribute emotions, intentions, or any kind of mental state to non-human animals; Descartes regarded animals as automata. Vanquished elsewhere, behaviourism persisted in relation to the animal mind. Primatologists and other ethologists have, however, vastly enriched our understanding of the behaviour and mental life of many animal species. And one revelation of such research has been that learning and culture are more widely distributed across the animal world than previously recognized. Around the world, chimp communities in entirely separate locations use different tool-based techniques to discover and harvest termites. These techniques appear to have been invented and then transmitted through social learning. To the extent, then, that our notion of 'culture' describes learned practices, transmitted socially rather than genetically, and distinctive of particular communities rather than universally adopted, it appears that culture is not the unique possession of humans. Our picture of animals as automata driven only by instinct falls into doubt.

This recognition of learning and culture among some non-human animal species, however, needs to be joined with recognition of the ways in which human cognition, learning, and culture far outstrip what we see in chimps and some other species, in complexity and degree of development. Michael Tomasello—a major contributor to the research on joint attention—identifies the *ratchet effect* as a critical part of the explanation of the centrality of enculturation to human behaviour, and its much more modest role elsewhere in the biosphere: the ability of humans to transmit and *preserve* inventions, through language and other means of representation and communication, so that our knowledge and ability to manipulate the world continually accumulate.[94] This marks us off from other species, even those evolutionarily close cousins with whom we share a great deal of genetic material and quite a bit of anatomical form. Now we may ask: does Tomasello shed light on *homo sapiens* as well as on other great ape species, via the concept of the ratchet effect? If so, it seems hard to deny that these insights have been gleaned through the naturalistic, comparative study of human and other species. Not that this is an easy task; as Sperber remarks, 'Underscoring the uniqueness of humans is all too easy. The challenge is to explain it in a naturalistic perspective.'[95]

From Thick Description to Thick Explanation

One of the more influential ideas across the humanities over the past forty years has been the notion of 'thick description', first proposed by Ryle and adopted by Geertz as a definition of ethnography.[96] Ryle asks us to imagine two superficially identical bodily movements: a boy whose eye twitches, and another who winks in a conspiratorial manner. Ryle adds another layer of complexity by postulating a third variation, where a boy parodies a conspiratorial wink. Ryle's point is that, in order to describe properly each of these bodily movements, we must engage in 'thick description'. A 'thin' description of each episode, restricting itself to the observable movement of the eyelid and muscles around it, would fail to discriminate between the three distinct events. 'The thinnest description of what the rehearsing parodist is doing is, roughly, the same as for the involuntary eyelid twitch', Ryle argues, 'but its thick description is a many-layered sandwich, of which only the bottom slice is catered for by the thinnest description'.[97]

Geertz suggests that ethnography is nothing other than an 'elaborate venture in' such thick description: 'Ryle's example presents an image only too exact of the sort of piled-up structures of inference and implication through which an ethnographer is continually trying to pick his way.'[98] As an anthropologist, not surprisingly Geertz puts on emphasis on the culturally specific practices, 'structures of signification',[99] and symbolism that such thick description must bring into play. While advanced by Geertz in relation to his home disciplines of social anthropology and ethnography, Geertz's theory of thick description is widely celebrated as an account pertinent to the study of culture in general, from literary and film studies to art history and cultural studies.

Geertz provides us with a rich and compelling analysis of one important kind of activity in the human sciences, one that is deservedly influential. My goal here is not to displace it, but to pair it with a parallel and equally 'elaborate venture' in *thick explanation* (though I should say that in suggesting that there is a parallel between the two activities, I do not mean to imply that there are point-by-point similarities). The notion of thick explanation will allow us to draw together various threads from the preceding discussion of naturalism, especially those bearing on the 'depth' of our knowledge and our degree of confidence in it, as well as the dual attention to the personal and subpersonal levels. Thick explanation might be thought of as a model or ideal of the naturalistic explanation of artistic and cultural phenomena.

What makes for a thick explanation? Before we can answer that question, we first need to establish the idea that explanation may come in degrees and may operate at different levels—that, as with description, explanation can vary in its 'thickness'. That explanation comes in degrees is implied by the way we use the language of explanation in both ordinary and specialist contexts. David Lewis writes of 'explaining well and badly', for example, while John Dupré avers that evolutionary considerations might be 'part of the full explanation' of particular phenomena.[100] It only

② subpersonal mechanisms underlying
moral experience)

makes sense to talk of 'full' explanations, however, if explanations can be less than 'full', that is, in some sense partial or limited. While some explanations may be flat out wrong, and some exceedingly accurate, in between these poles we find explanations that may be *incomplete* or *superficial*, but not simply mistaken. That is, an explanation may specify some of the factors relevant to an outcome, but not all of them; or an explanation might provide only a superficial description of a causal factor. An explanation may be more or less thick in at least these two dimensions. Say I'm involved in a collision with another car. The collision happens because it is snowing, I'm driving fast, and I get distracted when a bird flies towards the windscreen. If I cite only one of these three factors, my explanation is incomplete; if I say that the road was slippery but fail to mention that it was snowing, then that part of my explanation is vague or superficial. In these and perhaps other ways, explanations may vary in their degree of explanatory adequacy.

So what allows us to maximize the completeness and the depth of an explanation? Two strategies are particularly significant. The first involves a commitment to going beyond person-level explanations, and engaging especially with the subpersonal explanatory level. This is not to *reject* the level of personal explanation—to hold that we can explain nothing by reference to the beliefs, desires, and intentions of human agents; I've already argued that intentionalist interpretations constitute a type of explanation. As Robert van Gulick contends: 'The personal-level experience of understanding is...not an illusion...The fact that my ability is the result of my being composed of an organized system of subpersonal components which produce my orderly flow of thoughts does not impugn my ability.'[101] But it is to insist upon integrating the personal with the subpersonal. If I restrict my analysis of a film sequence to folk psychology and the concepts of the practitioner, I can offer an explanation, but a relatively 'thin' one. Reference to subpersonal phenomena enables a 'thicker' explanation, by revealing the mechanisms that filmmakers intuitively exploit. Across this work, and particularly in Part II, I aim to put this principle into practice through a variety of case studies focusing on the subpersonal mechanisms underlying emotional experience (see, for example, the treatment of affective mimicry in Hitchcock's *Saboteur* (1942) and *Lifeboat* (1944) in Chapter 5). So more particularly, we can say that thick explanations are thick, at least in part, by virtue of their reference to both personal and subpersonal mechanisms. While anthropological thick descriptions move 'sideways', into cultural context, scientifically informed thick explanations move 'downwards', into the subpersonal domain 'beneath' intentionality.

I have noted in passing the second (and more general) strategy by which we may seek to thicken our explanations, in discussing the distinction between scientific method and knowledge. The more we subject our assumptions and beliefs to sceptical pressure, actively examining the logic of arguments and bodies of evidence we ordinarily accept on trust, the more confident we can become regarding our beliefs and the thicker our explanations are likely to become. At least this is one way things can go once we start this process of self-conscious examination; it's also

① subpersonal produce orderly flow of thoughts

possible that our confidence in certain assumptions and the explanations that ordinarily underpin them will wilt in the face of sceptical heat. But either way, by engaging in such reflection we are engaging in a process by which we can thicken our explanations—make them more comprehensive, more exact, and more robust. And one important resource we have at our disposal in probing the assumptions, beliefs, and explanations that we begin with is the scientific method (or again, methods, if we are concerned to stress how the general principles of a scientific attitude to studying the world manifest themselves in different ways in different types of science).

There is another sense, however, in which naturalistic explanations are precisely *not* thick—at least not in a full-blooded way. This is the sense made famous by Bernard Williams in his discussion of 'thick concepts', that is, concepts which combine descriptive and evaluative elements: 'good' and 'bad' in this sense are thin, purely evaluative concepts, while cruel, kind, majestic, and mawkish are all thick concepts, at once describing something and expressing a judgement about it.[102] And then there are purely descriptive concepts—long, tall, short, and shallow— which can be used evaluatively in certain contexts ('the bath's too shallow'), but which are not intrinsically value-laden. Now, it is clear that a naturalized aesthetics cannot aspire to an entirely value-free form of discourse, for that would be to disallow reference to the very aesthetic properties and experiences that we are interested in explaining! And in Chapter 4, we will specifically examine the way in which certain perceptual experiences are 'thick' in both Geertz's and Williams's senses, that is, by virtue of value-laden, culturally specific ideas (such as the humility bound up with 'the flavour of green tea over rice' memorialized by the Ozu Yasujirō film bearing that name). It is, however, one thing to *describe, explain, and refer to values* and value-laden phenomena; it is another thing to *engage in evaluation*. So while the naturalized aesthetician must make reference to value-laden concepts and phenomena, they must also hold evaluation at bay and prioritize description and explanation.

Thus from a naturalistic perspective, there is a very marked contrast between criticism and theory. For criticism is clearly a kind of thick discourse, blending descriptive, explanatory, and evaluative claims. Criticism is the home of aesthetic judgement—of assessments of the aesthetic value or merit of particular works or groups of works—and as Nick Zangwill argues, aesthetic judgements are intrinsically value-laden.[103] But there is more to aesthetics than aesthetic judgement, and more to the study of film than criticism. Just as there is room in the study of language for both linguistics and literary criticism, so there is room in aesthetics for the explanatory goals of theory and the evaluative goals of critical judgement.

Of course, scientific practice and naturalistic philosophy are value-laden activities in that both are bound by the values of truth-seeking and truth-telling. Neither can science pretend to escape the shaping influence of the ethical and ideological values embodied in society more generally; science is contingently affected by all manner of political and moral views, shaping what research is funded and how questions are formulated, for example.[104] In this sense science as it is actually practised is anything

① criticism / theory

but a 'value-free' zone. But these moral and political currents are, so long as we aspire to the truth-tracking ideal of science, things to be transcended. Though hedged around on all sides by evaluative questions, science itself—and by extension naturalism as a stance towards philosophy and aesthetics—aims to bracket all values bar one: describing and explaining the world as accurately as possible.

No Ghosts Need Apply

At different times, we may stand in relation to artworks in different ways—as artists, as appreciators, or as theorists; and sometimes these roles will overlap and interpenetrate. Nonetheless making art, appreciating art, and explaining art do represent three different activities, each defined by a distinctive goal. When these goals and activities are muddled up, or when we mistake one for another, it is easy for confusion and misunderstanding to arise. Thus, when Michael Chanan implies that recent psychological research on continuity editing merely confirms a body of knowledge discovered by filmmakers more than a century ago, he confuses what is at stake in making and theorizing, and mistakes the nature of the claim being made by the psychologists.[105] Certainly practitioners make discoveries about the world, especially about the media with which they work, and such discovery is particularly salient with radically new media. Nobody is trying to steal those achievements from artists. But such practical know-how, directed towards the goal of producing compelling artworks, is very different to theoretical knowledge, which seeks to explain why the techniques of practitioners work as they do and to place our understanding of these techniques in relation to our knowledge of pertinent aspects of the rest of the world. In other words, the theorist is interested in discovering how film 'hangs together' with, among other things, optics, acoustics, chemistry, computing, and psychology. And, while much know-how is precisely a kind of unstated, tacit knowledge embodied in practice, theoretical knowledge is expressed in propositional form in hypotheses, observation statements, and models. The know-*how* of artists enables them to create artworks that furnish us with knowledge of *what* it is like to be a certain kind of person, or to be in a certain kind of situation. Artworks may also state or imply propositions about the world, but rarely do they provide us with systematic, theoretical knowledge *that* the world works in a certain way. In short, whatever points of contact may exist between them, theory construction is not in direct competition with artistic practice.

As a form of theory, naturalized aesthetics is primarily concerned with explanation. Boiled down to its essence, to approach something naturalistically is to assume that it is explicable—that we can explain its existence and dynamics by mechanisms that we already recognize or that we can discover; that we do not need to put it beyond explanation by claiming it transcends the material world and is somehow *sui generis*—'of itself' and floating free of contact with the rest of the universe. As George Santayana put it:

We are not compelled in naturalism...to ignore immaterial things; the point is that any immaterial things which are recognized shall be regarded as names, aspects, functions, or concomitant products of those physical things among which action goes on...Naturalism will break down, however, so soon as words, ideas, or spirits are taken to be substantial on their own account, and powers at work prior to the existence of their organs, or independent of them.[106]

Naturalists will nevertheless sometimes be seen pursuing what might seem to be some very strange supernatural ideas; both William James and C. D. Broad, within their generally naturalistic approaches to the mind, made space to consider spiritualism and paranormal phenomena.[107] But that is because they were open to the possibility that as yet undiscovered mechanisms would be discovered which would drag such supernatural phenomena into the orbit of naturalism; that we might find the mechanisms explaining the ghost within the machine. After all, if we go back far enough in history, many natural phenomena—lightning, magnetism, eclipses—must have seemed miraculous and beyond all explanation; and yet they have all been caught in the net of the natural. The history of naturalism is in part the history of reclaiming areas of human experience once governed by supernaturalism and superstition for rational understanding and explanation. In this respect the ethos of naturalism is perfectly summed up by Sherlock Holmes's remark: 'No ghosts need apply.'[108]

The same may be true for those aesthetic concepts that seem most resistant to naturalistic explanation. 'Genius', for example, might be explained by some combination of genetic disposition, early education, and intensive practice in some domain, producing extreme 'outliers', individuals whose ability seems far in excess of even skilled practitioners in that domain. Alternatively, one might argue, as does Peter Kivy, that genius is a phenomenon with respect to which we face 'cognitive closure'—in other words, an understanding of genius lies beyond human cognitive capacities, as quadratic equations presumably lie beyond the ken of all non-human animals (and a good many humans too).[109] Cognitive closure arguments are necessarily highly speculative, but note that such an argument is still naturalistic in spirit, being founded on the recognition that every type of biological mind will have its strengths and weaknesses, capacities and shortcomings. Within a naturalistic framework, we have no reason for thinking that human minds or any kind of mind will somehow transcend all epistemic limitations.

Naturalism is thus not a cure-all or a Key to All Mythologies. It is a form of theorizing, and as such it is constrained by the limits of that kind of activity. Theorists don't aim to make artworks, nor are they in the business of the poetic description and evaluation of artworks; that is the vocation of criticism. As we will see in Chapter 8, a naturalized approach to aesthetics can help us recognize the singular character of works of art, by showing how they emerge from—and stand out in relief against—a background of patterns and regularities. But a naturalistic, explanatory approach won't, generally speaking, make us better artists or appreciators or interpreters. In this sense the explanatory focus of naturalism is also its limitation. Neither, it should be stressed, is naturalism to be strictly identified—rather than allied—with science. Even in Machery's characterization of philosophy, with its dramatic move towards the empirical, philosophy is still given a distinctive role and that role has to do with methodological, conceptual, and argumentative self-consciousness. Philosophy is the pursuit of empirical knowledge by (typically, though not exclusively) conceptual means: 'philosophy is in the business of examining, criticizing, reforming the findings, theories, methods developed by scientists and of grasping the implications of sciences for our understanding of the world and our place in it'. On the model of theory construction, the philosopher must engage substantially with empirical research, but they need not be involved in the business of empirical research.[110] And that is why the book you have in your hands counts as an exercise in naturalized aesthetics and theory construction rather than one of science.

2

Triangulating Aesthetic Experience

To study Metaphysic, as they have always been studied appears to me to be like puzzling at Astronomy without Mechanics.—Experience shows the problem of the mind cannot be solved by attacking the citadel itself.—the mind is function of the body.—we must bring some *stable* foundation to argue from.—

Charles Darwin

I can calculate the motion of heavenly bodies but not the madness of people.

Isaac Newton

There are many concepts and phenomena within the domain of aesthetics that one might approach in a scientific spirit: aesthetic form, style, and value might all be tackled in this way, as might the very existence of beauty and aesthetic activity as fundamental features of human life. Depending on the particular focus of our enquiry, the methods of various particular scientific disciplines will come to the fore. In this chapter, I will be concerned with the prospects for a scientific approach to *aesthetic experience*, which I take to be a defining feature of the aesthetic domain: to engage in an aesthetic activity—whether as a creator of art or as an appreciator of nature or art—is to engage in an activity which is consciously experienced, in an important sense; indeed, when such experiences go well, they are not merely *had*, but *savoured*. They become the object of a particular kind of self-consciousness. Taking aesthetic experience as our point of departure is, for this reason, doubly interesting: not only is aesthetic experience a *sine qua non* of the domain of aesthetics, but insofar as it is a type of conscious experience, it would be regarded by many as one of the least scientifically tractable dimensions of the field of aesthetics. If, as many hold, consciousness in general is not amenable to scientific study, what hope is there that a sub-species of conscious experience will be any different? Taking the art of film as my primary example, I will argue that, on the contrary, we have good cause to be optimistic.

With aesthetic experience in our sights as the particular target of our investigation, how do we go about approaching it? One of the problems with 'experience' as a phenomenon, of course, is that it is precisely not physical—at least not in the sense that we can measure and hold it. In this respect, note how aesthetic experience throws up a very different, and arguably stiffer, challenge than do aesthetic form and style, both of which are physically instantiated. We can begin by considering some basic aspects of film form: all films have a particular duration and a particular aspect ratio (that is, relative width to height), both of which we can sense approximately, and measure precisely. Different styles of filmmaking will employ editing to a greater or lesser degree, a fact which (at least) informed and observant spectators will register, and which can be quantified exactly through edit counts and average shot lengths (produced by dividing the duration of the film by the number of shots within it).[1] But aesthetic *experience* would appear to be just the point at which scientific methods lose their grip. 'There is something odd about any attempt to make experience an object of [experimental, scientific] inquiry', writes George Dickie, 'as if experience were of the same type as a piece of copper, a frog, or even an example of behavior.'[2] How are we going to measure and compare my experience of *Avatar* (James Cameron, 2009) as exhilarating with your experience of it as disorienting? Or, for that matter, my exhilarating experience with your exhilarating experience? For even where there is agreement about the kind of experience a work of art seems to prompt, it is difficult to see how one goes about investigating the experience scientifically. On one view, this is where the purely qualitative, descriptive, and interpretive work of film (and, more generally, art) criticism assumes control. Indeed, on a traditional view, such criticism kicks in much earlier in the proceedings, allowing scientific methods at most a negligible role. Critical interpretation, from this perspective, is the method that refreshes the parts other methods cannot reach.

How, if at all, can we vault this barrier lying between the tangible and the experienced? A clue lies in what has already been said. In describing film duration and aspect ratio, I made coordinated mention of both concrete features and experienced qualities: watching *Avatar*, we 'sense'—that is, we know from our experience—that we are watching a widescreen film of long duration; and we will also know from experience whether we are watching the 2D or the 3D version. But it will take a stopwatch to establish the exact duration of the film, a ruler to calculate the precise aspect ratio, and quite a bit more empirical research to learn about the differences between 2D and 3D filming and projection. The key point here, though, is that the evidence of experience, and the evidence that can be gleaned from scientific quantification of duration, aspect ratio, and 'dimensionality', cohere with one another. In each case, what we 'sense' to be the case is confirmed, and given more precise form, by the empirical techniques. I do not mean to suggest that experience and measurement can never come apart, and that human perception and cognition are infallible. Optical illusions are the clearest counterexamples to any such claim, but there are many less dramatic instances. We might, for example, significantly misjudge the actual duration of a film, or we might find it difficult to gauge, just by looking at it, the exact aspect ratio of a given film (Figures 2.1a–2.1c). The epistemic limitations of human perception and cognition will be vital in what follows (and are important in the more general case for an aesthetics aided and informed by scientific methods).[3] But the fact that experience and physical form (as established through empirical methods) can and perhaps usually do resonate

Figure 2.1 Aspect ratios. Top (a): *San taam/Mad Detective* (Johnnie To and Wai Ka-fai, 2007; aspect ratio 2.35:1). Middle (b): *Der Stand der Dinge/The State of Things* (Wim Wenders, 1982; aspect ratio 1.77:1). Bottom (c): *Werckmeister Harmóniák/Werckmeister Harmonies* (Béla Tarr, 2000; aspect ratio 1.66:1). Seen in isolation, viewers may find it difficult to judge the precise aspect ratio in which a given film is projected.

with one another gives us a starting point for our assault on Mount Experience. How, though, do we get beyond the foothills?

Triangulation, the 'Natural Method'

Here I want to draw on an approach advanced by Owen Flanagan in relation to the more general problem of consciousness—the problem, that is, of explaining the existence, nature, and function of consciousness within the natural order. Flanagan calls his approach 'the natural method', and in passing uses the metaphor of 'triangulation' as a way of characterizing it.[4] As a first approximation, we can think of such triangulation as a refined version of the simple, two-part schema I've sketched, in which perceptual and cognitive experience on the one hand, and the physical form of the stimulus on the other hand, are mapped onto one another.

At the heart of triangulation is the principle that at the outset of enquiry we take seriously not just two, but *three* factors—three levels of analysis with their attendant types of evidence—that we have at our disposal with respect to mental phenomena:

- the *phenomenological* level (what, if anything, it feels like when we undertake some mental act)
- the *psychological* level (what sorts of psychological capacities and functions our minds possess), and
- the *neurophysiological* level (what seems to be happening in the brain when we exercise these capacities or have these experiences).

In other words, we have evidence pertaining to our *experience* of mental phenomena, the *information processed* by the mind in relation to particular mental functions, and the physical *realization* of the mental. Having put these varieties of evidence on the table, we can then attempt to 'triangulate' the object of enquiry. Triangulation involves locating or 'fixing' the object in explanatory space by (to follow the metaphor) projecting lines from each body of evidence, and following them to see where they intersect. Where any two, or all three, forms of evidence mesh in this way, so each of them is corroborated. Finally, however, and very importantly, Flanagan argues that '[a]s theory develops, analyses at each level are subject to refinement, revision, or rejection'.[5]

According to Flanagan, then, no item within these bodies of evidence is insulated from revision or rejection—so elimination of even long-established, cherished beliefs and theories is certainly possible. In addition, no straightforward methodological hierarchy among the three levels of analysis is established: no one of the three types of evidence necessarily overrules the others.[6] Rather, the assumption is made that, while *particular* posits within each level may be shown to be false or faulty, the three levels themselves are interdependent and thus all necessary in a comprehensive investigation of the mind. Something like Neurath's boat comes to mind. Otto Neurath likened scientists to

sailors who on the open sea must reconstruct their ship but are never able to start afresh from the bottom. Where a beam is taken away a new one must at once be put there, and for this the rest of the ship is used as support. In this way, by using the old beams and driftwood, the ship can be shaped entirely anew, but only by gradual reconstruction.[7]

In a similar fashion, researchers working on the mind can move around among the three levels, and they can reconstruct (question, empirically investigate, reconceptualize) particular items at a given level while 'standing' on other assumptions made at the same time, on the other levels. Wilfrid Sellars gave expression to the same basic idea while emphasizing the roots of science in and relevance for ordinary practical action and everyday theorizing, arguing that 'empirical knowledge, like its sophisticated extension, science, is rational, not because it has a *foundation* but because it is a self-correcting enterprise which can put *any* claim in jeopardy, though not *all* at once'.[8]

Flanagan initially presents triangulation as a methodological principle, but his explication suggests that it is more than a recommendation. Staying true to the spirit of Flanagan's argument, I suggest that while triangulation is not quite the only way in which psychologists and philosophers of mind can proceed, it is nonetheless the most powerful way. Let us consider each of the three levels of triangulation more fully in this light, beginning with the phenomenological. While noting the limitations of phenomenology as a method of exploring consciousness, Flanagan suggests that 'it is incredible to think that we could do without phenomenology altogether'.[9] As we've already noted, our experience of things may be misleading. Based on experience, we ordinarily think that our visual system affords us a uniformly coloured and detailed visual field. Chris Chabris and Dan Simons postulate a related 'illusion of attention', characterized by the 'erroneous belief that we process *all* of the detailed information around us'.[10] Careful testing shows that both assumptions are wrong: only a small fraction of our visual field is in sharp focus at any given moment, and at the extreme peripheries our visual system represents the world in monochrome.[11] We are also subject not only to 'change blindness'—an inability to spot changes in our visual field not in the spotlight of focused attention—but to 'change blindness blindness', that is, we are resistant to accepting the reality of change blindness even when presented with evidence of it.[12] So, odd as it may seem, we can be wrong not just about the world, but our experience of it. The general impression I have of my visual perception misleads me with respect to the perceptual skills I actually do possess, when examined closely.[13]

The relevance of phenomenology to the study of the mind is not, of course, restricted to the exploration of ordinary consciousness—that is, the conscious experience of mature, healthy human individuals engaged in routine tasks. Two traditions of writing take as their subject and seek to represent different kinds of unusual or abnormal experience. First, there is the body of literature devoted to charting drug-induced experience, from Thomas De Quincey to Malcolm Lowry, Aldous Huxley, William Burroughs, Gilbert Shelton, and Irvine Welsh; from the 1950s onwards, many films have exploited similar territory, from *The Man with the Golden Arm* (Otto Preminger, 1955) to *Chumlum* (Ron Rice, 1964), *Easy Rider* (Dennis Hopper, 1969), *Trainspotting* (Danny Boyle, 1996), and *Requiem for a Dream* (Darren Aronofsky, 2000). Another tradition of writing focuses on what it is like to apprehend the world with various kinds of psychological deficit, brain damage, or 'neuroatypicality'. What is it like not to be able to recognize or express emotions? What is it like not to be able to recognize individual faces, or when visual facial recognition is divorced from emotional recognition? How does the world look to someone who lacks the capacity to see movement? What is the experience of an autistic person like? In relation to such questions we find an intriguing convergence between neuroscientists like Oliver Sacks, for whom the experiential dimension of the neural conditions he investigates has always been a critical dimension, and artists working in various media who take such experience as their subject matter—Andrew Kötting with his film *Mapping Perception* (2002), for example, or Mark Haddon in his novel *The Curious Incident of the Dog in the Night-Time* (2003). In Chapter 4 I pursue this link between the exploration of atypical states of consciousness in art and literature and the tradition of 'Romantic science' exemplified by Sacks.

So phenomenological evidence is fallible; but it does not follow that it is always false or wholly unreliable. In any event, whether our experience is veridical or otherwise, *the experience itself still needs explaining.* To discard phenomenal evidence of conscious mental experience would be tantamount to discarding a key dimension of the *explanandum*, that is, the very thing that we want to explain. So we can neither do without phenomenological evidence, nor treat it as infallible and absolutely authoritative.

What does it mean to talk of evidence at the level of psychological function or information processing? It is important to underline at the outset that I use the expression 'information processing' to encompass all forms of cognition—'hot' and 'cold'—which aid us in navigating the physical and social environments that we inhabit. As the case studies coming up on suspense, empathy, and the startle response indicate, emotions, embodiment, and the environment are all central to our repertoire of information-processing capacities. Emotions, I suggest in Chapter 5, furnish us with a motivational centre of gravity. In the same spirit Jesse Prinz characterizes emotions as 'bodily radar detectors that alert us to concerns. When we listen to our emotions, we are not being swayed by meaningless feelings. Nor are we hearing the cold dictates of complex judgments. We are using our bodies to perceive our position in the world.'[14] Neither does the word 'information' exclude matters of value, for our concerns will often be moral, political, aesthetic; our emotional lives are inextricably bound up with the good, the just, and the beautiful, and the world we occupy is in part a value-made world, comprised not only of rocks, trees, and tables, but of temples, parliaments, and art galleries.

Beyond this initial but fundamental point, some examples will help clarify the nature of evidence at the functional, information-processing level. In the experiments on change blindness, do subjects notice changes in their visual field? Here the experimenter aims to tease out our capacity for attending to such changes; the experiments furnish us with evidence relating to an aspect of visual attention. In the Wason selection task—fundamental to arguments about the modularity of mind, and the existence of a specialized 'cheater detection' module—how many subjects correctly solve the puzzle when posed in terms of regulating a social contract, rather than as a more abstract problem? Here the psychological function under the spotlight is our capacity to solve certain kinds of mathematical and social problems, and the experiments provide us with evidence about that capacity.[15] To take a third example, in experiments on the attentional blink, how many subjects register information from the images shown in the window of the blink? Here the goal is to illuminate the degree to which we have the capacity to process information—to register and retain it—beneath the level of conscious attention. In each of the three cases, the evidence bears on a psychological capacity, irrespective of how it is neurologically implemented, and whether or not it is accompanied by consciousness (though all mental capacities and acts must be neurologically realized, and many are experienced consciously).

Explanations on the level of psychological function such as these are, as with phenomenological explanations, important but limited when viewed in isolation, because '[t]here are always more functional hypotheses compatible with the facts than can be true'.[16] Flanagan offers the case of 'auditory splitting' as an example.[17] In the relevant experiments, subjects hear distinct audio streams in their left and right ears, but they are told to pay conscious attention to the left audio stream. Subsequent testing shows that subjects do 'take in' and process information from the right audio stream, even though they have no conscious experience or memory of doing so. The orthodox psychological explanation is that information from the left channel is both decoded semantically and retrievable from memory because we attended to it consciously, while information from the right channel is decoded but enters our mental economy non-consciously, and is thus not available for conscious memory retrieval. Our auditory system is sufficiently complex that auditory inputs may be processed and memorized in a variety of ways.

Flanagan points out, however, that there are other possible psychological explanations: perhaps we do consciously experience both left and right audio streams when they occur, but the directive to pay attention to the left channel results in our *forgetting* our fleeting conscious experience of the right channel stream. We do, after all, routinely forget events that we were conscious of at the time of their occurrence. On this analysis, it looks like conscious attention comes with semantic decoding, since we are said to be conscious of the sound at the time that we hear the right channel stream (in contrast to the orthodox explanation, according to which we decode right channel information without awareness); but consciousness has a weaker relationship with episodic memory (having consciously attended to something does not guarantee that we will be able to recall having the experience, or retrieve how we came to possess the information encoded in memory). Our functional mental economy, in terms of the relations among hearing, decoding, and memorizing, looks different on the two interpretations. *Some* explanation of auditory splitting—whether one of these two or some other account—must be correct, but analysis at the level of information processing alone will not determine which is correct.

Neuroscience may play a vital role here, in pushing us towards one of the two (or more) psychological explanations on offer for any given mental phenomenon. Pursuing the example of auditory splitting, Flanagan imagines the point at which neuroscience is able to detect a distinctive pattern of neural activity subtending auditory consciousness for each ear. Running the experiment again, we find the pattern present for both ears. The neural evidence would thus, in this scenario, favour the second hypothesis, suggesting that the unattended sound in the right channel is consciously experienced for a moment, but no memory of the momentary episode is formed (even though the information contained in the right channel is processed semantically, and in that sense enters semantic memory). In this way, the findings of neuroscience are able to constrain and direct psychological theorizing. Just as, in Darwin's words, Newtonian mechanics provided a stable foundation for astronomy, so neuroscience may prove to be such for psychology.

Neuroscientific evidence, however, does not straightforwardly trump phenomeno-logical or psychological evidence. 'The study of the brain alone will yield absolutely no knowledge about the mind unless certain phenomena described at the psycho-logical or phenomenological level are on the table to be explained,' Flanagan notes. 'Imagine an utterly complete explanation of the brain framed in the languages of physics, chemistry, and biochemistry. What has one learned about mental function? The answer is nothing, unless one's neuroscientific inquiry was guided in the first place by the attempt to map certain mental functions onto the brain.'[18] The term 'neuropsychology' makes this intrinsic relationship explicit.[19] In the case of auditory splitting, neuroscience comes into play on the heels of phenomenal and psychological phenomena—evidence that while we consciously experience only the left channel, we process information from both channels. We have something on which to hang our neuroscience; we are not blindly poking around in the brain for just any flashing synapses.

This is not to suggest that there cannot be cases *led by* neuroscientific data; recall Jaegwon Kim's observations in Chapter 1 on the potential significance of discoveries at the level of realization.[20] For example, there is some evidence that the perception of left facial profiles triggers brain activity that is not triggered by right profiles.[21] But what are we to make of this in *mental* terms, if not by asking whether there is any phenomenal, psychological, or behavourial evidence with which the brain activity meshes. Does anyone experience the left profile of a face differently from the right profile? Is there any evidence for greater perceptual acuity with respect to left over right profile perception? Is there any evidence of practices of perception or repre-sentation in which there are marked preferences or differences of treatment in relation to left and right profiles? Or, to take a better-known body of research that I discuss at length later in this chapter and in Chapter 3, the discovery of mirror neurons—neurons that are active both when a subject performs and observes an action—was an accident. Giacomo Rizzolatti and his team (including Vittorio Gallese, who has gone on to investigate the role of mirror neurons in movie spectatorship, and to whom we return in Chapter 4) were undertaking experiments on the premotor cortex of macaque monkeys, focusing on how the neurons in this brain region respond to objects of different sizes and shapes. Evidence that the neurons discriminated for movements and actions arrived, so to speak, uninvited.[22] Once discovered, hypotheses were formulated concerning the functions of these neurons, and their possible links with aspects of experience.[23]

In short, in cases where unanticipated data about brain activity emerge, the evidence pushes us to make functional psychological and phenomenal hypotheses, without which the neural activity remains theoretically 'meaningless'—that is, it remains just a description of brain activity. Not for nothing have neuroscientists labelled one major type of brain scanning *fMRI—functional* MRI. The method of triangulation, then, makes an important ontological assumption. While any particular phenomenological, psychological, or neurophysiological claim may be overturned, and while not all mental activity has a phenomenological character, none of the *levels* can be eliminated.

As we have seen, Flanagan characterizes his approach as the 'natural' method— and it certainly is a natural and appropriate method for physicalists, for whom the mind emerges from, or supervenes upon—in one sense or another—the brain. We can see this even more clearly in the case of colour perception, as it has been discussed by one of the original and staunchest of 'neurophilosophers', Paul Churchland. Indeed, Churchland does not merely analyse human colour perception as an instance of triangulation; he advances it in support of the still stronger *identity theory*—the idea that mental activity just is neural activity.[24] Churchland begins by describing our current understanding of the colour visual system in neurophysiological and psychological terms. According to the Hurvich-Jameson opponentprocess theory, our colour vision depends on the functioning and interaction of neurons in the visual pathway, located both on cones in the retina and in parts of the brain. These neurons calculate or 'code' for particular colours according to the wavelength information that they receive. The specific arrangement of cones and neurons that characterize the human visual system gives rise to a 'spindle' of colours, that is, a graphic representation of the relations of similarity and dissimilarity among the colours that humans can perceive. The Hurvich-Jameson theory explains why it is that our visual system codes for colour in this way. But where, you may ask, is our *experience* of colour in this scheme of explanation?

Our experience of ordinary colours is the form in which we humans register—not infallibly, but generally reliably—the complex of light waves hitting objects in our visual field. Sensory experience is the interface between the mind and the physical world; our different modes of sensory perception are the means by which 'the mind opens out onto its environment and assembles for itself a representation of outer reality'.[25] That we have such conscious, qualitative experience of light wavelength is no more (or less) mysterious than the fact that we possess consciousness at all. Churchland introduces his most intriguing twist at this juncture, however. The Hurvich-Jameson theory implies—indeed, *predicts*—that there are types of colour experience which will not be triggered by ordinary perception, but which are possible given the physiological design of our system of colour perception. These 'rogue sensations'[26] can be triggered only by rare—and usually artificially induced—visual cues, and include our experience of 'impossible', 'self-luminous', and 'hyperbolic' colours. The sensation of 'impossibly' dark blue can, for example, be induced by focusing visual attention on a yellow patch for a sustained period (at least twenty seconds), and then shifting attention to a black patch. We will then experience an afterimage distinctly blue in hue, but as dark as the surrounding black—even though, in ordinary visual experience, anything with a hue must be lighter than pure black. Here we see 'a color that you will absolutely never encounter as an objective feature of a real physical object, but whose qualitative character you can nonetheless savor in an unusually produced illusory experience'.[27] Like other optical illusions, these 'chimerical' colour experiences do not veridically represent objects in the world, but arise from the layout of our visual system. If that system is stressed or stretched in particular ways, these are the colour qualia—the qualities characterizing our perceptual experience—that arise. We are close to the territory of perceptual 'expansion' here, explored in Chapter 1, where our perceptual capacities are 'pushed' in this way by design (more specifically, by the design of artworks). And to introduce a theme that we will pick up in Chapter 3, we can say that perceptual architecture shapes mental function and experience. The character of our perceptual and cognitive experiences is partly determined by the structure of our physiology and psychology. From the point of view of the informational function of perception—the provision of accurate knowledge of the external world—non-veridical colour experience is nothing more than noise in the system; but artists have been exploiting the characteristics of our perceptual systems for millennia. And as I noted in Chapter 1, a parallel point holds for change blindness: a limitation in our visual system that can lead to error has been exapted for the artful purpose of cinematic continuity.

Churchland's argument, then, is relevant for us in two ways. First, although the mind–brain identity theory remains controversial, Churchland's analysis supports the more modest thesis of triangulation: namely, that our understanding of conscious experience will be advanced by seeking convergence among our three levels (the phenomenological, the psychological, and the neurological). As we will see in greater detail in Chapter 4, colour qualia have been one of the prime examples used to undermine the possibility of a science of consciousness;[28] yet Churchland manages to derive predictions from neural evidence that, it appears, are borne out at the phenomenological level. Moreover, as with the example of auditory splitting, chimerical colour experience is particularly pertinent to aesthetics. Film in particular—and the visual and aural arts more generally—trades in the creation of audiovisual experience. We might expect to find filmmakers exploiting these features of our perception—and we do.

Consider first cases related to auditory splitting. Many films briefly combine multiple, competing streams of speech or other sound, sometimes split between channels, sometimes flowing together in a monophonic field of sound. Overlapping dialogue is something of a trademark in the work of both Orson Welles and—heightened by

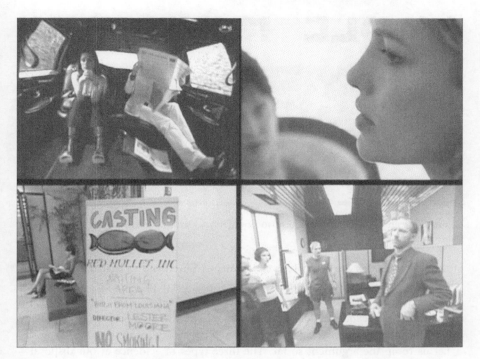

Figure 2.2 *Timecode* (Mike Figgis, 2000) includes auditory splitting at transitional points, where the sound shifts from one visual quadrant to another.

the emergence of multi-channel sound—Robert Altman. Mike Figgis's four-screen *Timecode* (2000) divides our visual and at points our aural attention, though it generally uses the sound mix to direct the viewer's attention to one of its four visual quadrants (Figure 2.2). More stridently experimental filmmakers—including Jean-Luc Godard, Paul Sharits, and Alexander Sokurov—have created more sustained passages in which our auditory attention is torn between multiple streams of sound (Figure 2.3). (Outside of film, a very lengthy example of auditory attention split between two verbal streams is found in the Velvet Underground song 'The Murder Mystery'.[29])

Sharits is also one of a small group of filmmakers who have explored the use of 'flicker', the rapid alternation of frames dominated by contrasting hues, a technique which elicits afterimages and in this way relates to Churchland's rogue visual experiences and the structure of the human visual system he describes. Other filmmakers who have worked with this method include Peter Kubelka, Stan Brakhage, Robert Breer, and Tony Conrad. The interests and achievements of Brakhage in particular—treated further in Chapter 4—in films such as *Rage Net* (1988) (see Figure 4.1) and *Glaze of Cathexis* (1990) as well as in his theoretical writings, are founded to some degree on an elaborate play with colour perception, eliciting many

Figure 2.3 Jean-Luc Godard launches two simultaneous streams of speech at the spectator in *Made in USA* (1966).

of the fleeting, otherworldly colour experiences Churchland describes.[30] In various works by these filmmakers, we see both *representations* of phosphenic, non-veridical colour experience (where imagery on the screen depicts such experience) and *representation-by-enactment* of such experience (where the film is designed to trigger actual afterimages and other entoptic phenomena).[31]

Let us recap the argument so far. The three types of evidence at our disposal—those related to phenomenal experience, psychological function, and neural implementation—do not exist in a simple hierarchy, but rather in a tail-chasing form of interdependence. Many (but by no means all) mental activities are consciously experienced; this experience makes these mental phenomena salient, and provides some evidence of their character. Psychological evidence—evidence for the existence of both conscious and non-conscious mental capacities—points us towards the functional specification and explanation of the human mind. Phenomenology and psychological theory can both be mistaken, however, and neuroscience is one important resource for either cross-confirming and corroborating, or highlighting problems with, these other forms of evidence. Each level of analysis taken alone is vulnerable: phenomenology is elusive and intangible; psychology ungrounded and unconstrained; neuroscience blind and inert.

Triangulation, then, is more than mere pluralism, since it goes beyond the idea that the complexity of the world—and human experience of the world—must be investigated through a variety of methods. It might be regarded as a particular form of *consilience*—that 'jumping together' of separate bodies of evidence that reinforces the plausibility of each taken individually.[32] What distinguishes triangulation as a form of consilience is that it occurs across distinct types of evidence and levels of enquiry, rather than meshing together different bodies of evidence on a single level—as one might, say, in seeking to integrate neural accounts of the perceptual and emotion systems; or psychological theories of memory and imagination. And in triangulating the phenomenological, the psychological, and the neurophysiological levels, our explanations are thickened. Note also that the division of labour among researchers in different fields and disciplines—philosophers of art and film, psychologists, and neuroscientists—across the three strands of triangulation is not as straightforward as it might appear. Art and film theorists certainly frequently advert to phenomenological evidence in setting out their arguments. But they also engage in psychological theorizing, seeking to place aesthetic cognition within human cognition more generally, and they often draw upon psychological and neuroscientific evidence.[33] In addition, in the close analysis of works of art, art theorists and critics are themselves pursuing a kind of empirical research (mostly qualitative, but sometimes quantitative, as we've seen in the case of average shot length analysis)—a point that is often insufficiently appreciated. It would thus be a gross caricature to think of philosophers, theorists, and critics of art (as a group) working narrowly only with the evidence of introspection and intuition. And the same is true for psychologists and neuroscientists: while each group 'stands' in a particular part of explanatory space and attends especially to the requisite type of evidence, each also typically engages with one or both of the other levels of enquiry.

Tracking Suspense

Let me turn now to the first of my two main examples, in which I explore the potential of triangulation to illuminate particular types of aesthetic experience: the case of *anomalous suspense*.[34] Suspense is an emotion typical of an important class of narratives, where our attention is focused on, and we experience anxiety about, the outcome of the narrative (or some part of it). Watching *Speed* (Jan de Bont, 1994) for the first time, I wonder how on earth Keanu Reeves is going to get the passengers off the rigged bus alive, and fear that he won't; suspense is just this blend of *hope* for an outcome with *fear* of its opposite. (I return to the issue of issue of emotional 'blending' in Chapter 8.) So far, so familiar. But what about those occasions where we experience suspense in full possession of knowledge of the outcome? Think of the many contexts in which this is a factor—not only repeat viewings of fiction films, but occasions when we've learned the outcome in advance through a conversation or 'spoiler', and historical narratives where we already know the outcome, as for example with *Titanic* (James Cameron, 1997) and *United 93* (Paul Greengrass, 2006). If suspense is premised on ignorance of an outcome, how can suspense arise in contexts where we seem to know the outcome? Such suspense is 'anomalous' with respect to the standard case, and in need of an additional or alternative explanation.

There are several possible responses to the anomaly. Perhaps it isn't really suspense we are experiencing in these cases? We can still be gripped by sympathy for the passengers on the doomed flight in *United 93* even if we know the outcome, appalled at what they had to live through. Watching Roman Polanski's *Macbeth* (1971), I know just where this story is headed because I studied the play ad nauseam in high school—and in any case, tragedies depend upon a sense of inevitability. In cases where we know that the outcome of a suspenseful narrative is bad, our emotional state has this character: grim fascination with the unfolding of a tragic, horrific, or otherwise undesirable sequence of events. And in cases where we know that a suspense narrative turns out well, perhaps the emotion we feel is a form of occurent, empathic suffering with the central character(s). (We will look at empathy itself again later, revisiting it in more detail in Chapters 3 and 7.) Knowing that things will end happily does not simply erase or neutralize unhappy events as they happen: we might empathize with Keanu Reeves and his fellow passengers as the bus hurtles along, even if we know that they will all survive. (Compare: when I visit the dentist, I loathe the experience even if I know that the visit will not last forever.) On this theory, then, our fallible phenomenology gets revised: we may think initially that we are experiencing suspense, but further reflection on the work of art itself and our response to it reveals that we do not experience suspense as we have defined it, but rather appalled fascination or empathy with the current state of a character. Our understanding of our experience is revised in the light of a fuller appreciation of the psychological possibilities: suspense is not the only candidate on the table.

Neuroscientific evidence suggests a different possible solution to the anomaly. Our perceptual and cognitive skills can broadly be divided into those which are fast, bottom-up, and 'informationally encapsulated', that is, largely immune to the influence of our existing beliefs, and those which are deliberative, top-down, and thus heavily inflected by what we already believe.[35] If we think of suspense only in relation to our deliberative, top-down cognition, anomalous suspense seems like an intractable problem—for if suspense responses are dependent on integration with our existing background knowledge, and we know the outcome of a story, how can we experience suspense in relation to it? But if we think of suspense as largely, or at least in some significant measure, dependent on bottom-up processes, then it is really no mystery at all that our minds continue to process the narrative as suspenseful and we continue to experience suspense even in cases where we know the outcome. Bold emotional expressions, fast cutting, rousing music, and clearly delineated actions stir up our senses, generating suspenseful anxiety even as we may say to ourselves—drawing on those other, top-down mental capacities—'he doesn't fall down the cliff', or even 'it's only a movie'. The screeching violins, stabbing motions, and the terrified face of Janet Leigh still work on the umpteenth viewing of *Psycho* (Alfred Hitchcock, 1960) (Figure 2.4). As David Bordwell has put it, as far as our senses are concerned, 'every viewing of a movie *is* the first viewing'.[36]

There is an important connection here with Diana Raffman's arguments concerning 'nuance ineffability' explored in Chapter 1. Recall that Raffman's model of music perception postulates that our ability to discriminate subtle nuances of pitch outstrips our ability to categorize or memorize those subtleties; instead, our memory for pitch operates at the coarser level formalized in musical notation systems. Quoting Raffman and

Figure 2.4 Anomalous suspense and 'bottom-up' emotion in *Psycho* (Alfred Hitchcock, 1960).

extending her arguments beyond pitch to timbre, Theodore Gracyk suggests that timbre has

an expressive impact in direct experience that will be absent in our memories of it...no matter how well we know the structure of a musical work or recorded performance, the local qualities always promise 'the thrill of the unexpected: you never know exactly what you will hear.' You do not know, because you do not remember them with precision. Their precise quality is only known perceptually, while perceiving them.[37]

That Bordwell's arguments on suspense in film and the arguments of Raffman and Gracyk on music perception resonate in this way is no coincidence, as they share a common influence in the generative theory of tonal music elaborated by Ray Jackendoff and Fred Lerdahl in the 1980s.[38]

The distinction between fast, bottom-up processes and slower, top-down processes is a classic functional distinction, but it is backed up by neuroscience which confirms that different types of cognition are subtended by specific patterns of neural activity. Neuroscientific research on suspense should, in principle, be able to discover what sorts of cognition come into play when readers or viewers engage with suspenseful narratives, and crucially, whether and where there are differences in the profile of cognitive activity for perceivers knowing the outcome on the one hand, and those ignorant of the outcome on the other. This might point us in the direction of either one of the two theories of anomalous suspense canvassed here: if knowledge of the outcome of a narrative results in a marked decrease in the intensity of bottom-up processing, or if there is some other strong contrast in the overall profile of cognitive activity, we would have reason to favour the theory that something other than suspense—in the prototypical sense—is occurring. On the other hand, if knowledge of the outcome of the narrative makes no significant difference to the nature or intensity of our neural and other physiological responses, the hypothesis that anomalous suspense is indeed authentic suspense—and generated largely by bottom-up processes—would be strengthened. However things actually might fall out, the crucial point to appreciate here is the power of triangulation as a method: we are most likely to solve the problem of anomalous suspense by examining the way in which *all three* layers of evidence—experiential, informational, and 'realizational'—come together. No one of these levels is sacrosanct, or capable of delivering an authoritative answer on its own; but neither should the implications of any one of them be discarded too swiftly. As Flanagan notes, triangulation involves finding a kind of reflective equilibrium among the three layers.[39]

Fixing Empathy

My second example of triangulation in action, like my first, concerns a common (and frequently intense) type of emotional response: *empathy*. Understood as the process of 'feeling into' (from the German, *Einfühlung*) another person or object, empathy has been widely referenced as an important constituent of our experience of certain types of art; one of the early German theorists of empathy, Theodor Lipps, described empathy as 'the inside of mimesis'.[40] The concept is invoked most commonly in relation to narrative film and literature, in both informal, and formal theoretical, contexts. Often it is claimed that empathy with characters is either essential for, or typical of, a full appreciation of at least certain kinds of narrative. In its original context, however, as a term of art in German psychology and art history, empathy had more to do with a kinaesthetic 'feeling into' geometrical forms and architectural structures, like arches. If we add to this the fact that, long before the coining of the term empathy, the same or very similar phenomena had been noted by earlier philosophers using other terms—notably David Hume and Adam Smith—one gets a sense of the central place that empathy and related phenomena have held within philosophy and psychology in general, and aesthetics in particular.

The investigation of empathy is particularly ripe for triangulatory treatment. Anecdotal, phenomenological evidence on the idea of empathy abounds; people frequently talk about feeling the feelings of others, and 'empathy' is one of the words they use to label this experience. At the psychological level, over the past quarter century we have witnessed the development of a debate between those who ascribe our ability to attribute states of mind to others to an implicit 'theory of mind', and those who ascribe that ability to an empathic or 'simulative' capacity whereby we 'try on' and seek to elaborate those states.[41] And most recently evidence for a neural 'mirror system' in humans has been advanced, which many have taken as relevant for theories of empathy. The existence of a rich (if recent, in the case of the debates around simulation and mirror neurons) body of evidence and theorization across all three levels—phenomenological, psychological, neurophysiological—makes the concept of empathy an ideal candidate for at least attempted triangulation.

How exactly are mirror neurons relevant to the project of triangulating empathy? As I've noted in passing, mirror neurons are neurons which fire both when a subject *executes* and *observes* an action, and appear to be present in both humans and many other primates. The existence of a neural 'mirroring system' in humans is significant because it provides evidence in support of the psychological theory of simulation, and the phenomenological intuition that we sometimes share the emotional states of others. In other words, there is a certain kind of psychological state in which we do not merely *feel for* a fellow human being, but *feel with* her. In contemporary psychological and aesthetic theory, this is the contrast between sympathy and empathy. While many have doubted the existence of empathy, questioning the reliability of our phenomenology, and the coherence of the psychological theories that posit such a state, mirror neurons specify a neural mechanism that may underpin the experience of empathy and the psychological function it performs. (The debate around mirror neurons thus constitutes another example of the method of theory construction discussed in Chapter 1, the discovery of mirror neurons contributing to the existence, ontological, and psychological questions attached to empathy.)

According to one influential account, mirror neurons furnish us with a special route to understanding a range of motor and emotional states experienced by others, one that depends upon the 'direct mapping' of neural activity from an observed to an observing person.[42] What makes such understanding 'special'? In ordinary cognition, we grasp the states of others—including their motor intentions and feelings— through inference: we see a smile and recognize it as an expression of happiness; we witness someone reaching to grasp an object and we recognize their intention to pick it up. Such 'cold' cognition contrasts with the 'hot' cognition enabled by the mirror system, where the neural mirroring response triggered by the sight of the smile or the grasping gesture involves a kind of imaginative mimicking or simulation of the action, rather than a mere categorization of it. As Andy Clark notes, drawing on terminology from Churchland, mirror neurons point to an action-oriented, 'motorocentric' form of perception, in contrast to a 'visuocentric', action-neutral form; perception of this type is a kind of latent action.[43] Further downstream, the understanding of the gesture or expression—whether derived from the mirror system or 'cold' inference—will be integrated with other background information we already possess about the context of action.

Mirror neurons do not provide direct evidence for the existence of empathy and the truth of the simulation theory. When we look at brain scans showing the mirror system in action, we are not seeing empathy. But insofar as we hold to the assumption that neural activity subtends mental activity—that the brain is the engine of perception, emotion, and cognition—we can reasonably assume that the neural activity underpins important cognitive work. And when we integrate the data concerning mirror neurons with what neuroscience tells us about those parts of the brain involved in motor activity and emotion, we can conclude that we have reason to believe in the reality of empathy, understood as a state of emotional matching and mirroring between human subjects. If the psychological hypothesis of simulation calls for further evidence to substantiate, elaborate, and refine it, research on and evidence of the mirror system is the response to that call. The case is by no means closed, but the intersection of phenomenological, psychological, and neural evidence strengthens the case for empathy. Empathy and simulation theory gain plausibility, and the burden of argument falls on the sceptic to provide some alternative explanation of mirror neuron evidence, perhaps by showing how this evidence knits as well or better with an alternative combination of psychological hypotheses and experiential intuitions. Note that in this case, even if the apparent convergence of empathy with the mirror system turns out to be wrong, triangulation as a method still holds. As in the case of anomalous suspense, the point of triangulating the phenomenological, the psychological, and the neural is to examine the extent to which a given hypothesis is or is not supported by a convergence of evidence across the three levels.

The Brain and the Body

There is a second area of neuroscience that potentially sheds light on empathy, much less remarked upon than the discovery of mirror neurons—the body of research on the brain's mapping of bodily image, vividly explored in V. S. Ramachandran's *Phantoms in the Brain* (co-authored with science journalist Sandra Blakeslee).[44] One of the exemplars of Ramachandran's 'phantoms' are those ghostly limbs which amputees continue to sense after they have been removed. The flipside of these phantom limbs are 'alien' limbs, which occur where cortical damage destroys that part of the neural map representing the limb, leading to the subject's sense that the limb does not belong to them and is controlled by someone else.[45] The significance of such alien and phantom limbs extends well beyond the case of the amputee, however: on the one hand, some individuals born without particular limbs nevertheless sense the presence of a limb (suggesting a genetic basis for normal human body image), and, on the other hand, clinical and experimental evidence shows that the brain's map of the body can be redrawn, reflecting either permanent changes in the topography of the body or illusions which mislead our senses with respect to the extension and boundaries of the body (suggesting that there is a considerable degree of elasticity and plasticity to the neural map). Once more we encounter the fallibility—though not the chronic unreliability—of human (self-)perception.

This second point probably accords with what most of us would expect: our brains possess generally accurate maps of our bodies. A neural body map is broadly isomorphic with the body that it represents; the boundaries of the body are as the map represents them. This map may be partly innate but it is modified by the reality of the body we come to possess, a body which changes, usually gradually, over time;

thus, for example, our neural map adjusts to reflect increasing physical height (otherwise we would routinely misjudge our height relative to the height of potential obstacles—not good for surviving or thriving).[46] Common sense does not seem to accommodate, however, evidence that the neural map of the body is so plastic that—at least given the right conditions—our image of the body can extend well beyond the actual physical boundaries of the body, either giving us the impression that particular body parts are dramatically distended relative to their real size, or, equally intriguingly, that inanimate objects can in some sense be assimilated within our body image. It is this latter possibility that takes us closer to empathy.

Ramachandran has discussed two sorts of case that are relevant here. The first concerns experiments he has undertaken which show that many human subjects can be led to *sense*, proprioceptively, a table at which they are sitting as if the table were a part of their own body.[47] In one such experiment, the subject sits at a table, with their arms under the table and concealed from their view by a screen immediately in front of them. The subject's vision is, instead, directed towards the table, which is tapped and stroked by an experimenter. At the same time, one of the subject's arms—under the table—is also tapped and stroked by the experimenter, the rhythm and intensity of the two sets of movements being synchronized and matched as closely as possible. The effect on roughly half[48] the subjects tested is that they come to locate the sensation of tapping and stroking at the point where the table is being stroked and tested, rather than where their arm literally lies.[49] In order to eliminate the possibility that subjects reporting this effect were simply using language in metaphorical fashion, or were exaggerating the character of the experience—'confabulating' their experience,[50] perhaps out of a desire to please the researcher and themselves—Ramachandran employed galvanic skin response (GSR) measures in order to gain quantifiable, objective data which might go some way towards corroborating the evidence from introspection. And he discovered that GSR responses to sharp blows to the table were commensurate with those that would be expected if such blows were directed against the actual body of the subject. Ramachandran comments:

It was as though the table had now become coupled to the student's own limbic system and been assimilated into his body image, so much so that pain and threat to the dummy [the table] are felt as threats to his own body . . . perhaps it's not all that silly to ask whether you identify with your car. Just punch it to see whether your GSR changes. Indeed the technique may give us a handle on elusive psychological phenomena such as the empathy and love that you feel for your child or spouse. If you are deeply in love with someone, is it possible that you have actually become part of that person?[51]

Note that Ramachandran is, in effect, putting the method of triangulation into practice here. Although he has not set out to examine empathy, the convergence of phenomenological and physiological evidence leads him to the psychological concept of empathy, which might be explained in part by the plasticity of neural body mapping.

More recent research in a similar vein has thrown up even more remarkable results. Valeria Petkova and Henrik Ehrsson have demonstrated in a series of experiments that it is possible to displace a subject's overall sense of bodily location into the body of an alternate subject—a dummy or another person—by combining synchronous tactile stimulation of the type used by Ramachandran with the visual point of view of the alternate (relayed by cameras on the head of the alternate to the subject via a head-mounted display). In other words, the subject does not merely sense an object as if it were part of their body; rather, the subject's sense of what body they occupy has been relocated. The effect is sufficiently robust that it persists even when a subject views their own actual body (via the relayed visual perspective of the alternate). Differentiating this experience from the experience of recognizing oneself in a mirror or other visual representation, Petkova and Ehrsson note that 'in the body-swap illusions, the visual, tactile and proprioceptive information [from the location of the alternate] is mapped directly onto the multisensory neuronal populations that represent one's own body in ego-centric coordinates'.[52] Once more we see a process of 'intermapping' between experience, psychological function, and neural realization.

The final sentence in the quotation from Ramachandran takes us to the second kind of case discussed by him that may be relevant to empathy. In the cases discussed so far, the bodily image of the self is extended to assimilate objects that are not literally part of the self (plastic arms, dummies, tables, cars, and at the limit—other human bodies). There is a 'melding' of the physical self with, or relocation to, some other bit of the world, but the literal, physical self remains the experiential centre of gravity. This is true even in the Petkova and Ehrsson experiments, where the subject's bodily sensations are repositioned spatially but are otherwise unaffected. In the second kind of case, by contrast, the self is not only extended to some other chunk of the world, but is remodelled around it. The relevant example here from Ramachandran concerns men who suffer from 'so-called sympathetic pregnancy or couvade syndrome'—a condition which can include many of the changes associated with actual pregnancy, 'including abdominal swelling, lactation, craving for strange foods, nausea, even labour pains'.[53] In such cases, 'I' has made way for 'you'—the literal self remodels itself, as far as possible (which, it seems from this case, is a remarkably long way!) on the self who constitutes the 'target' of empathy. Perhaps, though, it makes more sense to think of the difference between the two kinds of case as a difference in degree rather than kind. If we are capable of assimilating tables and cars into our bodily self-image, the integrity of the self as traditionally conceived may be a misleading idea. In place of a unified self with fixed and permanent boundaries, we have a self whose sense of physical and psychological extension may vary.

What bearing does all of this have on our experience of art, and of film in particular? With the more detailed and materially grounded account of empathy enabled by triangulating phenomenological, psychological, and neural evidence in place, we are in a better position to propose and explore hypotheses concerning the functioning of empathy in artistic experience. It is plausible to suppose that film-makers may exploit our empathic capacities in the way that they represent action and emotional expression. Hitchcock, in particular, sought empathic effects through precisely wrought renderings of gesture and facial expression. In a famous sequence in *Strangers on a Train* (1951), for example, Hitchcock's meticulous crafting of the action, sustaining our attention to the grasping motions and expressive exertions of Bruno (Robert Walker) as he reaches for a cigarette lighter stuck in a drain, invite us to 'feel into' his emotions (I return to this sequence in the context of a fuller discussion of empathy in Chapter 7, Figures 7.1a–7.1h). More generally, many films create one or more 'scenes of empathy'—scenes in which viewers are exposed to sustained close-ups of emotive facial expressions, often combined with affective aural cues, apt to elicit empathic feelings via the mechanism of mirror neurons (see the discussion of and stills from *Los amantes del círculo polar/Lovers of the Arctic Circle* in Chapter 7, Figure 7.3).[54]

It is important to recognize, however, that the proposal here is *not* that empathy amounts to a wholesale 'identification' with an empathic target character, in which the spectator loses her sense of self for the duration of the experience. The experiences of bodily extension and swapping revealed in the experiments just discussed require the combination of very specific, highly coordinated visual *and tactile* cues which we do not find in cinema as we know it. With the emergence of virtual reality technology and 4D cinema, however, direct manipulation of tactile experience (through gloves, suits, and seats) has been incorporated within the apparatus of filmmaking and projection, so that the experiences of bodily extension and relocation are at least conceivable. The still more outlandish cases of empathic transfer, like phantom pregnancy in men, however, are clearly even more complex and require extraordinarily specific conditions to arise (assuming that the phenomena are real in the first place). These more radical instances of identity transformation via empathic responsiveness to the condition of another thus have less direct pertinence for our understanding of film spectatorship, and our experience of artworks more generally.

Behavioural Evidence, Social Cognition, and Critical Analysis

Three other questions might be posed in relation to the model of triangulation. First, how do the model's three levels of description and evidence relate to the types of behavioural evidence so central to psychology? Second, what relations obtain among the phenomenological, the psychological, the neurophysiological, and the *social*? And third, when we bring the model of triangulation to bear on our experience of artistic and aesthetic phenomena, what role might close critical analysis of films and other artworks play?

Behavioural evidence—evidence of how humans act under particular circumstances, with whatever degree of awareness and self-understanding of these actions—is central to experimental psychology. You don't have to be a behaviourist to recognize the importance of behavioural evidence. The evidence of human behaviour may be particularly critical for behaviourism, but even psychologists who grant the need to posit internal mental states still typically draw extensively on the evidence of what humans do as a way of inferring what inner states and capacities they must possess. On a traditional view, the three types of evidence posited within the model of triangulation look like anything but behavioural evidence, since the phenomenology of an experience, the information processing of the mind, and the activity of the brain are all unavailable to ordinary inspection. Certainly, it seems right to say that the character of an experience, and the neural activity subtending that experience, are not forms of expressive or observable behaviour. But the alert reader may have noticed reference to 'behavioural evidence' in my exposition of triangulation. And this is no accident. As we have seen, in considering the nature of psychological evidence, it is often behavioural evidence—what people (fail to) notice in certain contexts, for example, or how easily subjects solve certain kinds of problem in particular contexts—that allows us to make claims or pose hypotheses about the types of information processing our minds can undertake. In this sense, evidence of psychological function is certainly bound up with behavioural evidence, if not reducible to it.

Phenomenological and neurological evidence might also be regarded as types of behavioural evidence, if we expand our conception of behaviour beyond expressive and observable behaviour. To take a simple example that we will return to later in the chapter, when humans witness the sun setting, they typically have a reddish-orange visual experience. The details will vary endlessly of course, but the broad colour character of the experience is predictable. Although intersubjective—radical scepticism aside, we can be confident that we share the nature of such experiences with other human subjects whose visual system is mature and intact—the experience is precisely not observable: it is 'private' in this sense. Sometimes we may issue utterances like 'just look at that shade of orange', but these are contingent add-ons, descriptions of the experience unnecessary for the experience itself. The critical point is that the experience is a reliable kind of response, and such responses seem to fit comfortably within a conception of behaviour that goes beyond observable behaviour. On this view, our reddish-orange experience is a piece of behavioural evidence.

A parallel case can be made with respect to neurophysiological evidence. Such evidence would be a paradigm case of non-behavioural evidence if we restrict behaviour to that which is observable. But we can identify certain neural responses as reliably as we can certain experiences: a snake or snake-like object will almost certainly trigger activity in the amagdyla. Is that neural activity any less a kind of behaviour than the bodily reaction that follows? Brain and body are all part of our physiology. Emerging medical evidence and practice exemplify this point in startling fashion: some patients deemed to be in a permanent vegetative state, based on the traditional observable criteria of eye, verbal, and motor responses, exhibit patterns of neural activity which suggest a level of cognition and even consciousness may remain intact.[55] There is good reason, then, to treat neural evidence as a kind of behavioural evidence, one not playing an expressive role and not ordinarily observable, though available to inspection via brain scanning (a tool explored later in this and the next chapter). As we will see, however, there is a trap here—the trap of neural behaviour*ism*—that we need to avoid. I return to this issue towards the end of this chapter.

What of social dynamics and processes? How do they relate to the model of triangulation? It is tempting to regard the levels of the phenomenological, the psychological, and the neural as comprising a description pitched at the level of the individual subject, and then add an additional level to capture the social dimension of human behaviour and cognition. But this would be to misrepresent how the social dimension enters into *each* of the levels of triangulation. The brains of individuals do not develop in isolation from the social activity of the subjects who possess them; and many systems within the brain are dedicated to interpersonal psychological functions (consider the mirror system, or the brain's highly developed capacity for recognizing and memorizing individual faces). Much of the behavioural evidence we draw upon in delineating the mind is evidence of human social behaviour. Even the theatre of experience—on the face of it, as private as anything can be—is shaped by the interactions among subjects; as we saw in Chapter 1, self-understanding is sometimes transformed by dialogue with others. And since human nature is by nature social and cultural, so our experience, psychology, and neurophysiology must in important ways be shaped by the social forces and cultural traditions in which we operate. I return to these themes in Chapter 3 by way of the idea that the human mind develops and flourishes as part of a 'community of minds', and in Chapter 7 via an exploration of the 'extended mind' thesis, which contends that human mentality depends in myriad ways on the physical and social environment beyond the skin and skull of the individual agent, and that human cognition is not 'brainbound'.

My third question concerns the relationship between detailed critical scrutiny of artworks and the model of triangulation. Does the focus on inner states, neurophysiology, and psychological function simply remove us from attention to the formal and stylistic properties of works themselves? The actual criticism that I engage in throughout this book I hope provides an ostensive answer—an emphatic 'no!'—to this question. But we can tease out the underlying theoretical principle here. A film is constituted by the artistic choices and decisions—the acts—of the filmmaker. In that sense, a film is evidence of the filmmaker's behaviour, behaviour from which, as we have seen, we can reasonably—if not always straightforwardly or infallibly—infer their intentions, beliefs, and attitudes. And perhaps the central intention for any filmmaker is the intention to craft an *experience* for the spectator and to shape their behaviour—minimally to hold their attention, but often to change their attitudes and sometimes to exhort them to action (a theme I return to in Chapter 4). In this way, attention to artworks, though apparently at a remove from the levels of triangulation, always takes us back to them.[56] Artworks are the products of feeling and thinking human agents; it should be no surprise then that our understanding and appreciation of them is shot through with the language of the mind and may draw upon the resources of phenomenology, psychology, and neuroscience.

Neural Behaviourism

It is important to stress, however, that neural evidence—whether pertaining to neural mirroring, body maps, visual attention, suspense, or whatnot—does not speak for itself. We must triangulate this evidence with phenomenological and psychological evidence bearing on our understanding of the actions, emotions, and intentions of others. An experiment on the perception of that great American institution, the Super Bowl ads, reveals some of the problems that can arise from overheated interpretation of neural evidence, without due regard for the two other levels of analysis. A team of neuroscientists, led by Marco Iacoboni, conducted fMRI scans on viewers as they watched ads for the 2006 Super Bowl, and conducted interviews with them afterwards.[57] In his commentary on the experiment, Iacoboni first notes that parts of the mirror system were strikingly active during a Michelob ad, leading him to suggest that '[t]he activity in these areas may represent some form of empathic response', or perhaps 'the simulated action of drinking a beer'. 'Whatever it is,' he concludes, 'it seems a good response to the ad.' Presumably Iacoboni means that the neural evidence shows that the subjects were in some sense 'taking on' the actions depicted in the ads (and the ads are thus 'good' in the sense that they appear to be fulfilling their function).

But on the account developed here, all the neural evidence shows is that the subjects *understood* the action depicted (in part) through that 'direct mapping' onto the premotor cortex that can be described, psychologically, as simulation. It is a big further step to suggest that such understanding affects our *desires*. And the neural evidence presented tells us nothing of the total pattern of neural activity or, at the psychological level, of the relation between understanding-through-simulation and other dimensions of the cognizing of the ad: granted that the evidence suggests that subjects understood the actions in the ad in a 'direct experiential' fashion, we don't know from this evidence whether they were delighted by the thought of drinking beer, indifferent to it, or hostile it; nor whether they might have found the ad itself—as distinct from the action it depicts—amusing, uplifting, manipulative, or clichéd. The neural evidence here, at least as presented, is too limited and far too coarse-grained for any judgement to be made beyond that concerning understanding-through-simulation.

The problem is repeated in even more egregious form later in the commentary, when Iacoboni suggests that the validity of negative verbal reports of female subjects to 'ads using actresses in sexy roles' was undermined by scans showing the mirror systems of these subjects firing up 'quite a bit, suggesting some form of identification and empathy'. Again Iacoboni assumes that the mirror system response goes beyond understanding and indicates an endorsement of the desires and values implicit in the 'sexy roles'. It is at least equally plausible that the negative verbal reports provide a valid indication of the subjects' moral stance towards the actresses—as valid as the neural evidence is for the 'direct understanding' of the actions of the actresses. Iacoboni is quite right to note that, when interviewed, people often 'say what they [believe they] are expected to say'—we have already encountered the possibility of such confabulation in discussing Ramachandran's experiments. But Iacoboni has no grounds for the claim that the neural evidence he reports shows us that the brains of these female interviewees 'seem to say the opposite' of what the women state verbally.

There is still another example of overinterpretation of the neural data in the essay. Iacoboni discusses a third ad, for FedEx, in which a caveman is crushed by a dinosaur, noting that activity in the amygdala—a brain region associated with emotional responses, in particular fear—spikes dramatically at the moment the caveman is flattened. 'The scene looks funny and has been described as funny by lots of people, but your amygdala still perceives it as threatening, another example of disconnect between verbal reports on ads and brain activity while viewing the ads.' Surely a more plausible interpretation of the data is that the activity of the amygdala provides us with only part of the overall story. How is the activity of the amygdala related to the activity of other parts of the brain? Iacoboni doesn't tell us. The fact that the amygdala lights up when watching a representation of a fearful event is signifi-cant, suggesting as it does that at least aspects of our emotional responses to actual events carry over directly to responses to fictional representations. But the verbal reports that stress the humour of the ad may still be fundamentally accurate— statements that describe the overall phenomenal experience created by the global activity of the brain. Again, the problem is not just the slender amount of neural evidence presented, but the very idea that brain activity alone speaks for itself—a fallacy that we might label *neural behaviourism*.

What Do I Know?

One other important point arises from the cases of anomalous suspense and empathy. In setting up the former, I posed the question: what about those occasions where we appear to experience suspense in full possession of knowledge of the outcome? Once we take into account the heterogeneity of an individual's mental capacities—the mix of fast and slow, bottom-up and top-down—it should be apparent that there is no simple *I* who could be in *full possession* of the knowledge. We do exist as persons, that is, as more or less coherent, goal-oriented, conscious entities, but as we saw in Chapter 1 the capacities we recognize as typical of persons are built up from a host of *subpersonal* processing capacities. The investigation of such capacities is the province of physiology and psychophysiology, using such techniques as eye tracking (saccadic eye movement), electromyography (muscle movement), GSR, and, not least, fMRI and other kinds of brain imaging.[58] Most of the time, these subpersonal processes are integrated effectively enough such that we can function as purposeful creatures, a necessity for rational and moral agency that Michael Smith labels the 'coherence constraint'.[59]

Sometimes, however, the system orchestrating these subpersonal mechanisms falls apart, as in the case of jet lag and the body clock discussed in Chapter 1. Even when the system remains intact, if we look closely enough, we can see the strains in its functioning—as when the sudden sight of the shark in *Jaws* (Steven Spielberg, 1975) compounded by a musical 'stinger' in the score for the film, makes me jump out of my skin, even as another part of my mind recognizes that it's just a piece of rubber.[60] Or, to refer to some examples we've already encountered, when my body gets agitated with suspenseful anxiety over the fate of a character, even though I know—having seen the film before—that the character will live happily ever after; or when I experience a chimerical colour as a result of pushing my visual system in unusual ways, knowing all the while with another part of my mind that the colour is an artefact of my visual system and does not represent light waves in the world. So our traditional conception of selfhood is misleading in two ways: it is neither as *internally unified* nor—as we saw in the discussion of bodily self-image being extended and relocated—is it as *spatially contained* as we are inclined to think. A naturalized understanding of the self, which accepts and embraces these facts as they are revealed by scientific investigation, can also lead us to a more nuanced conception of aesthetic response and experience, which pushes beyond the mostly conceptual and sometimes sterile debate that has dominated the field of aesthetics historically.

We cannot pick up my experience of red, or your experience of the peculiarly horrible dilemma facing the central characters in *The Wind that Shakes the Barley* (Ken Loach, 2006), with tweezers, and weigh them on a set of scales. But then, neither can we directly observe subatomic particles or extinct species. Much of what we readily acknowledge as the object of science depends on inference and reconstruction. To appreciate properly the prospects for a scientifically informed aesthetics, we need to work with a more capacious and sophisticated definition of science than high school biology and chemistry—the dissected frog and magnesium over the Bunsen burner— afford us. To be sure, the inaccessibility of conscious experience to direct observation is of a particular kind that can't simply be assimilated with the other cases I allude to here. But setting consciousness, and our conscious experience of aesthetic objects, into this context appropriately deflates the sense of implausibility that may initially strike us when we contemplate approaching aesthetic experience scientifically. Scientific practice long ago came to encompass the unobservable and the indirect; without them, we would not have the science and the scientific history that we do in fact possess. Triangulating the phenomenological with the psychological and neural may yet allow us scientific insight into the 'madness' of people to match our understanding of the motion of heavenly bodies.

3

The Engine of Reason and
the Pit of Naturalism

If the mind happens in space at all, it happens somewhere north of the neck.
What exactly turns on knowing how far north?

Jerry Fodor

We propose that a crucial element of esthetic response consists of the activation
of embodied mechanisms encompassing the simulation of actions, emotions and
corporeal sensation, and that these mechanisms are universal. This basic level of
reaction to images is essential to understanding the effectiveness both of everyday
images and of works of art. Historical, cultural and other contextual factors do
not preclude the importance of considering the neural processes that arise in the
empathetic understanding of visual artworks.

David Freedberg and Vittorio Gallese

It is hard to escape the brain these days—everywhere one turns, one encounters
brain-scan images, claims about the neural basis of various human behaviours, and
whole new sub-disciplines based on the application of neuroscientific ideas or
techniques to traditional domains of enquiry, as in 'neurolinguistics', 'neurophilosophy', and 'neuroeconomics'. Another such emergent field of enquiry is 'neuroaesthetics', which seeks to illuminate our understanding of aesthetics by examining the
brain processes and structures upon which aesthetic experience appears to depend.
Among those neuroscientists who have been ploughing this furrow, Semir Zeki and
V. S. Ramachandran—both eminent in their own fields—have attracted the most
attention. Zeki is known for his arguments concerning object constancy (our ability
to perceive the integrity of objects, in spite of changes of angle, lighting, distance, and
so on), visual abstraction (visual experiences of colours and forms, rather than of
objects per se), and what the visual arts can tell us about these phenomena;
Ramachandran caused a stir with his proposed eight 'laws' of aesthetic experience.[1]
Many other researchers are at work in what is consolidating itself as a research
programme.[2] All of these developments have taken place against the backdrop of—or
perhaps they are simply constitutive of—the gradual move from 'cognitive science' to
'cognitive neuroscience', a shift expressive of the changing self-understanding of the
broader domain of enquiry.[3]

Why should we care? What does, or might, this have to do with the study of art in general or film in particular? There are several reasons why aestheticians and film scholars might turn their attention to these developments in neuroscience. First, in addition to the specific field of neuroaesthetics, which has focused almost wholly on still depictions, there are now several teams of researchers tackling related questions on other art forms, including film. Uri Hasson and his collaborators, for example, conducted early research in 'neurocinematic studies'; other teams of researchers working on related terrain include Talma Hendler, Gal Raz, and their colleagues at Tel Aviv University, Pia Tikka's NeuroCine research team at Aalto University, Helsinki, and Vittorio Gallese, Michele Guerra, and their colleagues based at the University of Parma.[4] Such research has one foot in an existing research tradition in film studies, namely cognitive film theory, which has gradually become more interested in neuroscientific research just as its 'parent' research field, cognitive science, has come under the sway of the brain. Moving in the other direction, neuroscientific research on such fundamental mental capacities as perception, emotion, empathy, and memory is also relevant to art and film, as we will see in the course of this chapter. Moreover, neuroscientific research (on film, on art, or on aspects of human psychology more generally) is pertinent not only to cognitive film theory, but to any approach to film with a significant psychological dimension, including phenomenological and psychoanalytic film theory. If Deleuze and some of his followers are prepared to allude to the brain, they ought, in good faith, to be prepared to follow those allusions to the place where research on the brain is actually conducted.[5]

A second reason that neuroscience matters to the study of film is that it matters to film practitioners—or to some of them, at any rate. In parallel with scholarly work on film and the brain, we also see filmmakers venturing into 'neurocinema', that is, the application of neuroscientific tools to filmmaking. So far, this practice has taken at least three forms. First, brain scanning has been used as an extension of the venerable practice of test screenings, where scans provide another way of assessing the kind of impact particular moments in films possess; more generally, and not surprisingly, brain scanning is now being used as a tool in the advertising industry, spawning the idea of 'neuromarketing' (an example of which we have already explored in Chapter 2—Marco Iacoboni's study of the 2006 Super Bowl ads). The second practical application of neuroscience in the world of motion pictures concerns what we might call 'neural interactivity' in narrative film and in game design, wherein brain signals transmitted from headsets worn by players and viewers affect directly the game world and the progression of the narrative, as in the game *Focus Pocus* and in the films produced by MyndPlay.[6] A third practical application of neuroscience involves the conversion of neural data into animated moving imagery, a technique designed to represent mental imagery in filmic form—in effect, to realize not merely brain scanning, but *mind* scanning.[7] Jeff Zacks speculates about a fourth possible application in the form of 'Magnovision'—cinema supercharged by the application of another neuroscientific technique, transcranial magnetic stimulation (TMS), whereby parts of the brain are stimulated by controlled magnetic fields:

Imagine you are watching a car chase. The Mustang's brakes are out, and the car is headed for a cliff. As the car swerves, we zap the part of your brain responsible for your sense of balance and you feel for a moment as though your body is turning suddenly. At the last instant the hero the dives out of the car and hits the ground. We zap the part of your brain responsible for body sensation and you feel a touch as the protagonist makes contact.[8]

Unlike the other neurocinematic tools, then, Magnovision would involve direct manipulation of the brain, rather than scanning and exploiting neural activity in response to movie experience. Magnovision is a speculative idea, of course, and even the existing techniques and the practices based on them are still in their infancy, so it is too early to say much about their character or value. But that they exist at all is surely of note.

Perhaps there is a third, more general, reason for arts disciplines to take note of the *3.* burgeoning world of neuroscience. The current prominence of neuroscience is driven by the emergence of new technologies that are providing a picture of unprecedented detail of brain anatomy and function. Many scientists and philosophers believe that this new abundance of data will transform our understanding of phenomena across a wide range of fields. As we will see, there is much debate around these claims, but an adequate debate cannot be had without the participation of those individuals in possession of the requisite expertise—and in the case of 'neurocinematic studies', that means *both* neuroscientists and film scholars. Make no mistake: neuroscience will continue to spread into the making and the study of film and the arts in general. Film scholars and aestheticians can stay in their comfort zone and pretend it is not happening, or they can look outward with an open mind as well as a sceptical eye, assessing just what neuroscience might or might not have to offer to our understanding of the arts.

I make a start on that project of assessment here. I begin by exploring some of the controversies surrounding contemporary neuroscience, and some of the arguments offered against its extension into new domains. This discussion will be largely philosophical, and the connections here with film and the arts will not always be obvious; it is, nevertheless, essential to a proper understanding of what is at stake. With a sketch of these critical concerns in place, I turn to two aspects of our cinematic experience—startling in response to films, and empathic mirroring of characters' states—where, I argue, insights from neuroscience can deepen and enrich our understanding of the phenomena at stake.

Meet the Neurosceptics

Not everyone is impressed with or pleased by the rise of neuroscience. Jerry Fodor has given vivid expression to a long-standing tradition of scepticism among philosophers and psychologists of a functionalist stripe who question whether the mind can be illuminated by evidence about the brain. Fodor decries in particular the vogue for brain scanning, which he sees as an undisciplined 'gold rush' for neural data unconstrained by the formulation of clear and testable hypotheses.[9] The classic functionalist worry, however, hinges on the 'multiple realizability' of mental states—the idea, that is, that mental states do not depend on any one form of hardware or physical implementation. On a grand scale, this points towards the possibility of artificial intelligence, or the intelligence of organic entities with a different biochemical basis from our own; on a more modest scale, multiple realizability points towards neural plasticity—manifested, for example, in the ability of the brain to reconfigure itself after injury, restoring mental capacities through neural interconnections very different to those preceding injury.[10] If mental function does not depend on some specific physical substrate or organization of material, why would we expect to learn much about mental phenomena by looking at the brain?

Peter Hacker (like Fodor, a philosopher) and Maxwell Bennett (a neuroscientist) have together advanced a still more wide-ranging critique of contemporary neuro-science, stressing the confusions that, they argue, arise from speaking of neural processes in the language of personal agency.[11] As we saw in Chapter 1, Hacker and Bennett refer to this as the *mereological fallacy*—where a property or a capacity properly attributable only to a whole person or organism (perceiving, thinking, experiencing, acting) is attributed to a part of that organism, namely the brain or some part of it. Iacoboni provides a clear example in his fMRI study of Super Bowl ads: 'The scene looks funny and has been described as funny by lots of people, but *your amygdala still perceives it as threatening*, another example of disconnect between verbal reports on ads and brain activity while viewing the ads'.[12] My analysis of Marco Iacoboni's study in Chapter 2 shows that Hacker and Bennett are right to urge caution around such claims, but we have also seen in Chapter 1 that, used with care, such metaphorical language is both warranted and illuminating, and in any case difficult to avoid.

Perhaps the most voluble and prolific of the neurosceptics, however, is Raymond Tallis—author of *Aping Mankind: Neuromania, Darwinitis, and the Misrepresenta-tion of Humanity* (2011),[13] and of various other works inveighing against the contemporary development of neuroscience. Tallis's views are worth engaging with for a number of reasons. Tallis is a (now retired) professor of geriatric medicine who boasts expertise in clinical neurology, and who has sustained a remarkable second career as a philosopher and a writer. Accordingly, one might have expected him to have considerable sympathy with the rise of neuroaesthetics and with the various tributaries of brain research that wend their way into the territory of the humanities and social sciences.[14] But Tallis is profoundly sceptical of many of the claims made by and on behalf of contemporary neuroscience. This scepticism takes us to the second reason for exploring Tallis's perspective in detail. In works such as *Not Saussure* and *In Defence of Realism*,[15] Tallis was an early and significant critic of post-structuralism. He has long been critical of the tendency among humanist scholars to import and regurgitate half-digested ideas from various scientific and pseudo-scientific disciplines, such as Saussurian semiotics and Lacanian psychoanalysis; his critique of the currently fashionable appropriation of neuroscientific and evolution-ary ideas and language by non-specialists represents a continuation of this theme. Given the significance of this earlier work, Tallis's current work surely deserves a hearing, even (or perhaps especially) from those of us sympathetically disposed towards the idea of neurocinematic studies.

Around the time of the publication of his book *The Kingdom of Infinite Space* (2008),[16] Tallis appeared on the UK's BBC Radio 4 show *Start the Week*. The book is concerned with the various features and functions of the human head, but pointedly *excludes* consideration of the brain. Tallis describes *The Kingdom* as 'affirmative action for the body', underscoring his argument that human thought and behaviour cannot be understood as arising from the brain alone; the motor and expressive capabilities of the body must be given their due. Tallis also remarked that the book is intended as

a way of getting hold of our curious situation of being embodied subjects … a way of putting forward a view of humanity that doesn't fall into either a supernaturalist viewpoint, or fall into the pit of naturalism. I think we cannot be explained as having fallen from the sky—I'm a good Darwinian, Dan [Dennett] will be glad to know—at the same time we are extraordinarily distanced from the rest of the animal kingdom that was generated by the standard Darwinian processes.[17]

Tallis's critique of 'neuromania' (and its sibling 'Darwinitis') focuses, then, on 'the pit of naturalism'. So what is the conception of naturalism that Tallis finds so objec-tionable? Once again it's important to underline that the naturalism at stake here has nothing to do with naturalism as a literary or artistic style; naturalism here is rather a philosophical stance. Naturalism in this sense is the project of explaining human behaviour based on the assumption that the human species is a part of the natural world, and that consequently the methods and knowledge of the natural sciences will play a central role in such an explanation. Tallis regards such naturalism as a 'pit' to be avoided because of its alleged failure to acknowledge and accommodate the gulf—cognitive, behavioural, and existential—between humans and other animals. 'The word is out in academe and more broadly among intellectuals that human beings are really beasts—and rather nasty ones at that—or zombies', writes Tallis. 'Those who view us as zombies argue that we are wired in, via our evolved brains, to the outside world in such a way as to ensure replication of our genetic material. We are disposable phenotypes, utilized by the genome to ensure its own survival.'[18] One of the key ideas in this passage is that 'we are wired in, via our evolved brains, to the outside world'. What does this idea amount to? And how does it relate to the naturalistic stance?

In this passage, Tallis invokes a familiar contrast—between the behaviour of non-human animals, regarded as governed by evolved instincts and reflexes, and human behaviour, understood as characterized by deliberation and reflection. In Tallis's account, an evolutionary perspective on human behaviour compels us to do away with this contrast, instead regarding humans as 'beasts' or 'zombies'—presumably in the sense that human behaviour on this account is determined by evolved reflexes or reflex-like responses embodied in the brain and the nervous system more generally, thus leaving no scope for rational deliberation. Tallis's main target in this passage is genetic determinism à la Richard Dawkins, according to which the individual human agent is (from a genetic point of view) nothing more than a vehicle for genetic replication; we are 'wired' to do the bidding of our genes.[19] The 'wiring' metaphor in this context naturally extends to encompass the nature of the relationship between the actions of the individual agent and the environment in which the agent exists, with the 'evolved brain' acting as the intermediary between the level of the gene and the level of the organism. According to Tallis's version of evolutionary theory, it is the brain that ensures that the individual is 'wired into the world' in such a way as to prioritize genetic reproduction. Behaviourism, with its emphasis on physical stimuli and observable behavioural responses, and with its denial of the scientific credibility of mental phenomena, lurks not far behind the bogeyman of genetic determinism here. As Tallis writes: '[i]f you reduce human life to responses to stimuli, then you will seem to be justified in seeing us as biological devices programmed to respond to stimuli'.[20]

Behaviourism is not Tallis's principal target, however. While dismissive of behaviourism, his real concern is with cognitive science, the movement that supplanted behavioural psychology. Indeed, an equally important source of Tallis's hostility towards the language of 'wiring' is its origin (or at least widespread use) in cognitive theory.[21] In this context, 'wiring' is used to refer to the physical constitution of thinking agents—like human beings—and is an extension of the analogy between the human mind and the computer fundamental to mainstream cognitive science: the human mind as an information processor. A contrast is typically drawn between those aspects of our physical constitution which are 'hard-wired' (innate and developmentally predetermined) and those which are 'soft-wired' (shaped by learning), though it is better to think of these as end points of a continuum—for even those aspects of our being that are heavily influenced by experience and learning, such as language, will nevertheless develop within certain fixed parameters. Tallis's objections to the wiring metaphor can be boiled down to two elements. The first is that such talk is reductive, appearing to treat humans as entities that can be exhaustively described in terms of physical properties; the second, related worry is that the language of wiring appears to leave no space for the rationality and flexibility of human action.

Another work by Tallis on the distinctiveness of *homo sapiens*, *The Knowing Animal* (2005),[22] articulates his own contrasting view: unlike all other animal species, Tallis argues, humans are 'uncoupled' from—rather than 'wired' into—the world. 'Lots of triggers of our behaviour are very abstract', Tallis remarked on *Start the*

Week; 'we are not wired into the world the way other animals are', he continued, paraphrasing the passage from *The Kingdom* already quoted. Humans have the ability to grasp situations and problems, consider the possible solutions, and weigh up their respective pros and cons. On the level of immediate action, we are capable of inhibiting (or stimulating) our instinctive desire for food or for sex, for example; on the level of long-term, strategic planning, we are able to transcend the imperatives of our genes, most obviously by choosing not to engage in reproduction. Even where we do engage in reproduction, we are not merely acting instinctively: we are choosing to act one way rather than another way within a field of possibilities. This description is, of course, nothing more than a thumbnail sketch of a traditional (and in many ways powerful and plausible) picture of the distinctiveness of human behaviour, one which takes for granted both the normal development of the individual and a social context that enables the individual possessed of these rational capacities to act on them. But the sketch is sufficient to ask two questions: is this contrast between human and non-human animal behaviour tenable? And does the contrast, as Tallis claims, undermine naturalism?

Normative Panting

In *The Kingdom* Tallis discusses laughing and crying—behaviours in which the head plays a starring role—under the rubric of 'normative panting'. Citing William Hazlitt (and Aristotle indirectly), Tallis argues that laughter and crying are uniquely human behaviours; important types of response to the gap between our perception of the ways things *are* and the way they *ought* to be.[23] Laughter is 'normative', then, in the sense that it is a response involving recognition of a standard or norm that some event or state of affairs fails to match, rather than simply a response to that state of affairs. For Tallis, this normative element is an example of the complexity of human behaviour, and its distance from behaviour driven by simple instincts and reflexes. Normativity is one of the key ways in which we are 'uncoupled' from the world, and is one of the main reasons that 'aping mankind'—comparing human behaviour with the behaviour of other primates and exploring human behaviour more generally in the context of evolutionary theory—should, according to Tallis, be avoided.

But there is a curious and telling inconsistency here. By referring to laughter as a form of 'panting', Tallis underlines the physiological similarities between laughter and homologous non-human animal behaviours, thereby gesturing towards the evolutionary roots of laughter. To be sure, when discussing tickling among chimpanzees, Tallis stresses both that their panting takes a different form from human laughter, and that the objects of chimpanzee laughter do not extend to the cognitively elaborate, physically absent, normative cues that are, on his account, the characteristic triggers of human laughter. But, rhetorically at least, the cat is out of the bag: the link between human laughter and its evolutionary precursors has been made. As we will see, this link points to the way in which the unique features of human existence can be accommodated within a naturalistic perspective, and the way in which such a perspective can be enlightening. As his language implies, Tallis is in fact a type of naturalist. He is moved to argue against naturalism—and cast it as a hellish 'pit'—only because of an overly narrow and rigid conception of what is to count as naturalism.

Like most philosophers who are resistant to a naturalistic perspective on human behaviour, Tallis repeatedly stresses the uniqueness of human behaviour—the fact that, whatever similarities might obtain between, for example, human and chimpanzee behaviour, no such comparison will capture the particular capacities and attributes distinctive of human beings. True enough; but how much of a problem is this argument for naturalism? In itself, it does not really pose a problem at all. *Every* species will possess one or more unique features—if only the feature that each species is *just that species and no other*. (And on the latest estimate, there are currently 8.7 million species on earth; that's a lot of uniqueness to go around.) As Helena Cronin puts it:

to erect a biological apartheid of 'us' and 'them' is to cut ourselves off from a potentially useful source of explanatory principles ... Admittedly we're unique. But there's nothing unique about being unique. Every species is in its own way.[24]

One vivid exploration of this explanatory resource is Mark Rowlands's *The Philosopher and the Wolf*, a comparative study of human, simian, lupine, and canine psychology, which brings out the distinctiveness of each lineage and species. Species uniqueness per se, then, does not constitute grounds to reject naturalism.[25]

Consider a related point: pick any two disparate points on the tree of life—say, a bacterium and an earthworm or the same earthworm and a zebra—and we will be struck by the gulf between these forms of life. Two factors, however, make the gulf between humans and other animals, and especially other primates, more salient in everyday thought than the remarkable differences between many other species. The first factor is simply the fact that, when it comes to comparisons between humans and other species, we occupy one of the points of comparison subjectively. No matter how much we try to look upon our own species dispassionately, as a biological phenomenon to be studied scientifically, it is hard to lay aside the 'view from within'. We are always, in this sense, contending with a kind of 'species egoism'; with a type of anthropocentrism. The second factor that makes the existential and behavioural gap between us humans and our fellow primates stand out is the fact that we share so much genetically with them—more than 99 per cent with our nearest relations, chimpanzees. Given this genetic intimacy, why the behavioural distance? Two points are particularly pertinent here. First, as these facts tell us, relatively small genetic differences can go hand-in-hand with very large behavioural differences. And second, it follows that some significant part of the gulf between humans and other primates cannot be directly attributable to our genetic makeup, but must instead be explained by the interaction between our genes and our environment—including the environment of culture in which humans develop.

What all this suggests is that we need to look in more detail at the specific content (and history) of *human* uniqueness in order properly to assess Tallis's argument. This state of affairs returns us to Tallis's characterization of *homo sapiens* as the 'uncoupled animal'—the animal who is not 'wired into the world' in the way that other species are so wired; the animal who lives in what Wilfrid Sellars famously christened the 'space of reasons'.[26] It would be foolish to deny that rational deliberation is indeed an enormously powerful capacity possessed uniquely, or at least to a unique degree, by human beings.[27] But is it adequate to sum up human psychology as rational—as entirely characterized by detached and careful reflection? If we are looking for an accurate description of human psychology, as distinct from an idealized account of it, it should be obvious that we cannot simply describe *homo sapiens* as the 'reasoning animal'. This is the general burden of the now vast literature on 'bounded rationality', and reasoning under time-bound, uncertain, or other sub-optimal conditions. Human cognition is comprised of a combination of numerous heuristics—cognitive shortcuts that are efficient and effective in the right context, error-prone in others—along with the more abstract reasoning skills described by logic. What is key here is that the heuristic responses are typically spontaneous and immediate; 'quick and dirty', as the saying goes, rather than reflective and deliberative.[28]

As Tallis himself points out, many emotions and other behaviours, including laughter and yawning, are 'contagious'. Such behaviours are triggered beneath conscious intention, by the laughing and yawning of those around us. On one influential account, emotions in general are 'gut reactions', rapid appraisals of the relevance for us of events that we encounter; appraisals that are then typically re-evaluated but which nonetheless constitute our initial response and form the baseline of any reappraisal.[29] All of these forms of affective and cognitive response are, in other words, evidence of our animal natures in exactly Tallis's sense: they demonstrate how we are, in many ways, precisely 'wired into the world'.

So much for Tallis, and the 'broad spectrum' critics of neuroscience—those with general doubts about the coherence of neuroscience and its relevance to psychology and other disciplines. How have the interventions of neuroscience been received specifically within the philosophy of art? Critiques of neuroscience from within this domain tend to be more moderate, if not less serious. John Hyman's commentary on the arguments of Zeki and Ramachandran stresses the mismatch between the intended scope and ambition of these theories, and their actual limitations.[30] Hyman dubs Ramachandran's account 'the Baywatch theory of art', arguing that while on the one hand it explains only a limited range of types or aspects of art, on the other hand it seems to explain the attention-grabbing nature of many phenomena outside the purview of art and aesthetics.[31] In a related vein, Vincent Bergeron and Dominic Lopes have underlined the very different definitions of 'art' and 'the aesthetic' operative in the work of neuroscientists and art theorists—often unacknowledged differences which threaten to render useless the experimental work undertaken.[32]

David Davies, meanwhile, highlights two ways in which neuroscientific research on art may miss its mark.[33] First, in an echo of Fodor, Davies argues that brain research may provide nothing more than an 'implementation story' about already acknowledged features of aesthetic or artistic experience; on this view, learning that, say, the seat of some emotional response is the insula rather than the amygdala does not enrich our understanding of the aesthetic phenomenon. Second, noting the contrast between descriptive questions about the nature of our actual responses and normative questions about 'merited' responses, Davies stresses the centrality of the latter in philosophy of art and queries the ability of empirical research to address them. Things rather work in the other direction, according to Davies: experimental work must make normative assumptions which, if they are acknowledged and defended at all, will be on the basis of conceptual argument. Here Davies's argument joins with Tallis's in playing up the strongly normative character of human behaviour—another dimension of our uniquely 'uncoupled' existence. I return to these concerns and criticisms again in the conclusion of this chapter.

The enthusiasm for all things neural, then, is matched by doubts coming from many directions. My aim so far has been to consider some of the worries raised by critics of contemporary neuroscience and to show that they are often groundless, overstated, or at least in need of further elaboration and defence. I hope to have created some space for naturalism in general and for a neuroscientific approach to the arts in particular. Within that space it is important not merely to set out certain areas of neuroscientific research and show, in a broad-brush way, how this research maps onto questions about film and the arts, but to pinpoint the specific, novel, and irreducible contributions that have or might be made by such research. I attempt this here by exploring what neuroscience might have to teach us about the ways in which filmmakers seek to elicit, and the ways in which spectators experience, two particular forms of affective response: the *startle response* and *empathic mirroring*. We can best appreciate the value of neuroscience, and in particular how it may go beyond the provision of 'implementation stories', when we arrive at a fine-grained analysis and explanation of such specific phenomena.

Startling Sounds and Sights

When we jump at a loud or unexpected noise or at a sudden, dramatic change in our field of vision, we are experiencing the startle response. Startling in this manner is a brainstem reflex: we cannot, at least under normal circumstances, exert significant control over it. We can no more stop ourselves startling at a loud, unanticipated gunshot than we can halt the shrinking of our pupils when we move into a field of bright light. The startle response depends on specific neural pathways, leading from the visual and acoustic systems through to the motor cortex.[34] Signals carried on this pathway cause the characteristic motor 'jerk' of the torso and limbs, along with an eye blink and distinctive facial expression. Being evolutionarily ancient, the startle response is found in many species, and its evolutionary function is not hard to discern: in potentially threatening situations, the startle response propels us into a state of heightened attention.[35] In this sense, the startle response is very clear evidence of both 'the continuity of species'—of the evolutionary continuity between humans and other animals—and of the way in which we (like other animals) are 'wired into the world'.

How have filmmakers drawn upon the startle response? In reading the last paragraph, many readers will doubtless have recalled examples from horror movies and from thrillers. The 'startle effect' (or 'jump scare') is a staple of such films, just as the lachrymose response invited by the sight of the crying human face is a key ingredient in melodrama. Robert Baird suggests that the startle effect as an integral feature of the horror film can be traced to producer Val Lewton, who referred to such effects as 'busses', named after his first use of the technique in *Cat People* (Jacques Tourneur, 1942), where we are startled by the sudden and unexpected appearance of a bus from off-screen.[36] *Iron Man* (Jon Favreau, 2008) furnishes us with a more recent but similar example. Tony Stark (Robert Downey Jnr) is being escorted by a group of American soldiers in a Humvee across a desert landscape in Afghanistan. The scene begins with a shot framing in the centre of the vehicle a boom box on which plays the AC/DC song 'Back in Black', first heard at high volume, before settling after a few seconds into its function as diegetic background music. The camera tilts up from the boom box to reveal, through the windscreen, two other Humvees in front of the one in which the camera is situated (Figure 3.1a).

Stark is a flamboyant character—a celebrated inventor equally well-known as a playboy. Incongruously, he cradles a cocktail (Figure 3.1b), and after a few seconds, he starts to banter in good-natured fashion with the soldiers. The soldier sitting alongside Stark in the back of the vehicle asks if he can get a photo with him. Stark assents and strikes a pose (Figure 3.1c), while the solider in the front passenger seat frames the shot, the action focusing on the framing and staging of the photo. Across the thirty or so seconds that have elapsed since the scene began, then, the film has worked to focus the spectator's attention on the initially tentative, but increasingly relaxed and humorous, interaction between Stark and the soldiers. The AC/DC song, Stark's cocktail, and his irreverent jesting create a sociable atmosphere within the Humvee, an atmosphere that is at odds with and distracts us from the treacherous environment outside the vehicle. A micro-narrative is created around the taking of the photograph, which we expect to be completed. A complex but stable overall rhythm emerges from the blending of editing, figure movement, and the AC/DC song; the auditory dynamics of the scene are similarly stable.

All of these factors set up the startle response cue—a sudden and tumultuous blast as the Humvee in front of Stark's vehicle is destroyed by a rocket-propelled grenade or a missile (an explosion that resonates through every speaker in a surround sound system). The explosion is rendered visually across three rapidly cut shots—beginning in the background behind the soldier taking the photo (Figure 3.1d), continuing in a shot of the convoy,[37] and concluding with a return to the framing inside Stark's vehicle, as debris from the destroyed Humvee lands on top of it.

Figures 3.1a–3.1d Setting up the startle response in *Iron Man* (Jon Favreau, 2008).

Now, it is obviously the case that our appreciation of this scene and the film as a whole depends upon a whole array of mental capacities that go far beyond the brief, involuntary, reflex reaction that is the startle response. In order to make even basic sense of the action, viewers need to understand the dialogue, to interpret facial and vocal expressions, and to figure out the spatial relations among the agents and features of the setting. If their understanding is to go beyond rudimentary comprehension, spectators will in addition need to bring to bear a great deal of culturally specific knowledge—about Marvel Comics, Robert Downey Jnr, and the 'war on terror', for example—on the unfolding action. None of this knowledge, however, makes startle cues like the explosion in *Iron Man*, and the primitive response that it triggers, any less significant, any less a designed feature of the film that exploits a real and important feature of human psychology. Here the startle cue performs a number of functions: it marks a major narrative development (indeed, a plot point); it symbolizes in concrete form the danger posed by the Afghan insurgents; and it delivers a thrilling 'whomp'—one of those powerful bodily sensations so characteristic of action and horror movies, very much akin to the visceral, stomach-in-mouth pleasures of fairground rides.

With such disreputable associations in mind, Baird notes that the startle effect has been '[m]aligned as mindless and a hallmark of B-movies and exploitation fare'.[38] Cultural prejudice of this sort, however, should not stop us from seeking a deeper understanding of such genres, nor of the dispositions and capacities upon which they depend. Tallis and other traditionalists might be inclined to agree that the startle response is, precisely, 'mindless'—a reflex response of the body bereft of flexibility and variability. But such a stance is untenable. Unless we are prepared to embrace Cartesian dualism, human psychology cannot be regarded as dividing conveniently into a wholly mechanical, bodily dimension and an entirely voluntaristic mental dimension. Tallis's own adage regarding 'affirmative action for the body' is ironically apt here. Tallis emphasizes that the brain cannot be understood properly in isolation from the body.[39] But it is equally true that cognition itself cannot be understood properly when detached from its neural and bodily grounding, since the cognitive capacities an organism possesses depend, at least in some ways and to some degree, on that organism's (neuro-)physiology. As we saw Darwin putting it (in the epigraph to Chapter 2), 'the mind is [a] function of the body'.

In any event, the startle effect is not uniquely associated with the horror film or with other popular genres, even though it has certainly been exploited most frequently and routinely in these types of film. *Ran* (1985), Kurosawa Akira's free adaptation of Shakespeare's *King Lear* (1606), shows the effect at work in a much more 'exalted' cultural context.[40] In the film, the Lear-figure Hidetora (Nakadai Tatsuya) has ceded effective leadership of the Ichimonji clan to his first son, Taro (Terao Akira), while Hidetora retains his role as titular leader of the clan. Initially in residence at Taro's castle, Hidetora leaves after arguing with him, eventually moving into the castle of his third son, Saburo (Daisuke Ryu). Taro and Jiro (Hidetora's second son, played by Nezu Jinpachi) together mount a sustained and bloody attack on Saburo's castle.

Across a lengthy sequence, we witness the extraordinary carnage of battle (Figure 3.2), and the gradual progress of the attacking armies towards the capture of Saburo's castle. All diegetic sound from the battle—the clash of armour, the galloping of horses, the cries of injury and death—is suspended, however; in its stead, we hear only Toru Takemitsu's mournful, Mahler-inspired score. Until, that is, we see Taro, leading the offensive army and entering Saburo's castle on horseback— at which point he is shot in the back, a single, loud gunshot terminating the musical cue abruptly and marking the restoration of diegetic sound.

As in the *Iron Man* sequence, a striking change in the overall rhythm of the scene, initiated by the occurrence of an unanticipated event incarnated by a sudden loud sound, prompts the startle response. And here, the force of the startle is both to underline a dramatic turning point, and to remind us of the physical brutality of war. The startle effect caps a process of defamiliarization, whereby our appreciation of what is being represented is heightened by the shift in style. First, we witness slaughter on a mass scale, through the stylized, 'operatic' phase of the sequence, when only the score is audible; then, with the re-entry of diegetic sound, the realistic potential of the visual imagery is drawn out. The startle generated by the gunshot marks the dividing line between the two styles; the effect of defamiliarization therefore turns on this moment. (We return again to the notion of defamiliarization in Chapter 4.)

Thus far in this discussion of the startle response, I have assumed that the response itself is an invariant feature of human physiology; what variation of

Figure 3.2 The battle sequence in *Ran* (Kurosawa Akira, 1985).

function we see arises from the contexts in which it is spontaneously triggered or exploited by design, as in *Iron Man* and *Ran*. In fact, to some extent, context may affect the form as well as the function of the startle response. 'Unlike the knee-jerk, the sneeze, or the flinch', writes Baird, 'startle reflexes are modified by emotional and cognitive states.'[41] According to Peter Lang and his collaborators, 'the vigor of the startle reflex varies systematically with an organism's emotional state...the startle response (an aversive reflex) is enhanced during a fear state and is diminished in a pleasant emotional context'.[42] Baird points to the 'threat scene' as evidence of horror filmmakers' understanding, whether fully conscious or more intuitive, of this fact. In such a scene, a character is presented as fearful of a hidden, often indeterminate, off-screen threat; after depicting the character's anxiety for a period, the immediate space around the character is subjected to a sudden intrusion, typically from an unpredictable direction or in an unpredictable manner. The threat phase of the sequence primes us for the startle response; in an anxious and fearful state, we are more likely to be startled. (Baird suggests that this is why we find the startle effect much more frequently in horror and thriller films than in any other filmic context.) Threat scenes thus perform a balancing act between priming and misdirection: an unsettling, fearful mood is created, but within that broad affective context, our attention is taken away at the critical moment from the precise spatial location of the threat. (On the relationship between moods and emotions, and the priming of the latter by the former, see the discussion of *Heimat* in Chapter 6.)

Baird analyses the bus scene from *Cat People* as an important historical exemplar of the threat scene. Alice (Jane Randolph) is seen making her way through the streets at night. She senses that she is being followed by someone or something, and glances several times to screen left. After this pattern has been sustained over some seconds, a bus abruptly and noisily enters from screen right. Note here the role and force of the deictic gaze, that is, our impulse to track the gaze of others; Alice's glances to the left pull our attention in that direction as well. The sequence from *Iron Man* is closer to this antecedent than the sequence from *Ran*. In the former case, general knowledge of war zones and particular knowledge about attacks on military convoys in Afghanistan put us on alert. The relaxed social atmosphere in the Humvee—Stark's cocktail, AC/DC hammering away, the badinage and business around the taking of the photo—are designed to distract us from the possibility of an attack, however; our visual attention in particular is (mis)directed to the right of the frame (where the photographer lines up the camera) and away from the centre of the frame (where the Humvee in front will explode) (Figure 3.1d). In the *Ran* sequence, the sense of threat is somewhat dampened and flattened by the suspended diegetic sound, and the fatal bullet is less visibly intrusive than the bus (in *Cat People*) or the missile (in *Iron Man*); even so, the basic constituents (character, implied threat, and sudden intrusion) are in place here as well.

There is also some evidence that the startle response may be subject to more idiosyncratic and elaborate cultural variations in the form of 'culture-bound syndromes'. Members of Malaysian, Indonesian, and some other Southeast Asian cultures recognize a condition called *latah*, which roughly translates as 'jumpy'. Afflicting mostly middle-aged, economically deprived, and socially marginal women, those suffering from the condition appear to have a strong innate predisposition towards being startled, but this predisposition is combined with some element of learned performance (playing up of the startle response) through 'matching' (mimicry of the startling event) and 'automatic' obedience to a command following the startle.[43] In an interview with anthropologist Ronald Simons, Cik Alimah binti Mamad gives the following account of the behaviour of a *latah* (the same term is used for the condition and a person suffering from it):

When she's sitting quietly we can take a piece of wood and bang it, or we can poke her in the ribs over and over and she'll become *latah*. She gets startled! Then if we order her to hit or dance, she'll hit or dance. And she'll do whatever we tell her to do with what she's holding. Whoever is in front of her will be hit. That's what a *latah* does![44]

To some extent, *latah* resembles the practice of acting out and playing up startle and fear responses among Western horror movie audiences; though in this context, the practice is not so elaborately developed, and appears to be restricted to the time and space of spectatorship. On the one hand, then, *latah* appears to be grounded in the startle response; on the other hand, *latah* appears to be a cultural extension of the response, where the effects of learning and context are very evident. 'The nearer the onset of the original response (speaking of microseconds), the more innate, "hard-wired" the response', Baird argues in relation to the startle response; 'conversely, the further from onset, the more learning, context, and personality [influence] behavior'.[45] As with the film sequences discussed, there is no difficulty, in principle or in practice, in recognizing both the invariant physiological basis and the variations achieved through particular uses and cultural elaborations of the startle response. For this reason, we can acknowledge that the response 'wires us into the world' without denying that the response figures as just one part of the immensely complex and flexible cognitive and behavioural repertoire possessed by human beings.

How do such culture-bound syndromes fit into the naturalistic, biocultural framework under development in this book? Jesse Prinz suggests that although such syndromes are sometimes found in only one population, and sometimes flare up for relatively short periods, 'there is often overlap [among related syndromes] across the globe, suggesting that each culture cobbles together different clusters of coping mechanisms that are potentially available to all of us'.[46] Biology enables culture, and culture extends biological capacities, in variable ways. Human nature is a composite of biological and cultural processes (a thesis I pursue further in Chapter 6).

Mirror Thrills

Another element in the human cognitive repertoire is the set of interrelated capacities usually gathered under the label *empathy*—a term which is used to refer to a variety of phenomena, ranging from the conscious, imaginative effort to 'perspective take' or put oneself in another's shoes, to affective mimicry and emotional contagion, whereby we 'catch' the emotions of others through a process of low-level, non-conscious, involuntary mimicry.[47] As we saw in Chapter 2, the study of empathy is one of the contexts in which the discovery of mirror neurons has been so significant. Recall that mirror neurons are active both when subjects perform an action, and when they observe that same action being performed. There is evidence that a neural 'mirror system' exists in humans for 'somatosensory' experiences (tactile, proprioceptive, and pain-related sensations), basic actions (grasping objects, switching switches), and basic emotions (including disgust and sadness).[48] In terms of the model of triangulation advanced in Chapter 2, the mirror system, then, is the *neural* substrate that 'implements' our *psychological* capacities for sensory, motor, and affective mimicry, and the *experiences* that may characterize these processes. Gallese—one of the team who discovered mirror neurons—with Guerra and other colleagues has developed an *embodied simulation* model of film spectatorship in just these terms.[49] The psychological abilities realized by the mirror system, in turn, appear to be central to the intensely social character of human existence: sensory and affective mimicry enable a rapid, almost seamless, grasp of the basic affective states of the individuals and groups with whom we interact, while motor mimicry enhances not only our ability to recognize with ease and facility the intentions of others (as these are embodied in basic actions), but also our ability to pick up new motor skills (such as those at stake in sporting activity or musical performance, as well as in more utilitarian tasks). In this context, as Margrethe Bruun Vaage has put it, *seeing is feeling*: the mirror system allows us to simulate the sensations, emotions, movements, and actions of those we observe.[50]

Mirror neurons are not unique to humans—indeed, as we saw in Chapter 2, they were first discovered in macaque monkeys, and research on mirror neurons in humans is still at an early (and in many ways controversial) stage. The passage of discovery, however—from macaques to humans—nevertheless underlines, and indeed encapsulates metaphorically, the continuity of species. No matter how massively humans may have evolved—biologically and culturally—in a distinctive direction, we share many ancient physiological, psychological, and behavioural traits with other animal species, particularly primates (as Darwin stressed in *The Expression of the Emotions in Man and Animals*, to which I return in Chapter 5).[51] We have an important instance here of the fruitfulness of one of Cronin's ethological 'explanatory principles', that is, the strategy of setting human behaviour in the context of other animal behaviour: were neuroscientists not prepared to propose and test hypotheses about humans based on non-human characteristics or behaviour, no one would even be exploring the existence and nature of the human mirror system.[52] In the present context, however, the key point about mirror neurons, and the sensory, motor, and affective mimicry that they implement and enable, is not so much that they tie us with our evolutionary ancestors and cousins, but that they *'wire' us into each other*. In the words of Gallese, Christian Keysers, and Giacomo Rizzolatti, mirror neurons enable a 'direct experiential' form of understanding the actions and emotions of our conspecifics.[53] Or in the words of Iacoboni: '[w]e empathize effortlessly and automatically with each other because evolution has selected neural systems that blend self and other's actions, intentions, and emotions... Our neurobiology... puts us "within each other"'.[54] And, as with the startle response, filmmakers have not been slow to exploit this capacity.

127 Hours (Danny Boyle, 2011) provides a recent and vivid example of the way that filmmakers may draw upon our ability to mirror the experiences of others. The film relates the true story of Aron Ralston (played by James Franco), a mountain climber who goes on a solo biking and climbing trip in the Utah desert. While climbing in a narrow canyon, a rock fall results in one of Ralston's arms becoming trapped beneath a boulder. From the outset, the film is intent on giving expression to Ralston's sensory experiences—the intense pace of his life, the rush of pleasure he takes in climbing and biking, the dry heat of the south-western desert landscape.

The credit sequence of *127 Hours* is a montage of large-scale collective events, including sporting events such as a marathon, the Pamplona bull run, and a swimming gala; significantly, for our purposes, during these scenes of sporting spectacle almost as much emphasis is laid upon spectatorship of the events as on direct participation in them. The bold gestures and often extreme states engendered by sporting activity provide fertile ground for filmmakers and make our mirroring responses highly salient. The various forms of empathy—sensory, motor, and affective—are not, of course, prompted uniquely by witnessing sporting endeavours; any form of physical action, expression, or sensory experience can act as a prompt to empathic mirroring. But it is no accident that many films generate drama around and through sporting encounters—like the tennis match in Hitchcock's *Strangers on a Train* (1951) (analysed in Chapter 7) or the boxing bouts in *Raging Bull* (Martin Scorsese, 1980) and countless other fight movies. Along with the action film, the sports film is one of the major sites for the generation of what we might call 'mirror thrills'—intense, bodily sensations triggered by and tracking those of the characters on screen.

Cues for such mirror thrills are present in concentrated form during the climax of *127 Hours*. By this point in the plot, Ralston has been trapped in the canyon for approaching five days. His water supply has run out, delirium from exhaustion has set in, and there is no realistic prospect that he will be discovered by other hikers or climbers, such is the remote and obscure nature of his location. Ralston faces a stark choice: die a lonely death from heat exhaustion and dehydration in the canyon, or find a way to release himself from the imprisoning boulder. Ralston chooses survival—by amputating his trapped arm using a blunt penknife. The film goes to great lengths to get us to feel the excruciating quality of his situation—that is, both the literal pain of the trapped arm, and the larger anxiety arising from his isolated entrapment and impending death in the canyon. In the climactic scene of the amputation, all three types of mirroring come into play, because Ralston is both an agent and an object in this scene. That is, the film invites us to mirror the *sensations* of his trapped and dying arm (the constant weight of the boulder, the cutting and ripping of skin, the breaking of bone); the strenuous efforts—*motor actions*—of Ralston as he contorts his body to break his arm and cut himself free; and his *facial* and *vocal expressions* of pain (Figures 3.3a–3.3d).

What might Tallis make of my emphasis on the role of mirror neurons in explaining our experience of *127 Hours*? Tallis's writings are curious because—as we might expect given his medical background—many of them are larded with discussions of human physiology, including neurophysiology, which run alongside his emphasis on the distance between humans and the rest of the animal kingdom. As a consequence of his emphasis on the most sophisticated aspects of human cognition, however, Tallis is in danger of caricaturing human psychology and the place of human existence in the natural world. (We will see the same problem of overstatement at work in relation to culturalist treatments of language, cognition, and emotion, in Part II in general and in Chapters 6 and 8 in particular.) Attention to the subpersonal roles of the various neural systems discussed here—those underpinning the startle response and empathic mirroring—acts as a corrective to such a caricature. As we have seen, humans are 'wired into the world' in the sense that a great many human reactions are spontaneous and unreflective; non-conscious, autonomic responses and literal reflexes represent an extreme on the spectrum of types of human response, but they can hardly be ignored. And more specifically, humans—like the members of many other species—are 'wired into' the minds of their fellows by virtue of somatosensory, motor, and affective mimicry, psychological capacities realized by mirror neurons. These capacities allow us to track, virtually effortlessly, the basic emotional states of those around us, and assist us in imitating and in learning new motor skills. Of course such capacities do not describe the human mind exhaustively; neither can they be regarded as exemplars for all forms of human mental activity. But they cannot be written off as trivial or unreal facets of the human behaviourial repertoire.

So What?

Let me conclude this chapter by offering some thoughts in response to an inevitable, and good, question: what exactly is it that the neuroscientific elements of the analyses I've offered can be said to add to our understanding? What can we learn about the startle response and empathic mirroring that we didn't, or couldn't, know from the existing sources of knowledge at our disposal (including reflection on our experience,

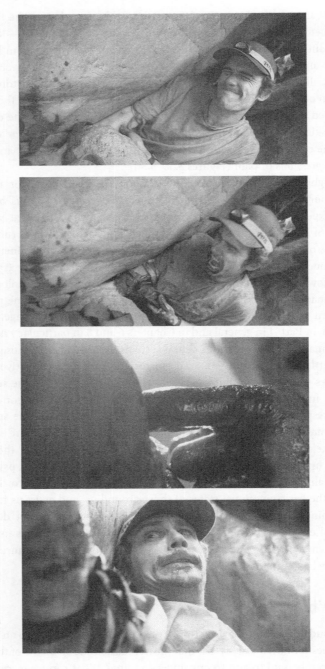

Figures 3.3a–3.3d Eliciting embodied horror in *127 Hours* (Danny Boyle, 2011).

exploration of the practices and discussions of filmmakers, and psychological theories of these phenomena)?

First and most basically, to reiterate a claim from Chapter 2, we gain knowledge about the very existence of the phenomena. Empathy has been disputed for as long as it has been an object of speculation; evidence of a mirror system provides a new form of evidence in favour of its existence. In this respect, the discovery of mirror neurons bears comparison with the emerging evidence of the existence of the Higgs boson particle; in each case, experimental evidence has provided empirical support for theoretical postulates. The startle response might seem less fragile as a postulate, so robust is the evidence from ordinary experience. But what is not obvious from such experience, or from the reflections of practitioners, of critics, or of viewers, is the *precise* nature of the startle with which we all have casual familiarity. How is the startle response realized physiologically and neurally? To what degree, and in what ways, is it affected by learning and by cultural context? How do these factors bear upon the role of the startle response in our experience of films? Experience and reflection are vital, but systematic observation and controlled experimentation add a further, fine-grained level of detail to our understanding of the world.

This fact points to the second way in which neuroscience adds something new to the sum of knowledge we possess about psychological phenomena like the startle response and empathic mirroring. Neural evidence sheds light on the functional nuances of the phenomena that elude ordinary experience and reflection. In this respect, neuroscience is like any type of scientific observation that transcends the limits of ordinary human perception; the brain scanner joins the telescope, the microscope, stop motion and x–ray photography, radar and sonar, and so on—all technologies which allow us to see (or otherwise detect) new aspects of our world, or to see familiar aspects of it in greater detail.

In these ways neuroscience contributes to the process of theory construction explored in Chapter 1, furnishing important evidence of the *existence* of a psychological process, as well as a nuanced picture of the *character* of that process. Together these contributions afford an answer to the worry, articulated by Davies and others, that neural evidence might amount to nothing more than an 'implementation story'—the view, that is, that all we will learn from neural evidence is that certain types of cognition depend on this or that part of the brain, without learning anything about the character of those types of cognition, or the value that we attach to them in our theories of art and the aesthetic. The blunt answer to this worry is that *cognitive architecture is shaped by neural architecture*; or to put it more circumspectly, it is methodologically unwise to rule out the possibility that cognitive architecture is importantly shaped by our brain anatomy and chemistry. The way we think is shaped by the kinds of brain we have; the kinds of mind that we possess arise from our evolved physiology.[55]

Take vision as an exemplary case. We see the world the way we do as a result of the physiology of our visual systems: animals with an array of eyes and cones different from ours will apprehend a different field of vision and discriminate different colours in the environment. The mantis shrimp has three eyes, for example, each possessing sixteen colour receptive cones (compared with the three cones in human eyes), providing the shrimp with extraordinary visual acuity within its ecological niche. Or consider memory. Neuroscientific research into memory has confirmed the hypothesis that memory is not a single, homogeneous capacity, but a composite of different information-retaining skills supported by different neural subsystems; such research also shows how intimately related are the apparently very distinct processes of memory and imagination. Neuroscience has similarly moved beyond the traditional picture of the five senses, breaking several of these sense mechanisms down into distinct senses, as well as bringing to light the high degree of cross-modal interaction among the senses.[56] In sum, then, the cash value of neuroscience lies not merely in assigning mental functions to neural locations, but rather in discovering and refining facts about mental functions themselves. Andy Clark defends a related idea by floating a notion of 'microfunctionalism', in which neuroscience plays a critical role in specifying mental functions at a very fine-grained level of description.[57]

How do the startle and mirror responses appear in the light of these considerations concerning the relationship between cognitive and neural architecture? In the case of the startle response, we have seen how the 'vigour' of this reflex varies with the mood of the subject, is subject to a modest degree of influence from learning, and some-times acts as the kernel of elaborate cultural syndromes. In the case of mirror responses, brain research is gradually giving us a picture of how the targets of empathic response (sensations, emotions, actions) may vary across primate species, and, among humans, may vary according to background and experience. None of these insights is transparent from experience or even from systematic reflection upon our experience, our ordinary habits, or our artistic practices. In all these cases, neuroscientific evidence may feed back upon and change our conceptual assump-tions, rather than leaving them untouched. On this account, we do not possess a conceptual 'grammar' that is simply given and timeless in all respects, a grid that empirical research can do no more than fill in with implementation stories. Instead, neuroscientific research—empirical research in general—may call us to revise and even abandon the conceptual map and assumptions that provided our starting point. Once more, such research exemplifies the method of theory construction expounded in Chapter 1.

With this in mind, it is worth revisiting the 'wiring' metaphor one more time. I've noted that, from a physicalist perspective, any and all mental functioning is dependent on 'wiring' of some sort or another; minds must be realized at the material level, whether biochemically in the form of brains, or perhaps via silicon or some other material—the jury is still out on the extent to which mentality and intelligent behaviour can be realized artificially. What we learn from the domains of computer science, artificial intelligence, and robotics, is that all tasks and functions, from the simplest to the most elaborate, must be underpinned by wiring in this sense. The light switch on the wall depends on a simple mechanism; the computer on which I write a more complex one; both instantiate not only literal wiring, but 'wiring' in the general sense of 'material realization and implementation' at stake here. In his *Start the Week* dialogue with Tallis, Dennett turned the 'wiring' metaphor—introduced by Tallis, as we have seen above—back on Tallis in just this way: 'We all know what "sweet" is for, we all know what "sexy" is for—what's "funny" for? That is, why should we [our brains] be wired up ... why should our endocrine and paracrine systems be all tuned up for us to get pleasure out of humour?' Short of the intervention of spirits, souls, or ectoplasm, there is no getting around this. We live in the material world, and we are part of it. Even in our most sophisticated guises, we are realized through the material form of our physiologies, which shape the capacities that they enable. The complex social worlds and mental properties that humanists concern themselves with emerge on the basis of this material substrate. We are not only wired into the world; we are constituted by wiring.

We need to acknowledge a third and final way in which neuroscience may contribute to what we know. Even where neural evidence adds little detail to our picture of a phenomenon and only seems to confirm what we already knew, in reality it does or can do much more than that. It is important not to confuse here the *dramatic novelty* of some body of scientific knowledge with its strictly *epistemological value*. Scientific findings arising from controlled experiments that broadly confirm hypotheses derived from everyday experience and folk theory may not be very sexy, because they leave the landscape of ordinary belief and practice unchanged. Commenting on his quantitative analysis of shot-length dynamics, Yuri Tsivian asks:

What do we learn about films from calculating their average shot lengths? I once applied this method to compare the average shot length of Kuleshov's films against the films made by his teacher Yevgenii Bauer, and when I put my data side by side with world-wide data collected by others, I felt my heart beat faster, for it turned out that between 1917 and 1918 the cutting tempo of Russian films had jumped from the slowest to the fastest in the world. Not that the difference could not be detected without all the timing and counting, but I felt proud and excited that now we could not only intuit but also demonstrate this.[58]

From an epistemological point of view, then, such findings are significant, adding the kind of systematic and quantitative evidence provided by scientific methods to the looser, anecdotal, and experiential evidence already in our possession. The point here is not to denigrate these latter forms of evidence, but just to point up the limited sense in which we can be said to 'already know' something based only upon them. Knowledge arises not only from the dazzling and unexpected finding, but also from the gradual accumulation and correction of detail, as well as the convergence among the different sources of knowledge upon which we draw.

4

Papaya, Pomegranates, and Green Tea

...there is some deceiver both very powerful and very cunning, who constantly uses all his wiles to deceive me. There is therefore no doubt that I exist, if he deceives me; and let him deceive me as much as he likes, he can never cause me to be nothing, so long as I think I am something...this knowledge...I maintain to be more certain and evident than all I have had hitherto.

René Descartes

Consciousness, then, does not appear to itself chopped up in bits. Such words as 'chain' and 'train' do not describe it fitly as it presents itself in the first instance. It is nothing jointed; it flows. A 'river' or a 'stream' are the metaphors by which it is most naturally described. In talking of it hereafter, let us call it the stream of thought, of consciousness, or of subjective life.

William James

Notwithstanding Descartes's confidence in his own consciousness, and James's influential characterization of conscious experience as a flowing 'stream', for much of the twentieth century, consciousness was put on the back burner of philosophical and scientific debate (though debate was hardly extinguished—consider the import-ant works by C. D. Broad and Gilbert Ryle, as well as Edmund Husserl and the tradition of phenomenology).[1] Numerous forces conspired to put it there, but three factors might be singled out as particularly important. First, Freud: notions of an 'unconscious' dimension to the mind and behaviour certainly existed before psycho-analysis, but there is little doubt that Freud and his followers put the notion at centre stage, making it the fulcrum of the psychoanalytic theory of mind. Within the tradition of psychological behaviourism, consciousness perhaps fared even worse. While psychoanalytic theorists may routinely doubt the reliability of conscious avowals and states of minds, behaviourism denies, or at least remains agnostic about, their very existence, restricting itself to observable behaviour, the billiard balls of stimulus and response. Even the advent of cognitive psychology—the paradigm-shifting force which overturned behaviourism and in certain ways began to rehabilitate the study of consciousness—continued (and continues) in its own way to keep consciousness at arm's length. As we saw in Chapters 2 and 3, the historically dominant framework within cognitive psychology conceives of mental activity as *computation*, and the mind as an *information processor*; and to the extent that our chief model of an information-processing device—the computer—lacks consciousness, so the analogy does not make *conscious* computation very salient. A great deal of cognitive theory has concerned itself with information processing which is always or normally non-conscious—like the brain computations allowing you to see this page and to make sense of the words you are reading. Of these traditions, the first and the third—psychoanalysis and cognitivism—have exerted considerable influence on the study of film and the arts. Perhaps it is not surprising, then, that the relationship between consciousness and film art remains largely uncharted territory. The goal of this chapter is to provide a preliminary map of the terrain, with some suggestions concerning lines of future enquiry.

Despite the situation I have described, the study of consciousness has been all the rage for a decade or more, to the extent that 'consciousness studies' has now established itself, with all the paraphernalia of an academic discipline—journals, symposia, conferences, dedicated departmental centres and graduate-level courses, a steady flow of book publications, along with internal debates and controversies, which sometimes spill into the public domain.[2] What explains this resurgence? The emergence of cognitive theory made reference to internal states—thoughts, intentions, beliefs, feelings—respectable once more, while also engendering a new confidence that the nature of mind, so conceived, could become the subject of scientific investigation. In the words of Steven Pinker: 'When we talk about how computers work, you can't get around imputing internal states to them. Computers have memories, they have goal states, they execute plans. If you can do that about a hunk of metal, and you're not being unscientific, why should it be unscientific to say those things about a human being?'[3] The initial emphasis on non-conscious states—or computations for which consciousness did not appear to be an important feature—eventually led to consciousness, in the form of the question: if our minds can crunch so much information non-consciously, why would we have evolved consciousness at all? In short, what are the functions of consciousness? As Jaegwon Kim notes, functionalizing conscious states of mind lies at the heart of the project of naturalizing the mind. If we can demonstrate the functions performed by the qualitative dimensions of mental states, we have taken a big step (indeed the critical step, according to Kim) towards locating the mind in the physical world and the natural order.[4]

One way of approaching this question is to consider the types of cognition that involve consciousness.[5] Our thinking becomes highly conscious when we face challenging or novel tasks. Learning to type, or drive a car, initially requires great conscious deliberation over the sequence of movements and steps involved. Mastery of such tasks is characterized in part by greater speed and fluidity in their execution, which goes hand in hand with an attenuation of conscious attention. As I type this sentence, I don't consciously think about the location of individual letter keys—that aspect of the task has become automatic for me, freeing up processing capacity for the more demanding job of coming up with an overview of consciousness and its relationship with film. And once a skill like typing or driving has been mastered, finding ourselves becoming conscious of it usually impedes performance. But some tasks always seem to require conscious attention, as V. S. Ramachandran notes:

> Imagine you are driving your car and having an animated conversation with your friend sitting next to you. Your attention is entirely on the conversation, it's what you're conscious of. But in parallel you are negotiating traffic, avoiding the pavement, avoiding pedestrians, obeying red lights and performing all these very complex elaborate computations without being really conscious of any of it unless something strange happens, such as a leopard crossing the road...Intriguingly, it is impossible to imagine the converse scenario: paying conscious attention to driving and negotiating traffic while unconsciously having a creative conversation with your friend.[6]

Ramachandran characterizes the conversation that requires conscious attention as 'creative' in character, but any use of language—beyond the smallest of small talk and the most vacant of affirmatives—would seem to depend upon such attentiveness. Very little language use falls into the category of Brian O'Shaughnessy's 'subintentional' behaviour (discussed in Chapter 1).

Consciousness also serves a vital function in affording detailed and vivid apprehensions of the world, adjusting the salience of particular elements in a situation and the urgency of particular tasks. Greg Currie and Ian Ravenscroft consider

> an orthopaedic surgeon with a broken toe and no pain sensations. He might have as good a knowledge as anyone of the nature of the damage, the likely effect of certain movements, the best way to move. Compared with the pain, that knowledge is a poor guide to action; unless he stays immobile, he is likely to make the damage worse, despite his expert knowledge.[7]

The pain provides the surgeon with information about the location and nature of his injury—information that he can use, along with the clinical data about the injury and his general knowledge of anatomy. Such phenomenally rendered information—or 'phenomenal information properties', to use an expression Daniel Dennett credits to Peter Bieri[8]—about the state of the body is not, of course, infallible; neural maps of the body can misfire and mislead, leading to phenomena like referred pain, phantom and alien limbs, and the strange extensions and displacements of the self explored in Chapter 2. But these are, precisely, exceptions to the rule, malfunctions of a nervous system that has evolved in part as an organ of *proprioception*, that is, an organ whose function it is to provide information about the state of the body's position in space. Pain is an extreme instance, forcing the damaged state of a body part into the spotlight of conscious attention, and thereby giving it high priority. In this respect, physical pain functions much as fully fledged emotions do, providing detailed phenomenal knowledge of the world in relation to the goals and desires of the experiencing agent, enabling them to plan and to act in the light of this

① conflating conscious & attentive?

knowledge. Indeed, perception itself provides this kind of information. Currie and Ravenscroft continue: 'Think how it is when the lights suddenly go out; you know quite well where you are in the room and what things lie in your path to the door. Still, progress is painfully slow without the rich and vivid awareness of the room's layout given in perception.'[9] As we will see in Part II, Currie and Ravenscroft (along with a number of other theorists) liken emotional experience to perception, in part on the grounds of these functional and phenomenological similarities. Perception, pain, and emotion all inform us about the world and our situation within it, and they do so by furnishing qualitative experience. Things look and feel a certain way; there is 'something that it is like' to sense particular things or to be in the grip of particular emotional states.

The more conscious a perception is, the more fine-grained it tends to be. Thus parts of the visual field that we fixate foveally, in the course of consciously exploring it, will either be immediately available in consciousness, or poised for access in working memory, while those parts of the field which hover unscanned in peripheral vision are registered much more roughly. So it is that we can be blind to very significant elements in a visual array before us if we have devoted little or no conscious attention to them, as we have seen in earlier chapters in relation to the phenomenon of 'change blindness'. In fact there are two related but distinct phenomena relevant here: change blindness and 'inattentional blindness', referring to the failure to perceive, respectively, stable features of a visual array, and apparently striking changes to a visual array.[10] These forms of 'blindness' may be driven either endogenously, that is, by the nature of the visual goal or task set for the viewer, or exogenously, that is, by the cues in the viewer's visual field. Thus, we may fail to see certain features in the visual field because we are actively looking for other features (as in the invisible gorilla experiment, where subjects are instructed to follow the basketball), or because the power of particular visual details overrides our attention to other details (as in a match-on-action edit, where the salience of a moving object captures our attention and obscures the presence of the cut which occurs in the course of the object's motion).[11]

These forms of perceptual 'blindness' play an important role in relation to principles of image composition in film, as well as principles of continuity editing. The conventions of continuity editing keep our attention fixed on elements carefully controlled for continuity; other details across a sequence may be less consistent, but perceptual blindness makes it unlikely that we will pick them up.[12] (The phenomenon of 'blindsight'—registration of information by the visual system with absolutely no conscious awareness of vision—might appear to undermine this relationship between consciousness and perceptual detail, but in fact it supports it. Blindsight demonstrates that perception can occur without consciousness, but the 'resolution' of such unconscious perception is coarse, compared with that delivered by conscious perception.) Broadly, then, it seems that consciousness attends certain types of cognition in novel situations, where detail and vividness of perception and flexibility of mind and action are at stake, providing an adaptive advantage over creatures lacking such attributes. Given the centrality of novelty and vividness to artistic practice and experience, we should not be surprised to find consciousness playing a crucial role in relation to art and its appreciation—a point I return to in the final section of this chapter.

The question of the function(s) of the conscious mind has come to be known as one of the 'easy problems' in debates around consciousness. The hard problem arises from the very fact that consciousness exists; 'why is all this processing accompanied by an experienced inner life?'[13] A brain is a complicated thing, but it is made of nothing more than flesh and blood. How does it give rise to a conscious mind? How can meaning emerge from meat, subjectivity from synaptic firing? There are a variety of responses to the hard problem, each generating new problems. Substance dualism, which owes its modern philosophical origin to Descartes, holds that consciousness doesn't arise from physical matter; it somehow coincides with it in human beings, residing as the 'Ghost in the Machine'.[14] Physicalists generally hold that consciousness supervenes on material brain states, prompting the search for the 'neural correlates of consciousness', that is, the specific brain states which correlate with— and thus are plausible candidates for the causation of—conscious states of mind. But as many sceptics would maintain—physicalists among them—we still don't have a clue as to *how* it could be that a physical event, no matter how complex, could give rise to glimmers of consciousness. 'How could a physical system such as a brain also be an *experiencer*?' asks David Chalmers. 'We do not just lack a detailed theory; we are entirely in the dark about how consciousness fits into the natural order.'[15] Chalmers himself adopts property dualism: there may be no separate nonmaterial substance constituting consciousness, but the properties of conscious states are irreducible to any currently conceivable physical description.

A more extreme scepticism—the 'new mysterian'—holds that an understanding of the relationship between matter and mind is permanently out of our reach, in the same way that calculus is beyond the ken of guinea pigs. Smart as we are relative to other species, there are going to be some problems that are beyond our comprehension, just because we don't have the right kind of or sufficiently powerful minds.[16] Still another response to the hard problem goes by the name of 'panpsychism', whose advocates argue that the solution to the hard problem lies in not restricting consciousness to ourselves, or even to animal life in general; if we meat machines possess consciousness, perhaps consciousness is much more widely distributed in the physical universe than your average physicalist is wont to admit.[17] One other colourful member of the troupe warrants mention here: the eliminativist thesis that consciousness—at least as traditionally understood, as intrinsically private and ineffable subjective experience, the unique 'what it is like' to be a certain individual in a state and situation—does not exist.[18] None of these arguments is easy to swallow: the interest in the hard problem of consciousness seems inversely proportional to the plausibility of available solutions to it.

Consciousness Analysed

Although reference to 'consciousness' in general is standard in the contemporary debate on consciousness, implicit in that designation are numerous types and levels of conscious experience. Breaking the overarching concept of consciousness down into various subtypes marks an important step towards its understanding. The first distinction we might draw lies between perceptual or 'primary' consciousness,[19] on the one hand, and self-consciousness, on the other. For an entity to have perceptual consciousness, it must have conscious awareness of some object or phenomenon— the increasing intensity of light, let us say, as the sun rises. Such consciousness might be momentary and episodic, or more continuous. One step on from this, an entity that possesses a conscious perceptual sensitivity to the state of its body we might say possesses 'sentience'. Another elaboration involves the integration of perception with memory, setting the stage for personal identity, conceived in the Lockean tradition as an at least partly continuous, temporally extended conscious experience. In the context of medicine, the Glasgow coma scale provides a measure of these aspects of consciousness in brain-injured patients, based on a combination of eye, verbal, and motor responses, ranging from deep unconsciousness to normal (self-)awareness.

Fully fledged self-consciousness involves a level of awareness well beyond, even if continuous with, these basic levels of consciousness. To have self-consciousness is to have knowledge of, and to attend to, the nature of one's being in the world. Classically, the emphasis in debate on self-consciousness has lain on our awareness of ourselves as thinking, free-willing agents, transcending our status as physical, animal beings. We see this in Descartes's arguments for dualism in the *Meditations*, as well as in Kant's account of the antimony between the self as part of the fabric of causality, and as an autonomous agent, in *The Critique of Pure Reason*.[20] A more contemporary picture would lay emphasis on the embodied nature of human existence, acknowledging our place in the physical and biological realms, while emphasizing the character and limitations of such embodiment. Such self-consciousness does not eradicate or transcend more basic forms of consciousness in human experience, however. Much of the time we consciously attend to the task at hand, whether that be a relatively humdrum exercise (fixing a nail to a wall), or a more demanding and notionally 'exalted' activity, such as focusing intently on an aesthetic object (a film or a piece of music, say).[21] At the very least, for much of the time *self*-consciousness drops into the background as we engage with the world; as Eric Schwitzgebel has memorably captured the point, we are not aware of the sensation of pressure on our feet unless we actively turn our attention to monitoring that part of our body.[22] Constantly sustained and intense self-consciousness is probably pathological and maladaptive.

Consciousness varies around other axes too. Consciousness comes in different grades; we can be conscious of things to different degrees. Watching a film, I am most conscious of those elements that grab my attention from moment to moment, like the flow of conversation and play of facial expressions between two characters. But at the same time I have some awareness of a large array of secondary and peripheral factors, such as the score and sound design of the film, the quality of the light in the depicted space, and objects in the space behind the characters. Theorists of film music often mark just this distinction in contrasting 'hearing' with 'listening', where the latter describes focused attention on the soundtrack, the former a still conscious but more peripheral, and 'lower grade', form of attention.[23] The dynamic and flexible nature of the stream of perceptual consciousness ensures that at any given moment, however, the items occupying the spotlight of conscious attention may change—a change in ambient sound breaks through into conscious awareness, and I ask myself, why do things sound different? Has a door been opened offscreen? What else might explain the shift in ambience? The technique of the *sound bridge*, where the sound of a scene drops out and is replaced by the sound of the succeeding scene a few seconds before the visual cut, is one example of standard practice which exploits the mobility of conscious attention. And here we have another example of the way that patterns of attention can be driven exogenously, that is, by external cues. In Miguel Gomes's *Tabu* (2012), to take one striking example, the shift from standard to 'silent' film sound conventions mid-way through the film leads us to focus consciously on the sound and keenly anticipate the transition to a new space of action.

Psychologists have also marked a distinction between 'declarative' and 'representational' memory that hinges on the degree to which the memory can be brought to consciousness. A declarative memory is one that we can describe and discuss in language, a memory of which—whatever its veracity—we feel we have a more or less complete understanding. I can recall vividly the occasion of my learning about the sudden and untimely death of a colleague. I know how it made me feel and I know why, and I can describe both the qualia of the state and its causes. Representational memories, by comparison, are elusive but potent states. Visiting a house I was familiar with in an earlier phase of life, I experience a definite unease, but I can neither recall nor articulate the cause of the unease. The sights and sounds of the house trigger certain memory associations; I consciously experience a certain kind of emotion, but cannot bring to consciousness the earlier experiences causing the emotion. Greg Smith has argued that films may exploit this form of memory through 'emotional markers'—filmic motifs, like musical cues or lighting schemes, which redundantly mark a character or an action with a particular emotional tone without drawing great attention to themselves.[24] Drawing on Smith and taking Christopher Nolan's *Memento* (2000) as a case study, Karen Renner discusses in detail the facial expressions of Leonard (Guy Pearce), the evocative descriptions of his experience in voice-over and dialogue, and the main theme from David Julyan's score as instances of such emotional markers.[25] The upshot of this strategy is that spectators have an intense experience of the emotion in question, with a very incomplete conscious knowledge of the devices in the film that have given rise to this experience.

Although the model of mind here is not psychoanalytic, and in particular does not posit a mechanism of repression whereby certain experiences are actively 'buried' beneath conscious attention, the concept of representational memory does acknowledge the existence of *unconscious sources* of conscious states of mind—mental states which are not merely currently non-conscious or only peripherally conscious, like the objects of secondary awareness as I watch a scene in a film, but wholly unavailable to consciousness.

To complete our sketch of the varieties of conscious experience, we need to acknowledge the place of dreaming as a form of consciousness. Dreaming as a form of consciousness? Well, yes—insofar as we experience things in dreaming, it is a form of consciousness. The claim will only seem odd because of the legacy of psychoanalysis, which explains the functions of dreaming by recourse to its particular conception of the unconscious. Contemporary psychological research into dreaming, however, paints a very different picture, identifying the functions of dreaming in terms of memory and learning—dimensions of mind which we associate primarily with fully conscious, waking experience.[26] There are *two* conceptual revisions at stake here: first, simply appreciating that while there is obviously an important difference between dreaming and being awake, when we dream we do not lack consciousness— as we do during other phases of sleep. And second, emerging evidence suggests that dreaming has evolved to enhance aspects of the conscious mind, not to provide a playground for experiences repressed by the conscious mind. The idea that film viewing is akin to dreaming goes back pretty well to the origin of cinema, and psychoanalytic film theory has erected elaborate theories on the basis of what was originally an evocative metaphor. This revised 'cognitive' conception of the dreaming mind, brought within the orbit of conscious cognition, raises an intriguing question. We certainly don't literally fall into a dream state when we watch films; but is it possible that we do enter a neural-cum-mental state distinct in certain ways from the mental state we possess when we engage with the world? A state so systematically in contrast with our waking navigation of the world that it warrants identification in the way that we identify dreaming as a distinct type of mental experience? Or to recall a parallel question addressed in Chapter 1, is there a distinctive mental state which constitutes 'aesthetic attention' or the 'aesthetic attitude'[27]—a form of consciousness systematically distinct from ordinary, 'interested' consciousness, characteristically prompted by artworks and other natural or artefactual aesthetic prompts?

Consciousness in the History of Film

A phenomenon as central to human existence and identity as consciousness is bound to be manifest in the history of an art form in innumerable ways. We can, nevertheless, pick out a number of ways in which the idea or the fact of consciousness has not merely been present in film but an explicit object of fascination or enquiry. The conscious mind—or at least the particular types of conscious state that comprise it—is integral to the earliest extended work of film theory in English, Hugo Münsterberg's *The Photoplay*.[28] Münsterberg focused on the way in which the development of technique and form over the first two decades of cinema sought (on his view) to mimic the mental mechanisms of attention, memory, and emotion. Few subsequent theorists put such an emphasis on the role of these basic conscious mental processes in shaping cinematic form; and, as we have seen, psychoanalytic theory played down their relevance, stressing instead the idea that a film, like a human subject understood in psychoanalytic terms, should be understood in terms of the dynamics of the unconscious. Some recent theory has shown a renewed appetite for conscious mental processes, in terms of their significance for both the design of films and the experience of film viewing, but little work shows much interest in the fact that these mental processes *are* conscious. Such research has focused on the functional roles of various types of perception, memory, and emotion, rather than their qualitative character *as* conscious experiences. The real successors to Münsterberg's early ruminations are not to be found in any body of film theory, but in particular traditions of filmmaking, at least with regard to the evocative representation of consciousness. Perhaps this should not surprise us: if our goal is to generate fine-grained representations of perceptual, emotional, and cognitive experience, art is the natural arena in which to realize this goal. As Frank Cioffi might have insisted, sometimes what we want is a vivid representation or expression of some phenomenon, rather than an explanation of it.[29]

The most obvious stamping ground for the representation and exploration of the conscious mind has been the tradition of art cinema.[30] One of the defining features of such cinema, and one that can be traced back to its roots in the 1920s movements of German Expressionism and French Impressionism, is an emphasis on the rendering of subjective experience.[31] Filmmaking in this mode confirmed the thrust of Münsterberg's thesis, exploring the representation of visual experience, but also expanding the range of mental states given expression to include fantasy, dream (which, to reiterate a point above, we may regard as an important form of conscious experience), drug-induced and sundry other 'altered' states, often with a focus on extreme, deranged, or otherwise abnormal conditions. Art cinema also expands the techniques through which subjectivity can be rendered, and often foregrounds them, sometimes by making the boundary between subjective and objective action indeterminate. From Federico Fellini's *8½* (1963) and Luis Buñuel's *Belle de Jour* (1967), through the work of David Cronenberg, Claire Denis, and Lars von Trier, to contemporary examples like Gomes's *Tabu* and Peter Strickland's *Berberian Sound Studio* (2012), filmmakers have depicted the interpenetration of reality and fantasy; in Chapter 7, I analyse a typically intricate example from Julio Médem's *Los amantes del círculo polar/Lovers of the Arctic Circle* (1998). Not that such techniques are wholly absent from more mainstream traditions of filmmaking. Indeed, in certain periods and genres, they have been highly visible; dream and fantasy sequences were fairly common in *films noir* and female gothic pictures of 1940s Hollywood, and have become a staple of contemporary American serial television dramas, in such

(1) *fine-grained representation of experience*

shows as *The Sopranos* (David Chase, 1999–2007), *Lost* (Jeffrey Lieber, J. J. Abrams, and Damon Lindelof, 2004–10), *Mad Men* (Matthew Weiner, 2007–15), *Damages* (Daniel Zelman, Glenn Kessler, and Todd A. Kessler, 2010–12), *The Walking Dead* (Frank Darabont, 2010–), and *Ray Donovan* (Ann Biderman, 2013–). But, by and large, it is within art cinema that the dramatic representation of consciousness has been explored most tenaciously.

One director who confronted a particular conception of human consciousness in the classic, postwar era of European art cinema was Michelangelo Antonioni. Antonioni's *L'Eclisse/The Eclipse* (1962), the third of his famous trilogy, bears the marks of the widespread influence of Sartrean existentialism during this period. The film is restrained in its overt rendering of the subjectivities of its central characters—especially when compared with the examples given above—instead directing our attention to their outward behaviour and the surface of the physical world. But the diffuse discontent and unfocused anxiety of the characters makes itself felt, hanging like a cloud over the entire film. András Kovács has argued that the characters suffer from the angst characteristic of those living in the disenchanted state described by Sartre: the absence of any traditional metaphysical guarantee leaves them facing 'Nothingness', all too conscious of the contingency of the world, their fragile and insignificant place within it, and the weight of their own decisions in shaping their destinies.[32]

Consciousness has also been explored in the still more rarefied atmosphere of avant-garde filmmaking. Structural films—essentially a manifestation of 1960s art world minimalism in the context of avant-garde film—were given an early and influential interpretation as 'metaphors for consciousness'. The stripped down form of a film like Michael Snow's *Wavelength* (1967) was held to represent, and invite the spectator to contemplate, nothing less than human 'apperception' (self-consciousness) itself. The gradual, 'stammering' zoom across the loft space that forms the backbone of *Wavelength* represents, on this argument, not merely certain objects and the occasional event but, at a deeper level, the conscious subjectivity itself which might apprehend particular objects and events. What role does minimalism play here? Only by drastically minimizing what we normally perceive and cognize *through* consciousness can consciousness itself become the focus of consciousness (precisely, self-consciousness), via the agency of the film-as-metaphor. Only by eliminating or attenuating the action available to be viewed through a window are we likely to attend to the window itself. In proposing this interpretation of Snow's work, Annette Michelson was in part inspired by the repeated use of cinema as an analogy for conscious experience in philosophical and psychological writings—an image found in the writings of William James, Henri Bergson, and Edmund Husserl, and still active in the work of Oliver Sacks.[33] Citing Gérard Granel, Michelson likens the method of philosophical phenomenology to 'an attempt to film, in slow motion, that which has been, owing to the manner in which it is seen in natural speed, not absolutely unseen, but missed, subject to oversight'. Michelson, also describes Münsterberg's *The Photoplay* as 'an early and remarkable attempt at a phenomenological analysis of the cinematic experience'.[34] Reciprocally, structural filmmaking offers back to philosophy this metaphor, now incarnate in film itself.[35]

Such filmic reflections on consciousness are not, however, the unique possession of such ostentatiously serious traditions of cinema as art and avant-garde cinema. Consciousness has been fertile material for Hollywood as well. Many contemporary science-fiction films thematize aspects of consciousness: *2001* (Stanley Kubrick, 1968) and *I, Robot* (Alex Proyas, 2004), for example, both dramatize the possibility that a computer might develop consciousness and assert independent agency on the basis of it. Ridley Scott's *Blade Runner* (1982), about the hunting down of a group of advanced, renegade androids, explores the impact of doubt about the reliability of memory, uncertainty as to the duration of a human life, and the ever-present threat of death (and the demise of consciousness).[36] We also find within contemporary Hollywood the 'comedy of consciousness', in films that exploit some of the absurdities implicit in our confused and often paradoxical assumptions about consciousness. Films like Carl Reiner's *The Man with Two Brains* (1983) and *All of Me* (1984), and Spike Jonze's *Being John Malkovich* (1999), create humour from the dualist idea that the conscious mind can be decoupled from its physical seat and relocated in other bodies, and even objects. In *Being John Malkovich*, Malkovich's personality makes its way through several individual bodies, finally arriving, in rather sinister fashion, in the body of a child; while in *All of Me*, the soul of the character played by Lili Tomlin cohabits with Steve Martin in 'his' body, before taking up residence in the body of Victoria Tennant (with a brief stay in a bucket along the way: a joke that resonates with the doctrine of panpsychism—the idea that consciousness, in different grades, is pervasive in the universe).[37] Humour arising from the perplexities and paradoxes of consciousness is hardly restricted to Hollywood, however: in Wong Kar-wai's *Chung Hing sam lam/ Chungking Express* (1994), the protagonist addresses a limp and dripping bar of soap in a bittersweet reflection on and projection of his own state of loneliness.

Inside the Stream of Consciousness

At the outset of this chapter I noted William James's influential treatment of consciousness as a continuous 'stream' of experience. James's focus on the phenomenological character of consciousness returns us squarely to the question of the relationship between the arts and the sciences, discussed in Chapter 1, and to the methodology of triangulation, developed in Chapter 2. While science generally excludes the first-person perspective, in an effort to discover the 'view from nowhere', such an exclusion is impossible to maintain in the science of mind; a strictly neurophysiological description of the physical processes underpinning consciousness would be unable to explain anything about our mental capacities or experiences. (And the same is true even if we think of cognition as embodied and extended: so long as the focus is narrowly restricted to the physical systems upon which the mind depends, our theory of mind will be hobbled.) The model of triangulation addresses this shortcoming by proposing that we attempt to cross-reference and bring into alignment evidence at the phenomenological, psychological, and neurophysiological levels. The door is thereby opened to admit, at least in a limited and principled fashion, the first-person perspective within a scientific approach to the mind.

This area of convergence between the goals of art and the science of the mind can be seen from both sides of the divide; and some theorists, notably Nelson Goodman and Catherine Elgin, make it the fulcrum of their approach to the arts.[38] On the one hand, it is clear that many artists seek to enhance our understanding of the world, and we regard many works of art as having 'cognitive' value—they contribute, that is to say, to our 'cognitive stock' and afford us knowledge of the way things are. In particular, illuminating the inner lives of characters has been a central ambition for a great many artists, ranging across period, style, and medium; it is one of the most ancient and central vocations of artistic representation. My brief sortie into the representation of consciousness in film only scratches the surface of this deep and enduring concern. On the other hand, there is a tradition of scientific research and writing on the mind that fully embraces the phenomenological dimension. Oliver Sacks may be the best-known contemporary exponent of this tradition in the English-speaking world, which extends back to the Soviet psychologist A. R. Luria. Other notable contemporary figures include neuropsychologists Paul Broks and Jonathan Cole.[39] Suzanne Corkin's *Permanent Present Tense* (2013, on patient H[enry] M[olaison]), and Jean-Dominique Bauby's *The Diving Bell and the Butterfly* (1997, as well as Julian Schnabel's adaptation of the memoir, 2007) are both kindred exercises in triangulating the neural and the phenomenological.

Two titles give us an indication of what is distinctive about this tradition of writing: Luria's *The Man with a Shattered World* and Sacks's *The Man Who Mistook his Wife for a Hat*, both of which evoke the distinctive kinds of experience associated with particular kinds of brain damage, disease, or developmental atypicality.[40] The convergence of this tradition of 'Romantic science' with artistic representations of the mind can be traced, in the context of film, in the range of film projects made about Temple Grandin, Professor of Animal Science at Colorado State University. Grandin is a subject of fascination as an autistic person whose condition appears to give her special insights into the perception of animals, on the basis of which she has introduced various innovations in animal welfare. In a clear echo of Sacks, a 2006 episode of the BBC Science show *Horizon* on Grandin was titled 'The Woman Who Thinks like a Cow'. As with Sacks's writing, the goal here is to combine a neurological understanding of autism with an exploration of the psychological and phenomenological facets of the condition, through sustained focus on an individual. The example is particularly rich because there are two layers to the phenomenological enquiry: an attempt to represent 'what it is like' to be Temple Grandin, and an attempt to represent her empathic insights into the experiences of cattle. Grandin has also been the subject of an episode of Errol Morris's *First Person* documentary series

('Stairway to Heaven', 2001) and of an HBO television feature, *Temple Grandin* (Mick Jackson, 2010). The title of Morris's series speaks directly to the issue at stake here. Across these films, the common interest of scientists and artists in the character of first-personal experience, especially in its atypical and exotic variants, is abundantly evident.

Qualia and (Film) Art

In 1982 Frank Jackson introduced the world to Mary the colour scientist.[41] Mary has been raised in an artificially contrived black-and-white world, but as an expert colour scientist she has nevertheless acquired a complete understanding of all there is to be known about the physics of colour. One day Mary is exposed to coloured objects: does she now learn anything new—that is, does she obtain new *knowledge*? Jackson (and many others) held that she does, and that no amount of propositional knowledge concerning the physical underpinning of colour experience will deliver knowledge of (for example) what it is like to see red, the distinctive subjective 'raw feels' that constitute conscious experience. The character of conscious experience as given by qualia is, as such, *sui generis*, and according to Jackson, exposes the falsity of physicalism as a metaphysical doctrine (the thesis that reality is constituted wholly by physical elements, their properties, and their relations).

How does Jackson's thought experiment and the 'knowledge argument' that it supports—that knowledge of the qualia that constitute conscious experience is a distinctive, irreducible form of knowledge—bear upon the making and appreciation of films? Like all art forms, film trades in the domain of phenomenal experience. The visual arts furnish us with novel visual experiences; the sonic arts provide us with new aural experiences; and the literary arts, while not directly rendering novel perceptual experiences, instead evoke phenomenal experiences through the imaginative positing of actual and fictional agents, spaces, and situations. Films characteristically work on all of these fronts. This emphasis on the conscious, qualitative character of our experience of art may strike many contemporary literary and art theorists as peculiar, or worse, naïve and even pernicious. But remove conscious qualia in the domain of art and you truly have, to adapt Kant's well-known phrase, a system without purpose. The knowledge argument matters for a theory of art because it impinges on what we understand art to provide us with, and how we value it. If art can provide us with knowledge, and if it is uniquely or especially well-placed to furnish us with particular kinds of knowledge, then phenomenal knowledge—knowing what it is like to perceive and experience from a particular point of view—must be a frontrunner. If the knowledge argument fails, then one of the grounds for attributing to art a special and unique epistemic role in human existence would appear to be under threat.

That apparent threat, however, can and indeed has been neutralized—not least by Jackson himself. In order to appreciate this, it is worth tracking the fortunes of the knowledge argument in Jackson's own later thinking. In *From Metaphysics to Ethics* (and other essays) Jackson commits himself to articulating a staunchly physicalist framework for the understanding of all phenomena, including the qualia of perceptual experience; one chapter of this work is given over to the case of colour perception.[42] And in an essay reflecting on the original thought experiment concerning Mary, Jackson argues that the uniquely 'quick and easy' character of sensory experience, relative to other forms of discovery which require a less immediate and more laborious collation of various types and sources of information, drives the misleading intuition that something more or other than the acquisition of knowledge about the physical world is at stake in our sensory grasp of it. As Jackson puts it, we are subject to a strong (but mistaken) intuition 'that Mary learns something about how things are that outruns what can be deduced from the physical account of how things are'.[43] Sensory experience simply *is* the central form in which humans and other animals gather knowledge about their environment; to restate a formula from Chapter 2, sensory experience is the interface between the mind and the physical world. In the Gibsonian terms used by Joe Anderson, our 'complex sensory systems . . . extract information from the environment by sensing patterns in these phenomena'; or, to recall the words of Brian O'Shaughnessy, through our senses 'the mind opens out onto its environment and assembles for itself a representation of outer reality'.[44] So Mary does learn something when she experiences red for the first time: she learns about properties of the physical process that only sensory experience can give direct access to; but she is not thereby accessing some mysterious mental world constituted by a different substance. Whether what she experiences could be deduced from the physical account is harder to say, though the later Jackson (writing on colour) clearly holds out this hope.[45] In other words, Jackson himself joins those who doubt that the story of Mary and the original argument secure the *metaphysical* conclusion that Jackson was aiming at—that physicalism is false, or at least that we have strong reasons to doubt it.

Jesse Prinz nonetheless notes that 'just about everyone is willing to grant that Jackson's argument establishes an *epistemological* conclusion. The concepts involved in knowing what experiences are like differ from the concepts involved in knowing about brain states as such: one cannot infer one class of concepts from the other.'[46] As we established in Chapter 2, no amount of description of brain states, no matter how fine-grained, will—on its own—give us an account of mental function and experience. So the language of qualia and of experience may be irreducible to the language of neuroscience and the physical, but not because the physical coexists with some ethereal mental substance. Rather, brains are complex physical entities which possess or give rise to mental *properties*—as we have seen Darwin putting it, 'the mind is [a] function of the body'—and we need the concepts and language of phenomenology and psychology in order to represent those properties. We have already seen some of the ways in which films and artworks in general may contribute to the challenge of representing the mind, in all of its elusive subtlety; Jackson's focus on qualia allows us to revisit, develop, and refine this claim. A route to restoring the special epistemic role of art is thereby opened up.

What, then, can we say about the kinds of qualia created by different sorts of art? And how do the arts go about creating such qualia? Ozu Yasujirō's *Ochazuke no aji/ The Flavour of Green Tea Over Rice* (1952) provides a good starting point. The title of the film refers to the traditional and simple meal of rice with green tea. The meal—which is shared in harmony by a married couple, who have been rowing over the course of the film—is symbolically laden, representing the virtues of a quiet, unpretentious, and relaxed attitude to life. But what is key here is the way that whatever symbolic value the meal has is embodied in the *taste* of the meal, or rather, for viewers of the film, in the way that the taste of the meal is evoked by the film. What this brings to mind is another, rather more famous instance of the evocation of a specific taste in a work of narrative: Proust's description of the madeleine in the opening pages of *À la recherche du temps perdu/Remembrance of Things Past*.[47] What both examples remind us of is the extent and depth of connectedness between the subjective experience of something as apparently simple as a taste, and the network of memory, cultural association, and symbolism it can become integrated with: the way a whole life can be conjured up by a taste or a smell, and the way 'thick' percepts and sensations like this—qualia laden with memory, association, beliefs, desires, values—can be created and evoked by works of art. (In Part II, I approach this phenomenon afresh from the perspective of emotion; see Chapter 8 in particular.) Other films which similarly evoke a dense network of associations through sensory imagery include Ozu's *An Autumn Afternoon* (1962), the Japanese title of which is *Samma no aji*—literally, 'The Taste of Samma', evoking 'the brief season in late summer when *samma*, a variety of mackerel, is at its most savory';[48] Sergei Parajanov's *Sayat Nova/The Colour of Pomegranates* (1968); and Trần Anh Hùng's *Mùi đu đủ xanh/The Scent of Green Papaya* (1993).

The work of Stan Brakhage, introduced in Chapter 2, takes us into the matter of art and qualia from a different angle. Brakhage was an experimental filmmaker whose films can most straightforwardly be likened to Abstract Expressionism. Some of Brakhage's films are purely abstract; many contain representational elements, but even where they do so, the films retain a strongly abstract quality, in the sense that they put before us fields of textured light that do not depict objects, characters, or events (Figure 4.1). (Though very different in other respects, the films of John Smith often generate a similar interplay between representation and abstraction, in relation to both artefacts and natural phenomena: consider the transformation of the painting stick in *Dad's Stick* (2012), Figure 1.1, and the seascapes in *Horizon (Five Pounds a Belgian)* (2012), on the cover of the present work, into luminous colour fields.) In a famous passage from his essay 'Metaphors on Vision', Brakhage asks us to

Imagine an eye unruled by man-made laws of perspective, an eye unprejudiced by compositional logic, an eye which does not respond to the name of everything but which must know each object encountered in life through an adventure of perception. How many colours are there in a field of grass to the crawling baby unaware of 'Green'? How many rainbows can light create for the untutored eye?[49]

Figure 4.1 Abstraction in Stan Brakhage's *Rage Net* (1988).

Brakhage's films work against our natural inclination to find objects in the visual arrays we are presented with, instead presenting us with colours, forms, and textures which refuse to 'attach' themselves to stable depicted objects. It is in this sense that the films create an 'adventure of perception', in which we are confronted with strikingly novel visual experiences. Comparing Brakhage's art with the example of *The Flavour of Green Tea over Rice*, we can mark a distinction between Brakhage's ambition to create radically new qualia—ones which cannot be adequately described through familiar concepts or predicates like 'green'—and Ozu's ambition to evoke for us a familiar quale, even as he renews our awareness of it and bestows special significance upon it.

One way in which this conception of the distinctive knowledge furnished by art has been articulated is through the notion of *defamiliarization*, first propounded by Viktor Shklovsky in 1919. Ordinary cognition, Shklovsky argues, works to 'automatize' the perception of objects and execution of tasks with which we have become familiar:

And so... life fades into nothingness. Automatization eats away at things, at clothes, at furniture, at our wives, and at our fear of war.

If the conscious life of many people takes place entirely on the level of the unconscious, then it's as if this life had never been.

And so, in order to return sensation to our limbs, in order to make us feel objects, to make a stone feel stony, man has been given the tool of art. The purpose of art, then, is to lead us to a knowledge of a thing.[50]

Shklovsky's account of ordinary cognition, then, prefigures in outline one of the central ideas in cognitive neuroscience discussed earlier in this chapter—that we become most conscious of an activity when it is novel, and as it becomes habitual, so it recedes from (processing-hungry) conscious awareness. The expansive dimension of art explored in Chapter 1—its tendency to stress and stretch our perceptual, cognitive, and emotional capacities—puts this process into reverse, breaking up routines and forcing phenomena back into consciousness. The vocation of art to defamiliarize or 'make strange' ranges across all aspects of experience, from simple object perception to emotionally charged personal relationships and social events. The contrast between Brakhage and Ozu can be illuminated in these terms as well: where Brakhage works at (or even before) the level of object perception, Ozu focuses upon the experiences of family and community life. The contrast should not be oversimplified, however: many of Brakhage's films represent existential themes like birth and death, and as we have seen, Ozu shows the interpenetration of perception, emotion, memory, and personal life. Both filmmakers are concerned with 'life' in the broadest sense but each tackles the task of representation through a different point of entry.

The role of art in creating new qualia, and renewing our awareness of familiar qualia, does not end with the art object itself and the perceiver's engagement with it. On this view of the function of art, one of the major roles of criticism is to *evoke* the qualia created by particular works of art. Criticism in this mode sustains the focus on and renewal of the qualia of experience achieved by art, by describing and evoking *what it feels like* to engage with specific works of (film) art. The aim of such criticism is to describe, and thereby enable us to imagine, the set of 'phenomenal information properties' (to recall the phrase used by Dennett) that, taken together, uniquely characterize the experience a given work of art is designed to elicit. And here the target of such description will be both the qualia represented by the work (the flavour of green tea over rice), as well as the unique qualia furnished by the work itself (*The Flavour of Green Tea over Rice*). The role of criticism in this respect is perhaps most obvious in the form of impressionistic passages, where critics attempt to capture the experience of viewing a film through metaphor and adjectival description. But, in this respect at least, such impressionistic criticism is continuous with more technical analysis. For those with the relevant knowledge, describing a cue within a film score as a 'major seventh with a sharp attack and equally rapid decay', or a film sequence as an example of 'metrical montage at a tempo of ten frames a second', will serve to bring to mind the characteristic feel of the sequences in question. Again, it is important not to misunderstand the contrast here between impressionistic and more technical analysis: technical analysis enables precise description where it is possible, but as we have seen in the discussion of Diana Raffman's work in Chapters 1 and 2, there may be aspects of perceptual experience beyond the reach of such analysis,[51] and this is where more indirect, especially metaphorical, description may play an essential role. (We return to these issues again in Chapter 8.) Not all impressionistic analysis is mere *belle lettrisme*. The vocation of art is the creation of novel and highly nuanced adventures in perception and cognition. The work of artists like Brakhage and Ozu is the call to which evocative criticism is the response, and the savouring of the qualia of conscious experience is central to both enterprises.

PART II

Science and Sentiment

5

Who's Afraid of Charles Darwin?

Most of our emotions are so closely connected with their expression, that they hardly exist if the body remains passive . . . a man may intensely hate another, but until his bodily frame is affected he cannot be said to be enraged.

Charles Darwin

Perhaps I'm wrong, but to me the great gift of cinematography is the human face. Don't you think so? With a camera you can go into the stomach of a kangaroo. But to look at the human face, I think, is the most fascinating.

Ingmar Bergman

The Art of Film in the Age of Evolution

Over the course of its short history, the study of film has principally been defined as a humanistic discipline. It is a field of study, that is to say, concerned with those phenomena that are traditionally regarded as distinctively human, including art and culture. For this reason, I doubt that it will surprise anyone to find the phrase 'the art of film' lurking within the introductory subtitle of this chapter. Like it or loathe it, filmmaking is self-evidently a central part of contemporary culture, and it has been commonplace to think of film as 'the art of the twentieth century'—not only in the sense that the cinema rapidly emerged over the first twenty years of the last century as an aesthetically novel and economically powerful institution, but one which impacted on the practice and self-definitions of most of the traditional arts. Our understanding of film continues to act as the platform for our understanding of subsequent audiovisual media: television, video, and digital media. But the acceptance of film as an authentic art, with all of the formal, expressive, and symbolic power of literature, drama, and painting, was a fraught affair. Most serious theoretical writing about film up to the 1950s concerned itself with justifying film as an art, and with teasing out those aspects of film which made it distinct from all earlier forms. And although the battle is in many ways long since won—the study of film has been around in the academy in the Anglo-Saxon world for around fifty years—even today one often encounters a casual condescension to film on the part of many influential commentators, suggesting that it is still regarded in some quarters as a glitzy but insubstantial upstart, a glamorous newcomer whose seductive appearance flatters to deceive.

So much, for now, on the art of film. But what about the more mysterious—even alarming—part of my subtitle? What is the phrase 'the art of film' doing sitting cheek-by-jowl with the name Charles Darwin and the process he discovered, evolution by natural selection? In referring to the 'age of evolution' I mean to evoke two periods, of radically different orders. The first is our own historical moment, as the time in which Darwinian theory has come of age. But 'the age of evolution' also refers to that epoch of human (pre)history when, biologically speaking, the species *homo sapiens* took shape; the 'environment of evolutionary adaptedness', roughly coincident with the geological epoch of the Pleistocene. This is the special concern of evolutionary psychologists, who ask the question: how has the evolutionary history of the human species created a legacy of psychological features, functions, and preferences which (directly or indirectly) still impacts on us today, millennia after the environment in which these features were adaptively formed has disappeared? How, for example, does our evolutionary inheritance bear upon such things as morality, beauty, art, and fiction? In particular, one might ask, does evolutionary psychology have anything to tell us about the art of film?

While you're recovering from that thought, I want to insert a brief note on the more general issue which frames the one I've just set up—an issue at stake throughout this work—namely, the relationship between the humanities and the natural sciences. As we've seen in the context of the two cultures debate, these labels are often used to conjure up a picture of the pursuit of knowledge as governed by two warring power blocks, implacably opposed to one another (with the social sciences sometimes occupying a non-aligned role, siding with each of the parties on particular occasions). According to this view, natural science is the domain of fact, quantification, and prediction; human science the arena of qualitative experience, interpretation, and the unique, unpredictable act. And never the twain shall meet.

Though widely (if rather vaguely) held, this simple dichotomy is deeply misleading. The first thing to note is that the traditional distinction itself implies that *some principles*—though perhaps exceedingly general—are shared between even the most disparate disciplines: we do, after all, talk of both natural and human *sciences*. An alternative, 'third cultural' view of the pursuit of knowledge underlines this commonality, bringing the natural and human sciences closer together. Complementing this recognition of shared principles operating at the most general level, however, we also need to recognize the *differences* among disciplines *within* both the natural and the human sciences. (For example, does prediction occupy the same place in evolutionary biology as it does in physics?) Once we recognize this variation within the two big power blocks, the idea of a single, paramount divide between them begins to dissolve. This is not to collapse the natural and human sciences into some grand, undifferentiated union of all human knowledge, but rather to recognize a continuum or variegated field of disciplines in place of two large zones, opposed and discontinuous but each internally homogeneous. Here I'll aim to demonstrate the problems with the supposed dichotomy between the natural and the human sciences through a case study, on emotion, which brings the two domains together. But I want to approach emotion through one more related, preliminary topic.

That topic is *fiction*—central to any consideration of the art of film, and a phenomenon which has drawn the attention of evolutionary psychologists. Fiction looks like one of those strange things that couldn't possibly have an evolutionary explanation, because it is hard to see how stories about non-existent people and places could have been much help in terms of survival. But since we have fiction, the evolutionist would insist that it must have descended to us either because it was *selected* as something that enhanced survival (that is, it is an adaptation), or, perhaps more plausibly, because it is a *byproduct* of something else that was an adaptation. Brian Boyd argues in favour of the first option: fiction and narrative constitute a cognitive extension of play, helping to hone skills that are key to survival and reproduction for humans, including those related to social cognition, cooperation, and creativity.[1] On the byproduct view, what is adaptive is our capacity to *imagine*: one thing that sets us apart from other species is our ability to 'simulate', in our minds, circumstances which we *might* encounter, or indeed which we have encountered in the past. From this perspective, fiction is to the imagination as strawberry cheesecake is to fruit—a cultural elaboration of a biological adaptation. In simulating possible scenarios, we are able to 'rehearse' how things *might* go in circumstances that we have not actually experienced (or, in the case of imagining past experience, we can reflect upon how things *might* have gone differently). The imagination, in other words, enhances our foresight and supercharges our ability to *plan*; and it is not hard to see how this improves our 'fitness' in the environment of human action.[2]

Fictions, in turn, engage our emotions, and emotion too is a subject about which evolutionary thinkers have had quite a bit to say. Most of us would accept that our emotions are part of our basic biology, but would equally quickly agree that emotions are a crucial part of our social and cultural life, and still more specifically that our experience of (most) art is emotionally coloured. So emotions span the apparent gulf between our biological, evolutionary inheritance, and the sophisticated, endlessly varied phenomena of our modern cultural existence. The terrain of emotions is thus an especially appropriate testing ground for the idea that evolutionary theory and the humanistic study of film can be thrust into a productive dialogue.

What, then, has evolutionary theory had to say about emotion, and of what relevance might this be to the way we understand and engage with films? The dominant tradition in Western thought has regarded emotion as a burden to human existence, an impediment to reason—a view manifest (in somewhat different ways) in thinkers as varied as Descartes, Kant, and the playwright Bertolt Brecht. And if anything, this is a view of emotion even more entrenched in popular culture than it is in the esoteric realms of philosophy and art theory—think of those models of supreme rationality, Spock and Data from *Star Trek*, whose special intelligence and insightfulness is directly related to the absence or suppression of emotion in their mental economies.[3] And one doesn't need to listen to news coverage for very long before encountering some manifestation of the idea that someone is being led astray by their emotions, or not taking a sufficiently detached—unemotional—view of a situation.

To be sure, there have always been thinkers representing a different view of the emotions, one which grants them an important, even revered, place in human existence (Augustine and Hume spring to mind). But Darwinian thinking poses the sharpest challenge to the hostile, anti-emotion tradition by asking the question: why would emotions—these subversives of rationality—have been naturally selected at all? Evolutionary theory offers two compelling answers to this question. First, emotions provide us with a kind of *motivational gravity*, a ballast allowing us to grip the world and act decisively within it, rather than drifting among an array of equally weighted options. Second, emotions provide a *rapidity* and *intensity* of response to a changing environment which reasoning alone cannot provide. Emotions are signal boosters, functioning to rivet our attention on particular features of a situation. This, recall, is part of the answer to Jaegwon Kim's question concerning the functions of qualia, as we saw in Chapter 4 (a crucial question to answer for a naturalistic account of mind and of art). Given that we live in a changing and sometimes hostile environment, our chances of survival are enhanced if we have a kind of inbuilt 'rapid reaction' force alongside our more precise, but much slower, mechanisms of reasoning. Whether it's a wild animal or a car suddenly bearing down upon us, it's mighty handy that we have an instinctive startle response to unexpected loud noises and fast movements (as explored in Chapter 3); that we leap out of the way immediately, rather than calmly assessing the nature of the moving object (its size, speed, and intentions), by which time we might well have become roadkill. In short, emotions are characterized by an *ecological rationality*—given certain environmental or ecological conditions, particular emotions will serve you far more effectively than would reason divested of all emotional attachments.[4]

The evolutionary view of emotions enables us, indeed exhorts us, then, to take emotions seriously—rather than regarding them as an irrelevance, a distraction, or an embarrassment. This is as true for art as it is for life; and it is surely true for film. Many genres are named, directly or indirectly, after particular emotions (thrillers, horror movies, Liebesfilm, weepies), while other film genre terms have become indelibly affect-laden (melodrama). More fundamentally, *film depends for its existence to a greater extent than any preceding art on the interplay among emotions as these are expressed in the human face and voice (as well as in posture and gesture).*[5] Take a look at any mainstream feature film—and a great many other films as well— and it will be obvious that the visual landscape of these films is dominated by shots in which facial expression is legible (whether in close-ups or longer framings), while their corresponding soundtracks resonate with the cadences and intonation of emotionally expressive human voices.

As an initial example, consider the opening sequence from *Rio Bravo* (Howard Hawks, 1959) in which several distinct expressions are sharply etched for us through a series of shots and framings—the furtive look of anguished expectation worn by Dude (Dean Martin); Joe's (Claude Akins) gloating smile; and the Duke's (John Wayne) expressions of disgust and anger (Figures 5.1a–5.1d). Or, to take a more recent example, consider the shot from *24* (Joel Surnow and Robert Cochran, 2001–10) in which a split-screen effect is used to juxtapose contrasting facial expressions—of concern (on the part of Kiefer Sutherland's protagonist, Jack Bauer), and happiness (on the part of his antagonist, Gaines, played by Michael Massee) (Figure 5.2). Note the way that, in spite of the split-screen pyrotechnics, we are still offered a clear view of both characters' expressions, in Bauer's case through a combination of profile and frontal shots.

Another kind of evidence for the foundational significance of facial expression in film is offered by films which depict characters who have lost the power of facial expression. Take, for example, the burnt airman's face in *The English Patient* (Anthony Minghella, 1997) or the facial prosthesis masking the disfigured face in the Spanish film *Abre los ojos/Open Your Eyes* (Alejandro Amenábar, 1997); or again, from earlier in film history, the face of the protagonist in *The Man Who Laughs* (Paul Leni, 1928), scarred into a permanent grin. Consider also the classic French horror film, *Les Yeux sans visage/The Eyes Without a Face* (Georges Franju, 1959), in which the protagonist Dr Génessier (Pierre Brasseur) not only hides his daughter Christiane's (Édith Scob) damaged face with a mask, but grafts the face of an abducted young woman Edna (Alida Valli) onto it; we are treated to visions of the masked Christiane (Figure 5.3), Edna's face entirely wrapped in bandages, as well as Christiane's face as the new skin is rejected. Why are such images so potent? Expressions of emotion point in two directions: inwards, towards the agent's felt state of being, and outwards, to others perceiving and interacting with the agent. Faces without the capacity to express emotion are thus striking and troubling because they deprive us of such a basic means of social interaction. The consequences of an inability to express emotion facially (whether caused by disfigurement or neural disorders, like Parkinson's disease), or an inability to recognize expressions of emotion (as found in the condition of 'emotional agnosia') can be as severe as the complete destruction of emotional orientation experienced by some victims of brain injury.[6]

An important problem of principle, with practical ramifications, should be noted here. Frame enlargements ('screen grabs', in the age of DVD and Blu-ray) capturing facial expressions are of considerable illustrative value. But the practice of 'capturing' a facial expression in such a still also highlights the fact that expressions are dynamic events, little 'episodes' in the lives of faces with a dramatic arc all of their own. Facial expressions possess an apex or 'dramatic climax' at which they are at their most recognizable, and it is for this reason that we usually have a reasonably clear sense of what sort of emotional state a person or character is in, based on a still representation. In extracting (and abstracting) a still image from the moving medium of

Figures 5.1a–5.1d Facial expressions of emotion in *Rio Bravo* (Howard Hawks, 1959).

Figure 5.2 Contrasting facial expressions in *24* (Joel Surnow and Robert Cochran, 2001–10).

Figure 5.3 The masked, disfigured face in *Les Yeux sans visage/The Eyes Without a Face* (Georges Franju, 1959).

cinema, however, one cannot fail to notice how many subtle but telling additional cues to the emotional state are lost. This fact is made particularly salient in the perceptual theory of J. J. Gibson, who treats human vision 'not as a snapshot but as a flowing optic array'[7] in which visual input is constantly updated by movement. On this view, moving depictions are more 'basic' than still depictions, even though motion picture technology comes much later in human history. Visual artists working with still media are likely to develop strategies addressing this problem in a way that is simply not demanded of filmmakers. For this reason, stills from films, illustratively useful as they are, may be incomplete or even misleading in the way that they render emotional expression in a manner qualitatively different from paintings and photographs.[8]

It is at this juncture that evolutionary theory makes a more specific contribution to our understanding of film as an art. Inspired by Darwin's *The Expression of the Emotions in Man and Animals* (1872), there is now a large body of literature on the nature and functions of facial and vocal expression of emotion, which discriminates among types of emotion, their degree of cultural variability, their qualities and functions. For Darwin, and for many writing and researching in his wake, the expression of an emotion is partly constitutive of it, rather than a secondary phenomenon following the emotion proper: 'Most of our emotions are so closely connected with their expression, that they hardly exist if the body remains passive ... a man may intensely hate another, but until his bodily frame is affected he cannot be said to be enraged'. William James would later push further in this direction in his theory of emotion: 'Without the bodily states following on the perception, the latter would be purely cognitive in form, pale, colorless, destitute of emotional warmth'.[9] These, then, are the foundations of the bridge between the art of film and the science of emotion: the evident significance of emotional expression to film, and the importance accorded to the expression of emotion by Darwin and his followers. But before we can appreciate the full relevance of the Darwinian account of emotions, we need to take a brief diversion, back through the history of thinking about film.

Facial Expression, Montage, and the Kuleshov Fallacy

When filmmakers, critics, and philosophers first began to reflect on the nature of film in the 1910s and 1920s, they took as their basic task the need to specify what made film a distinctive art form, which was neither merely a passive technology of recording nor a mere parasite on older forms of art (be it theatre, painting, or literature). For the Soviet filmmakers of the 1920s, *montage* was the aspect of film that made it distinctive. It was the capacity of film to take diverse shots, often derived from entirely disparate or unrelated locations, and weave them together into a new whole, that seemed to the Soviet theorists to be the most original power of film, and one unique to it. And they can hardly be faulted for this insistence; the power of film editing is indeed astonishing. But while montage theory captured a certain truth, it was also a thesis with flaws. It turned out to be one of those truths whose very light obscures other 'adjacent' truths, whose existence can only re-emerge over time, as the novelty of the original insight wanes.

The most pertinent item of montage film theory for us to consider here is the 'Kuleshov effect'. In a demonstration of the potency of editing, Lev Kuleshov edited together a shot of the actor Ivan Mosjoukine displaying a neutral expression, glancing off-screen, with shots of several different objects—respectively, a bowl of soup, a child in a coffin, and a sunny landscape. According to Kuleshov and his protégé Vsevolod Pudovkin, audiences who viewed these variations not only made the inference that Mosjoukine was, in each case, looking at the object, but ascribed different affective states to Mosjoukine—hunger, sadness, and happiness— and marvelled at his performative skill (even though it was the same shot of the actor on each occasion). Thus the power of editing: what we see in each shot is far less significant, on this account, than the meanings and emotions which arise out of the editing together of shots. Our interpretation of Mosjoukine's situation and state of mind changes according to the shots that are juxtaposed with the shot of him.[10]

Evolutionary studies of facial expression, however, give the lie to the notion that shots of faces are *entirely* plastic, and can be moulded by contextual shots to suggest *any* kind of emotional state. On the contrary, the work of Paul Ekman—the most well-known contemporary evolutionary scientist of facial expression, and the editor of the third edition of Darwin's *Expression of the Emotions*—provides extensive evidence that a range of 'basic' emotional expressions (for happiness, sadness, disgust, anger, fear, and surprise) are easily and quickly recognized *cross-culturally*.[11] A shot of a smile, a grimace, a frown, or an angry sneer—to take some key examples—cannot easily be overridden by adjacent shots which might suggest some other emotional state; for the basic emotions, facial expression is itself a powerful determinant in evoking highly specific emotions.[12] The force of these basic emotional expressions is surely something that the sequence from *Rio Bravo* draws upon and reveals, as do the shots of Begbie (a fictional character in *Trainspotting* (Danny Boyle, 1996), played by Robert Carlyle) and Kevin Keegan (a real football manager, here famously fulminating against rival manager Alex Ferguson, also in 1996) (Figures 5.4a–5.4b).[13]

Such facial expressions don't tell us everything about the dramatic situation of which they are a part. As we said of the startle cues in *Iron Man* in Chapter 3, such elements have to be interpreted in context, and that context will include many culturally specific things (knowledge of saloon bars, whisky, and spittoons in the case of *Rio Bravo*, for example). Or consider again the still from *24* (Figure 5.2). We can judge that Gaines, in the bottom right-hand frame, is probably in some sort of happy state, based on his expression alone; but we can't know that the particular form of this happiness is, in fact, sadistic delight—Gaines's pleasure in the power he wields over Jack Bauer (visible in the juxtaposed frames)—unless we know the context of his expression. Similarly, in order to fully understand Kevin Keegan's expression,

Figures 5.4a–5.4b The sneer as a basic emotion expression in fictional and real contexts.

one needs to know about his role (at the time) as manager of one of England's major football clubs, and how much rides on the fortunes of these clubs in English culture.

It is, nevertheless, important to disentangle here the question of *context* and the question of *cultural specificity*. Even if certain expressions are universally recognizable, it does not follow that they are hermeneutically self-sufficient and self-explanatory. This point is central to Errol Morris's forensic investigation of the circumstances surrounding the infamous photographs taken by American soldiers at the Abu Ghraib detention centre in 2003, gleefully celebrating their abuse and torture of prisoners. One photograph that Morris focuses on in particular shows US Army reservist Sabrina Harman posing with a broad smile and a 'thumbs up' gesture alongside the battered corpse of prisoner Manadel al-Jamadi (Figure 5.5). Harman's smile doubtless tells us something about her state of mind, and the fact that most viewers find the juxtaposition of the beaten corpse and the smile deeply disturbing shows just how 'hard-wired' is the relationship between happiness and smiling. But the burden of Morris's analysis is to show how complex the situation in Abu Ghraib was, and that we cannot understand the full implications of the photographs without

Figure 5.5 Sabrina Harman and Manadel al-Jamadi in Abu Ghraib prison (2003).

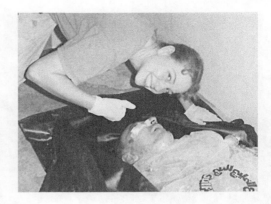

knowing more about the context in which they were taken.[14] We cannot assume that we can take images, or the expressions depicted in them, at face value.

Context is thus always necessary to allow us to understand the exact meaning of an expression. But cultural variation bears on this only incidentally; even if we are completely at home culturally, we still need immediate context to understand an expression fully. Note that the sequence from *Trainspotting* in which Figure 5.4a appears does not provide us with this kind of context. This is one of a number of freeze-frames shown during the film's closing credits, depicting the central characters in typical situations, with characteristic expressions. The still might evoke particular situations in the film, but it doesn't unambiguously refer to any one of them. Nevertheless, the emotional 'zone' occupied by Begbie, and the character traits that go along with it—angry aggression and domineering masculinity—are pretty unmistakable, in spite of the limited contextual information furnished by the sequence. *The key point, then, is that basic facial expressions play a crucial role in giving us an initial orientation towards a situation, on the basis of which we then apply our contextual knowledge.* There is thus a fallacious implication in the theory of the Kuleshov effect, at least in its stronger forms: the implication that the context of an individual shot, as established by editing, will entirely determine our interpretation of the contents of the shot.

It would be wrong, however, to say that the evidence for basic expressions reveals the claim for the Kuleshov effect to be completely false. A key aspect of Kuleshov's demonstration was the *neutral* expression of the actor—a feature which cuts both ways.[15] On the one hand, you might say that Kuleshov rigged his 'experiment' by using a shot of a man showing no strong emotional expression, so as to (over) emphasize the power of editing. On the other hand, you might say that he chose this 'expressionless' shot *in recognition of* the power of facial expression—for *only* with a neutral expression would the contextual power of editing become so apparent. Kuleshov was, in effect, controlling the variable of facial expression. We can see the truth of this through the following example, from Alfred Hitchcock's *North by Northwest* (USA, 1959). Cary Grant plays Roger Thornhill, an advertising executive

Figure 5.6 'Stupefied amazement' in *North by Northwest* (Alfred Hitchcock, 1959).

who has been framed as a secret agent. In one scene he tracks down a diplomat at the UN in New York, who he thinks will be able to extricate him from this situation. Thornhill shows the diplomat a photograph of a person who he hopes the diplomat will recognize. A second later the diplomat is murdered by a knife thrown into his back (Figure 5.6); a further fraction of a second passes before Hitchcock cuts to the assassin and we grasp just what has happened. This is the key moment for us.

Kuleshov argues that our understanding of any given shot will change as the context of the shot changes. So in this case, at first we think that the diplomat is expressing *surprise* at the photo, but then as our contextual knowledge broadens, we (re)interpret the expression as one of 'stupefied amazement', which Darwin characterizes as 'closely akin to terror'.[16] This, I think, captures the basic character of our experience, but equally, it overlooks the extent to which the diplomat's expression *immediately* appears incongruous. The expression just doesn't look like one of surprise at the contents of the photo—the eyes and mouth are open too wide; the diplomat's gaze shoots forward rather than down towards the photo; the onset of the expression is extremely rapid, and accompanied by a gasp. As Darwin argued, surprise and terror may be on same continuum of emotion, but they are nevertheless distinct in important ways. So the effect Hitchcock is looking for, or at least the one that he achieves, is not a shift from one firm interpretation of the expression to another (as the Kuleshov effect would predict), so much as momentary confusion over what is happening, precisely because the apparent explanation (surprise at the photo) is subtly, but palpably, inappropriate. The additional contextual information serves to clarify a complex set of cues, rather than reversing (and thus utterly transforming) our interpretation of the diplomat's expression and situation.[17] This kind of ripple in the surface of the action is one of the things that makes Hitchcock a great director, and one of the constituent elements that he draws on in creating this effect is the force of distinct, basic emotional expressions.

Is the notion of the Kuleshov effect no more than a museum piece? Hardly. Arguments and assumptions of this type concerning the power of editing over other aspects of film technique, and particularly performance, are still very much alive. Consider, as a parallel example, Howard Goodall's analysis of Bernard Herrmann's score for Hitchcock's *Psycho* (1960). Goodall claims that the extended sequence of shots showing Marion Crane (Janet Leigh) driving away from Phoenix (Figure 2.4) would take on an entirely different emotional character if they were juxtaposed with upbeat music, rather than the unsettling harmonies and jagged rhythms of Herrmann's score. That much is certainly true; there can be no doubting the 'added value'[18] that sound and music bring to the film image in general, nor of the importance of Herrmann's score in shaping our experience of the story of Marion Crane and Norman Bates in particular. Goodall cannot resist implying, however, that Leigh's facial expression is entirely inert, and that her performance plays no significant role in conjuring up the mood of the scene. 'What's remarkable about [Herrmann's cue for the scene] is how much impact it has on the pictures. Without it, what we're looking at is someone driving along in a car, and there's nothing dramatic, tense, or worrying about that.'[19] But what Goodall implies by this claim is manifestly false: across the sequence Leigh's face betrays many symptoms of anxiety and agitation (nervous sideways glances, lip biting, strained squinting into the headlights of oncoming traffic as she drives long into the night). In this respect the example differs from the classic Mosjoukine case, for Leigh's face is not expressively neutral. To be sure, a different score would interact with these facial expressions to obtain a different effect to the one actually achieved with Herrmann's score (as Goodall demonstrates); but that does not secure the claim that Leigh's facial expressions are playing no significant role. We are back to a version of the Kuleshov fallacy: only context—here provided by the score, rather than editing—counts in determining the meaning or emotional character of a given facial expression. In this respect, Goodall's otherwise very compelling analysis of the musical character of Herrmann's score and its contribution to the film strikes a false, if very familiar, note.

Beyond the Basics

Notwithstanding their significance, basic expressions are not the whole story. The use of a neutral facial expression in Kuleshov's experiment also draws our attention to all those types of expression which exist alongside basic emotion expressions. These would include expressions associated with the so-called 'higher emotions', like love, which admit of more cultural variation,[20] and expressions modified by, in Ekman's words, culturally specific *display rules*—that is, cultural conventions which govern *who* can express what *sort* of emotion in which *social contexts*. The classic example here concerns the different display rules evident in American and Japanese society, but let me take one closer to home: the gender-related display rules governing the facial expression of fear in Hollywood films. Lead male characters get frightened in American movies, but they are far less apt to express this facially than either their female compatriots or minor male characters; think of such 'facially laconic' icons as Robert Mitchum or Clint Eastwood.

And consider these stills from *Jurassic Park* (Steven Spielberg, 1994) (Figures 5.7a–5.7b). In the first still, the expression of fear exhibited by Jeff Goldblum is markedly less extreme—more contained—than Laura Dern's expression. But when we turn to a minor male character in the second still, the look of terror on his

Figures 5.7a–5.7b Emotional expression and display rules in *Jurassic Park* (Steven Spielberg, 1993).

face is every bit as extreme as the expression on the face of the girl next to him. The fact that minor male characters express fear as vigorously as female characters is important in establishing that the suppression of expressions of fear in male protagonists is a social display rule—rather than a genetically determined behaviour.[21]

Psychologists have also identified subtle cultural variations even in relation to basic emotion expressions. Dacher Keltner has speculated that Britons are more likely to use the 'social smile' than are their American counterparts.[22] An American smile is more likely to be a 'Duchenne smile', that is, a spontaneous smile expressive of the smiling person's happiness, which involves the muscles around the eyes as well as the mouth (named after French neurophysiologist Guillaume Duchenne, a major influence on Darwin). Keltner likens a social smile—a smile adopted to convey politeness or to provide reassurance to interlocutors rather than to express the happiness of the agent—to the effect of Botox, which leaves the upper part of the face motionless (in essence, the *orbicularis oculi* muscle around the eye fails to contract as it does in a spontaneous smile).[23] To the extent that this contrast in smiling behaviour arises from a greater emphasis in British culture on the display of social politeness and deference, this may be another instance of display rules at work. Note, however, that recognition of cultural difference of this type is not evidence against the argument that a smile is a universal expression of happiness. Americans, Britons, and everyone else smiles, and members of all cultures exhibit both Duchenne and social smiles. Patterns of cultural variation stand out against this robust background of common behaviour.

So there is plenty of room within a Darwinian account of emotions for neutral, suppressed, culturally specific, or otherwise ambiguous expressions. And this is a good thing, for as Michael Newman argues, 'in cinema as well as in real life emotions may be expressed in subtle or partial ways that do not involve the classic facial patterns we think of as an "angry face" or a "surprised face"'.[24] Such 'partial' or incomplete expressions form an essential complement to more transparent basic emotion expressions in the dramatic fiction film. Indeed, some directors, like Otto Preminger and Robert Bresson, have developed unique styles in which oblique or ambiguous facial expression plays a key role. Moreover, the emphasis here on facial *expressions* of emotion—visible, physiological manifestations of inner states— should not be taken to overlook the role of these same expressions in social communication. Such communication, crucially, includes various types of deliberate 'mis'-communication: think of the deceptive, taunting smile in the sequence from *Rio Bravo*, or of Jack Bauer's recurrent need in *24* to adopt fake expressions in order to extricate himself from perilous situations. Closely related to such outright deception is the pervasive use of the social smile, which as we have noted acts as a signal of reassurance, assent, or deference rather than an expression of happiness. Consider nurse Carol Hathaway in *ER* (Michael Crichton, 1994–2009), played by Julianna Margulies, as one of television's great compulsive social smilers.

The psychologist Alan Fridlund places great emphasis on the social and communicative role of expressions, arguing that Ekman's view of facial expressions as direct expressions of felt states is incomplete and misleading.[25] Ekman, however, explicitly acknowledges the social role of emotional expressions.[26] Indeed it seems logically necessary that expressions standardly do provide us with reliable information about the inner states of others, in order for the more elaborate paraphernalia of concealment and pretence—adopting false expressions, suppressing emotional responses, and so forth—to work at all. Social smiles could not have their reassuring effect if smiles were not tied with the expression of happiness. The underlying lesson drawn here from Ekman's work concerns *recognition* of emotion expressions. An expression may be recognized, however, without it following that it is recognized *as* an expression of the emotion with which it is associated. We may work with the default assumption that an angry expression betrays a feeling of anger, but in many circumstances we quickly perceive that the angry expression does not signal anger—as when we realize that someone is performing an expression, for example. But in such cases, we continue to regard the expression as an 'angry expression', even though it is not in this context expressive of anger. As in so many respects, Darwin got there first: 'Laughter is frequently employed in a forced manner to conceal or mask some other states of mind, even anger.'[27] Context plays an important role in helping to determine whether a particular instance of an emotional expression is an expression of the emotion it standardly signals.

The complexities concerning context and the social norms regulating the display of emotions drive us to recognize a further important point: the emotions experienced by agents within a scenario can be conveyed *situationally* as well as *expressively*. That is to say, sometimes our understanding of a dramatic situation is sufficient for us to infer the emotions likely being experienced by the characters in the situation, even without the assistance of expressive cues. This, so to speak, is the baby that must not be thrown out with the bathwater of the Kuleshov fallacy. Imagine another variation on the sequences analysed from *Jurassic Park*, in which we witness a character being confronted by a dinosaur but betraying no visible emotional reaction. So long as we can assume that the character is an ordinary human agent (rather than, say, an affectless android), we are still most likely to conclude that the character experiences fear while suppressing its expression (which, in this kind of context, we might construe as strategically valuable—not a display rule, but a survival tactic). We are able to make inferences of this type so readily because emotions are embedded within and learned from *paradigm scenarios*—schematic dramas that define the roles, feelings, and reactions characteristic of particular emotions.[28] By the same token, when we encounter a person or character lacking facial or other expressions, and without any situational information, we are usually at a loss as to how to interpret such a figure. John Smith wittily reflects on this kind of perplexing circumstance in *Frozen War* (2001), the first of his series of *Hotel Diaries* (2001–7), in which the filmmaker finds himself confronted by suspended newsreel footage late at night in his hotel room. Shorn of any expressive or situational clues, the figure frozen on Smith's screen becomes quite inscrutable. (A television caption tells us that the item under discussion concerns the post-9/11 strikes on Afghanistan, but we can glean nothing about the role or stance of the figure depicted.) Werner Herzog in *Pilgrimage* (2001), and Christian Marclay in *The Clock* (2001), explore related strategies by presenting us with a succession of facial expressions without full or precise contextualization.

The importance of situational understanding in the apprehension of emotions was recognized by Rudolf Arnheim early in the history of film theory, who noted in *Film as Art* that '[m]uch facial expression is comprehensible only because it is part of a situation'.[29] The insight also receives support from Fritz Heider and Marianne Simmel's classic study, and accompanying animated film, on the attribution of states and traits to others, which shows how our situational understanding is sufficient to attribute basic emotions even to animated geometric figures with few expressive features.[30] In more recent times the point has been elaborated theoretically and supported empirically by research in both psychology and film. Arvid Kappas underlines the complex relations between facial expressions and emotions, noting that not all emotions issue in facial expressions, nor are all facial expressions the product of concordant emotions: as we've noted, a smile can mask unhappiness as well as express pleasure.[31] Newman, meanwhile, argues for the importance of both the multimodal nature of emotional expression—emotions are conveyed through vocal, gestural, and postural as well as facial expressions—and situational context in our grasp of characters' emotional states.[32] In other words, our understanding of emotions is supported by an array of (under normal circumstances) redundant, mutually supporting mechanisms.

Some theorists take this a step further, treating the role of situations in emotional apprehension as support for a kind of radical externalism about emotions. On such a view, emotions become properties of situations rather than of the agents interacting and responding within them.[33] But this is a revision of our concept of emotion which flirts with incoherence, or the metaphysical extravagance of the panpsychism we encountered in Chapter 4, for we will be required to say that when Scottie (James Stewart) experiences vengeful fury towards Madeleine at the climax of Alfred Hitchcock's *Vertigo* (1958), it's the situation rather than Scottie that actually possesses the emotion. But situations do not have nervous systems, and are not loci of experiences. In Chapter 7, I explore the theory of the extended mind, which allows us to recognize how human emotions and other mental states might indeed depend upon aspects of the world beyond the brain and body of the individual agent. But it is a further step beyond the version of the theory that I defend to say that the experiential centre of gravity of an emotion is displaced from the individual agent and into the world itself.

Evolution and the Aesthetic Sculpting of Emotional Expression

The sceptic might still ask the question: did we need these evolutionary studies of emotion to know that some emotions are plainly and forcefully legible? Well, when Ekman started out in the 1960s, he began with the—at the time—widespread assumption that all facial expressions were culturally specific and none were universally recognizable; Darwin's thesis had fallen completely out of favour.[34] And such relativism, it must be said, has been dogmatically assumed for much of the history of academic film studies. So evidence from evolutionary psychology has been crucial in establishing the plausibility of the basic emotion model, with its cross-cultural, universal implications. What's more, the fact that basic emotion expressions are universal lends support to another idea important to many early and classical film theorists—namely, the notion that film was a peculiarly 'internationalist' medium, that it constituted a kind of universal 'language'. Writing in 1924, Béla Balázs extolled the power of film to capture facial expression and gesture, which he characterized as the 'aboriginal mother-tongue of the human race'.[35] And in the late 1920s, many filmmakers and critics became agitated about the loss of this internationalism, as the talkies displaced silent cinema and the 'universal language' of facial expression was overlayed and obscured by the babble of particular verbal languages. The opening of *Rio Bravo*, with its choreography of expression and gesture in the absence of dialogue, was conceived by Hawks in this spirit, as an homage to silent cinema. Extending this technique to a new extreme, Sergio Leone made the sustained, speechless exchange of glances a structural principle in his Westerns, as seen in the epic prologues of *Il buono, il brutto, il cattivo/The Good, the Bad, and the Ugly* (1966) and *C'era una volta il West/Once Upon a Time in the West* (1968) (Figure 5.8).

Figure 5.8 The sustained, speechless glance in the work of Leone—the opening shot of *Il buono, il brutto, il cattivo/The Good, the Bad, and the Ugly* (Sergio Leone, 1966).

As we watch a fiction film, then, our ability both to recognize and to respond to facial expressions is brought into play, just as so many other of our ordinary perceptual, cognitive, and emotional capacities are engaged. In this sense, fiction films were creating 'virtual realities' for spectators long before the phrase was invented; virtual in the sense that the worlds depicted by fiction films are at once *imagined* realities and yet *sensuously apprehended. Basic emotion expressions play a vital role here as a bridgehead not only between universal and culturally specific experience, but also between actual and fictional experience.* In Figure 5.4, Begbie's expression is as recognizable as Kevin Keegan's, and both are meaningful cross-culturally (though neither is hermeneutically self-sufficient). Small wonder, then, that the face was so important to some early film theorists: facial expressions underwrote both the special realism, and the internationalism, that seemed to be the peculiar possession of the cinema.

But this is still not the end of the story with regard to the significance of the Darwinian account of facial expression. In addition to the universal expression and recognition of a certain range of emotions, there is also evidence that when we see such emotions expressed in others we *mimic* them in ourselves. In other words, as we move through social space, we don't only perceive and categorize the emotions of others, we *feel* them, albeit in attenuated form—a phenomenon which has been discussed in terms of, among other concepts, *affective mimicry* and *emotional contagion* (notions which relate to the concept of *empathy*—a topic on which I expand in Chapters 2, 3, and 7).[36] The adaptive origins of such mimicry can be traced to an alarm-and-rescue function—the evolutionary ancestor of altruism—in which individual members of social species would be sensitive to, and feel as if their own, the emotional states of their conspecifics.

A striking instance of affective mimicry occurs at the climax of Hitchcock's wartime espionage thriller, *Saboteur* (1942). The saboteur (Norman Lloyd) has been cornered at the top of the Statue of Liberty, and in desperation climbs out from the viewing deck onto the torch. Now there is nothing very subtle about the symbolism here: an enemy of democracy splayed helplessly on one of its most famous icons. But Hitchcock handles this action in a curious fashion. As the saboteur dangles from the torch, Hitchcock peppers the sequence with close-ups of the saboteur's expressions of pain and terror—shots that are apt to elicit mimicry on our part, so that we quite literally feel the saboteur's fear in some measure.[37]

Now up to this point, the saboteur has been a pure object of hatred and disgust—unsurprising given the film's wartime theme and context. This brief passage inviting mimicry creates an unexpected emotional crosscurrent, however, as for a few moments the saboteur's fear, and his vulnerability, become palpable for us. The imagined satisfaction of running the traitor to ground and vanquishing him are undercut by these shots. Perhaps Hitchcock was trying to suggest how *we*—the defenders of liberal democracy against the Nazi threat—are capable of complex, sympathetic reactions even to our enemies; and that even in victory we might regret that the battle had to be fought at all. What is certainly true is that in a later wartime thriller, *Lifeboat* (1944), which comes to a very similar climax in which a German U-boat captain is pushed overboard the lifeboat when his malicious intentions become apparent, Hitchcock avoided any shot of the captain at all—let alone a close-up making his expression maximally legible and inviting affective mimicry.

The kind of play with our sympathy and antipathy for villainous characters that we find in *Saboteur* can be traced throughout Hitchcock's career, but it seems that he came to feel (or was made to feel) that such play was out of place in a political, 'propagandistic' film, in which our allegiances should remain clear and unambiguous throughout. In interviews, Hitchcock has given an aesthetic, rather than political or moral, explanation for the shift in approach evident in *Lifeboat*: the climax of *Saboteur* 'fails' because it tries to generate anxiety for the villain, rather than the hero.[38] Hitchcock oversimplifies things here, however: the original conception of the scene involved the creation of anxiety for the hero *through* anxiety for the villain, by tying the hero's well-being to the villain's survival (the hero has been wrongly identified as the saboteur, and only the real saboteur can exonerate him).[39] This conception is only vestigially present in the film itself. Comparing these aspects of *Saboteur* with *Lifeboat*, it seems that Hitchcock's change of tactic is even more dramatic than my analysis implies. The occlusion from view of the U-boat captain certainly prevents affective mimicry (via facial expression) with him, but the 'lynching' of the captain by the Allied figures hardly presents them in a sympathetic light at that moment either. Hitchcock thus shifts from 'compound sympathy' in *Saboteur* to 'reciprocal antipathy' in *Lifeboat*.

Now let us review the spectrum of claims that comprise my analysis of these sequences: on one end, we have the argument that Hitchcock exploits universal expressions (of distress and terror) and a biological response mechanism (affective mimicry) to those expressions. At the other end, we have the argument that Hitchcock came to regard the creation of sympathy for the Nazi figure, at least at the climactic point in the story, as aesthetically, politically, and morally inappropriate. All in all, this is an argument that shows how an aspect of the biology of emotions is enlisted in a cultural and political cause. The biology of affective mimicry doesn't determine anything about the politics of the sequence; rather it exemplifies what Stephen Jay Gould calls *biological potentiality*, that is, the way in which our biological capacities can be exploited in various ways and to various ends.[40] Neither is the meaning of the sequence being 'reduced' to the biological level, any more than the meaning of *Iron Man, Ran,* and *127 Hours* were so reduced by exploring their use of the startle response and bodily empathy in Chapter 3. Hitchcock's exploitation of affective mimicry in the sequence is but one link in an explanatory chain. We do not have to make a choice between an evolutionary, biological explanation, and a purely cultural one; and if we do make that choice then we weaken our explanation. The multilevelled, 'biocultural'—or as I characterized it in Chapter 1, the 'thick'—nature of this explanatory account is its strength, not its weakness.

Through most of this chapter, I have been happily running together discussion of emotional expression in film with emotional expression in everyday life. It would be naïve, however, to suggest that facial expression, as an aspect of film acting and filmic depiction more generally, can be understood wholly as a matter of the imitation of facial expression in life. *Any* film art is going to modify, shape, and redirect facial expression to some degree, if only by *bracketing, clarifying,* and *intensifying* expressions which strike us as otherwise quite ordinary. There will always be a process of *aesthetic reshaping* in play—that is, depending on the particular artistic goals of the work in question, facial expression will be moulded in ways that support those goals.

Among directors whose careers began in the silent era, Carl Theodor Dreyer stands out for his sustained development of a distinctive visual style centring on facial expression. As David Bordwell notes, however, putting one's finger on what makes Dreyer's treatment of the face unique is tricky, since '[a]lmost every director of narrative films privileges the face over other parts of the body'. In Dreyer's early films, Bordwell finds a systematic dialectical between tableaux composition on the one hand, and shots of the face which isolate and abstract it from its surroundings on the other, 'creating a physiognomic space distinct from the tableau'.[41] In *La Passion de Jeanne d'Arc* (1928), Dreyer pushed this principle to an extreme, creating a film in which much of the drama is conveyed through the interplay of facial close-ups (Figures 5.9a–5.9b). Little wonder, then, that Balázs was among the first to recognize and celebrate Dreyer's work, constituting as it did an exceptionally distilled example of the 'microphysiognomy' characteristic, according to Balázs, of silent cinema.[42] In later films, such as *Vredens Dag/Day of Wrath* (1943), Dreyer's interest in the face as part of the tableaux composition remains evident (Figure 5.9c).

The face has continued to be an object of special fascination for some directors in subsequent periods and other traditions. Closest to Dreyer, there is Ingmar Bergman, who was particularly emphatic about the importance of the close-up of the face, writing that 'proximity to the human face is without a doubt the cinema's most special feature and mark of distinction...The objectively composed, perfectly directed and played close-up is the director's most powerful means of influencing the audience. It is also the most flagrant proof of his competence or incompetence.'[43] Such a commitment to the expressive power of the face is abundantly evident in Bergman's films.

Here, though, I want to outline briefly the strategies of three other directors all of whom develop performative and compositional treatments of facial expression in strong contrast to the bold expressions characteristic of Hawks and Hitchcock, Dreyer and Bergman: Robert Bresson, Kitano Takeshi, and Wong Kar-wai. (I continue the exploration of facial expression in modernist cinema in Chapter 6 through discussion of Edgar Reitz's *Heimat*).[44] Kitano has achieved renown as both an actor and a director, often appearing in the lead role in his own films. In works such as *Sonatine* (1993) and *Hana-bi/Fireworks* (1997), Kitano has developed a style of performance that presents the face as a blank, expressionless mask, broken only by the occasional smile and facial twitch (Figure 5.10). Given that Kitano has worked extensively within the gangster genre, we

Figures 5.9a–5.9c Carl Theodor Dreyer's use of the face in close-up in *La Passion de Jeanne d'Arc* (1928) and in longer framing in *Vredens Dag/Day of Wrath* (1943).

Figure 5.10 Emotional reticence in *Sonatine* (Kitano Takeshi, 1993).

might regard his approach to facial expression as an extreme stylization of the macho culture of inexpressiveness (the same culture that I mentioned earlier in relation to Hollywood's tough guys). (Bearing in mind the arguments concerning cross-cultural dynamics and interaction set out throughout the present work, it should not surprise us to find such commonalities between in some ways distant cultures.) Kitano himself cites the influence of Japanese theatrical traditions, and has said that his aim is to make the intentions and feelings of his characters enigmatic. We might think, therefore, of Kitano as pursuing an *aesthetic of emotional reticence*.

Bresson developed a still more consistently austere style of performance, in which facial expression as such is displaced, in two ways: his performers modulate their expressions only very subtly, and Bresson will often cut to parts of the body other than the face at moments of dramatic intensity. In *L'Argent* (1983) for example, a series of vital climactic moments are clinched by shots of, respectively, a hand, a ladle, and a cup of coffee. The effect is a kind of ritualization of human action, by which Bresson aims to remove his characters from the sphere of ordinary human psychology, asking us to regard them instead as governed by a kind of spiritual destiny. We might label this strategy an *aesthetic of spiritual transcendence*.

The films of Wong Kar-wai depend on a more recognizable, naturalistic style of performance, but one that is overlaid by a compositional stylization which often presents characters obliquely: in profile or from behind, partially hidden behind other objects, sometimes obscured by layers of translucent material (curtains, rain) or made hazy by special effects. Consider the frames here from *Hua yang nian hua/In the Mood for Love* (2000) all of which are taken from shots that sustain this sort of oblique perspective towards a character (Figures 5.11a–5.11d). Note also the strong

Figures 5.11a–5.11d Oblique and elliptical depiction of emotion in *Hua yang nian hua/In the Mood for Love* (Wong Kar-wai, 2000).

contrast between Wong's blocking here, and the much greater frontality of character positioning in the still from *24* (Figure 5.2), facilitating much more direct access to the emotional states of characters. Bordwell has suggested that Wong's work is defined by an *aesthetic of the glimpse*,[45] in which characters' emotional states are often, as it were, at one remove from us—echoing the way that the romantic desires of his characters are perpetually just beyond their grasp. Not that Wong's work is unvarying in this regard, however: *Yi dai zong shi/The Grandmaster* (2013) climaxes with an eleven-minute exchange of frontal close-ups between the central romantic leads that Dreyer and Balázs might have admired.

Hawks, Hitchcock, Dreyer, Bergman, Bresson, Kitano, Wong: each of these directors, I have argued, has developed distinctive artistic strategies in relation to facial expression. The fact that the approach of Hawks and Hitchcock is more naturalistic, however, in the sense that their performers adopt expressions which are manifestly similar to those we encounter in life, while in the cases of Bresson and Kitano we find an attenuation of emotional expression which we would find disturbing or even pathological in life, doesn't render the evolutionary perspective on emotional expression irrelevant. Directors like Bresson and Kitano provide a kind of 'negative evidence' for the relevance of evolutionary accounts of expression: understanding how facial expression ordinarily functions sharpens our understanding and appreciation of the aesthetic sculpting of expression by particular directors. We understand these aesthetic strategies more deeply when we see what they occlude, foreground, and transfigure, relative to the ordinary functioning of facial expression.[46]

One aspect of the title of this chapter remains to be explained. *Who* is afraid of Charles Darwin? I think we can boil down contemporary opposition to Darwinian theory, at least as it is applied to social and cultural matters, to three groups: creationists (of course), humanists (of a certain sort), and many of those on the political left. Creationists I shall leave aside; I doubt that anything I could say would assuage their fears. The criticisms levelled by humanists and leftists, however, concern me more. Traditional humanists and leftists often argue that an appeal to natural science, and especially evolutionary theory, necessarily results in explanations which are reductive, deterministic, and politically reactionary. Through the case study on emotion and its expression that I've presented in this chapter, I have sought to point up the inadequacy of conventional wisdom on these matters.

I hope it is clear that I am not arguing that the concerns of artists or critics can be reduced to those of natural scientists, let alone that science and (film) art are the same thing (the latter in particular is a straw man that ought to be burned and discarded forthwith). The human sciences really are distinct from the natural sciences. But I am arguing for the pertinence of knowledge gained from the natural sciences to the *theoretical* understanding of art. Artists, whatever else they are, are craftspeople, who use the techniques of a given medium to fashion objects or performances that are designed to elicit particular responses. Good artists possess a vast *practical* knowledge of how the medium that they work *with* works *on* audiences; and one of the roles of the theorist of art is to explicate this knowledge with an explicitness and clarity which we do not expect from practitioners. Among the array of things that such practical knowledge encompasses is a knowledge not just of our cultural assumptions, habits, and shibboleths, but a knowledge of our universal, biological endowments.

The humanities and the natural sciences each give emphasis to different aspects of the world we inhabit, and humanistic knowledge cannot be replaced by the deliverances of natural science. But the world we inhabit is, in an important sense, one world—a world populated by different cultures and characterized by different levels of experience (animal and human, rational and emotional, mental and physical), but one world all the same. An insular humanism that disdains scientific insight, in the misguided belief in its complete autonomy from the business of the natural sciences, is a much impoverished one. For this reason, the humanities cannot simply turn its face away from the hypotheses and discoveries of science, including evolutionary science; and a human science confident of its own grounds and legitimacy will not feel the need to do so.

6

What Difference does it Make?

Humans are animals and everything we do lies within our biological potential.

Stephen Jay Gould

We, alone on earth, can rebel against the tyranny of the selfish replicators.

Richard Dawkins

Wittgenstein once derided the 'science of aesthetics', ascribing to it the apparently absurd goal of telling us 'what coffee tastes good'.[1] Wittgenstein's remark condenses a number of ideas relevant to the present work—chief among them the thought that the field of aesthetics is or might, in some sense, be defined as a *science*; that the business of the field of aesthetics is mainly or exclusively the phenomenon of 'taste' or evaluation; and that the matter of taste is intrinsically elusive, unpredictable, and idiosyncratic— and thus beyond the reach of any method which might be described as 'scientific'. Scepticism about aesthetics *as* a science, and of the relevance of scientific knowledge more widely *to* aesthetics, has, of course, been widespread since Wittgenstein dropped this pearl of wisdom. Writing during the heyday of Wittgenstein's influence on Anglo-American aesthetics, George Dickie argued that scientific, empirical knowledge, whatever its value elsewhere, simply had no role to play in our thinking about art and the aesthetic.[2] During the same period, as we saw in the Introduction, C. P. Snow's well-known critique of the deepening schism between the 'two cultures'—the human-istic ('literary intellectual') and the scientific, existing as largely independent bodies of thought and debate—received short shrift from F. R Leavis, who was, like Wittgenstein, confident of the conceptual and methodological autonomy of the humanities. In the German philosophical tradition, the same split is recognized in the distinction, perhaps most famously associated with Wilhelm Dilthey, between *Geisteswissenschaften* and *Naturwissenschaften*. More recently, and more immediately connected with our domain, Greg Currie has asked whether cognitive film theory might be better off sticking with folk psychology when considering questions of cinematic meaning— thereby suggesting that film theory might have little or nothing to gain by enlisting the big guns of scientific psychology.[3] Meanwhile, other fronts have been opened on the authority of science by post-structuralism, science studies, and by some strands of 'post-analytic' philosophy.

As the earlier chapters I hope have demonstrated, while the tide may not have turned, the waters are now much choppier. Running against the currents of scepticism, the last thirty years have seen the emergence of what we might call *cognitive aesthetics* (exemplified, for example, by the work of David Bordwell on film, Diana Raffman on music, Blakey Vermeule on literature, and Bruce McConachie on theatre) and *evolutionary aesthetics* (exemplified by the anthropologist Ellen Dissanayake, philosophers Denis Dutton and Stephen Davies, and 'literary Darwinists' such as Brian Boyd, Joseph Carroll, and Jonathan Gottschall)—the study of the creation and perception of art in the light of cognitive psychology, and evolutionary biology and psychology, respectively. Along with these movements we need to note various precursors and tributaries, including the cognitivist approach to art history pioneered by E. H. Gombrich, the tradition of *empirical aesthetics* (a lineage that goes back to Gustav Fechner and Hermann von Helmholtz, and continued in the work of Daniel Berlyne, Colin Martindale, and the recently established Max Planck Institute for Empirical Aesthetics in Frankfurt) and *neuroaesthetics* (best known through the interventions of V. S. Ramachandran and Semir Zeki). While none of these research programmes might purport to tell us exactly which kind of coffee tastes best, they are all fundamentally engaged in the business of situating—understanding and explaining—our experience of art in the context of human experience conceived naturalistically, that is, conceived as the experience of a particular sort of species under particular environmental conditions, and amenable to investigation by scientific methods. This broad programme of research does accommodate the idea that we humans do have certain evolved preferences and predispositions. Far from seeing art as a phenomenon that transcends our past and present material conditions, the ambition of cognitive and evolutionary aesthetics is to embed our understanding of art within them; to explain how distinctive aesthetic and artistic phenomena emerge from the general features of evolved human behaviour and cognition. In short, the overarching ambition of the programme is to develop and articulate a *naturalized aesthetics*, in the sense described in Chapter 1.

Of course, the goal of any given piece of research in any one of the specific fields described above may be much more modest or 'piecemeal', aiming simply to illuminate a specific aesthetic phenomenon via a concept borrowed from one or other of the natural sciences. In the long run, however, the viability of such 'locally' motivated borrowings will depend on the general coherence of integrating knowledge from the natural and the human sciences. So even where the question of the possibility of a naturalized aesthetics is not explicitly articulated, any argument which breaches the divide between the 'two cultures'—no matter how circumscribed its immediate concern—will implicitly invoke it. By the same token, the demonstration of the pertinence of this or that particular scientific concept to this or that specific aesthetic problem will provide much of the ammunition for the claim that a naturalistic approach to aesthetics in general is coherent and viable.

The emotions are of particular significance in this context for several reasons. The emotions are evidently an integral feature of ordinary existence; to live a normal human life is to live a life permeated with emotion. The emotions we experience ebb and flow in their intensity, but the complete absence of emotion is rather rare, and usually signals a pathology caused by a damaged emotion system (as seen for example in Antonio Damasio's studies of individuals suffering from damage to the frontal cortex).[4] Perhaps not surprisingly, then, emotions are widely regarded as central to our experience of most forms of art, though the nature and place of emotion in relation to art is the subject of much debate. So the emotions provide a central case study for the wider project of cognitive and evolutionary aesthetics.

Moreover, the study of emotion over the last 150 years provides in microcosm a picture of one of the fundamental controversies in the study of human behaviour at the heart of this book. On the one hand, there is the view that the emotions are (wholly or largely) universal, biological adaptations, apt to be explained by the methods of the natural sciences—to be treated as material phenomena with neural and physiological underpinnings, amenable to objective examination, dissection into distinct dimensions and variables, and thus controlled experimentation. By contrast there is the view that emotions are (wholly or largely) culturally varied phenomena, apt to be explored and understood by the methods of the human sciences—by the detailed exploration of cultural self-understanding as evidenced by the practices and artefacts of a culture, including the use of and debates around the concepts and language of emotion. In other words, the study of emotions, in general and in relation to art in particular, has been and is a key site for the conflict between *scientism* (the idea that nothing is beyond the purview of science) and *culturalism* (the idea that nothing human lies outside the scope of culture). The brand of naturalism advanced in the present work attempts to steer a course between these two positions, adopting some of the insights of both while avoiding their problems.

Culture and Biology

The culturalist account of emotion treats emotions as 'culturally constructed'. The emotions we feel and to which we ascribe meaning are on this view so thoroughly embedded within the particularities of culture that little in the way of emotional experience, beyond perhaps generic physiological arousal, can be said to be held in common across cultures. On this view, emotions 'reflect people's adherence to and participation in different ways of life', to borrow J. L. Mackie's characterization of moral codes.[5] Standing in strong contrast to this account is the theory of emotions as hard-wired 'affect programmes', in which emotions are defined in large part by specific neural and physiological architecture. On this account, emotions—or at least, the basic emotions, introduced in Chapter 5—are universally evident, with little or no significant variation in their expression or meaning across cultures. As Darwin put it, 'all the chief expressions exhibited by man are the same throughout the world'.[6] They are thus almost certainly part of our genetic inheritance. Where the strong biological account regards the experience of an emotion as akin to the perception of 'basic' (focal) colours—the perception of which appears not to vary across cultures[7]—the culturalist regards an emotional experience as more like the assumption and enacting of a socially prescribed 'role'.[8]

Each of these radical views recommends that we study the emotions through quite different methods—the methods of humanistic interpretation (such as the 'thick description' advocated by Clifford Geertz, discussed in Chapter 1), in the case of culturalism, and the methods of natural science, in the case of the biogenetic account. I will argue here that neither position—at least in their most extreme forms—is very plausible, or adequate to the task of providing a rich understanding of the emotions and their role in the arts. As Kim Sterelny insists, there is no

culture/biology divide, either in human phenotypes or in human environments. The environment does not segment into biological and cultural aspects. Food, for example, does not divide into items eaten solely for social or ritual reasons (communion wafers are the exception, not the rule) and mere metabolic servicing, when we shovel anything digestible down our throats. Finding, preparing, and eating food typically serves social as well as metabolic ends, and answers to cultural as well as ecological constraints.[9]

In his study of human violence, evolutionary psychologist Steven Pinker similarly stresses both the importance of culture in the explanation of human behaviour *and* the interaction between cultural norms and evolved psychology.[10] Returning to a theme from Chapter 1, I will thus also argue against the idea that a single 'method', characterizable in traditional terms as scientific-explanatory or humanistic-interpretative, is sufficient to this goal. Instead I will argue for a *biocultural* view which rejects the dichotomous views of both emotion and the study of emotion.

Before I turn to the biocultural model in detail, I want to say a few more words about the culturalist position, specifically regarding the motivations and logic that underlie it. The culturalist account of emotion is rooted in the fundamental philosophical insight that, among animals, humans are uniquely self-conscious and self-reflective. As we saw in Chapter 4, we are not merely conscious of various states of mind and body, but conscious that we are conscious of these states. As a consequence, we are able to 'stand outside' such states, and wonder about their origins and value to us, as both individuals and as members of communities; we possess the ability to assess rationally our states of being and mind. Now this self-conscious or 'self-interpreting' characteristic—characterized by Hegel as humanity's 'alienation' from an animal state of being[11]—is, I think, the ultimate justification for the culturalist dismissal of the relevance of the biological in the study of human life. The fact that we can stand outside whatever instincts, preferences, and predispositions we have inherited genetically renders these factors inert, it is implied. But there is a fallacy here. The fact of self-consciousness does not entail that the capacities and traits we inherit exert no pull on us. Consider the way in which perceptual illusions work upon us: we can come to know that the two parallel lines in the Müller-Lyer illusion are the same length, by measuring them, but we can't *perceive* them as equal in length; our visual experience is impervious to our knowledge. Similarly, my taste for meat may survive my decision to become a vegetarian on ethical grounds. Thus, it does not follow, from the fact that we are able to stand outside ourselves and reflect on our natural predispositions, that we can simply transcend these predispositions— that we can wipe the slate clean. In short, self-consciousness does not entail complete individual or cultural plasticity.

Moreover, even if we do grant a very high degree of such plasticity, culturalism is no better placed with respect to the question of determinism, and the scope of individual free will, than is bioculturalism. The individual can be conceived as thoroughly determined by socio-cultural forces—as in the once influential Althusserian model of 'interpellation'—just as much as a puppet of genetic evolution. Equally, other varieties of both culturalism and bioculturalism allow varying degrees of individual 'elbow room'. The question of individual free will is thus distinct from the question of the degree of independence of culture from biology. (A belief in *absolute freedom* is not plausible, but neither is it necessary for our intuitions regarding the autonomy and variability of culture. Perhaps it is more intractable as a symptom of a desire for human perfectibility.) Thus culturalists who believe that they are getting a high concentration of individual autonomy from culturalism have not read the philosophical small print.

The underlying logic of the biocultural view of emotion can be stated quite succinctly. Only a madman or a fool would deny the significance of culture—and thus of cultural variation—to human life. But from where does culture come in the first place? How does culture arise, if not from certain evolved features of the human species? Culture simply is a central feature of human nature, paradoxical as this may sound. Here it is valuable to mark a distinction between *metaculture*, that is *culture in general*—those evolved features of human psychology which both enable and demand culture—and the *specific cultures* which answer to this universal need. In stating that '[c]ultural learning is a cultural universal', Elliot Sober indicates how specific cultural ideas and practices sit against and are channelled through a back-drop of features uniform across cultures.[12] Culture in this general sense arises from the combination of three features of human nature: the intensely social cast of the human mind; its power and plasticity; and the variability of the environments in which human societies have survived and thrived. The enormous flexibility of the human mind has clear adaptive advantages, and in this sense there are grounds to think of culture itself as an adaptation.

More specifically, argues Richard Dawkins, culture may be regarded as a part of the *extended phenotype* of the human species; as much a part of our biology as the web is a part of the spider's biology.[13] While the genotype is the set of genes defining a species, the phenotype is the collection of attributes manifested by the genotype in an environment over the course of ontogeny.[14] The concept of the phenotype thus traditionally refers to the characteristic bodily form or 'morphology' of the species, but the concept has been 'extended' to encompass 'extracorporeal adaptations', like the beaver's dam and the spider's web.[15] Culture, and cultural variation, arise from and depend on our biology in just this way. Sober breaks cultural learning down into the transmission of traits via *vertical* (parent–offspring), *horizontal* (among peers), and *oblique* (intergenerational but not with kin—for example, between mentor and protégé) relationships, arguing that such learning is 'an important feature of the human phenotype'.[16] If the phenotype includes culture, as Sober's account of cultural learning implies, then it follows that culture is encompassed by biology. As Torben Grodal has suggested, the existence of cultural variation does not reflect the absence or transcendence of biological imperatives within human experience, but rather the complexity of human biology—the fact that we are shaped by a multitude of (sometimes competing) instincts.[17]

The metaphor of 'construction', then, so beloved of culturalists, is effective in making cultural difference more salient than cross-cultural similarity, but it is incoherent if it is offered as some sort of 'argument' showing the independence of culture from biology. Out of what is culture 'constructed', if not the tools and capacities bestowed upon us by our evolved natures? As Daniel Dennett argues, if we shy away from admitting our evolved biology into our explanations of culture, we will find ourselves reaching for 'skyhooks'—entities which we conjure up in order to fill explanatory gaps but which themselves float mysteriously without explanatory support—whence culture, or art, as the product of the 'human spirit'.[18] Dennett contrasts skyhooks with 'cranes', which, unlike skyhooks, 'have to be designed and built, from everyday parts already on hand', and 'located on a firm base of existing ground'.[19] In Dennett's terms, culture emerges and is built from the cranes of human biology.

It is thus nonsensical to speak of biology and culture as if they were *simply* opposed or 'alienated'. Every cultural act or event depends, ultimately, on some biological capacity; and conversely, even our most basic, instinctual, 'purely' biological needs must manifest themselves in a cultural context, given that such contexts are the naturally evolved settings for human action. As the anthropologist Donald Brown puts it, '[i]t is wrong to think that there is some sort of zero-sum game—even worse, a winner-takes-all game—between universals and the culturally particular or between biological and sociocultural approaches to anthropological problems'.[20] Of course, many fundamental physiological functions and processes in an important sense admit no cultural variation whatsoever. No set of cultural beliefs can change the fact that we see the still frames comprising a strip of film as a moving image when projected at the right speed. But even these physiological invariants occur in the context of cultural beliefs, so the invariant fact of filmic movement can be used in many ways. In just the same way, we saw in Chapter 3 that the hard-wired startle response can be used in films for a variety of purposes, and has been elaborated to varying degrees by different cultures (recall the *latah* of Malaysia). And the same is true for other basic physiological processes such as respiration, perspiration, sleeping, yawning, and defecation; processes which admit of either no, or very little, variation in their basic functioning. Beneath new culture lies old psychology; but the 'old psychology' of our biologically evolved dispositions can only be realized in and through particular cultural situations and habits. There is no 'pure' expression of biology, free of culture, but equally there is no expression of culture that does not depend more or less directly on a biological capacity. It's not that we should do away with our concepts of biology and culture. It is rather the relationship between them that is at stake here, and the problematic notion that culture is *essentially* divorced or alienated from biology.

Nevertheless, it is equally clear that, once culture is up and running, it throws up all manner of *byproducts*—effects, that is, which are not in themselves adaptive, but arise from ones that are adaptive. Dawkins quotes Ronald Pulliam and Christopher Dunford approvingly to the effect that cultural evolution 'owes its origin and its rules to genetic evolution, but it has a momentum all its own'.[21] This has important consequences for how we are to understand the idea of culture as an aspect of the extended human phenotype. For Dawkins, the legitimacy of extending the concept of the phenotype to 'extracorporeal' phenomena hinges on the fact that these structures still serve to enhance the odds that the genes of the organism will be passed onto the next generation. The beaver's dam is an adaptation precisely in this sense; the dam-building ability of beavers has been selected because, within the beaver's ecological niche, building a dam helps increase the chances that an individual member of the species will be around long enough to procreate. An 'animal artefact' like the beaver's dam 'can be regarded as a phenotypic tool by which that gene [the one responsible for the behaviour that produces the artefact] could potentially lever itself into the next generation'.[22] The dam in this sense is no different to, say, the beaver's teeth. Can we say that culture serves genetic survival in the same fashion and to the same extent? At a genetic level, culture offers fewer guarantees—is less effective from the viewpoint of the gene—than the more basic, physical animal artefacts that Dawkins discusses. *Is* culture plausibly thought of as an adaptation?

Dennett thinks we can conceive of culture in these terms, as is evident when he explicitly makes the link between culture and the extended phenotype.[23] What is not explicit in Dennett's account, however, is the way in which the conditions of inclusion within extended phenotypicality have been loosened by him. It is enough for Dennett that genetic evolution gives rise to culture; once in place, it need not continue to serve exclusively genetic ends. Given this, however, it may make more sense to think of culture as a byproduct rather than an adaptation. We might say that the psychological features underlying the emergence of culture—the power, flexibility, and sociability of the human mind—are adaptive, while holding that culture itself is a byproduct of these features. This allows us to make sense of and respect the fact that many cultural phenomena plainly do *not* serve genetic replication. A life of celibacy and devotion to the community beyond one's immediate kin is a common enough pattern in numerous cultures around the world, but it is a behavioural pattern with no payoff from the gene's 'point of view'. So while we can maintain that culture is a part of the extended human phenotype in that culture arises from our genetic evolution, and no mature human life is complete without development in and through cultural practices and representations, it is at best imprecise to claim, as Edward O. Wilson once notoriously did, that culture is 'on the leash' of our genes.[24] Too many particular cultural practices have evidently broken free of this leash. On the other hand, it is true that our genetic interests must, overall, be served to some considerable degree by the aggregate practices of a culture, or else that culture—and all the individuals and the genes which they bear—will be headed for a more or less rapid demise.

As part of the redrawing of our conceptual map, it is important to understand that in the scheme being proposed here 'biology' should not be understood as equivalent to 'genetics'. Genetics is obviously central to modern biology, but it is not the whole of it (Darwin, of course, had no concept of the gene). So long as biology also concerns itself with the phenotypes which develop on the basis of genotypes, this must be the case. If we accept that culture is part of the phenotype of the human species, then the logic of the biocultural position becomes clear: culture, as an aspect of the human phenotype, is a biological phenomenon, just as surely as is the beaver's dam. 'Humans are animals and everything we do lies within our biological potential', as Stephen Jay Gould puts it.[25] But culture is not thereby *genetic*, other than in the minimal and indirect sense that the human genotype includes genes for those aspects of mental plasticity, power, and sociability from which culture, and cultural variability, emerges.

So even strongly culturalist accounts must acknowledge some role for biology. Not only are culture and biology difficult to disentangle in human affairs, as Sterelny vividly demonstrates, but culture is dependent on biology. There are two aspects to this claim: one logical, the other empirical. The logical point is that the very idea of culture, and thus any particular claim about a culture, presupposes some background of basic human capacities that enable the development of cultures. A culturalist might insist on the enormous plasticity of human beings, but that very plasticity is then being presupposed as a basic attribute of the species. So in the case of emotion, a culturalist might plausibly deny that much is universal when it comes to emotions— they might adduce evidence to show that the circumstances eliciting emotions, the characterization of emotions, the expressions and other behaviours associated with emotions, and the regulation of emotion all show much more variation than consistency across cultures. But in showing this, they would necessarily make reference to lower-level items by virtue of which the comparison can be made: so they might, say, compare the 'affective life' or the 'feelings' or 'attitudes' of different cultures in order to reveal these marked differences, and in doing so they will have assumed something shared, albeit at a broader or lower level. For example, Catherine Lutz has no problem depending on a broad notion of 'emotional discourse' in her exploration of the Ifaluk even as she protests against the illicit 'naturalizing' of (what she regards as) parochially Western ideas about emotion; similarly, a generation earlier, Ray Birdwhistell saw no difficulty in leaning on 'emotional states' even as he argued there were no 'universal symbols' for such states.[26] But without implicitly universal concepts like 'emotional discourse' there would be no debate to be had; only if we assume that 'emotional states', or some kindred concept, applies universally, does it make sense to ask whether there are universal expressions corresponding to them. The positing of such concepts just seems to be dictated logically, once we agree that 'culture' describes an aspect of human existence, dependent on certain capacities of the species, an aspect of which points to variation which can be recognized— indeed which we are forced to recognize—when we compare human existence in different times and places. The culturalists can't have their cake and eat it: they can't have their differences without the concept of culture or the method of comparison, and this pairing of concept and method logically mandates a recognition of the human species as a biological kind.

But this logical admission doesn't specify where or at what level we will find the threshold between universal features and capacities of the species on the one hand, and culturally specific instantiations and elaborations of those features on the other hand. This is where the empirical aspect of the claim for the necessity of biology enters the picture. Granted that logically the very recognition of culture brings with it an assumption of underlying, shared biology, the ways in which biology and culture interact, with respect to different capacities, is a matter of empirical enquiry, as is the exact story of the emergence of culture from biological processes across evolutionary history and within the development of the individual. One may recognize the many pitfalls and the difficulty of empirical research, and acknowledge that we never reach more than plausible-but-provisional conclusions, but we cannot circumvent this empirical dimension. And given the fact that arguing the toss between culturalism and biologism on a priori grounds is a non-starter—because, as the logical argument shows, there is not really a choice to be made—the action will take place within this domain of empirical enquiry, and only a philosophical prejudice towards purely conceptual enquiry will make empirical debate seem like fruitless wheel-spinning.

For this reason I cannot entirely agree with Peter Goldie's lament that, when it comes to the debate between culturalism and evolutionary psychology, 'the best we can hope for is an endless debate about where to put the emphasis'—or rather, I can agree with the point, but not with the implied disappointment.[27] Much depends here on the force of 'endless': does Goldie mean 'provisional' or something more devastating, like 'undecidable' or 'arbitrary'? Scientific knowledge is by its nature provisional, and in that sense endless, but if we can reasonably argue about 'where to place the emphasis', then it cannot be a merely arbitrary or undecidable matter. Indeed, in his subsequent analysis, Goldie shows how, while always interacting in some way, the 'emphasis' on biology or culture falls differently with respect to different capacities (a reflexive eye blink is less 'developmentally open' than a sincere smile, according to Goldie). So the matter may be complex, and our theories always subject to revision, but that does not make the question of the relationship between evolution and culture trivial or fruitless.

Does the mutual dependence between human biology and human culture argued for here mean that biology and culture can never be in conflict? No. One of the ironies attending Dawkins's controversial place in contemporary debates around evolution is that, far from arguing for unadulterated genetic determinism through the concept of the 'selfish' gene, Dawkins is emphatic that humans are a species unlike any other precisely to the degree that they can transcend and exert a considerable measure of control over their genetic inheritance. The final line of the original edition of Dawkins's most famous work reads: 'We, alone on earth, can rebel against the tyranny of the selfish replicators.'[28] To this extent, Dawkins honours the arguments of earlier philosophers, like Kant and Hegel, who emphasized this special human characteristic. Biology and culture can certainly be in conflict—but to the extent that this formulation drives us back to the idea that biology and culture are two separate, internally coherent and self-sufficient systems, it is deeply misleading. Rather we need to recognize that within the sphere of 'bioculture' numerous different forces exist alongside one another, sometimes neatly codependent, sometimes delicately balanced, sometimes in conflict with one another. Sometimes the interests of genes and aspects of culture will conflict; but equally, we also find competition within the biological realm narrowly conceived, for example among the organs of an organism in the course of development.[29] The interaction among these forces need only be coherent enough for the system as a whole to persist; such interaction need not live up to some elevated and idealized standard of harmony and optimal functionality. Tension and conflict is thus an integral feature of culture as it is of the biosphere more generally, and it is thus a distorting simplification to suggest that the sole or prime location of conflict is the borderline between culture and biology; for there is no such borderline.

The Emotions in Biocultural Perspective

What do the emotions look like when understood as a biocultural phenomenon? From such a perspective, an emotion is a dynamic somatic and cognitive apprehension of the significance of some phenomenon—an object, a person, an event, a situation—by an agent. So conceived, an emotion is an 'embodied appraisal', to borrow Jesse Prinz's formulation.[30] The target or *object* of an emotion may be real or imagined; thus, for example, an event eliciting an emotion may be actual or fictional. Emotions are *dynamic* in that they are best characterized as processes rather than simple states; *somatic* in that they typically enlist various bodily systems, like the viscera and the peripheral nervous system, as well as the neural systems on which our cognitive states are usually held to depend. (In the next chapter, I examine the notion of the 'extended mind' and related theories that contest the assumption that cognition is 'brainbound'.)

An emotion begins with what Jenefer Robinson terms an *affective appraisal*, characterized by its speed and relative coarseness—it is, as we say, 'quick and dirty'; a 'gut reaction'.[31] In this respect, emotions are more like perceptions than beliefs: they register events in the environment in a direct fashion, they are fast (and are thus prone to similar sorts of error as perception), and perhaps, in some respects, they are cognitively impenetrable (that is, unaffected by background knowledge).[32] 'Like perceptions, emotions can be inaccurate or even unjustified', Prinz avers. 'But they can also be revelatory. They can deliver information that helps us assess how we are faring. They often allow us to pick up this information before we have made any pertinent judgments.'[33] The startle response—explored at some length in Chapter 3—while not usually regarded as an emotion proper, might be thought of as a model of this first, initiating stage of emotion—a dramatic, reflex physiological reaction which stops us in our tracks and redirects our attention. This initial appraisal is affective—'non-cognitive'—in the specific sense that it occurs, neurally, via particular pathways which bypass those parts of our brain responsible for fine-grained cognition (the frontal cortex).[34] Recognizing and characterizing the first stage of the emotional process in this way marks off the account of emotions presented here, informed by evidence from neuroscience and evolutionary theory, from more purely 'cognitivist' or 'judgementalist' accounts.

An affective appraisal sets in train a subsequent process of cognitive monitoring— where, once again, 'cognitive' is quite specifically defined in terms of cognition correlated with activity in the frontal cortex. Such cognitive monitoring itself begins rapidly, so it is only a matter of some additional fractions of a second before we might judge that, for example, what we took for a snake on the path is in fact a stick. But though it begins quickly, the process of cognitive monitoring may persist for much longer periods, through a series of cognitive reappraisals. How long will depend on the nature of the *emotion episode*—'the emotional transaction between a person and his or her environment', a transaction which may be 'composed of several subevents but that is perceived to have an internal consistency'.[35] Once I'm certain that the stick isn't a snake, no further appraisal is necessary (though the fright of the initial affective appraisal will keep me alert to further snake-shaped items that I might encounter on the path). But where, say, I've had an argument with a colleague over what I took to be a slight regarding the quality of my research, my initial cognitive evaluation of the triggering remark ('yes, he really did mean to offend me') might give way to a whole series of re-evaluations ('perhaps I offended him with that earlier remark'; 'he didn't mean to offend me, even if he did'; and so on). At the extreme, entire relationships can be characterized by the ambivalence of such a modulating series of appraisals.

Note also, as this second example suggests, that the initial rapid and coarse-grained affective appraisals characteristic of emotions can be triggered not only by simple physical events—the sight of a snake-shaped object, a loud noise—but by complex cognitions,[36] where we might speak of an emotional response to an 'internal environment'. Recently, for example, I was combing through several months' worth of bank statements when it dawned on me that I had been charged large amounts of interest on payments I had quite forgotten to make. The moment of realization was an emotional one; from virtual somnabulance, a rush of adrenalin woke me up and focused my attention on the penalty charges and their causes.

In other words, I was alarmed by the charges and, once cognitive appraisal had been achieved, aghast at my own stupidity and forgetfulness. It is not a coincidence that we sometimes describe such complex but sudden realizations with simpler physical models—'I felt the ground go from beneath me'; 'I felt like I'd been slapped in the face'—because such realizations can trigger affective appraisals of the same type and intensity as purely physical perceptions. *Upheavals of Thought*, the title of Martha Nussbaum's major work on emotion, provides another example of the casting of complex evaluative judgements in physical terms.[37]

The 'front end' of the emotion process—the initial affective appraisal—seems to be characterized by the limited but universal range of reactions associated with the notion of basic emotions: surprise, fear, happiness, anger, disgust, sadness, and possibly shame. These emotions include characteristic facial expressions, of the type discussed in Chapter 5. Subsequent cognitive monitoring, however, allows for more fine-grained distinctions that give rise to complex emotions—and it is evidently here that cultural and personal background will come to play an important role. Note, however, that on this theory, the complex emotions arise from the cruder, more basic, hard-wired, universal appraisals, and 'cluster' around them. This picture of the emotions—as falling into families, encompassing both basic emotions and more subtle, complex, cognitively differentiated and culturally informed emotions—goes back to Darwin, whose book on the emotions is largely organized around emotions clustered in this way.[38] Perhaps not surprisingly, this is also the view of the prime contemporary neo-Darwinist theorist of emotion, Paul Ekman, who recognizes within the family of 'happiness' (to take one case) at least twelve emotional subtypes, including amusement, wonderment, excitement, and other states most economically captured by terms in other languages, such as the Italian *fiero*, naming a feeling of intense satisfaction derived from the accomplishment of a sustained and difficult task.[39]

Note how much space is allowed for cultural variation here, even given the biological constraints on culture implicit in the biocultural model of the emotions. The complex emotions which admit of significant cultural variation are not summoned up out of thin air—or drawn on a blank slate—but built from and operate within a terrain defined and circumscribed by our evolutionary inheritance, as manifest in the basic emotions. There *is* indefinite scope for the elaboration, blending, and nuancing of such basic emotions within 'different ways of life', but the emotions defined by specific cultures, and thus the ones that we regard ourselves as feeling, do not float free of biology.

Finally, while we can for analytic or experimental purposes discriminate distinct emotion episodes, as I have been, in reality our emotional experience is characterized by feedback, overlap, and considerable flux: emotions often change their hue and sometimes their colour through cognitive monitoring, and various 'streams' of the overall emotional process will flow into one another, creating more or less complex 'blends' of the basic and the 'higher' emotions. Thus, for example, anger at some perceived slight may transform into embarrassment or regret at having reacted with anger, not because

I cease to believe that my anger is justified but because I believe that the display of anger in a particular social context was inappropriate (see the discussion of 'display rules' in Chapter 5). Michael Newman suggests that in one scene in *Welcome to the Dollhouse* (Todd Solondz, 1995), 'we might believe that [the central character] is *shamed* by being told she has no friends, *angered* by being the one who got in trouble when the instigators got off, *afraid* of being punished, and *remorseful* about having caused her teacher harm'.[40] We should also note that because much of the appraisal process— cognitive as well as affective—occurs beneath consciousness (a theme to which we will return in Chapter 7), and because it is so complex and mutable, the words we use to describe our emotions are best thought of as 'summary judgements' of typically quite extended and multi-layered emotional experiences.[41] Chapter 8 focuses on the unique properties of such episodes as they are embodied in narrative artworks.

The fluid complexity of emotional experience—with its varied degrees of con-sciousness and the interplay between immediate reaction and subsequent rounds of cognitive assessment—is well captured in the novel *Thinks...* (2002) by David Lodge. Ralph Messenger has just discovered that his wife Carrie has been pursuing an affair, and he has been turning over in his mind various arguments and counter-arguments about his situation and what he should do:

Ralph did not formulate these arguments in... explicit terms, but they were, as we say, at the back of his mind, as he raged inwardly at Carrie's treachery, her appalling choice of a lover, and the insult to his pride and self-esteem. Gradually they exerted a cooling influence on his thoughts of retribution and revenge. He grew calmer and more contemplative; his driving, dangerously fast at the beginning of the journey, had become more controlled by the time he reached the outskirts of Cheltenham; his mood, when he entered the house on Pitville Lawn, was surly rather than angry.[42]

Note also the significance of *mood* in the fictional action that Lodge narrates here. His use of the term roughly accords with the distinction, widely accepted in the philosophy and psychology of emotion, between strict emotions and their affective cousins, moods: while an emotion is an affective state directed towards an object (grief, for example, at the loss of a loved one), a mood is a more diffuse affective state lacking an object in this sense. One can simply feel more or less gloomy, or upbeat, or anxious, without this feeling being directed towards any particular object. In *Thinks...*, Ralph's anger—an emotion with a clear object, his wife's secret affair—gradually dissipates into a 'surly' mood. As Greg Smith has argued, these objectless affective states play an important role in orienting and priming us for more specific emotions, not least in our experience of fiction films.[43]

An Example: *Heimat* and Emotion

With this theory of the emotions in place, we can now ask: of what relevance is such an account—one informed in detail by psychological, evolutionary, and neuroscientific research on the emotions—to our experience and understanding of a work of film art? In Chapters 2 and 3 the focus was on the *elicitation* of affective responses from film spectators, in the form of states like suspense, empathy, and the startle response; and in Chapter 7 we return to explore empathy in more detail. Here, however, I pick up on the exploration of the *representation* of emotions, and our *recognition* of the emotional states of characters in films (albeit with an eye to the ways in which 'cold', cognitive recognition may blur into an 'hot', enactive, and embodied responses, at least in some contexts), initiated in Chapter 5. I want to take as my example here the epic German film cycle *Heimat*, comprised of *Heimat: Eine deutsche Chronik/A German Chronicle*; *Die zweite Heimat - Chronik einer Jugend/The Second Heimat: Chronicle of a Generation*; and *Heimat 3: Chronik einer Zeitenwende/A Chronicle of Beginnings and Endings* (Edgar Reitz, 1984, 1992, and 2004). My reasons for doing so are worth spelling out explicitly.

First, as a sophisticated and widely praised work of art, *Heimat* might be regarded as the (natural?) possession of the culturalist. To understand and appreciate such a work it is necessary to embed oneself in the culture from which the work arose. A corollary of this view is that only those fully educated and immersed in the relevant culture can hope to experience the work fully. That makes me—a British person with only indirect knowledge of German culture and history, and almost entirely ignorant of the German language—at least a partial outsider; what sense then can I make of this work, and on what basis?

Second, *Heimat* is not a Hollywood film. According to one line of argument, because Hollywood films—or at least, Hollywood blockbusters—are made with the ambition of succeeding in the widest possible range of international markets, they tend to ground themselves in universal situations and psychological capacities to a greater extent than do non-Hollywood films. That is, Hollywood films are a prime example of what Noël Carroll terms 'mass art'.[44] This second motivation for choosing *Heimat* is, then, the flip side of the first. Perhaps blockbusters, with their emphasis on primal thrills and spills, can be illuminated by evolutionary psychology, but what about works directed towards narrower audiences possessing specific sorts of cultural knowledge? In addressing this question and taking *Heimat* as a case study, I also aim to rebut the charge that a naturalistic approach has an in-built bias towards the 'average, standardised' work and is especially 'attuned to the dominant cinema'.[45]

My third and final reason for choosing *Heimat* as a case study pertains to a particular cultural tradition of considerable significance to the background and style of Reitz's epic work: the tradition of European artistic modernism. *Heimat* is a work of late modernism, one might say; it wears its air of self-consciousness and experimentalism lightly but persistently. To the modernist sensibility, the easy cross-cultural accessibility of Hollywood fare is an intellectually nutritionless gruel—or worse, a con trick, claiming to find universal interests where it in fact imposes culturally specific ones, 'naturalizing' culture in the derogatory sense of the term associated above all with the Roland Barthes of *Mythologies*.[46] In the most extreme cases, modernist artists explicitly set themselves 'against nature'.[47] Modernist filmmaking, then, promises to pose a different and more severe challenge to bioculturalism than the style of international popular filmmaking embodied by Hollywood product. I choose *Heimat* precisely as a difficult test for the biocultural account of the emotions advanced here.

I want to focus here on a single scene from the final installment of *Heimat 3*, 'Abschied von Schabbach'/'Goodbye to Schabbach'. Although the scene is of modest dramatic and emotional scale, it nevertheless exemplifies the emotion-laden interaction that constitutes the fabric of fiction films in general. Moreover, as the scene occurs in the last episode of the third series, after roughly fifty hours of drama, it carries considerably more dramatic weight than it might appear to, taken in isolation. The scene is concerned with two of *Heimat*'s central characters, Hermann Simon (Henry Arnold) and Clarissa Lichtblau (Salome Kammer). The Simon family constitutes the dramatic centre of gravity across all three series of *Heimat*. Hermann is the third son of Maria Simon, the figure around whom much of the first *Heimat* revolves. Hermann makes his appearance during the first series, and becomes the closest thing to a protagonist possessed by the second and third series. In the second series, which focuses on Hermann's early adulthood in Munich, Hermann enters into an intense, romantic relationship with Clarissa, a fellow music student. They split up, but some twenty-five years later, in the action narrated by *Heimat 3*, they meet by coincidence and enter once again into a romantic involvement.

The scene in question is significant in that it is woven into the storyline concerning Clarissa's strong sense of autonomy and independence, and her ambivalent relationship with her mother, Frau Lichtblau (Edith Behleit). Clarissa shares an intense bond with her mother, who raised her as a single parent. Advancing into middle age, however, Clarissa often finds her mother a domineering and suffocating presence. In the scene in question, Hermann and Clarissa are clearing Hermann's flat, which has become redundant now that they have consolidated their life as a couple around a restored house overlooking the Rhine, close to the village of Schabbach. The mood of the scene—its broad, orienting affective tone—is nostalgic, relaxed, and reflective, as the sale of the flat reminds them of times past. A note of deep anxiety sounds in the scene, however, when Hermann's buoyant enthusiasm regarding the future elicits Clarissa's admission that, following her illness—earlier in series 3, she has been afflicted by cancer—such feelings of unbounded optimism are no longer within her grasp. Hermann, Clarissa, and the property agent assisting them move towards the exit of the flat, discussing the business of some missing keys. As Clarissa exits the flat smiling, her eyes follow a pair of removal men carrying boxes down the stairs. Clarissa's eyes are thereby led to the sight of her mother who is ascending the stairs. This is the point at which the more marked 'emotional action' in the scene begins.

We can break down the emotion episode that the scene will dramatize into three phases or 'subevents'. The first of these begins as Clarissa catches sight of her mother. The smile on her face—expressing the generally easy-going and convivial mood of the scene thus far—quite suddenly disappears at this moment of recognition. Her face literally drops (Figures 6.1a–6.1b). This is the moment of affective appraisal—the initiating moment in a new cycle of emotion, marking the break with the previous mood and its associated emotions. The emotion Clarissa experiences is surprise, or some variant thereof; notably, however, her face does not manifest the characteristic expression of surprise (other than, perhaps, in the most attenuated fashion). The disappearance of her smile, however, along with the immediate and larger context, makes it quite plain that her response is one of surprise. (As I stressed in Chapter 5, in relation to the notion of situational understanding, our grasp of character emotions is not reliant only on the presence of facial expressions and other overt emotion cues.) The initial affective appraisal is very quickly succeeded by the process of cognitive monitoring, evident in Clarissa's movement towards her mother and the restoration of a smile, albeit of a more tentative sort (Figure 6.1c). Having digested the surprise and its cause—the unexpected appearance of her mother—Clarissa is now puzzling over its significance.

As Clarissa moves down the stairs to greet and assist her mother—who is struggling up the last of what appear to be several flights—a cut to a new shot reveals Hermann and the property agent moving out into the stairwell. Hermann's happy expression has disappeared as well, but where Clarissa regains her composure quickly and smiles again, if only mildly, as she approaches her mother, a look of troubled concern or *consternation* persists on his face (his knitted brows suggesting irritation, even a hint of anger). The property agent standing alongside Hermann, meanwhile, continues to smile blandly, as if there has been no fundamental change in the emotional tenor of the action (Figure 6.1d). Not only does she fail to grasp that the unheralded arrival of Clarissa's mother might be worrisome—rather than an occasion for joy—throughout the scene she appears to be oblivious to both Clarissa's and Hermann's expressions of concern.

A cut takes us back to a medium shot of the mother ascending the final flight of stairs, facing us, while Clarissa, with her back to the camera, descends them. During this action, Clarissa's mother reveals that she has not merely made her way from her retirement home in Wasserburg to visit her daughter and son-in-law, she has *run away* from the home, which she has come to loathe. This revelation initiates the second phase of the emotion episode, for it is at this moment that the deeper implications of her appearance at the flat start to become apparent. The contrast between the first and second phases of the emotion episode shows how emotions may be initiated by both complex cognitions and relatively simple physical events: where the initial surprise is triggered by Clarissa's mother's appearance, the alarm of this second phase is elicited by the cognitive apprehension that Frau Lichtblau has fled from her retirement home. The triggering of a new affective appraisal—and thus a new 'subevent' in the emotion episode—becomes evident when Clarissa turns back towards Hermann, her face now showing an expression of deep anxiety or alarm, most evident in Clarissa's frowning (resembling Hermann's expression from the moment of the mother's arrival) (Figure 6.2a). Here it is not merely a case of her

Figures 6.1a–6.1d An emotion episode unfolds in *Heimat 3* (Edgar Reitz, 2004).

smile disappearing, as at the moment of the initial affective appraisal, but rather of a new expression taking its place. A reverse shot of Hermann and the agent dwells on Hermann's continuing anxiety over the situation, compounded in his case by an evident disquiet with the presence of the agent, his eyes nervously flicking in her direction as he tries to maintain his composure.

Now sitting with her mother on the stairs, while Hermann and the agent look down on them from the landing above, Clarissa talks through the situation with her mother. We might mark the beginning of the third phase of the emotion episode at the point when Clarissa's mother declares her desire to move in with Clarissa and Hermann. I suggest this moment might mark a fresh affective appraisal because Clarissa reacts, immediately and physically, to this new twist: her face drops as she recoils, literally pulling away from her mother. But Clarissa is now well into the business of what Robinson, following psychologist Richard Lazarus, describes as *coping* with her emotion.[48] She is not merely cognitively monitoring it—thinking through what it is that she has reacted to affectively, what it means for her, for her mother, for her relationship with Hermann (or so we can reasonably surmise); she is also considering what it is appropriate and strategically wise for her to express visibly—to display—or to mask, and how to manage the demands made upon her by the situation which has prompted her emotional response. Thus, very soon after the affective 'jolt' carried by her mother's excited grasp of the idea of moving into the house on the Rhine, Clarissa produces the most palpable example in the sequence of a *social smile* (Figure 6.2b)—a smile adopted by her in order to offer reassurance to her mother, but one cutting against the grain of her own felt emotion (the characteristic dynamic of the social smile, as we saw in contrasting it with the Duchenne smile in Chapter 5).

In addition to the absence of muscular activity around the eyes, a social smile may possess other distinctive, tell-tale features arising from the combination of feeling and foresight experienced here by Clarissa, the underlying feeling 'leaking' through the strategically adopted expression. Discussing the 'leakage' of 'micro expressions' into the face, Ekman argues that '[a] false expression can be betrayed in a number of ways: it is usually very slightly asymmetrical, and it lacks smoothness in the way it flows on and off the face'.[49] While it is difficult to judge the symmetricality of Clarissa's expression, since she is depicted in profile at the moment she adopts the social smile, it is certainly true that her expression 'lacks smoothness', the smile only fleetingly and incompletely masking the underlying expression of perplexed concern.

The scene concludes with these various 'spikes' of emotional intensity levelling off, leaving us with a new, sober mood quite distinct from the mood that dominates the first half of the scene, before Clarissa's mother arrives. This disparity in mood is a qualified one: as I noted earlier, the gloomier mood is adumbrated through Clarissa's expression of anxiety over her health. And the new mood is not entirely downbeat— witness the genuine relief evident in the faces of both Clarissa and Hermann as the scene concludes (Figure 6.2c). Hermann's frown has finally dissipated. Nevertheless the mood we are left with contrasts palpably with the mood at the outset of the scene.

Figures 6.2a–6.2c The emotion episode draws to a close.

Ironically, the agent, still lagging behind the emotional pace, looks rather forlorn as Clarissa and Hermann relax at the end of the scene. One might wonder about the purpose of this character and her incongruous expressions: what might Reitz hope to achieve by making her so salient in the scene? A more straightforward treatment of this character would, I think, have involved blocking and framing her as part of the background, or perhaps providing some ruse for her exit. Instead, she remains an active presence in the scene, drawing Hermann's attention along with ours. The agent complicates and, to a degree, interferes with the main emotional axes of the drama, those running between Clarissa and her mother, Clarissa and Hermann, and Hermann and his mother-in-law. The agent's obtuseness is both puzzling and faintly comic; the main effect is to qualify the melodramatic intensity of the scene. In this sense, we can understand the agent as a manifestation of *Heimat*'s modernism. To be sure it is a small and subtle example; but the subtlety is part of the distinctive character of *Heimat*'s modernism. The agent's presence disrupts the flow of the central emotional drama, creating a few eddies and whirlpools in the course of its movement; a miniature Brechtian *Verfremdungseffekt*. This will seem like a less surprising claim if we remind ourselves of the more overtly modernist aspects of *Heimat*: its mutating use of colour and monochrome footage; its narrative disjunctions between and within episodes, redolent of the 'leaps' and 'curves' Brecht advocated in place of narrative continuity; and its focus on modernist musical aesthetics through the figure of Hermann, who emerges as the dominant figure in the series taken as a whole. It is also significant in this context that *Heimat* was conceived by Edgar Reitz in part as a rejoinder to the US television series *Holocaust* (Marvin J. Chomsky, 1978). The handling of the incongruous minor character in this scene is symptomatic of Reitz's refusal of the full-blooded, 'Manichaean' melodrama of *Holocaust*, along with his commitment to an alternative but still emotional form of drama: a kind of synthesis of Brecht's 'epic' and 'dramatic' modes.[50]

Culture and Emotion

What of the cultural dimensions of the situation that this scene dramatizes? Is there nothing here which demands explanation in less-than-universal terms? Of course, the action described involves particular characters and circumstances. Compared with much of the action of the first *Heimat* series—which encompasses the period of Nazi rule—however, the action here looks pretty 'generic', in the sense of not being highly distinctive of a particular culture. But the culturalist is not only, or even primarily, concerned with cases of such spectacularly distinctive social and political history. The culturalist is at least as interested in cultural particularity as it is manifest in the ordinary and everyday (and of course, one of the most remarkable features of the first *Heimat* is its representation of the period of National Socialism as a string of mostly everyday events). And at this level, two or three items do stand out.

First and most obviously, there is language. Fluent comprehension of a given language gives us direct access to a world of expressive and normative subtleties that we will otherwise struggle to grasp. But the culturalist tradition vastly overinflates the extent to which ignorance of a language bars us from comprehending actions undertaken by speakers of that language. Subtitles, and more extended critical commentary, do the work here. Comprehension of interactions conducted in languages with which we are unfamiliar will be relatively indirect and difficult, but not in principle impossible, as the more radical strains of culturalism would have us believe. Many languages possess simple terms for emotions that can only be translated into other languages using more elaborate phrases, that is, by taking emotions or attitudes embodied by simple terms in the translating language, and then qualifying and elaborating on these terms. Yiddish, for example, contains the word *naches*, which expresses the idea of pride in the achievements of one's children.[51] Or, to take a family of examples closely connected with the mood of nostalgia evoked by the sequence from *Heimat* explored here: Portuguese *suadade*, Welsh *hiraeth*, and German *Sehnsucht*, all express a particular variation on an emotional state of painful, nostalgic yearning. (Reitz's 2013 prequel to the *Heimat* cycle explicitly builds the German concept into its title: *Die andere Heimat—Chronik einer Sehnsucht*.) Just as *naches* articulates a specific form of pride, so these words express a particular form of longing. The nuances of each concept are attributable to the place of the word and concept within their respective languages and cultures; and yet it is perfectly possible to recognize these culturally specific terms as expressive of closely related forms of emotional experience. The act of translation forces us through a process of semantic unpacking of such single terms, teasing out their specific implications and associations.[52]

The meaning available through translation is thus less concise, less direct, and less automatic than the meaning conveyed in the original language; but there is no reason to believe that translation does not enable robust understanding of initially unfamiliar emotion concepts. Indeed, were this not the case, we would not be able to incorporate individual words from other languages into the lexicon of our primary language; there would be no *schmucks* or *schlubs*, and we would have nothing to *kvetch* about. Lack of fluency in a language obviously throws up practical difficulties in comprehension, but it does not erect a metaphysical barrier.[53] Radical scepticism is no more warranted here than it is in any other practical domain of communication. Moreover, since science only claims to deliver provisional and fallible knowledge about the world, radical scepticism is an ineffective sword to wield against it: if neither the everyday pragmatist nor the fallibilist scientist pretend to *absolute certainty*, the radical sceptic really has nothing at which to aim.

In what other ways does culture manifest itself, in addition to language? At the most basic level, there is 'local' knowledge of such things as geography. Few non-German viewers will have any precise sense of the location in Germany of Wasserburg; and this makes it difficult to gauge just how far Clarissa's mother has travelled, how much effort was involved, and what risks were taken. But it is easy to gain this knowledge, and once gained, we have no difficulty in working it into the stock of knowledge we draw upon to interpret the scene. A good many Germans are also probably ignorant of the exact location of Wasserburg as well; there seems to be no difference in principle between the way a German, and a non-German, viewer would plug, or cope with, this gap in their cultural knowledge.

Then there is knowledge of more intangible factors, like social norms—and one such norm that impinges directly on the action here concerns attitudes towards parents and older people. What obligations would children be expected to fulfil towards their parents in this culture? Is the housing of parents in retirement institutions accepted or frowned upon? Here the picture is much messier, in several ways. The very existence of retirement homes indicates their legality and perhaps their basic respectability, but attitudes to such institutions are likely to vary considerably among different social groups and individuals (just as, say, attitudes towards abortion or euthanasia vary). Much of the tension of the scene derives from the very fact that it touches directly on this delicate matter. But how do we cultural outsiders access all of this? The simple answer is: it is just the fact that these issues are *dramatized* in the scene that allows us, gradually, to understand them. To dramatize something is to make it salient, to bring it to the surface, to scrutinize it, to make apparent aspects of the phenomenon in question which would normally be implicit. Drawing upon our more basic capacities for grasping social interactions—including not only our knowledge of emotions through their expression, as explored in this chapter, but our capacity for joint attention discussed in Chapter 1, and our capacity for empathy addressed in Chapters 2, 3, and 7—we come to understand the ambivalence that Clarissa feels towards her mother: the blend of fear, concern, and duty that we witness in the scene. Ageing, and the care of parents and the elderly, are themselves universal, biologically given problems, and this provides any viewer with a starting point from which they can begin to discern the specific attitudes towards an aged and vulnerable parent in the scene, and to gauge the relationship of these attitudes to prevailing social norms.

Consideration of this example—of attitudes and obligations towards the elderly—raises a further important point. The scope of cultural norms and assumptions varies enormously. On the one hand, there are a multitude of assumptions which are shared by Western Europeans; others that are shared by Europeans more generally; still others that are common currency for some Europeans and North Americans. These facts motivate and license our use of such vague concepts as 'the West', or 'Anglo-American' culture. On the other hand, the notion of *subculture* arose in recognition of the fact that, at least in large-scale societies, there is likely to be significant variation and conflict among the groups comprising such a society. For these reasons there are few, if any, sharp boundaries between cultures. Cultures overlap and interconnect with one another in much more complex ways, and cannot be modelled on the geographical boundedness of nation states, nor even the more fluid form of language communities. Thus in thinking about many social norms, like norms pertaining to the treatment of the elderly, our assumptions about who will be 'inside' and who 'outside' the culture may need to be drastically revised. Granting the earlier point about the variation that is likely to exist within a large, modern society towards an issue such as care of the elderly, a British and German viewer are likely to share preconceptions about the issue and the range of attitudes it elicits, precisely because both are from modern European liberal democracies. Thus the ways in which and the extent to which one is an 'insider' or an 'outsider' to a culture may vary considerably depending on the specific dimension of culture at stake.[54]

Emotions as Cultural Bridgeheads

I said at the outset of this analysis of *Heimat* that while Hollywood films might be regarded as plausible objects of universalistic explanations, because they are fashioned to reach a wide international audience, works like Reitz's trilogy offer a sharp challenge to the naturalist theorist because of their greater cultural specificity. We can now see that this is only a half-truth, however. Art cinema, along with the film festival culture through which it now exists, are both themselves profoundly international phenomena. Given the complex entanglements among cultures, and the long and continuous history of interaction between societies through trade, war, and imperialism, art films like *Heimat* are far from obscure, inward-looking objects, closed to all but the members of their host culture. Moreover, as I indicated in Chapter 1, a naturalized aesthetics needs to accommodate cultural specificity even as it challenges culturalism; the present chapter lays out how that challenge is met.

Where, then, does all this leave us with respect to the question I ask in the title of this chapter, and repeatedly across this book: what difference does the array of scientific research on emotion that I've drawn on and alluded to make to what we might say about a film and our experience of it? The first thing to note is that it provides us with a keener understanding of what an emotion is, and allows us to propose critical descriptions and interpretations that are sensitive to features of the emotions of characters and spectators which might otherwise go unnoticed. In other words, we gain in descriptive and explanatory nuance.

Second, the fact that the scientifically informed theory of emotion advanced here proves to be sensitive to many of the expressions and gestures we witness in *Heimat* lends credence to the idea, advanced in Chapter 5, that most filmmaking, indeed most depictive art, works from a mimetic basis, adopting and adjusting the everyday forms of emotional expression—many of them universal or widely dispersed across numerous cultures—for particular artistic ends, rather than disregarding or rejecting them. *Heimat* is hardly a work of unalloyed aesthetic realism; and yet its performance style answers to many of the patterns of behaviour that we encounter in reality.

Third, and leading on from this second point, when we ascribe broad and basic emotion types to ourselves and others, in engaging with life and with movies, we are latching on to real features of the world—of the embodied agents we refer to as people or characters—rather than projecting or imposing 'assorted contemporary Western ideas...onto the experience of others', as Lutz would have it.[55] Our understanding will be incomplete without a proper understanding of cultural (and indeed, still more local) context, but it is not in principle false. Our apprehensions of the affective states of others through facial and other forms of expression may constitute rudimentary interpretations, but they are not intrinsic misinterpretations.

One of the questions I have been asking in this case study on *Heimat* is, in effect: how does this sequence mobilize our emotions? This is surely a reasonable question to ask in the context of aesthetic enquiry. And to answer it we must make recourse to a variety of types of knowledge, from the very specific (attitudes towards emotional drama within the German modernist tradition) to the much more general (the biological basis of human emotion and its expression). Once more, as I argued in Chapter 1, no simple division of labour between methods appropriate to 'explanation' on the one hand, and interpretative 'understanding' on the other, proves adequate to the task at hand.

Thus the biocultural account of the emotions advanced here suggests that, in engaging with works from cultures more or less distant from our home culture, our knowledge of emotion and emotional expression is one of the more important things that allows us to navigate them. Emotional expressions provide a kind of foothold for viewers which allows them to understand even highly complex, and culturally specific, ideas and representations (to be sure, in combination with other such footholds arising from other cross-cultural constants, as well as other kinds of 'local' knowledge spectators glean from films themselves). To this extent, the advocates of silent internationalism, like Béla Balázs, were right. As we saw in Chapter 5 and have seen again here, basic emotion expressions are not hermeneutically self-sufficient, since any such expression can only be fully understood in context; to understand an expression of anger properly, we have to know the object of the anger. By the same token, the meaning of an image or sequence cannot be a matter of context 'all the way down', as we would then face the problem of an infinite regress of contexts; indeed, the very distinction between 'text' and 'context' would be lost. So basic emotion expressions perform a vital role as expressive or semantic 'primitives', enabling the search for meaning to begin, *in media res*, irrespective of context.

When examined from the biocultural perspective, then, the interdependence of the universal and cultural dimensions of emotional experience comes to the fore, sharply contrasting with the unitary emphasis placed on culture by culturalists, for whom, in the words of Greg Smith, 'emotions cannot be understood outside of culture and the shaping forces of society'.[56] If we construe this statement to mean 'a given emotion episode cannot be understood *fully* outside of its context, including pertinent cultural norms', then it would seem that the biocultural position developed here is not irreconcilable with culturalism. But if we interpret Smith's statement as an endorsement of the view that 'emotions in general cannot be understood *at all* outside of culture', then no reconciliation is possible. Taken to such an extreme, the culturalist position leaves us with a mystery, for it is unclear how a developing child or a visiting adult could ever begin to understand a specific culture if there are no footholds beyond or beneath or threading through culture. But this is a feat that every reader of this book will have performed at least once in their lives. It is not the least of the virtues of the biocultural theory presented here that it explains this rather central fact about human experience.

7

Empathy, Expansionism, and the Extended Mind

Fever Pitch is about being a fan. I have read books written by people who obviously love *football*, but that's a different thing entirely; and I have read books written, for want of a better word, by hooligans, but at least 95 per cent of the millions who watch games every year have never hit anyone in their lives. So this is for the rest of us, and for anyone who has wondered what it might be like to be this way.

Nick Hornby

Some people thought he was crazy because they couldn't understand why a man would constantly be playing a guitar all the time. But basically what he was doing was making this instrument an extension of his body.

Billy Cox, on Jimi Hendrix

Commenting on the landmark Pink Floyd album *The Dark Side of the Moon*, bassist and principal songwriter Roger Waters characterized the album as 'the beginning of empathy'.[1] Waters wasn't advancing the novel hypothesis that the process or the concept of empathy sprang into being in 1974, when the album was released, but rather emphasizing a shift in the mood and lyrical content of the group's work, away from the delirious, if solipsistic, psychedelia of their earlier work—the mind turned in upon itself in the exploration of 'inner space'—and towards the outer world, especially the social world of other minds. In a very different context, neuroscientist Marco Iacoboni has employed fMRI scanning technology in order to ascertain the motives underlying political allegiances and voting behaviour. Identifying particular regions of the brain as responsible for the processing of empathy, Iacoboni claims to have gathered evidence showing that the sense of empathic connection with favoured political candidates is eroded by negative political adverts.[2] And more generally, Iacoboni argues that we are 'wired for empathy' (see the discussion of the metaphor of physiological, and more specifically neural, 'wiring' in Chapter 3).[3] Waters and Iacoboni could both very well be spouting nonsense. But the fact that they both make reference to the concept of empathy, in the very different contexts of biographical art criticism and what I suppose we should call 'neuro-social scientific' research, shows that the concept of empathy is alive and, possibly though not necessarily, well.

Regrettably I won't be lingering on *The Dark Side of the Moon* in this chapter. Instead, my goals here are twofold. First, I want to consider empathy in the novel context of the theory of the 'extended mind', as a way of illuminating the relationship between empathy and the narrative arts. The theory of the extended mind is part of a family of theories—other members of which include those concerned with embodied, situated, and 'enacted' cognition—which shifts the focus away from the role of the brain as the seat of cognition and towards the body and the environment beyond the skull. One issue in this context is the extent to which the insights on empathy drawn from neuroscience so far can be reconciled with the picture of cognition elaborated by theorists of the extended mind. My second aim here is to address some objections to the notion of empathy, and its place within our experience of representational art in general and film in particular, objections which become particularly salient when empathy is set in the context of the extended mind. So let's begin at the beginning: what sort of thing do I take empathy to be?

Personal Imagining, Empathy, and Subpersonal Scaffolding

Empathy is a kind of imagining; in particular it is a type of *personal* or *central* imagining. Such imagining takes the form of imagining perceiving or more generally experiencing events, in contrast to *impersonal* or *acentral* imagining, where we imagine that certain events have taken or are taking place, but without imagining that we perceive or experience them.[4] Consider the following as an example of personal imagining. I find myself gazing out of the window, down onto the relatively quiet, semi-rural, residential street on which we live. My eldest son is playing behind me, building a castle from wooden blocks, flying model planes in close to the towers, and bombing the hapless figures populating the structure. A car shoots by, its noise and sudden appearance startling me—it must be going at least 60 miles an hour, I think to myself. And this tips me into a brief, but quite disturbing, train of thought—of imagination—for a few seconds. What if, one day, we are outside on the street when one of these reckless drivers thunders by? What if we'd been outside just now, when that car sped by, and one of the children—lost in one of their own imaginative games—had veered into the road at the wrong moment? A queasy feeling passes through me; my breathing becomes irregular for a couple of seconds. We've all had this sort of experience—indeed, I suspect that, for some people, these alarming microfictions of catastrophe are quite common, part of the texture of their lives. In spite of the palpable emotional consequences of such personal imaginings, though, when we find ourselves thinking such thoughts—when, as we say, our imaginations run away with themselves—it is not as if we lose sight of where we actually are, of what actually is the case, of the fact that the imagining is just that: a vivid mental projection of a possible state of affairs. Our imaginations run away with themselves, but they do not hijack the mind as a whole.

In this type of case, I am imagining a variation on the actual state of affairs in which I find myself situated. I am imagining an alternative version of myself; many aspects of the scenario are carried over directly from the way the world actually is. Let us call such imagining *self-focused personal imagining*. Empathic imagining takes a slightly different form. In imagining how some other, *specified agent* sees the world, and in imagining how they think and feel, I empathize with that agent.[5] Call this type of imagining *other-focused personal imagining*—imagining the experience of others 'from the inside', in the words of Kendall Walton.[6] Such imagining allows us not merely to recognize or understand, but to grasp directly, according to the theory advanced by Vittorio Gallese explored in Chapters 2 and 3, the emotional frames of mind of others. And the purpose of such imagining, like the function of emotions more generally, is to lend our ascriptions of the mental states of others more 'bite'— that is, to assess them in terms of their urgency, salience, and relevance. In this respect empathy functions just as emotions do in general, affectively mapping out the world in terms of its potential harms and benefits.

On the account given so far, empathy involves the active, conscious use of the imagination; it emerges out of a desire to 'understand a particular individual, the person with whom one empathizes', as Susan Feagin puts it.[7] Empathy, however, does not take place or arise in isolation from other mental processes. In particular, as we have had occasion to note in Chapters 3 and 5, empathy is systematically connected with certain other, lower-level, 'pre-reflective' responses, in particular *motor* and *affective mimicry*, and *emotional contagion*.[8] Consider, as an example of the former, affective mimicry through facial expression. When we witness legible instances of the facial expressions associated with certain basic kinds of affective state—the so-called 'basic' emotions, explored in Chapters 5 and 6—we are apt to simulate the feeling associated with the expression, via the mechanism of facial feedback.[9] Emotional contagion is closely related, but where in affective mimicry we have some awareness that the source of the mimicked emotion lies in another person with whom we engage, in contagion we lack any such awareness of the source of the 'caught' emotion. Affective mimicry and emotional contagion can, I've suggested in earlier work, act as—in Walton's sense—prompts to, and props within, fully fledged imaginative projects.[10] I do not say these mechanisms always work in this way; the precise effect of the expressive faces in films, for example, is very much a matter of exactly how they are deployed—framed, lit, contextualized—by film-makers. *United 93* (Paul Greengrass, 2006), for example, gives ample screen space to the facial expressions of the hijackers—mostly expressions of anger and fear. And I think we do feel their fear by mimicry and contagion. But the film doesn't nurture a deeper imaginative engagement with the hijackers; no attempt is made to contextualize their immediate affective states in terms of their life stories.

On the other hand, the film provides relatively extensive context for many of the passengers on the plane, in this way fostering a fuller, more 'plenitudinous' imaginative engagement—specifically, an empathic, other-directed, personally imaginative engagement—with them.

This is an appropriate point at which to revisit the still emerging body of research on mirror neurons, discussed in Chapters 2 and 3, and the relationship between this research and the account of empathy I've sketched. Recall that mirror neurons are neurons which fire both when a subject executes and observes an action. They were first discovered, in the early 1990s, in macaque monkeys, but subsequent research has revealed that humans possess an even more active and extensive mirror neuron system.[11] By revealing its neural underpinning, the discovery of the mirror system provides further evidence in support of the existence of motor and affective mimicry, as well as specifying some of the mechanisms underpinning them (a good example of the method of theory construction discussed in Chapter 1). More recent research has consolidated the hypothesis that our understanding of at least some emotional states in others, including our old friends fear and disgust, is also mediated by a neural mirroring system. Such understanding constitutes 'direct experiential' knowledge of these emotions, achieved by the 'direct mapping' of visual and aural information concerning the emotions of others—in the form of expressions, gestures, and posture—'onto the same viscero-motor neural structures that determine the experience of that emotion in the observer'.[12] The mirror system does not constitute a complete neural underpinning for empathic simulation as it has been defined and debated by philosophers, but it does suggest how the simulation of higher-order states can work from the platform of motor and affective mimicry. Mimicry of basic actions and emotions may *scaffold* the imagination, including the empathic imagination, of more elaborate, finely specified states of mind.[13]

Strangers on a Train (Alfred Hitchcock, 1951) provides us with an example of the way in which vivid depictions of actions and facial expressions can scaffold more elaborate empathic imaginings. In one celebrated sequence, Hitchcock crosscuts between the desperate efforts of Bruno (Robert Walker) to retrieve a cigarette lighter that has fallen into a drain, with the no less determined attempt by Guy (Farley Granger) to win a tennis match (Figures 7.1a–7.1h). In both lines of action, Hitchcock presents us with highly legible close-ups of facial expressions (of concentration, exertion, anxiety, and pain) and motor actions (stretching, grasping, running, swinging) apt to trigger motor and affective mimicry of these very actions and affective states.[14] (Bruno's grasping for the lighter is particularly resonant in this context, since most of the early mirror neuron experiments involved subjects witnessing objects being picked up.) These mimickings may initiate, support, and enrich our broader imaginative efforts, also prompted by the film, to understand what it is like to be each of these characters—that is, to be in their situations possessing their distinctive character traits, histories, and goals. Thus we might centrally imagine Guy's immediate urgency as he attempts to finish off the tennis match, but also his anger towards

Figures 7.1a–7.1h Grasping, grimacing, stretching, and striking as cues for empathy in *Strangers on a Train* (Alfred Hitchcock, 1951).

Bruno and the excruciating injustice of his situation (in which he has every reason to resent his wife, but, appearances notwithstanding, has neither killed her nor connived with Bruno to kill her). The mirror system allows us to feel Guy's exertions on the tennis court, palpably connecting us with him, and thereby grounds and consolidates our imaginative appreciation of the larger complex of thoughts and feelings that he undergoes.[15] My hypothesis, then, is twofold: *Strangers on a Train* not only shows us how a film might strive to elicit 'motor resonance'[16] and affective mimicry, but also suggests how such mimicry might go on to scaffold fully fledged empathic imagining.

One might wonder, given the distinct types of mental process gathered under the umbrella of empathy in the discussion so far, whether the definition of the concept on offer here is really coherent. That worry might be fuelled further by considering the tangled history of the term. Introduced originally as a specialist term in psychology and art history in German, on the one hand 'empathy' has spread into ordinary English usage, and on the other hand revived—as this book testifies—as a term of art in psychology and philosophy of mind. The history of the term is further complicated by its relationship with the English 'sympathy'. In contemporary debate, empathy is typically contrasted with sympathy, but David Hume and Adam Smith used 'sympathy' to refer to a phenomenon we would label empathy. So long as our aim is to track and understand a *phenomenon*, however, rather than to give an account of the use of a *term* in ordinary or any other kind of language—or to describe a 'folk theory' of the phenomenon[17]—then the complex history of the term(s) used to refer to the phenomenon we are interested in need not derail the current project.

In this spirit, then, we can distil the description of empathy given in the discussion so far in the following way. Person A empathizes with target person B if and only if A personally (or centrally) imagines perceiving, cognizing, or feeling, partially or globally, the perceiving, cognizing, and feeling of B, where such imagining involves conscious, qualitative awareness of the state imagined. A may engage in such empathy on the basis of information gleaned from perceiving B, or information inferred or otherwise derived indirectly. Various 'sub-imaginative' forms of direct responsiveness to the mental states of others, such as contagion and mimicry, may initiate and/or bolster empathy (and perhaps typically do bolster empathy); these phenomena form a family with empathy insofar as all are characterized by A 'feeling with' B, such that if A feels anxious, B 'takes on' this anxiety (by contagion, mimicry, or volitional simulation). But contagion and mimicry alone do not constitute fully fledged empathy, which on this account requires the higher-level type of volitional imagining I have outlined.

It might be objected that the effort to render through literature or film 'what it is like' to be some other kind of person in a particular situation might afford only an 'imaginative grasp' of the situation, rather than the particular form of intersubjective relationship specified by empathy. There are several problems, however, with this counter-proposal. On its own, it is simply underspecified—if having an 'imaginative grasp' of a situation does not amount to simulating the states that one seeks to 'grasp',

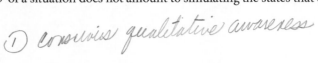
① conscious qualitative awareness

and in that sense empathizing with the person experiencing those states, we need to know what it *does* amount to. What might these alternative construals of 'having an imaginative grasp' look like? Consider these three possibilities.

- We recognize or understand what it would be like to be a certain kind of person in a certain situation in a purely cognitive sense—that the grief of a parent losing a child has a particular quality, for example, characterized by the ironic survival of the child by the parent. We can identify the state in terms of its relationship to various practices, norms, and other situations and states of mind. In this sense we come to understand or grasp the state, but without at any point simulating it (and empathizing with the subject by simulating it).
- Our imaginative grasp of the situation takes on an emotional character, but remains an 'acentral' one, a sympathetic (in the contemporary sense) rather than empathic response. Coming to know the character or person who experiences the grief of the loss of their child, we feel *for* them, but not *with* them. Of course, such feeling for a person necessitates the kind of intellectual or cognitive understanding of situations and states specified in our first option—we can't feel pity for a grieving individual unless we understand in this sense the nature of grief. So in this second option, we go beyond cognitive understanding to respond emotionally, but not in the form of empathy. Our emotional response is asymmetrical with the character's state—since they are responding to one situation but we are responding to their response to that situation. Empathy plays no role here, either as a prerequisite for understanding or a sympathetic emotional response, nor as an overall outcome of the process of engaging with the person or character.[18]
- A third possibility: having an 'imaginative grasp' of a situation might amount to 'in his shoes' imagining.[19] This form of imagining is closely related to but distinct from empathy as defined here. In such cases I might imagine how *I* would react in the situation of another—if I were in his shoes, *but possessed of my own rather than his traits, states, and history.* As I have implied through my initial example of personal imagining—the example of imagining the road accident—such imagining forms the ground of possibility for empathy. In being able to detach myself from *my* current actual state and situation and project myself imaginatively into an alternative situation, I open up the possibility of imagining how some other person might experience this situation. (Or, to put it differently, my imagining of the alternative situation might extend to include the dispositions and characters of the agents involved, in addition to its 'non-personal' elements—the setting, goals, and roles at stake.) Thinking in this way of the movement from self to imagined other in incremental terms demystifies the idea of empathy—there is no magical transplanting of one person into another, but rather the gradual and cumulative substitution of elements appropriate for myself with those appropriate for another. I have no particular anxiety

around crowds, but this character does, so imagining being trapped in a surging crowd at a football stadium comes out differently if I am engaging in 'empathic' or 'in his shoes' imagining respectively. Certainly, this is a process that admits of degrees, but to the extent that our imagining involves some degree of modelling on another person, empathic imagining is involved and we exceed the bounds of 'in his shoes' imagining. In our experience of fictions, these two forms of personal imagining typically run together, either in parallel or commingled.[20]

The problem with the first two options is that they fail to take seriously the qualitative, 'what it is like' dimension of statements like Nick Hornby's on his memoir *Fever Pitch*, set out at the beginning of this chapter, or the following remarks by David Cronenberg on his *Eastern Promises* (2007):

I think people go to the movies to live other lives...You want to get out of your own life and kind of become someone else for a while, even if you wouldn't want to stay in that life. There's a kind of vicariousness that's a part of all art, I think. So if you're going to be Nikolai [the film's protagonist, played by Viggo Mortensen], who lives a life that is fraught with danger, I want you to experience his life as it really is.[21]

I think it is implausible simply to deny that many authors and filmmakers regard empathic response, along the lines described here, as among the responses they seek from readers and viewers. Remarks by artists of this type are legion.[22] Perhaps such artists are simply wrong about the nature of the psychological transactions that their fictions initiate, in which case 'empathy' might be explained *away* by a kind of 'error theory'.[23] To be sure, there is often hyperbole in such statements, as in the case of Cronenberg's comments on *Eastern Promises*. But we have yet to see a really convincing version of such an error theory of empathy. An analogy from the history and philosophy of science may be helpful here. An error theory of empathy would treat it as equivalent to phlogiston in the theorization of disease—a conceptual artefact of a theory which turned out to misdescribe reality. Such a theory would seek an alternative explanation for our emotional interactions and 'readings' of others—the equivalent, in our analogy, with the transmission of disease—an alternative like the 'theory theory', for example (which takes our 'mindreading' ability to be a matter of folk theoretical inference rather than imaginative simulation). But on the argument advanced here, a large body of evidence suggests that empathy does name a real and important phenomenon which we can seek to theorize and explain, even if the concept is entangled with various existing folk and scientific theories of the phenomenon.

The third option is more plausible insofar as it addresses the qualitative dimension of our experience of artworks, but such 'in his shoes' imagining, I contend, is intimately bound up with empathy, both conceptually and in the actual practice and experience of engaging with fictions. 'In his shoes' imagining is not an alternative to the account framed in terms of personal imagining that I propose, but an oversimplified version of it. The three options taken together, however, do underline an important point. Our experience of engaging with characters in fictions and other narratives cannot be understood on the basis of empathy alone. There may be particular types of narrative in which empathy plays no significant role. But every type of response assayed in the discussion so far—purely cognitive understanding, 'acentral' sympathetic responses, contagion, mimicry, 'in his shoes' imagining, and, yes, empathy—plays a role in an account of the psychology of fictional response as a whole. And empathy is usually conjoined with other responses (a point to which I return in the final section of this chapter). The issue at stake here is to understand the nature and place of empathy in particular, within this array of types of response, more adequately.

Empathy and the Extended Mind

So much for an initial characterization of empathy; what about the *extended mind*? How might this innovative theory of mind shed light on the role of empathy in the narrative arts? Proponents of the theory of the extended mind hold that the human mind is distinctive in part because of the manner and extent to which it exploits features of the environment to enhance its cognitive capacities, including for example, memory, mathematical calculation, pattern recognition, and other forms of problem solving. Andy Clark and David Chalmers characterize the extended mind hypothesis as a form of 'active externalism, based on the active role of the environment in driving cognitive processes'.[24] The theory shares with Richard Dawkins's theory of the extended phenotype (discussed in Chapter 6) an emphasis on the 'extracorporeal' dimension of human (and other species') cognition; and it can be contrasted with 'brainbound' accounts of cognition, including those coming from neuroscience and traditional cognitive science, explored in Chapters 2 and 3. (One question we need to keep in mind here, then, is the extent to which the 'intracranial' emphasis of neuroscience can be integrated with the accent on the body and the environment defining the theory of the extended mind.) The use of pen and paper to perform long multiplication, physical rearranging of letter tiles in games like Scrabble, and slide rules are all offered as quotidian instances of the cognitive exploitation of 'environmental supports'. A similar idea is implicit in the explanation of change blindness discussed in Chapter 2: vision can work highly selectively because the environment acts a repository of immediately accessible information. Clark and Chalmers also point to language, which 'appears to be a central means by which cognitive processes are extended into the world. Think of a group of people brainstorming around a table, or a philosopher who thinks best by writing, developing her ideas as she goes.'[25]

What is key in such cases is that some part of the world is reliably *coupled* with the mind to form an integrated cognitive system; it is in this sense that the mind is extended into the world, structuring and co-opting part of it in order to augment its processing capabilities. Clark and Chalmers begin their essay with the image of a person working at a computer screen, her attempts to solve a spatial problem aided by the externalization of the problem on the screen before her. Equally we might think of a virtuoso musician—like Jimi Hendrix—playing their instrument, in terms of the intimate 'coupling' between person and instrument, and the enhancement of the musical cognition that this enables. Reiterated and systematic coupling leads to the 'looping' between organism and environment noted in Chapter 1, exemplified in the context of artistic cognition by sketching, storyboarding, and film editing.[26] As Clark puts it, 'Artistic intelligence...is not "all in the head"'.[27] A closely related proposal, due to Stephen Kosslyn, puts the emphasis on the extension of the individual mind by social means, that is, through other individuals and groups. Kosslyn argues that 'Evolution has allowed our brains to be configured during development so that we are "plug compatible" with other humans, so that others can help us extend ourselves.'[28] We will see shortly just how apt Kosslyn's description here of what he terms 'social prosthetic systems' is as a context for understanding empathy.

The extended mind thesis is a radical one that by no means commands the assent of all or even most philosophers of mind. But it comes in different strengths, and the version initially advanced by Clark and Chalmers is considerably stronger than is necessary for my purposes. Frederick Adams and Kenneth Aizawa mark a distinction between the extended mind thesis, and what they regard as the more modest 'extended cognitive system hypothesis'.[29] One of Clark and Chalmers's thought experiments concerns a character called Otto, who is afflicted with Alzheimer's disease.[30] Otto relies on a notebook to record crucial new information about the world, just as Leonard—who endures anterograde amnesia—relies on polaroids and verbal tattoos in Christopher Nolan's *Memento* (2000). Otto's vision and language skills are intact, and the notebook is always with him and poised for access, so Otto can quickly retrieve any information he has recorded there.

Now, according to Clark and Chalmers's extended mind thesis, the notebook is quite literally a part of Otto's mind. A 'key principle' of the extended mind thesis is 'that non-biological resources, if hooked appropriately into processes running in the human brain, can form parts of larger circuits that count as genuinely cognitive in their own right'.[31] On Adams and Aizawa's weaker thesis, the notebook is certainly part of a system established by Otto's mind to assist his memory, but the notebook itself lies outside his mind; it is not 'genuinely cognitive' because, while memories stored by the brain have direct or 'non-derived' mental content, the content of the notebook is 'derived' from and dependent on Otto's intracranial thoughts and intentions.[32] Otto's brainbound mind remains in the driving seat of an extended cognitive system; the elements outside the mind so conceived, though part of the system, do not have the same status as those elements bound by the mind in this traditional sense. And note that, though not all mental states are conscious, it doesn't look plausible to treat consciousness as arising from every element of the extended cognitive system—from the pens and paper beyond the skull as well as from the neurons beneath it. That way lies panpsychism (limned in Chapter 4). The physical seat of the conscious mind, as well as our phenomenal sense of its location, both appear to be located immediately 'north of the neck'.[33]

Alongside Adams and Aizawa's extended cognitive system hypothesis, two other models help us to recognize the distinctive way in which the human mind expands its capacities by exploiting external resources, without demanding drastic metaphysical revisionism. The first is the familiar concept of *technology*, understood as a kind of know-how for the making of artefacts that enhance our ability to manipulate the world. Filmmaking is a technology, obviously enough, but on this argument narrative and fiction are also (overlapping) technologies, the functions of which include the exercise and fine-tuning of our empathic capacity. Patrick Maynard, who defines technologies as 'extenders or amplifiers of our powers to do things', has advanced a comprehensive account of photography as a technology expanding our powers of visualization and imagination.[34] Maynard is also at pains to stress that 'filtering' or 'suppression' of our capacities goes hand in hand with such amplification.

The second model relevant here is afforded by the notion of *niche construction*, a concept of much more recent vintage, which highlights the relevance for evolution of the way in which organisms in general, and humans particularly emphatically, are not only adapted to their environments, but actively adapt them to their needs. '[I]t is readily apparent that contemporary humans are born into a massively constructed world, with an ecological inheritance that includes a legacy of houses, cities, cars, farms, nations, e-commerce, and global warming. Niche construction and ecological inheritance are thus likely to have been particularly consequential in human evolution.'[35] The human niche, it is worth adding, is partly constituted by values: human practices and artefacts alike are shaped to a high degree by moral, political, and aesthetic considerations. In a related argument, Michael Tomasello argues that 'the ontogenetic niche for developing human beings is a richly cultural one',[36] in which children learn through both unassisted imitation and 'absorption' of cultural practices, and through the active intervention of adults. A crucial feature of human cultural transmission, one that is both species-typical and species-unique, is what Tomasello dubs the *ratchet effect* (already encountered in Chapter 1): human cultural learning is cumulative, the robustness of the cultural transmission of human inventions enabling each generation to prevent 'slippage backward'.[37] In the words Kim Sterelny, humans are the 'self-made species', the species for whom cumulative niche construction takes centre stage.[38] Storytelling in general and fiction in particular are part of the niche that humans have constructed for themselves over evolutionary time—indeed storytelling and fiction are at once part of the niche constructed by humans, and mechanisms of cultural transmission by which the niche as a whole is both sustained and developed.[39]

So what is the relevance of all of this—the extended mind and the extended cognitive system theses, technology as a cognitive amplifier, niche construction and cumulative cultural learning—for the notion of empathy? There are, I think, two ways in which empathy might play a role within a theory of extended mentality. We might regard empathy as a *mechanism of the coupling* between the mind and that part of the world through which it extends itself (in which case it takes its place alongside other such mechanisms, like the visual perception and reading skills which enable Otto, in Clark and Chalmers's thought experiment, to couple his notebook with his mind). When we empathize with another person, we extend our mind to incorporate part of her mind. (Iacoboni, by way of Husserl, also uses the term 'coupling' to describe the work of mirror neurons in forging empathic connections between individuals.[40]) In doing so, we exploit some part of the environment around us—in this case, another human being—and thereby learn something about the environment. This is just the kind of process that Kosslyn has in mind when he discusses the 'social prostheses' through which 'others can help us extend ourselves'.

To put this in terms of a concrete scenario: imagine that I am standing, face to face, in a conversational exchange with Amy; her eye is caught by something behind me, and an alarmed expression appears on her face. Even before I turn to discover the object of her glance, I have learned something about her, and about the wider environment in which we both find ourselves—something significant and untoward has taken place and Amy is concerned about it. Registering her expression, a small jolt of anxiety runs through me. Much, of course, remains to be filled in; but empathy, triggered here by affective mimicry, has played a crucial initiating role, acting like a sentry alerting me to the presence of something likely to be relevant to me. I have learned something, and I have learned it in part by co-opting the perceptual and emotive capacities of another agent. (Of course, Amy's emotion and my mimicking of it are numerically distinct; she possesses and experiences her alarm, and I possess and experience my mimicking of her alarm. But my perceptual 'reach' has been extended by virtue of my uptake and mimicking of her alarm.) Such an exchange thus counts as an instance of 'social referencing', in which 'one person uses another person's affective response to a situation in order to assess the situation, guide his behaviour, and perhaps determine his own affective response'.[41]

So empathy may be a mechanism of coupling between the brainbound mind and its worldly extensions. Alternatively, empathy might be seen as one of those capacities—alongside memory—which is enhanced by the extended mind; that is, it might be seen as an end rather than (or perhaps as well as) a means in extended mentality. And if empathy is enhanced in this way, then it is the domain of representation, and especially the practice of narration, that constitutes the 'environmental support' created by the mind to drive its amplified performance. Public narration—exemplified above all by the narrative arts—is the anvil on which such extension is forged. We can think, for example, of the devices of filmmaking as *cognitive prostheses*, in much the same way that we think of other devices, like the telescope or microscope, as perceptual prostheses—devices that amplify our native perceptual capacities.

How, then, do the various forms of representation and narration augment empathy? They do so as part of a more general reinforcement of the imagination.

① *empathy in domain of rep. & narr.*

All developmentally normal humans possess an innate capacity to imagine things. We use our imaginations routinely and pervasively in the course of planning our lives, an activity which requires us to imagine and assess different paths of action that we might take in the immediate and more distant future. But now contemplate the difference between the kind and scale of imagining instantiated by, say, *War and Peace* (1869), or *Hamlet* (1599–1602), or *Heimat* (Edgar Reitz, 1984–2013), or *The Sopranos* (David Chase, 1997–2008) and the kind of imagining we can cope with unaided. 'The intrigues of people in conflict', writes Steven Pinker,

can multiply out in so many ways that no one could possibly play out the consequences of all the courses of action in the mind's eye. Fictional narratives supply us with a mental catalogue of the fatal conundrums we might face someday and the outcome of strategies we could deploy in them. What are the options if I were to suspect that my uncle killed my father, took his position, and married my mother? If my hapless older brother got no respect in the family, are there circumstances that might lead him to betray me?[42]

Pinker speaks here of a 'mental catalogue', but tellingly he follows his list of questions posed by well-known fictions by saying: 'The answers are to be found in any bookstore or video shop', indicating how the 'mental' extends out into, and is supported by, the physical environment.[43] So it is that we extend our imaginative capacity—and thus our capacity to ponder and perhaps even solve moral and social problems—by, to take another example of public narration, arraying a set on a stage and adding some props. As Walton has argued, our first acts of mimesis are those embodied by childhood games of make believe;[44] these games also constitute the beginnings, in the development of the individual, of *the extended imagination*.

Patrick Hogan and Lisa Zunshine have both objected to Pinker's account, partly on the grounds that his argument makes narrative as such essentially didactic.[45] Several things can be said in response to this charge. First, I enlist Pinker here only to argue that one significant function of narrative is to enable such strategic, action-oriented imagining. Second, Pinker's proposal may be more plausible if it is not put merely in terms of possible actions, but in terms of feelings and states of being which may lead to actions—what would it be or feel like to be a particular person in a specific situation? Take another literary example—the figure of Bonnie Clutter in Truman Capote's *In Cold Blood* (1966), who suffers from a form of chronic depression. In one scene, Mrs Clutter is discovered weeping in her room by a visiting family friend, Wilma Kidwell. As Mrs Kidwell comforts her, Mrs Clutter speaks:

'Wilma', she said, 'I've been listening to you, Wilma. All of you. Laughing. Having a good time. I'm missing out on everything. The best years, the children—everything. A little while, and even Kenyon [her son] will be grown up—a man. And how will he remember me? As a kind of ghost, Wilma.'[46]

Most of us, most of the time, don't think beyond stereotypes, generic ideas, and familiar imagery of conditions like 'depression'. Capote's precise delineation of

Mrs Clutter's mindset, as manifest in her agonized outburst, allows us to go beyond such schematic ideas. Once we can appreciate the specificity of Mrs Clutter's situation and her feelings, the idea that we might then contemplate the possible paths of action leading from her situation—what we might do, and what she might do, in her shoes—does not seem so farfetched. Theorists of emotion, after all, regard 'action readiness' as a typical element of an emotion (though Mrs Clutter may be a limit case, her depression precisely denying her the sense that there is anything she can do to help herself).[47]

Another consideration in relation to Pinker's account of strategic imagining aided and extended by fictional narratives: it might be that the classics invoked by Pinker are poor examples—either for the good reason that their complexity obscures this basic narrative function, or for the bad reason that we just can't stand the idea that *Hamlet* is, after all, in one respect at least, not that different to one of Aesop's fables. If we substitute, say, *United 93*, is it really such a stretch to say that the film helps us imagine what being on that flight was like for its passengers (or even, to a lesser degree, its hijackers)—and that this includes imagining deliberating over the options they had: compliance with the hijackers, resistance through subterfuge, or outright counter-attack?

Rachel Cooper, like Pinker though from the very different perspective of the philosophy of psychiatry, also notes that there are limits to our native capacity for empathy. In a deeply troubling passage, she quotes from the testimony of a prisoner of war given the choice between raping his own young daughter, or watching as she is raped by a prison guard. The prisoner opts for the second choice, but then is forced to rape his own daughter, all of this being witnessed by his young son. Cooper notes two impediments to empathizing with the prisoner. First, his experience is likely to be remote from our own; few of us have been imprisoned, let alone in the chaotic and lawless atmosphere of war; too many of the stepping stones between personal imagining and empathic imagining are missing. And second, many of us lack the will or the imaginative capacity to empathize with the prisoner; here we have not so much the much-discussed *imaginative resistance* so much as *imaginative akrasia*. We turn away, or our minds go blank, in the face of such a scenario.[48] Even reading the short, unadorned summary of the prisoner's story given above is difficult. Not that the failure of individual imagination is uniquely related to scenarios of extreme horror; oftentimes it is simply the peculiarity of the situation and the target of the empathy that impede empathy. Artistic narratives can step into this breach, giving us a collective context in which to strengthen our individual will, and giving us resources—Walton's props—to realize in imagination just what it would be like to be caught up in extreme or unusual circumstances, or to defamiliarize through empathy scenarios with which we have become habituated and overfamiliar.

The domain of artistic representation, then, provides us with the most striking and complex examples of extended imagining. But we shouldn't allow artworks to overshadow their more humdrum cousins. Gossip, everyday 'thought experiments' ('what are you going to do *if* you're made redundant?'), doodling and sketching[49] are all ways of playing out our thoughts with the aid of external supports, in the form of both purely physical props and (as in the case of empathy) other human agents with whom we converse and exchange ideas. Empathy and gossip are prime examples of the social prostheses postulated by Kosslyn. Such activities are tools that we use in the course of practical, social, and ethical problem solving each and every day, and they form the seedbed and training ground for the artistic imagination.

Extension and Expansion

Thinking of the narrative arts in this way brings my proposal into contact with another recent argument, already encountered in Chapter 1, concerning the basis on which we study the perception and cognition of artworks in relation to perception and cognition in non-aesthetic, 'everyday' contexts. Dominic Lopes argues that most empirical research on artistic cognition seeks to show how the appreciation of various sorts of artwork depends on the deployment of ordinary perceptual and cognitive capacities. Lopes distinguishes such an approach from a related but more sophisticated position that he designates *expansionism*, through a pair of proposals:

First, I propose that our engagement with most works of art, either as creators or as consumers, depends on the exercise of the very cognitive capacities we use to navigate our environment and to deal with others of our species. Second, I propose that in our engagement with works of art, these cognitive capacities are frequently extended in quite new directions, operating in ways not seen outside artistic contexts.[50]

If Lopes's first thesis is correct, we should expect that, in one sense or another, our ability to empathize with human agents will play an important role in our engagement with narrative representations—in the same way that our capacity to recognize basic emotion expressions carries over from the actual to the artefactual, as we saw in Chapter 5.[51] If Lopes's second thesis is correct, we might expect to find empathy 'flexing its muscles fully' in the context of narrative art, that is, functioning 'in new ways, perhaps in ways never evident' in extra-artistic perception.[52]

In what ways might empathy, then, be stretched and refined through its engagement by the narrative arts? In *scope* and *intensity*. Our ability to empathize is extended across a wide range of types of person and situation, and sustained and intensified by virtue of the artificial, 'designed' environments created by narrative artefacts. We are all limited, to a greater or lesser extent, in the opportunities we have to engage with situations, persons, and cultures dramatically different from our own. For those who want to take it up, fictional and non-fictional storytelling affords a limitless horizon of opportunities for engagement with alternative forms of life; and if empathy (along with its relatives) is as basic to human social life as the argument so far suggests, empathy will be one form of such engagement. The possibility of understanding 'from the inside'—that is, empathically imagining the thoughts and feelings of—human agents in social situations more or less radically different from our own is disclosed. We may come not only to see, but to feel, how an agent in a given situation concludes that there are only a particular set of viable choices open to them. The range of 'live options' perceived by the agent might be a much narrower range than we take them to possess if we assess their situation from the outside—that is, in narrowly rational terms and without an attempt to model or simulate her state(s) of mind.

Public forms of narration help us to sustain imaginative projects of this sort, allowing us to work through the details, and the possible dramatic patterns or 'arcs' of development, of such unfamiliar scenarios with a clarity and precision impossible without them. Consider once again the analogy with music: just as instrumentation and notation enable composers to create, and listeners to appreciate, musical form on an exponentially higher scale of elaboration than is possible without these material supports, so the novelist and the filmmaker, through the technologies of their trades, are able to sustain ambitious imaginative projects, thereby affording readers and viewers of their narrative works an opportunity to do likewise.

Along with this process of sustained elaboration and widening of the scope of empathy comes the possibility of *intensifying* our empathic responses. This might well sound highly counterintuitive, since we are, generally speaking, accustomed to thinking of the responses we have to representations as pale versions of the equivalent responses we would feel in real circumstances. Paul Bloom, for example, writes that our emotional responses to fictions 'are typically muted compared to the real thing. Watching a movie in which someone is eaten by a shark is less intense than watching someone really being eaten by a shark.' Similarly, Colin Radford avers that our reaction to a real death will be 'more massive, more intense and longer in duration' than to its fictional parallel, as the real death 'will not be alloyed—or allayed—by aesthetic pleasure'.[53] I can be moved by the untimely death of a sympathetic and central character, but not to the extent that I will be moved by the untimely death of an actual friend. My claim, however, is that the crafted environment of narrative artefacts enables the authors of such objects to shape, and thus to distil and concentrate, our responses to a high degree. As Carl Plantinga has demonstrated, mainstream narrative films commonly feature one or more 'scenes of empathy', in which a critical moment in the drama is capped and highlighted by prolonged and vivid depiction of a major character in the throes of emotion.[54] The climactic scene in *Saboteur*, analysed in Chapter 5, is such a scene, albeit a somewhat eccentric example because of the way that it invites empathy with the film's antagonist rather than its protagonist. A contemporary, and more conventional, example is the scene in *The Imitation Game* (Morten Tyldum, 2014) in which Alan Turing (Benedict Cumberbatch) laments the destruction of his computer 'Christopher'—named (in the film's storyworld) after Turing's intimate friend who dies in childhood.

As this biographical example underlines, what is at stake here is not a contrast between empathy in response to actual circumstances and empathy in response to narrative fictions, but the capacity of a wider class of narrative works, whether fictional or non-fictional, to intensify empathy. Such scenes of empathy, for Plantinga, are designed not only to elicit an empathic response, but to maximize the possibility and intensity of such a response by their sustained and detailed representation of facial and vocal expressions of affect. These expressions, as we have seen, are apt to trigger mimicry and contagion in the viewer, which may then scaffold imaginative empathy. Thus, in terms of both narrative set-up and stylistic presentation, the maker of a narrative film has the opportunity to 'engineer' an object precisely designed to elicit empathy; not for nothing do we speak of 'tear-*jerkers*'. Just as the culinary arts enable us to refine, and intensify, the flavours available in unprocessed, natural foods, so the makers of narratives may refine and intensify certain kinds of natural emotional response. It is in this sense, and only in this sense, that I propose that our empathic responses to narrative artefacts may be more intense than those to real circumstances.

Empathy Stays in the Picture

Unfortunately for me, the drift of my argument is in the opposite direction of that taken by at least some of those who would seem to be my natural allies. Responding to a number of arguments sceptical that empathy and imaginative simulation have any important role to play in our comprehension and appreciation of fictions, Greg Currie concedes that 'understanding real people and understanding fictional, and especially literary characters are very different activities'.[55] However, a number of points can be made in defence of the claim that empathy (and its relatives) play a significant role in our apprehension of fictions and other narratives. The first of these points concerns the distinction between the *quantitative* and the *qualitative* dimensions of the claim for the significance of empathy. Sceptics tend to assume that any claim for the centrality of empathy to the process of apprehending narrative must make it quantitatively dominant, or at least among the dominant modes by which we engage with stories; it must be something, so the assumption goes, that we are doing most or much of the time when we watch a movie or read a novel. But one may ascribe qualitative significance to empathy even if it occupies, quantitatively speaking, a rather small proportion of the time we devote to engaging with the fiction. Consider again Plantinga's argument, according to which mainstream films periodically elicit an empathic response from the viewer. These moments of empathy are clearly significant, because they occur at the climactic moments in the drama of the film, even though they might occupy no more than, say, 5 per cent of the duration of the film (and quite probably a good deal less than that).

Similarly, it is important to keep apart the *instrumental* and *intrinsic* value that we might attach to empathy. Although Currie acknowledges that there are some fictions which seem to call out for empathy with characters as an end in its own right, simulating characters' states of mind performs only an instrumental value in his scheme as a whole. Currie labels such simulation *secondary* imagining because it performs this instrumental role in relation to *primary* imagining—the business, that is, of imagining what is true-in-the-fiction.[56] But one might argue that empathy has intrinsic value in general in our experience of narrative; that empathy, so valued, is central to the institutions of narrative and fiction, and not merely of interest in the case of some exceptional narratives. In life, empathy is always functional, a means to an end; in narrative art, it becomes an end as well as a means. To know what it is like to be a certain kind of person in a certain kind of situation is something that we value for its own sake. The comments from Hornby on *Fever Pitch* and Cronenberg on *Eastern Promises* both exemplify this idea.

The distinction between instrumental and intrinsic value points to a tension in the literature on empathy concerning the *conditions* which are likely to elicit empathy in the context of narrative consumption, and the *purpose* of such empathy when it does arise. On the one hand we find the argument that empathy is most likely to arise when we have some, but very limited, knowledge of an agent in a situation. In such a context, empathy serves to probe and reveal more of what is or might be going on inside the agent; recall Feagin's claim that 'one engages in a simulation out of a desire to empathize with or understand a particular individual'.[57] Call this the *mindreading* function of empathy in relation to representational art. On the other hand, we also find the argument that empathy is most likely to arise—or in the case of radically unfamiliar cultural settings, can only arise—when we are furnished with extensive and detailed knowledge regarding the agent and their situation. Here empathy does not serve to uncover possible new information, but to put the information that we do possess under a new description, so to speak, allowing us to feel it 'from the inside'. Call this the *mindfeeling* function of empathy. In the case of mindreading, empathy operates at or near the base of the narrative understanding; in the case of mind-feeling, empathy arises at the apex of such understanding.

We can explore these two very different possibilities through the following three sequences from *Los amantes del círculo polar/Lovers of the Arctic Circle* (Julio Médem, 1998). The opening credit sequence of the film reveals a small plane grounded in a blizzard landscape. The image fades to black, and the new image which fades in is superficially similar, but difficult to recognize as such—a black and white photograph of the plane in a newspaper which is moving up and down. The newspaper flies into air, and then we see alternating shots of a woman (played by Najwa Nimri) running, from behind, up some stairs and into an apartment, with frontal shots of a man (Fele Martínez), apparently pursuing her. Inside the apartment, the man and woman embrace, but the woman possesses a strange, glassy stare, suggesting neither relief nor passion, even though her eyes well up with tears. Careful attention reveals other enigmatic features: the man's face can be seen in the woman's eyes in certain shots, a reflection which is hard to make sense of spatially (Figure 7.2). During these opening moments of the film, we're largely at a loss as to what is going on. Disdaining the sort of dense, redundant, and direct exposition characteristic of many narrative openings, the narration here is highly elliptical. According to the

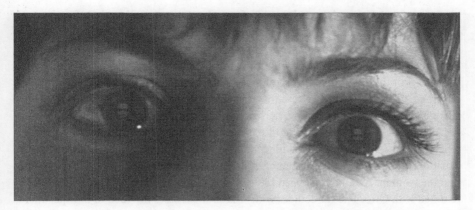

Figure 7.2 The enigmatic opening of *Los amantes del círculo polar/Lovers of the Arctic Circle* (Julio Médem, 1998).

Figure 7.3 Empathy as 'mindfeeling' in *Los amantes del círculo polar/Lovers of the Arctic Circle* (Julio Médem, 1998).

mindreading hypothesis, empathic imagining comes into play here quite naturally, as a means of fathoming what might be going on. In initiating such imagining, we draw on what information we can perceive and infer, and our imagining may be assisted by mimicry and contagion; indeed these processes may have nudged us towards empathic imagining in the first place.

By contrast, some way into the film we witness a scene in which Otto—the male protagonist we see in the opening sequence, and no relation to Clark and Chalmers's Otto!—grieves over his mother's death. Otto is shown in medium close-up, peering through a small window into the furnace room where his mother's body is about to be cremated (Figure 7.3). His father, stepmother, and stepsister Ana—also his lover— stand behind him. As the coffin bursts into flames, Otto's hostility towards his father—whom he blames for his mother's death—recedes, the two of them falling

① mimicry, affective contagion, emotional

into a grief-stricken embrace, the pain of loss clearly expressed in their facial, vocal, and bodily movements. As my commentary indicates, by this point in the film we have a very good handle on all the major characters and their interrelationships. According to the mindfeeling hypothesis, this richly developed context, along with the cues prompting mimicry and contagion present in the scene, solicits an empathic response. (The scene also represents an example of Plantinga's 'scene of empathy', albeit a relatively attenuated one, perhaps in line with the film's art house status.)

Lastly, in the final scene of the film, several shots from the opening sequence are repeated, but here they are extended, supplemented by other shots elaborating the situation, and placed at the fulcrum of a fully developed narrative. We now understand that the woman, Ana, has just been hit by a car, moments before she would have been reunited with Otto. The car collides with Ana as she crosses the road to the apartment, her attention fixed on the newspaper report of the crashed plane, in which she fears Otto may have perished. As she is thrown to the ground, the newspaper flies into the air; and in the cruellest of ironies, Otto arrives at the scene only seconds later. The embrace that we witness in the opening sequence is a fantasy of what would have happened had the accident not intervened; the glassy stare is the look of a dying person; the welling tears the sole sign of sentience; the reflection of Otto in Anna's eyes is created as he kneels by her stricken body. As with the scene of grieving, the mindfeeling hypothesis suggests that it is precisely the density of information available to us at this stage of the narrative that is likely to precipitate empathic imagining. Here such empathy functions as a vehicle of that complex rendering of extreme states of consciousness characteristic of modernist art cinema, discussed in Chapter 4.

The friend of empathy has still another card to play. We musn't confuse, the advocate insists, *occurrent* and *retrospective* empathy: that is, empathizing in the course of reading a novel or watching a movie, and empathizing after the fact, as we reflect on the experience of the novel or the film. Pretty much the entire debate on simulation and fiction has been geared to our occurrent experience of artworks, for obvious, and good, reasons. Our engagement with artworks is, or rather is assumed to be, at its most intense as we engage with them; the proof of the pudding lies in our occurrent apprehension of an artwork. Surely, though, we have to allow that artworks assume their significance within a wider frame of reference than that of our direct engagement with them, even if it all necessarily begins within that setting. We routinely come to realize things about artworks as we reflect on them after the fact—the significance of a line of dialogue suddenly comes to us; the connection between an early and a later scene drops into place. And while movies and stage plays are traditionally consumed in one continuous block, the narrative of a novel or a television drama is much more likely to be consumed in dispersed fashion, over days, weeks, or months—even years in the case of long-running television series—so occurrent engagement with the narrative may alternate with retrospective and indeed *anticipatory* engagement with it. Rereading or reviewing a narrative adds another layer to this picture. Thus in addition to its role in our occurrent experience of narrative artworks, empathy may be an important feature of our retrospective engagement with such narratives, rising up in the spaces between our occurrent engagement with them.

Finally, and by way of conclusion, the role(s) I am according to empathy in our experience of narrative works are sometimes deemed implausible, I suspect, because of some lingering, problematic, Cartesian assumptions concerning the operations of the mind. Those assumptions concern the *consciousness, singularity*, and *seriality* of the contents of the mind. To say that I might, as a part of my imaginative engagement with the scene in *Lovers of the Arctic Circle*, empathize with Otto's grief, is not to say that that imagined grief necessarily dominates my consciousness at any point. (Indeed, it might not break into consciousness at all: although the idea of unconscious emotions violates our current everyday concept of emotion, which ties emotions with consciously felt states, the evidence of unconscious perception ('blindsight') suggests that we should countenance the possibility of 'blind' (unconscious) emotions. Qualia may be typical but not necessary features of emotions.[58]) Nor is it to say that imagining Otto's grief 'from the inside' is the only activity undertaken by my mind at a given point in the course of viewing the scene. We know that the brain processes in parallel, and can be conceived as a 'locus of multiple, quasi-independent processing streams'; while there are limits to its capacities, normal business for the brain involves the processing of many items simultaneously, in different ways.[59] So in arguing that I might empathize with Otto during the scene of his mother's cremation, we should not cash that out in terms of Otto's grief bestriding my theatre of consciousness, loudly declaiming itself to the exclusion of all other mental operations; rather, we need to think in terms of 'a complex mosaic of simulations' taking place alongside other mental activities.[60] After all, we wouldn't think it odd to claim that at the same moment I am watching—and thus visually processing—the shot of the newspaper flying into the air in the final scene of *Lovers of the Arctic Circle*, that I am also remembering that I have seen this image before, recalling in which part of the film it appeared, and working out how it fits into the causal, narrative sequence of the film as a whole. If we can countenance the mind doing all these sorts of things simultaneously, why wouldn't we countenance empathic imagining as one, possibly subordinate, mental activity among many taking place? Just as, in the case of my self-focused personal imagining, I never lose sight of the fact that I am actually in the living room and my son is safely playing behind me, even as I experience the queasy sensation of fear at the thought of an accident, so in the case of this fictional imagining, I never lose sight of the overall dramatic situation and the emotions of the various other characters, nor of the fact that I am watching a fiction, even as I empathize with Otto.

8

Feeling Prufish

> ...addressing a picture with a general law feels rather like addressing a peach
> with a billiard cue—the wrong shape and size of instrument, designed for
> movement in the wrong direction.
>
> Michael Baxandall

> ...every scenario has its own feel.
>
> Ronald de Sousa

Over the past thirty years, film theorists have caught up with filmmakers and
viewers in recognizing the primary—indeed, you might even say primal—
importance of emotion in the life of movies. Most viewers of most forms of
filmmaking seek a focused and intense affective experience when they sit down to
watch a film, and filmmakers generally recognize this. I make no claim, of course,
that a film, or a good film, necessarily has a salient emotional dimension; merely
that films typically do possess this feature, and in most cases we will regard it as an
important feature.

What have theorists and philosophers of film had to say about the emotions
represented and elicited by films? Quite a bit in fact, as I hope to have demonstrated
across this work. But I want to take note of one particular characteristic of scholarly
research on emotion and film. Most of that research has been concerned with
'garden-variety' emotions—emotional states which are familiar from ordinary
experience and which perform a core role in our lives.[1] Discussion of *fear* in the
movies alone is sufficient to fill at least one library shelf. As one of the so-called 'basic
emotions'—along with happiness, sadness, surprise, disgust, anger, and perhaps
shame—it is readily apparent why theorists have taken stock of fear. Not all
garden-variety emotions—emotions which are familiar and widely recognized as
important, at least in a given cultural context—are 'basic' in this sense, however.
Love is an important ingredient in many film narratives, but love is often regarded as
a 'higher' emotion, in the sense that its cognitive component is more complex, and
more dependent on a particular cultural background, than is true for the basic
emotions. So fear may, in this sense, be more 'basic' than love, but both are
garden-variety or core emotions in terms of their familiarity and the importance
that we accord them.[2]

One influential proposal concerning the nature of such core emotions is due to Ronald de Sousa, who argues that emotions are defined and understood in part through *paradigm scenarios*. Such a scenario is 'a situation type, a kind of original drama that defines the roles, feelings, and reactions characteristic of that emotion'.[3] Grief, for example, might be understood through a scenario involving a parent responding with a mix of immediate, intense agony and prolonged sadness, to the death of a child.[4] De Sousa's concept has several virtues. The concept of a paradigm scenario brings out the important *cognitive* dimension of emotional states, underlining how they differ from simple arousal. To have an emotion is to recognize that one is in a certain sort of situation. But 'cognitive' should not be understood to imply 'internal' or 'subjective' in a narrow sense, since paradigm scenarios have an irreducible 'external' or *social* dimension; what the paradigm 'dramatizes' for us is how a given emotion is an appropriate response to a situation, comprised of multiple agents and a context or set of background conditions. (This emphasis on the external conditions of emotions makes the concept of paradigm scenarios fit well with the extended mind framework explored in Chapter 7.) And the concept of the paradigm scenario allows us to see how emotions are *learned*. Over the course of development, a combination of participation in and observation of such scenarios allows us to map the situation types, feeling states, and representations of both—most obviously, in the form of language—onto one another. As de Sousa puts it, 'the role of paradigm scenarios in relation to emotions is analogous to the ostensive definition of a common noun'.[5] What is more, fiction, depiction, and representation in general massively extend our opportunities for the 'indirect' observation of paradigm scenarios, and the learning of the cognitive and social dynamics of the emotions defined by them. We are educated in the ways of emotion through fairy tales, fables, songs, plays, paintings, novels, and films as much as through direct experience.[6]

A further feature of these scenarios is that they are *generic*, in the sense that they provide templates for understanding given situation-types and their associated emotions. The scenario would not be a *paradigm* scenario if it did not perform this coordinating function, enabling us to place social encounters with disparate surface features into underlying categories. My annoyance with a colleague as he hogs the photocopier may share few if any surface features with my irritation at my son's refusal to do the washing up, but both are instances of (mild) anger at the selfish behaviour of a member of a small community in which cooperation towards collective goods (availability of photocopying and clean dishes, respectively) is crucial for the functioning of that community. Bringing apparently disparate social encounters under the description of our generic paradigm scenarios is an important intellectual and social skill, for this is one way in which we bring coherence to our lives, recognizing patterns within them rather than simply careering through a succession of unique events. In this respect, life isn't so much one damn thing after another, but the same damn thing after another. Or at least, the same damn *things* over and over again.

Binding and Blending

All of this is well and good. But is our emotional life characterized *only* by such generic, garden-variety emotional states? And is the emotional traffic between films and viewers adequately captured by paradigm scenarios and the emotions they define?

Certainly, these states are important, as we can readily see from the important role of genre in the world of film. As we had occasion to note in Chapter 6, many genres are defined in part by the kind of emotional state they seek to elicit. Horror films are the most obvious case, since the genre itself is (nowadays, at least) labelled with the relevant emotion term: horror films are films which will (or ought to) horrify you. But emotion terms are ubiquitous in our thinking about genres more generally. The ancient genres of tragedy and comedy are characterized and contrasted through distinct emotional tones. The term 'melodrama' has come to denote an intense emotionality. In the film world, we speak of thrillers, (spine-)chillers, and weepies. Romantic comedies revolve around love and humour. Action-adventure films engage us by depicting and eliciting physical exhilaration. 'Gross-out' comedies depend upon a combination of disgust and humour; the 'comedy of humiliation'—think Larry David, Ben Stiller, Ricky Gervais— also commingles humour with a 'negative' emotion. Quasi-generic designations like 'film noir' have strong emotional associations. Even genres like the war or combat film, which are defined most obviously by a certain kind of subject matter, bring to mind characteristic emotions and affectively laden states of mind and body, such as fear, anxiety, courage, fortitude, and physical pain. Perhaps not surprisingly, then, generic, garden-variety emotions are important to genre films.

But what about finer-grained emotional states? Does the emotional appeal of film, or at least of some films, depend on the articulation or elicitation of emotions which slip through the net of paradigm scenarios? I will argue here that the *particularity* of the emotions represented, articulated, and elicited by films is indeed important. I will not argue, however, that acknowledging this mutually excludes recognition of the importance of garden-variety emotions, whether for genre or non-genre films. Just as we can appreciate *The Texas Chainsaw Massacre* (Tobe Hooper, 1974) as both a horror film and as a particular horror story, so the emotional experience or 'affective trajectory'[7] offered by a film can work on both levels. Indeed, one cannot fully appreciate *The Texas Chainsaw Massacre* as a particular film without understanding it against the relevant generic background, since the full resonance of many of its elements only becomes apparent when we see them against this backdrop.[8] But I do not offer up Tobe Hooper's film as an exceptional case; the dependence of the particular on the generic holds in general for narrative appreciation, at least in the context of narrative *art*. The particularity of a narrative, and the emotions it represents, may not matter much to us if the narrative serves a routine practical function— say, describing how to get from one place to another—but the specific character of a narrative will matter to us if we engage with it as an aesthetic object. In this sense, works of narrative art in general possess generic features, but are not exhausted by

represented, articulated & elicited

them. To say that a work possesses generic features or refers to generic conventions is not to say that it is wholly generic.

To make this point clear, let us compare narrative artworks with a more straightforwardly functional type of object: the humble nail. Both objects perform functions: nails pin objects together, while films entertain and sometimes enlighten and edify us. Within a certain range of variation, however, any nail is as good as any other nail. That is, if I need a 10mm nail, I don't need to search through my box of 10mm nails for any particular nail (so long as I can assume that any nail that I take from the box will lie within a given tolerance range). The individual characteristics of any given nail are of no interest to me, so long as they don't impede its function. Nails, in other words, are *fungible*: they are interchangeable with other objects of the same type. By contrast, the individual characteristics of a narrative film are typically important to us. Ingmar Bergman once likened making a film to fashioning an ordinary artefact, like a pot, but he immediately added that 'it was his pot and not quite like anyone else's'.[9] There may be a limit case where all we are looking for is some brute generic experience, as when we scan the channels late at night looking for some thrilling or comic or romantic action with which to wind down. But normally, even in the case of generic narrative fictions, we are interested in how effective a particular work is as an instance of a type—for example, how good is *this* thriller *as* a thriller? Answering such a question means assessing how the film, as a specific instance of the genre, embodies and works with the conventions of the genre. Moreover, it is plausible to hold that all fictions are related to genres, more or less directly. If there are 'bespoke', 'one-off' narrative fictions—fictions which do not seem to depend, even distantly, on a background of generic convention in order to be appreciated—it might seem that the dependence of the particular on the generic does not apply to them. But such fictions would still depend upon a tacit knowledge of recurrent situations and—crucially in the present context—paradigm scenarios, even where they do not draw on genre conventions per se. In pursuing the significance of the particular, then, I do not reject the significance of generic properties, including garden-variety emotions, either for genre films or for more idiosyncratic works.

In some sense, then, all films must work on the levels of both the particular and the generic, since particulars are invariably instances of more general categories. But perhaps it is true that the relative significance of generic and particular varies from work to work. Enter the mysterious state of 'prufishness'. 'Prufishness' has been proposed by John Benson as a term for the highly specific state of mind expressed by the character Prufrock in T. S. Eliot's 'The Love Song of J. Alfred Prufrock'.[10] Benson draws attention to a particular couplet, arguing that through these words Prufrock expresses a distinctive emotional state, even though he uses no emotion terms:

> I should have been a pair of ragged claws
> Scuttling across the floors of silent seas

Benson refers to this form of emotional expression as 'oblique description'[11]—'oblique' relative to the use of dedicated emotion vocabulary—and argues that it 'is more comprehensive in its range, and in the discriminations it can make' than forms of expression which restrict themselves to 'common emotion terms'.[12] Developing Benson's argument, we might say that more extended dramatic episodes, from scenes up to entire narratives, are also capable of representing and expressing highly particular emotional states. And they may do this without naming the emotions in play with single words or concise expressions (though the longer the narrative sequence in question, the more likely it will include, or evoke, the language of garden-variety emotions). Thus in coming to grips with Eliot's poem, we might draw upon a variety of paradigm scenarios and generic emotion terms, such as weariness, melancholy, and longing. But the power of the poem lies (in part) in conveying an emotional state with a unique and original 'flavour', dependent on just the set of circumstances evoked in it. We appreciate such a work in part *because* of the distinctive emotional tone that it creates.

Benson's example focuses on the impact and importance of a specific part of an artwork in expressing a distinctive emotion. Extending the scope of his argument to encompass more global levels of engagement, up to the level of the work as a whole, is vital in allowing us to appreciate the importance of the combination, interaction, and enchaining of emotions in the creation of a distinctive 'field' of emotion. We began to tackle this phenomenon in Chapter 4, in exploring the relationship between perceptual qualia and cultural context, and in Chapter 6, in relation to what William James famously described as the 'flux' of emotions.[13] In a similar spirit, Paul Ekman notes that

> emotions rarely occur singly, or in pure form. What we are reacting to in the environment often changes quickly; what we remember and imagine about the situation may change; our appraising changes; and we may have affect-about-affect. Typically, people experience a stream of emotional responses, not all the same ones. Sometimes each emotion may be separated by a few seconds, so that some of the initial emotional responses come to an end before new ones begin, and sometimes emotions occur in overlapping time, blending.[14]

Ekman draws our attention here to one set of parameters bearing on the way a multiplicity of emotions may be represented by a narrative work—those parameters involved in *individual* emotional experience. We may add to those another set of parameters: those arising from the *situation*, that is, the combination of emotions experienced by interacting agents. Just as the stream of emotions within an individual may be a complex, evolving entity, so the interplay of emotions among two or more individuals can be a multifaceted affair. And in all of this, we are speaking of emotions *represented by* and *expressed in* a work: still another layer of variation and complexity is added if we also take account of the differences between emotions so represented, and those *elicited* in the perceiver. Diverse emotions, then, may 'bind' together in our experience of narrative works in a variety of ways, in our understanding of individual characters, in the interaction between characters, and in the interplay between the emotions recognized, and those experienced, by the perceiver. In all these ways films may go beyond the garden-variety emotions.

linking

'Blending', or the interaction of emotions within the individual, is particularly critical in the emergence of more finely tuned emotional states. On the definition offered by Ekman, a blend is generated from the co-occurrence of basic emotional states. But there are many types of emotional blend, or ways in which emotions might blend together. Some blends are sufficiently commonplace that we might include them in the garden-variety category (which, recall, is not identical with the category of basic emotions). Thus, horror is often considered a blend of fear and disgust; Aristotle argues that tragedies seek to elicit both pity and fear; gross-out comedies seek a blend of amusement and disgust. (Note that we don't seem to have a word in English for this blend; 'grotesque' is close, but only implies amusement in some contexts.) Nostalgia mixes happiness prompted by fond memories with the sad recognition that the remembered events are long in the past (see the discussion of this emotion and the words used to designate it in various languages, in Chapter 6). Ekman discusses the blend of 'contempt and enjoyment' expressed through 'a smug contemptuous look'.[15] Closely related to such blends are *metaemotions* (Ekman's 'affect-about-affect'), second-order emotional responses to first-order emotions, as when I might be annoyed with myself, or embarrassed, for having become angry or shown anger over some incident. In such cases the first-order and second-order responses may coexist for some duration. Christopher Grau has analysed a powerful example of such a metaemotion in relation to *American History X* (Tony Kaye, 1998), where we come to feel not only horror at a vicious murder committed by the central character, but dismay at our own previous attraction to the character.[16]

Relatedly, there may be tension between two contrasting emotions that we experience simultaneously, or between an emotion that we authentically feel and a different one that we feel obliged to display. At the awards ceremony, the two stars Argle and Bargle are the two nominees for the Best Actor Award. They are also close friends. Argle is widely regarded as the favourite for the award, and though he is too modest to say it, he thinks so too. But Bargle wins. Argle knows that he is supposed to feel and display admiration for and happiness on behalf of Bargle, but he can't entirely contain his surprise and acute disappointment at not winning the award, which 'leaks' into his facial expression.[17] After all, he really is the better actor, Argle thinks to himself. Later, Argle is embarrassed at this immediate reaction, and ashamed when, looking back at a recording of the awards ceremony, he sees a look of nothing less than resentment flashing across his face as the applause rises for his friend and colleague Bargle. So there is tension between the admiration and the resentment, whether both emotions are felt or whether only one emotion is genuinely felt and the other merely 'acted out' and displayed. The two forms of tension are not identical, and the tension arising from two authentically felt emotions may be more intense, but it takes an act of concerted will to 'perform' an emotion which cuts against the grain of the one that we feel.

These cases suggest that there are at least three axes around which combinations of emotions vary:

- Temporal location: do the emotions co-occur or overlap in time, or are they successive?
- Degree of integration: if the emotions co-occur, do they truly blend (that is, fully integrate with one another, in the way that white and black blend into grey), or do they 'cohabit' as distinct emotions (patches of black and white rather than grey)?
- Degree of 'natural fit': are there constraints on which emotions can combine—whether as full-blooded blends or coexisting but distinct emotions? Certainly it seems that there are 'natural allies' (emotions that fit together ecologically, like fear and disgust) and 'odd couples' (emotions whose individual logic seems to keep them apart—such as disgust and admiration, or happiness and fear; essentially any combination of predominantly 'negative' and 'positive' emotions).

The exact nature of emotional blending has a bearing on the classic debate concerning negative emotions in the context of art: why are certain kinds of narrative designed to prompt negative emotions, like fear, disgust, horror, or embarrassment, and why do we seek to engage with them? Noël Carroll argues that, in the case of horror, what we really seek is narrative satisfaction; horror plays an important role in intensifying the pleasures of narrative—our relief at the vanquishing of the monster is the more intense the greater the imagined threat the monster poses—but we do not find the horror *itself* pleasurable.[18] The problem with this argument is that it seems to allocate to the emotion of horror too marginal a role in the genre after which it is named. I have proposed, alternatively, that our experience of horror is one in which fascination with and disgust at the horrific events in the narrative are, to use the terms proposed by Gary Iseminger, *integrated* rather than merely *coexistent*.[19] Two criteria might be used to decide whether the emotions in a given combination are fully integrated or merely coexistent. Is the emotion blend manifest in a single expression, like Ekman's 'smug contemptuous look'? (Is there an expression of 'fascinated horror'?) And, perhaps more importantly, are the constituent emotions combined and related in a *non-contingent* fashion? According to Carroll, horror fictions bring together narrative fascination and curiosity with horror; we want to find out what has happened and how the narrative will be resolved, but the cost of doing so is an encounter with the fearful and disgusting. Yet narrative fascination does not depend on horror, and for this reason, Carroll argues, the relationship between the emotions of fascination and horror is merely contingent. On my argument, by contrast, horror films embody a particular type of fascination that cannot obtain with other forms of narrative interest; the emotion of horror is a necessary constituent of the particular kind of narrative fascination built into horror films.[20] It is in this sense that I take the commingled blend of fear, disgust, curiosity, and fascination in art-horror to be a fully integrated emotional state.

The Role of Language

As we have seen, de Sousa places an emphasis on the role of language in the inculcation and promulgation of paradigm scenarios. It is worth considering further the role of language in the refining of emotional responses. On the one hand, language appears to play a crucial role in this process. Jenefer Robinson notes that, in coining the word 'prufish', Benson has given us a new item of emotion vocabulary, condensing into a single term the emotional state evoked by (Eliot's imagining of) Prufrock's imagining, giving a name to a feeling which hitherto had been, linguistically speaking, an unchristened fugitive.[21] And more generally, language does seem vital to that process of orienting and fitting basic emotions into the framework of a particular culture. As de Sousa points out, if a given 'paradigm scenario cannot be comprehended without complex linguistic skills...we shall not expect to find in someone who lacks those skills an emotion specifically tuned to that scenario'.[22] Consider the difference, for example, between stark and basic boredom (the state arising from lack of stimulation), and *ennui*—an emotion concept with particular overtones that arise from its development in a specific historical and cultural location. It is hard to see how we could grasp or experience the subtleties of ennui without language. One does not need to believe that concepts per se are dependent on language to accept that language brings enormously powerful resources to the range and flexibility of our conceptual schemes. It seems likely that human cultural diversity is thoroughly intertwined with the power of language to develop and refine our conceptual frameworks (and with these, our array of emotion concepts)—though neither linguistic determinism, nor strong cultural relativism, necessarily follow from this recognition (as I have already argued in Chapter 6).

And yet, as Robinson has stressed, there is a very important way in which language lags behind and struggles to capture the full dynamism of the emotion process. As we saw in Chapter 6, according to Robinson's theory an emotion begins with a relatively coarse non-cognitive affective appraisal, like *Threat!* for fear or *Offence!* for anger.[23] Each of these appraisals sets in train a particular suite of physiological responses; and each is underpinned by a particular profile of neural activity. Such appraisals, then, form the basis for something very similar to Ekman's basic emotions. But on Robinson's account, these appraisals are 'affects' rather than emotions proper. They 'evolve' into emotions through a process of *cognitive monitoring*, whereby we reassess, in a more deliberative fashion, whatever it is or was that prompted the initial affective appraisal. And this process of reappraisal can continue through many phases, up to the point where (usually) we can 'catalogue in recollection' what emotion we experienced: so, Argle might say, I was *resentful* that Bargle won the award.

But Robinson argues that this 'cataloguing' has the character of a 'summary judgement'—that is, it simplifies what has been a complex, evolving, multi-layered response to what is often an ambiguous situation that admits of different emotional

affect : emotion :: sense data : object n
sensation : perception

interpretations. Argle may settle on the idea that he was resentful of Bargle, thereby streamlining in memory the swirl of shock, disappointment, happiness, *and* resentment that characterized his response at the time. Or to imagine another example, when someone reprimands me for being rude, I might initially feel a mix of guilt and shame (for having been rude) and resentment (for having been rebuked). Eventually I settle upon the idea that I was indeed rude, and as that interpretation of the event takes hold, so my sense of guilt becomes more salient and consolidates in memory, while my memory of the resentment that was a constituent of what I initially felt recedes. For Robinson, the folk psychological attributions of emotion embodied by language fall off the pace of the emotion process, and are, in truth, more like hypotheses than descriptions or explanations. In this way they differ from the much faster, and less regulated, early phases of an emotional response. When our bodies register *Threat!* they are not merely floating a hypothesis—they are acting on a 'belief'. (More on those scare quotes shortly.) In a similar spirit, Carl Plantinga remarks that 'it often seems that language, far from circumscribing conscious experience, is desperately trying to keep up with it'.[24]

Our folk attributions do nevertheless possess some 'projective' power. Once we ascribe an emotion to ourselves at a certain point in the process of cognitive monitoring and reappraisal, we are likely to interpret the situation prompting the response in these terms, and through this feedback, respond authentically with that emotion. '[A]s soon as people begin to think of themselves as angry or euphoric', Robinson writes, 'they begin to make the affective appraisals, and take on the facial expressions, motor activity, and action tendencies characteristic of that emotional state'. Attributing an emotion to our ourselves can thereby become a 'self-fulfilling prophecy' (though I doubt that Robinson means that self-attributions always work in this way: we can surely attribute an emotion to ourselves, and then withdraw that hypothesis, treating it as mistaken).[25]

Why the scare quotes around 'belief'? Robinson's discussion of the limitations of our linguistically embodied folk psychology shares much in spirit with Paul Churchland's more general campaign to undermine the credibility of folk psychology as an account of mind. Analysing a scene from Edith Wharton's *The Reef* (1912), Robinson insists—in line with her emphasis on non-cognitive, affective appraisal as the foundation of emotional response—that George Darrow's *feeling* of all-encompassing rejection does not amount to a set of beliefs: 'Darrow does not *believe* that Anna is too cold and formal to be worth marrying; he does not *believe* that the waves and the weather are deliberately rejecting him.'[26] Emotions possess a cognitive element, but that element should not be regarded as amounting to a belief: fearing that p is not the same as believing that p.[27] Churchland's proposal is more radical. Robinson is still working largely within a framework of propositional attitudes, while insisting on the differences among such attitudes. Churchland, on the other hand, stresses the many domains of behaviour in which it seems undeniable that humans possess knowledge of the world, and yet where it seems entirely inappropriate to think of that knowledge being 'fixed' in propositional form of any sort, that is, held as beliefs, desires, hopes, fears, and so forth.

Churchland urges that we take seriously what neuroscience has begun to reveal about the mind: on the connectionist model that he favours, our minds represent the world by virtue of the fast, dynamic, and flexible 'vector-coding' of neurons, not (or not only) by the comparatively sluggish vehicle of our 'linguaformal' folk psychology.[28] He imagines a basketball player

frantically guarding a darting, leaping opponent. The player's visual perceptions of an adversary's every step, hesitation, and acceleration serve to guide his almost instantaneous motor responses, always tending to block the potential shot, intercept the potential pass, or prevent running access to the basket. The player doesn't have *time* to fix any propositional attitudes, nor time to deploy his deductive talents, so to infer therefrom some appropriate intentions and then act on them, even if he did fix an attitude or two. Anyone who mounts a defense using that strategy is doomed to a career on the bench ... the human perceptual system is here as active as can be, and active on a typical cognitive task, but the fixing of propositional attitudes seems not to be a part of the process.[29]

Language, and the folk psychology it enables, are evolutionary latecomers to the human mind; notwithstanding the ways in which language does bestow new capacities upon us, we ignore the epistemic and conceptual power of the *pre-* and *non-linguistic* mind at our peril—or at least at peril of a comprehensive understanding of the mind (as we saw, from another angle, in the exploration of the startle response and empathy in Chapter 3).[30] On both Churchland's and Robinson's views, then, our perceptual and emotional responses outstrip the capacity of language to render them (suggesting once more the kinship between emotion and perception, as discussed in Chapter 6). Just as we have no words for much of the perceptual knowledge that we possess, so we have no words for many of the complexes of emotion that we are capable of recognizing and experiencing.

We are now in a position to put together several threads running through Part II of the present work. In Chapter 5, I analysed the orienting role of basic facial expressions, that is, their role in providing participants and onlookers with an initial understanding of what individual agents are feeling. This function in turn enables these expressions to play a further role in guiding perceivers with regard to the norms of response—that is, in learning both how people typically do respond to given situations, and how they should respond to them. Developmental psychologists theorize that such 'social referencing' (briefly touched upon in Chapter 7) plays an important role in children's emotional education. Over the course of their first eighteen months, children master the routine of looking to see how their caregivers respond to situations—especially those which are unfamiliar or ambiguous—thereby learning how to 'match' specific situations and actions with particular emotions and expressions. Such social referencing is one of the mechanisms by which the paradigm scenarios for emotions are learned. Mature film viewers, of course, already possess a stock of knowledge concerning emotions and their expression; nonetheless, learning through a process of 'pictorial referencing'[31] is at play in films, in at least two ways. At the outset of a film, as viewers engage with a fictional world that is unfamiliar to them—the handholds of genre and other conventions only take us so far—the expressions of characters provide immediate information regarding who cares about what and whom, and in what ways. In this sense we learn about the fictional world by, among other things, reference to emotional expressions. But at the other end of the process, films may refine our existing affective knowledge, suggesting the appropriate forms of response to complex and idiosyncratic situations that exceed the bounds of paradigm scenarios. And as we will see, what we learn through such narratives may carry over from the fictional to the actual world.

The Role of Narrative

To sum up the argument so far: garden-variety emotions include both basic, and more cognitively complex and culturally dependent, emotions. Language is central to the way in which basic affects are developed into these more complex states, and gives us a resource in referring to ever more subtle and refined emotions (whether through single words, phrases, vignettes, or more elaborately described scenarios). When we ascribe emotions to ourselves, using the emotional lexicon of our language, we attempt to describe and explain what it is that we have felt. If accurate, this ascription is apt to consolidate that emotion, or our belief that we have experienced that emotion. If mistaken, wholly or in part, such ascription may still 'bootstrap' the emotion, such that the emotion may begin to take hold of us. But for all this, language is just one aspect of our embodied, emotion-laden cognition, and we should not overestimate its representational (descriptive) or projective ('bootstrapping') power.

Is language the only instrument by which our emotional landscape is refined? This is the point at which I can pick up and properly develop a thread of argument that I began to weave earlier in the chapter. Benson proposed the term 'prufish' to refer to a particular emotional state expressed by Prufrock, but his primary point is that Eliot evokes this peculiar state *not* by coining such a term, but through existing descriptive language, shorn of explicit emotion terms, employed to depict a compact dramatic scenario. Putting Benson and de Sousa together, I want to propose that one function of narrative art is to represent and elicit highly particular emotions or configurations of emotion, even as works of narrative art draw upon our understanding of more generic, garden-variety emotions. There is no tension here since, as we saw earlier, we can only get to the particular through the generic. While many narrative works will employ familiar paradigm scenarios in a relatively simple way, others will create scenarios evocative of emotional states, or combinations of such states, which are not (or not yet) paradigmatic. Speaking of their film on musician Nick Cave, *20,000 Days on Earth* (2014) (Figure 8.1), Iain Forsyth and Jane Pollard note that the film

(1) punctum breaks through studium

Figure 8.1 *20,000 Days on Earth* (Iain Forsyth and Jane Pollard, 2014).

attempts to convey a powerful, positive affective state, a kind of desire to realize imaginative possibilities:

Any time we make a piece of work we always start with the emotion that we want the person seeing the work to feel... We knew right from the start the emotion we wanted to leave you with when you came out of the film, and that is one of ... um ... I guess it ... it sounds trite, but we want to inspire, we want to make you feel the way that Nick makes us feel. His professionalism, his integrity, makes you want to be better, makes you want to do more, and we wanted you to come out of the film with that sense, that drive, to think 'I should just see that idea through'—that thing, that novel, that picture, that ... whatever it is, you know, I should bother, I should make that idea happen.[32]

Lacking any linguistic shorthand for this state of mind, they do their best to describe the emotion, but above all they characterize it ostensively—by pointing to the film itself, which (among other things) embodies just this affective state. In a parallel argument concerning the attitudes expressed by narratives, Ward Jones suggests that 'while some attitudes may have common names and familiar features... [a] huge range of patterns in our attitudes toward others is possible, and it may be that most of them are too rare to be named or too subtle and complex to be spoken about in everyday discourse'.[33]

In an echo of the passage from Ekman I quoted earlier, Robinson writes that 'our emotional life occurs in "streams" that change all the time in response to ever-changing appraisals, ever-evolving actions and action tendencies, ever-changing bodily states'.[34] Narrative artworks are highly effective vehicles for rendering this complex, dynamic, multimodal, multi-layered, and sometimes ambiguous process—because they can represent, and elicit, a range of perceptual and physiological responses rather than (merely) 'fix' these in the 'summary' language of folk psychology. Narrative *films* are particularly powerful in this regard, because of their basis in moving audiovisual depiction. Films engage us perceptually and proprioceptively; we follow a narrative film and respond to it emotionally by watching and listening to human (or human-like) figures interact in concrete environments, whether rendered through live-action cinematography, animation, or CGI. Language is but one element in this mode of narration.

A strong version of this thesis would imply that language is always apt to simplify, via a kind of 'compression' of data into verbal or propositional form, the complexity of a given emotional experience. We have here a version of Cleanth Brooks's 'heresy of paraphrase': the experience made possible by the material work of art itself, in all its subtlety and particularity, cannot be described in language without loss.[35] A weaker version of this thesis concerning the representational power of language, however, regards the glass as half-full rather than half-empty. This weaker version would rather emphasize the flexibility and expandability of our linguistically permeated conceptual mapping of the world, pointing to the way in which the coining of emotional neologisms, like 'prufish', can represent complex emotional configurations or dynamic processes. (German is rich with compound words designating finely individuated emotions: in addition to *Sehnsucht* and *Verfremdungseffekt* (from Chapter 6), consider *Schadenfreude*, pleasure in the suffering of another, and *Torschlusspanik*, the fear of diminishing opportunities as one grows older). If the strong version of this thesis concerning the representational character of language stresses what is lost in compression, the weak version emphasizes how much is retained and gained through compression. Thus Andy Clark argues that '[l]earning a set of tags and labels... renders certain features of our world concrete and salient and allows us to target our thoughts (and learning algorithms) on a new domain of basic objects'.[36] What both positions share is a recognition that language—no matter

how we think of it—cannot substitute for the richness, density, and nuance of perceptual and emotional experience generated by narrative films. Our experience of narrative films may be characterized by what Diana Raffman terms 'nuance ineffability'—an inability to remember and to express in language the fine-grained knowledge arising from our moment-to-moment perceptual experience (see the discussion of this phenomenon in Chapters 1, 2, and 4).[37] In the flow of viewing, we are sensitive to subtleties of facial and vocal expression, and to very precise 'internal shadings of emotional feeling',[38] which are embodied in the film but apt to be lost in translation when recalled in memory or recounted verbally.

Let us put some flesh on these arguments by considering some examples. I will focus on two cases, one very evidently borne out of generic conventions, the other less obviously related to genre. In *The Brave One* (Neil Jordan, 2007), Jodie Foster plays Erica Bain (Figure 8.2), a successful NPR journalist who is violently assaulted, with her fiancé, in New York's Central Park. He is killed in the attack; Bain herself takes many weeks to recover physically. The emotional trauma she suffers is, not surprisingly, much more sustained, and compounded by the seeming indifference and impotence of the police officers assigned to her case. After a series of frustrating encounters with them, Bain undergoes a kind of personality transformation: she copes with her situation by taking the law into her own hands. She buys a gun

① richness, density, & nuance

Figure 8.2 The self-alienated heroine in *The Brave One* (Neil Jordan, 2007).

illegally, begins to investigate the crime perpetrated against her independently, and intervenes in a string of other incidents, in the course of which she kills various other criminals. Eventually a clue enables her to track down her attackers, and with the connivance of a sympathetic police detective, she executes them. It will be obvious, then, that the film is an instance of the *genus* crime film, *species* vigilante, with one major twist on the standard conventions of the type: the victim-turned-vigilante is a woman.

The Brave One builds on that twist by accentuating the psychological trial endured by Bain. Rather than simply embracing her righteous anger wholeheartedly, as would be more typical in a story of this type, she experiences a kind of self-alienation, expressing this through the image of a stranger inhabiting her body (a version of the 'alien limb' syndrome, encountered in Chapter 4, writ large). Although she sees her rage through to its 'logical' conclusion by killing the men who murdered her husband, on several occasions she is stricken by doubt, and even revulsion, at what she has become. At one point, Bain is persuaded by her producer to use her radio show for a phone-in discussion of the vigilante active in the city (that is, Bain herself). Various callers celebrate, glamourize, and trivialize the actions of the vigilante, driving Bain to such a pitch of distress that she nearly turns herself in. While the film is a genre film, then, the emotional journey that it depicts cannot be adequately described using the shorthand of our ordinary emotional vocabulary. At the outset of the story, generic emotion terms may be sufficient: we recognize the love that Bain and her partner feel for one another, the fear that they experience when attacked, the grief and profound anger that Bain experiences after the assault. But as the story progresses, and the particularity of her temperament and her experience emerges, so that standard vocabulary becomes less adequate. We can attempt to describe that experience with more complex linguistic formulations, but ultimately it is *the totality of the film itself*—the story as it is realized through performance, cinematography, editing, and so forth—that gives expression to Bain's emotional trajectory. Even where linguistic descriptions and evocations of emotion appear in the film itself, in dialogue or voice-over, these form but a part of the overall representation of Bain's emotional state. And because it is the film as a whole that carries the burden of representation, the first task for criticism is to analyse the narrative as a whole, with an emphasis on its emotional dynamics.

I turn now to my second example, *Half Nelson* (Ryan Fleck, 2006). In this film, Ryan Gosling plays Dan Dunne, a committed but eccentric high school teacher in Brooklyn. A child of hippie parents, Dunne embraces a dialectical view of life, in the Hegelian-Marxist sense, seeing change at all levels as the product of opposing forces struggling with one another. He tries, and largely succeeds, in making this worldview vivid and accessible in the classroom. In addition, Dunne is the coach for the girls' basketball team, and, from what we can tell, is well liked and respected by his students and colleagues (with the exception of the school principal, who rides him for neglecting the core curriculum). But Dunne is also a drug addict, and the film traces the slow unravelling of his personal and professional life. At the centre of this downward spiral is the friendship he forms with one of his pupils, a black teenaged girl called Drey (Shareeka Epps). Drey catches Dunne smoking crack after a basket-ball game, but this acutely awkward—and for Dunne, potentially disastrous—incident leads to an unexpected intimacy.

Drey's parents are separated. Her mother is a police officer working long shifts; her father is virtually absent from her life (and the film). Her brother Mike has been jailed for drug dealing, taking the fall for a friend, Frank (Anthony Mackie). Frank tries to look out for Drey, partly out of self-interest, and partly out of a genuine sense of responsibility for her; Drey's attitude towards Frank is ambivalent. As Dunne's friendship with Drey grows and he becomes aware of Frank, Dunne tries to intervene and ward off Frank. But Dunne's addiction compromises his efforts in this direction. Little by little, Drey is drawn further into Frank's world. The film reaches its ironic climax when Drey discovers a stoned Dunne at a party to which she is delivering drugs on Frank's behalf. By this point, Dunne has been suspended at school, his personal life has fallen apart, and his cat has died of neglect.

So what can we say about the emotions represented by *Half Nelson*? Although the film might be seen as an off-beat high school comedy—and as the reference to the demise of Dunne's cat might suggest, there's plenty of comedy here, much of it black—the generic reference point doesn't take us far in specifying the emotional terrain of the film. Nevertheless, we can identify certain paradigm scenarios at work here in particular scenes: the embarrassment felt by Dunne when Drey discovers him smoking crack in the girls' restroom; the anger he expresses towards the referee during a basketball game. But what the film renders overall is Dunne's frail, painful, and often addled state of mind. A telling example occurs when Dunne decides to confront Frank, asking him to stay out of Drey's life. Dunne is so het up, out of a mixture of anger towards Frank and drug-induced jitteriness, that he can barely make his point, and is easily diverted by Frank's counterarguments and civility (including the offer of a 'drink') (Figures 8.3a–8.3d).

Figures 8.3a–8.3d Evolution of a complex emotional state in *Half Nelson* (Ryan Fleck, 2006).

There is no obvious, compact expression that comes to mind to describe Dunne's state: it is a peculiar, evolving admixture of happy, energetic enthusiasm, compromised by an undercurrent of slow-burning anxiety and despair. Raffman's point comes home to roost here: 'the grain of conscious experience will inevitably be finer than that of our schemas'.[39] In the DVD audio commentary on *Half Nelson*, the film's editor and co-writer, Anna Boden, notes that the title of the film is an allusion to a wrestling hold, and is meant to express the feeling of being caught in and unable to escape an uncomfortable situation. That elusive metaphor—it is nowhere spelt out within the dramatic action of the film itself—certainly captures some part of Dunne's predicament and state of mind, but again it is the film taken as a whole that renders more fully the particular 'shades of emotion'[40] which characterize Dunne's experience.

The Critic's Share

So we have moved from the generic to the specific, from garden-variety to more exotic emotions. Biology endows us with a set of basic emotional capacities which are then tuned to the needs and themes of particular cultures.[41] Narrative representations are an important vehicle for emotional paradigm scenarios, but narrative artworks can go beyond the articulation of generic scenarios, by representing unique situations which give rise to highly particular configurations of emotion. But now we need to recognize that traffic may flow in the other direction: that particularity may feed back into the culture at large and take on paradigmatic status. A narrative which represents a novel complex of emotions, whether experienced by a single subject of consciousness or expressed through an interaction among various agents, may spread memetically through a culture, becoming a vehicle for referring to this previously unnamed—and perhaps even unrepresented—emotional cluster.[42] Such a narrative becomes a template—a paradigm—through which we can interpret future situations, real or fictional, that we may encounter. Along similar lines, David Lewis suggests that

[s]ometimes reference to a fiction is the only way we have, in practice if not in principle, to formulate the truths that the fiction has called to our attention. A schlemiel is someone such that what is true of him strikingly resembles what is true in a certain fiction of a certain character therein, Schlemiel by name. Temporarily or permanently, first for those who know the story and then for others ... who don't, the word 'schlemiel' is indispensable in stating various truths.[43]

In this way, 'prufishness' might begin as an exotic emotion, lodged somewhere in the vicinity of self-doubt and regret and connected with a very specific character and situation, but there is always a chance that it will be adopted as a paradigm for other situations. In reviving and redeploying the term in the context of theoretical discussion, Robinson and I marginally increase the odds of this happening. If the term is so adopted, the exotic may start to travel in the direction of the garden-variety. When we speak of 'Hitchcockian dread', 'Proustian longing', or refer to Goncharov's Oblomov as an exemplar of laziness, we use particular scenes or entire narratives from the work of these artists as templates for varieties of emotional experience which are not adequately captured by 'fear', 'sadness', and 'laziness', or even 'dread', 'longing', and 'indolence'. In a less concise way, we might use the narratives of *The Brave One* or *Half Nelson* as models for episodes in our own emotional lives, or in those of others. The process comes full circle when artists themselves draw upon these newly christened affective states: episode 9 of the third season of *Breaking Bad* (Vince Gilligan, 2008–13) bears the title 'Kafkaesque'. In this way films help us to capture, distil, and grasp the nuance of particular emotional scenarios in all their shifting, multimodal glory.

We also need to take note of the importance of *critical appreciation* here. Recall that Benson, rather than Eliot or Prufrock, invents the word 'prufish'. The critical act—the verbal analysis and explication of the experience afforded by a narrative artwork—is essential if the work of a narrative in representing a distinctive configuration of emotion is to be recognized and disseminated, and thereby become available as a template. Criticism will often draw upon explicit emotion-laden vocabulary, in the course of mounting an evocative description of a film. Seeking to capture the distinctive emotional tone of Pedro Almodóvar's *Los abrazos rotos/ Broken Embraces* (2009), A. O. Scott writes of the film's 'exuberant melancholy', and coins the term 'Almodóvaria' to name the 'mixture of devastation and euphoria, amusement and dismay' elicited by many of the Spanish director's films. Thus Scott both draws on our familiar lexicon of emotion terms, and proposes a Benson-like neologism to designate the particular feel of Almodóvar's work.[44] But other techniques are available. Just as a narrative work need not denote or express an emotion or emotion complex through explicitly emotion-related vocabulary—whether existing or invented—so critical language may evoke the emotional qualia elicited by a narrative while making little or no use of emotion terms. Recall that a paradigm scenario sets out a situation in terms of a context or setting, roles, and feelings. As we saw in Chapter 5, sometimes a careful description or detailed depiction of setting and roles is sufficient for us to infer the emotions of the agents in the scenario. And sometimes, this descriptive technique overlaps with the use of metaphor.

We have already encountered an example of such a metaphor in *Half Nelson*—the title of the film prompts us to think about a physical situation and the feelings associated with it, and then apply them by analogy to the literal action of the film. Tom Tykwer's *The International* (2009) affords us with a second example. In the course of an interview on the compositional strategies of the film and its use of contemporary architecture, Tykwer states that his intention was to depict a 'seemingly perfect brave new world—Salinger [the central character, played by Clive Owens] representing the people who live in that world, being kind of stuck in a spiderweb, in a perfectly constructed spider's web, and he's in the net, he's trying to free himself. And the net is shaking a little bit, but it's seemingly indestructible.'[45] Tykwer's description is almost purely 'behavioural' in that the only mental state mentioned is Salinger's intention to free himself; but from this we can readily infer the emotions he is likely to be feeling. In the case of *Half Nelson*, the metaphor is verbally embedded in the film, as its title; in the case of *The International*, the metaphor is implicit in the film's visual design. In both cases, in interviews the filmmakers act as explicatory critics of their own works, helping us to recognize significant aspects of the design of the films. What this shows is a continuity between the work itself and critical appreciation of it, especially in respect of the role of language in rendering emotions. Films may exploit all the resources of language in narrating emotion-laden stories, from simple description to emotional predication and metaphor, and criticism will often build directly on such linguistic components of films. One measure of good film criticism, however, is that it will not be over-reliant or over-focused on such linguistic elements, and will seek to analyse and describe the audiovisual foundation of cinematic representation, showing us—as Tykwer does with his own film—how the non-linguistic dimensions of a film work, or are intended to work, upon us.

The Art and Science of Emotion

I have argued in this chapter that one of the reasons we value art—narrative artworks in particular—has to do with the way that they render and instantiate the particular, the individual, the singular. Although we find our way to individual works of art through more general categories, like the genre system in filmmaking, much of the interest and satisfaction we derive from narrative works has to do with their uniqueness. We go to see the latest *Scream* (Wes Craven, 1996–2000) or *Saw* (James Wan, 2004–) film—or watch the next season of *The Wire* (David Simon, 2002–8)—in keen anticipation of new storylines, new characters, new settings, as well as the familiar fixtures of these series. Moreover, narrative artworks can push beyond our routine understanding of human psychology (though some will realize this possibility to a greater degree than others). As Robinson puts it, 'Novels are not just illustrations of principles of folk psychology. They introduce both characters and readers to emotional states for which there are no one-word descriptions in folk psychology... Folk psychology generalizes; literature particularizes.'[46] The singular configuration of emotions that a narrative represents is thus an important dimension of its unique character.

This emphasis on the particular in art is traditionally contrasted with the value placed on the general in science. In their various ways, the sciences are ultimately interested in laws (or law-like tendencies and generalizations). The physicists in the CERN[47] laboratory are not interested in the particular subatomic particles zipping around the large hadron collider, except insofar as they can yield representative data regarding the laws of quantum physics. These contrasting emphases return us to a question at the heart of this book. If the point of art is to render the particular, what could be the relevance of science to the study of art? If I am right that, in the domain of art, 'feeling prufish' is at least as important as 'feeling fearful', doesn't this undermine the strategy of using the tools and data of science to explore emotion in art? Given the role accorded to scientific research on emotion in recent philosophical debate in general, and aesthetic theory in particular, this is not a trivial question.

Many are comfortable with an answer in the affirmative to my second question, allowing artists, critics, and theorists of the arts to pursue their interests in ('blissful') ignorance of the knowledge and the methods of science. But they are wrong to adopt this stance, on several counts. To begin with, we need to acknowledge that the arts and the human sciences are not *only* characterized by a concern with particularity. *Critics* may focus on the particular work, or the particular auteur or historical movement, but *theorists* in the humanities are concerned with questions at a much higher level of generality. Moreover, many narrative artworks imply generalizations through the particular stories that they tell. What the study of the emotions in art reveals is not that art and science repel each other, like identical poles of a magnet, but that they complement each other. On the one hand, most scientific knowledge depends on the investigation of particulars, in the form of replicable laboratory experiments (as well as 'natural experiments', which by definition cannot be replicated, at least not by design). Scientists, that is, must conduct their experiments on particular instances of the general phenomena that they investigate, even as their eyes are on the nomological prize. On the other hand, artists—and the critics who explicate and interpret their works—must employ our general categories of understanding, whether derived from folk or scientific theory or a mixture of the two, in order to contrive the particular objects, performances, and experiences that constitute art. In creating, analysing, and appreciating these particulars, the artist and the critic probe and refine our general categories. And since, as we noted earlier, the particular is dependent on the generic, the artist cannot leapfrog the general and land directly in the particular. In this sense, then, the artist is dependent on that (the general) which is the ultimate target for the scientist, just as the scientist is dependent on that (the particular) which is the focus for the artist.

Science and art each start from the same point—from our experience of the world, and our intuitions about it as they are embodied in folk theories. From where else would an artist or scientist begin? Perhaps from an established scientific theory, rather than folk theory; or perhaps from some exotic cultural theory that makes us think twice about our own folk theory; perhaps from a priori assumptions or some form of innate knowledge. However we map this out, there are a limited number of places to start, and the intuitions derived from experience will loom large wherever we are coming from. The important matter, in any case, is the direction in which scientific and artistic endeavours move from their starting points. While science marches towards generalization, art engages our attention in the particular (and where it lays claim to more general ambitions, it does so through the particularity of the individual work). '[I]f we really want to understand emotions in all their uniqueness and individuality...we would do better to stay away from the generalizations of philosophers and psychologists, and turn instead to the detailed studies of emotion that we find in great literature',[48] Robinson declares. Given the role of and value placed on scientific research and theory on emotion in her work and in the work of other participants in the contemporary debates on art and emotion, however, Robinson's statement here represents only one side of the story. Our understanding and appreciation of the particularity of artworks—and the emotions that they represent, express, and elicit—is greatly heightened by the general, scientifically informed theory of emotion that has flourished in these debates, to which the current work testifies.

Conclusion

Reconciling the Manifest and Scientific Images

> Having the goose which lays the golden eggs, the description of each egg already laid is a minor matter.
>
> William James

Where are we now? The present work has taken the reader on a tour exploring various ways in which knowledge and methods from the humanities and the sciences might fruitfully interact. Chapter 8 explored the significance of the particularity of each individual work of art, arriving at the conclusion that any theory of art must accommodate this dimension of our appreciation of artworks. Particularity is not the whole story, since a considerable amount of aesthetic and artistic traffic takes place at more abstract levels, such as those pertaining to genre, artistic movements, national and regional trends. But it is undeniable that a standard target for critical discourse is the individual work. Although this might be seen as posing difficulties for a naturalized aesthetics, I ended Chapter 8 by arguing that the generalities uncovered by science can nonetheless play an important role in the explanation, understanding, and appreciation of individual artworks.

The reflections of William James on the science of emotion, as it existed in his time, push us further in this direction. James writes:

as far as 'scientific psychology' of the emotions goes, I may have been surfeited by too much reading of classic works on the subject, but I should as lief read verbal descriptions of the shapes of the rocks on a New Hampshire farm as toil through them again. They give one nowhere a central point of view, or a deductive or generative principle... The trouble with the emotions in psychology is that they are regarded too much as absolutely individual things. So long as they are set down as so many eternal and sacred psychic entities, like the old immutable species in natural history, so long all that *can* be done with them is reverently to catalogue their separate characters, points, and effects. But if we regard them as products of more general causes (as 'species' are now regarded as products of heredity and variation), the mere distinguishing and cataloguing becomes of subsidiary importance.[1]

James concludes this passage with the punch line serving as the epigraph of this conclusion: 'Having the goose which lays the golden eggs, the description of each egg already laid is a minor matter.' He thereby identifies the dangers of an obsession with the particular instance, which can degenerate into a narrowly descriptive exercise cutting the object off from the various categories, contexts, and patterns of behaviour which are essential to a proper understanding of it. While we need to make space to recognize the unique features of artworks, as we saw in Chapter 8, we also need to be wary of the trap identified by James—the compulsion to detail what is special about every token, at the cost of attention to the character of each token as a type.

Worries about the fit between the arts and naturalistic explanation persist, however. Asked in an interview why he titled one of his books on art *Unnatural Wonders* (2005), Arthur Danto replied: 'there's no natural law that covers what goes on in art'.[2] Seen in the context of the interview, the statement reveals at least two confusions. Danto's point is that scientific practice will never replace art as a vehicle of human expression and meaning-making; and neither will science provide the tools for discerning the 'embodied meanings' of artworks. But as we have seen, the ambition of naturalized aesthetics is to provide a theory of aesthetic and artistic phenomena in the light of our more general, scientifically informed understanding of the world; it is not advanced as a method by which individual works are to be interpreted, and still less as a substitute for art making. Danto is right that science can't substitute for art, though artists have long drawn upon scientific theories for instruments and inspiration, and some types of art require exact quantification on the part of their makers. On my argument a naturalistic, scientifically oriented theory of art is not a rival to art, but a rival to non- or anti-naturalistic theories of art. Understanding the scope and goals of naturalized aesthetics, and how it fits within the range of practical, theoretical, and critical activities undertaken by aestheticians, is crucial to a fair assessment of its value and prospects. If the first confusion arising from Danto's statement is that it mistakenly puts art making and naturalistic theory into competition with one another, the second concerns the kinds of explanation encompassed by naturalism. The explanatory ambition of naturalized aesthetics need not be understood as a search for covering laws that govern aesthetic and artistic phenomena, but rather as the search for singular causal explanations of such phenomena. Alfred Hitchcock's *Lifeboat* (1944) may be a unique, complex object that resists assimilation to any single covering law, but we can illuminate many of its particular properties by investigating it in the light of the science of emotion (as I sought to demonstrate in Chapter 5).

Frank Cioffi is similarly cautious with regard to the ambitions of naturalism, offering only 'two cheers for the coroner's report'—such a report being Cioffi's symbol of the explanatory goal of naturalism. Cioffi is right to stress that there are a variety of other ways of approaching the world beyond seeking explanations. Writing the acknowledgements of this book a few minutes ago, for example, I wasn't engaged in explanation. There are also acts of Wittgensteinian 'further description' focused on clarifying and giving a perspicuous overview of phenomena that we already understand intuitively; in Cioffi's words, 'there are aesthetic perplexities which don't find their natural consummation in the discovery of causal connection'.[3] Neither should we forget the business of evaluation so central to film and art criticism.

Moreover, as we have seen in Chapters 4 and 8, another central goal of criticism is the evocation of the particular character of artworks and the distinctive qualia that they prompt in us. In those chapters I have offered a theory of the place of qualia in our appreciation of artworks. But note that formulating such a theory only involves acts of critical analysis and the evocation of the qualities of particular works in a secondary way, as material to test the theory; a theory of art criticism is itself no more an act of criticism than a theory of science is an exercise in scientific investigation. So while it is true that aesthetics, broadly construed, encompasses more than explanation, by the same token it is important not to confuse naturalism with scientism, precisely because naturalism (or at least, the variety on offer here) happily admits that there are questions and activities beyond the purview of the sciences. 'Respect for science, and an enthusiasm for learning from it', as Philip Kitcher puts it, 'are fully compatible with rejecting scientism.'[4] Naturalism simply insists that explanation is a significant part of the enterprise of philosophical aesthetics.

I began this book with a discussion of C. P. Snow's claims concerning the divide between the sciences and traditional culture. Writing in the same period as Snow, Wilfrid Sellars made a parallel distinction between the 'manifest image' and the 'scientific image' of the world—a distinction between the way in which the world appears to us in ordinary experience on the one hand (in which persons and the 'space of reasons' play a central role), and the understanding of the world that we gain through science on the other.[5] Sellars's contrast was considerably more intricate than Snow's, treating the empirical impulse as an aspect of ordinary human understanding which, when elaborated and purified in the form of modern science, comes into conflict with other aspects of that 'manifest' understanding. In this sense science is continuous with ordinary human cognition, even if science eventually comes to challenge certain aspects of the manifest image of the world (as is evident from our changing understanding of the shape of the earth, of disease, and closer to the themes of this volume, of perception, emotion, and empathy).

An abiding concern for Sellars was the question: how do these two pictures of the world, so often at variance, 'hang together' with one another? Sellars himself was committed to achieving a 'synoptic vision', a 'true stereoscopic view' that 'blends' or 'joins' the manifest and scientific images.[6] While it is certainly true that our everyday understanding of the world is shaped and informed by scientific discovery, it may be too much to ask for an entirely harmonious integration of these two perspectives. One of the lessons of modernist art, however, is that things can hang together in a disharmonious way; that a work can exhibit a certain degree of fragmentation and still be recognized as a work. (Note that this is an example, then, of another face of the third culture: an instance of the arts providing an insight into the world, here furnishing a model of the relationship between the scientific and the manifest images.) That may be a more realistic model for the manner in which the manifest and scientific images of the world can coexist. At this point in human history, both are necessary and inescapable, but they can no more fuse than can our (manifest) experience of the surface of the earth as a flat plane seamlessly meld with our background (scientific) knowledge that the earth is spherical in shape.

Another area where the manifest and scientific images of the world are in tension concerns our understanding of perception itself, and the nature of mind more generally. According to the manifest image, perception gives us access to the world as it is (an assumption sometimes described as 'naïve realism'); illusions and mis-perceptions are aberrations that prove the rule. The dominant view of perception in the cognitive sciences gives us a very different understanding of perception. Accord-ing to this alternative picture, our minds give us access to the world by *representing* it. The colours that we perceive are not mind-independent phenomena; colours come into being in our perceptual apprehension of the world. Nonetheless, when we perceive the grass as green, we are perceiving the grass and responding to features of the grass (roughly, the frequency of the light waves bouncing off it) as a percept. This is, then, an apt moment to stress that, notwithstanding the attention paid to the various forms of radical externalism in these pages—those theories emphasizing the dependence of the mind on 'extracranial' factors, like the body and the world—*Film, Art, and the Third Culture* remains resolutely committed to the *representational theory of mind*. According to this theory, a wide variety of core mental states—including perceptions, beliefs, desires, emotions, memories, anticipations, and imaginings—represent the world as it is, or has been, or might be. As we saw in Chapters 1 and 2, we possess neural maps of our own bodies allowing us to coordinate our movements within the world, and 'body clocks' orienting us to the diurnal rhythms of the world, but these representational mechanisms are not infal-lible. Insofar as our beliefs can be mistaken and our senses can deceive us—to take just two of this array of mental states—neither cognition nor perception can coher-ently be thought to deliver unvarnished apprehensions of the world; but it is does not follow that we perceive only 'sense data' or inner representations. Rather we perceive the world, transparently, *through* our mental representations of it. As I have argued in Chapter 2, our different modes of sensory perception are the means by which 'the mind opens out onto its environment and assembles for itself a representation of outer reality'.[7] What's more, the concept of mental representation is intimately related to an array of other concepts—intentionality, meaning, and consciousness among them—which it is far from easy to dispense with, not least in an account of art and aesthetic experience.

The capacity of an organism to navigate and act in the world by representing it is in the first instance a biological phenomenon; organisms have evolved minds in order to cope with, survive, and sometimes thrive within the world; and minds are adapted to the different 'niches' within the external environment that they occupy.[8] Because the mind is the original representational device, we need to understand external representations (paintings, movies, language) in the context of mental representation (rather than the other way around—small wonder that gen-erations of philosophers have found fault with efforts to model mental on external representation). In Chapter 7, I have defended a version of the theory of the extended mind, which invites us to understand external representations precisely as extensions of the mind.

Kendall Walton's arguments concerning the 'transparency' of photographic representation help us see the connections here, that is, to understand how mental and external representation can be seen as subspecies of the same phenomenon. As we saw in Chapter 1, Walton argues that when we look at a photograph, we perceive not only the photograph itself, but the object it represents; we see the photograph itself directly, and we see what the photograph depicts *through* it, that is, indirectly. In claiming that photos allow us to see spatially or temporally remote objects, Walton suggests that our powers of perception are augmented and extended by them. In this way photographs resemble devices like telescopes, eyeglasses, and mirrors—visual prostheses, each of which aids vision in a different way. Moreover, his theory also indicates how there is no mutual incompatibility between perception and (the mediation of) representation: we see a chair through its photographic representation, just as in an ordinary, non-photographic perceptual episode we see the chair through our perceptual representation of it.[9] Insisting on the representational character of the mind does not place us behind a veil of mere sense data, or prevent us from engaging with the world itself. On the contrary, the representational capacities of the mind are the very tools that enable us to get hold of the world. As Jerry Fodor puts it, 'There is a gap between the mind and the world, and (as far as anybody knows) you need to posit internal representations if you are to have a hope of getting across it. Mind the gap.'[10]

I conclude this book by focusing on ideas from Walton and Fodor—two of our most distinguished philosophers—in part to underline once more the nature of naturalized aesthetics and the broader project of a third culture advocated here. Such naturalism emerges from an ongoing dialogue between empirical research and conceptual reflection on the assumptions we make, the questions we ask, and the existing frameworks through which we understand the world. Good empirical research requires attention to its conceptual scaffolding, and good philosophical theorizing demands alertness to the relevance of empirical findings about the world. From such dialogue, robust theory construction, as outlined in Chapter 2, is possible. Nonetheless, such a broad, collaborative enterprise allows for, perhaps even best flourishes in the context of, a division in labour in which it is the particular responsibility of philosophers to sift, interrogate, and synthesize the ideas, evidence, and argument relevant to particular domains of enquiry. It has been the goal of this work to exemplify just such an approach to the art of film, the many other art forms from which it emerged and with which it remains in creative exchange, and the world of aesthetic experience more generally.

Notes

Introduction

1. C. P. Snow, 'The Two Cultures', *New Statesman*, 6 Oct. 1956, 413–14, <http://www.newstatesman.com/cultural-capital/2013/01/c-p-snow-two-cultures>.
2. Over the years, commentary on the two cultures debate has been published by, among others, Stefan Collini, Roy Porter, Anthony O'Hear, Roger Kimball, Lisa Jardine, Raymond Tallis, Frank Furedi, and Onora O'Neill. O'Neill's 'The Two Cultures Fifty Years On' was delivered as the Rede Lecture in 2010, fifty-one years after Snow's contribution to the same series. For a recent overview, see Guy Ortolano, *The Two Cultures Controversy: Science, Literature and Cultural Politics in Postwar Britain* (Cambridge: CUP, 2009).
3. William Seeley e.g. writes of 'a culture of mutual distrust' between philosophers of art and cognitive neuroscientists working on aesthetic phenomena: 'What is the Cognitive Neuroscience of Art…And Why Should We Care?' *ASA Newsletter*, 31/2 (Summer 2011), 1.
4. In certain contexts it is important to make further distinctions—between, for example, the natural sciences, the social sciences, and the humanities; between artistic practice and the theoretical, historical, and critical investigation of art and culture; or between the life sciences and the physical sciences. I follow both Snow and the wider consensus since (at least) the late 19th century in assuming that behind these more specific contrasts, however, lies the question of the relationship between the natural and the human sciences (where the latter encompasses disciplines in the humanities and the social sciences). For a contemporary treatment of the divide, especially as it pertains to debates around empathy (the subject of Chapter 6), see Karsten R. Stueber, *Rediscovering Empathy: Agency, Folk Psychology, and the Human Sciences* (Cambridge, MA: MIT Press, 2006).
5. Wilhelm Dilthey, *Introduction to the Human Sciences: An Attempt to Lay a Foundation for the Study of Society and History*, tr. Ramon J. Betanzos (Detroit: Wayne State University Press, 1988). Derek Freeman explores disputes in anthropology in the light of Dilthey's conception of the sciences in *Dilthey's Dream: Essays on Human Nature and Culture* (Canberra: Pandanus Books, 2001). Kant's discussion of the third antinomy is to be in found in his *Critique of Pure Reason*, tr. Norman Kemp Smith (Houndmills: Palgrave, 1929), ch. 2, section 2.
6. Snow uses the expression 'literary intellectuals' in the longer and better-known 1959 version of the essay, delivered as the Rede Lecture, published first in the journal *Encounter* and subsequently as a book (Snow, 'The Two Cultures: The Rede Lecture' (1959), 4 and throughout). The most recent edition provides an introduction by Stefan Collini: Snow, *The Two Cultures*.
7. Snow, 'The Two Cultures: The Rede Lecture' (1959), 14–15.
8. A further parallel between the intellectual landscape Snow describes and Viennese logical positivism is evident when he notes the attitude of disdain held by many scientists towards some types of philosophy, including both metaphysics and existentialism.

9. See e.g. Paul M. Churchland, 'Eliminative Materialism and the Propositional Attitudes', *Journal of Philosophy* 78/2 (Feb. 1981), 67–90, and Patricia S. Churchland, *Neurophilosophy: Towards a Unified Science of the Mind-Brain* (Cambridge, MA: MIT Press, 1996). The bark of the Churchlands is often worse than their bite, however; in Chapters 2 and 8, I aim to demonstrate how Paul Churchland's neurophilosophy may be enlisted in explaining important aspects of colour perception and motor experience as these function in the arts. For another example of replacement naturalism, see Alex Rosenberg, *The Atheist's Guide to Reality: Enjoying Life without Illusions* (New York: W. W. Norton & Co., 2012). Rosenberg actively embraces 'scientism', typically used as a derogatory label for the kind of position described here as replacement naturalism.

10. Snow, 'The Two Cultures: A Second Look', 71; John Brockman (ed.), *The Third Culture* (New York: Touchstone, 1996), 18.

11. These terms and the contrast they invoke are advanced by Richard Feldman, 'Naturalized Epistemology', *Stanford Encyclopedia of Philosophy*, 5 July 2001, <http://plato.stanford.edu/entries/epistemology-naturalized>.

12. Steven Pinker, 'Science is Not Your Enemy', *The New Republic*, 6 Aug. 2013, <http://www.newrepublic.com//article/114127/science-not-enemy-humanities>.

13. Dilthey, *Introduction to the Human Sciences*; F. R. Leavis, 'Two Cultures? The Significance of C.P. Snow', *The Spectator*, 9 Mar. 1962, reprinted with other material by Leavis and commentary by Stefan Collini, as F. R. Leavis, *Two Cultures? The Significance of C. P. Snow* (Cambridge: CUP, 2013).

14. Jesse J. Prinz, *Beyond Human Nature: How Culture and Experience Shape our Lives* (London: Penguin, 2012), 285–8.

15. Vincent Bergeron and Dominic McIver Lopes note the importance of such conceptual ground-clearing if empirical research is to be relevant to the questions asked by art theorists and aestheticians, in 'Aesthetic Theory and Aesthetic Science: Prospects for Integration', in Arthur P. Shimamura and Stephen E. Palmer (eds), *Aesthetic Science: Connecting Minds, Brains, and Experience* (New York: OUP, 2012), 63–79.

16. Mitchell S. Green, *Self-Expression* (Oxford: Clarendon Press, 2007), 16–17.

17. Green, *Self-Expression*, 16; Michael Tomasello, *Origins of Human Communication* (Cambridge, MA: MIT Press, 2008), pp. xi and 6; Vittorio Gallese and Michele Guerra, *Lo schermo empatico: Cinema e neuroscienze* (Milan: Raffaello Cortina Editore, 2015), 52–3, 122–5; Richard Wollheim, *Painting as an Art* (London: Thames & Hudson, 1987), 100.

18. Quoted in Arthur C. Danto, 'Christian Boltanksi', in *Encounters and Reflection: Art in the Historical Present* (New York: Noonday Press, 1991), 257. See also Danto's remarks on *Fountain* in *The Transfiguration of the Commonplace: A Philosophy of Art* (Cambridge, MA: Harvard University Press, 1981), 94.

19. Noël Carroll, *Beyond Aesthetics: Philosophical Essays* (Cambridge: CUP, 2001); Immanuel Kant, *The Critique of Judgement*, tr. James Creed Meredith (Oxford: Clarendon Press, 1952).

20. For a discussion of related views of aesthetic experience, and a defence of such in the context of empirical doubts, see Sherri Irvin, 'Is Aesthetic Experience Possible?' in Gregory Currie, Matthew Kieran, Aaron Meskin, and Jon Robson (eds), *Aesthetics and the Sciences of Mind* (Oxford: OUP, 2014), 37–56.

21. G. Gabrielle Starr, *Feeling Beauty: The Neuroscience of Aesthetic Experience* (Cambridge, MA: MIT Press, 2013), p. xi.

22. Colin McGinn, 'Storm Over the Brain', review of Patricia S. Churchland, *Touching a Nerve: The Self as Brain, New York Review of Books*, 24 Apr. 2014, <http://www.nybooks.com/articles/2014/04/24/storm-over-the-brain>.
23. See the references to the work of these scholars in Chs. 3 and 4.
24. Frank Jackson, 'Epiphenomenal Qualia', *Philosophical Quarterly*, 32/127 (Apr. 1982): 127.
25. The first phrase is Fodor's: 'Diary', *London Review of Books*, 21/19 (30 Sept. 1999): 68, <http://www.lrb.co.uk/v21/n19/jerry-fodor/diary>. The second and third are from W. Teed Rockwell, *Neither Brain Nor Ghost: A Nondualist Alternative to the Mind-Brain Identity Theory* (Cambridge, MA: MIT Press, 2005).

Chapter 1 Aesthetics Naturalized

1. Not only analytic philosophers, however—see e.g. Terry Pinkard, *Hegel's Naturalism: Mind, Nature, and the Final Ends of Life* (New York: OUP, 2012).
2. David Macarthur, review of Jack Ritchie, *Understanding Naturalism* (2008), *Notre Dame Philosophical Reviews*, 10 Nov. 2009, <https://ndpr.nd.edu/news/24219-understanding-naturalism>.
3. Geert Keil, 'Naturalism', in Dermot Moran (ed.), *The Routledge Companion to Twentieth Century Philosophy* (London: Routledge, 2010), 254.
4. Robert Sinnerbrink, *New Philosophies of Film* (London: Continuum, 2011) is one of the few exceptions, recognizing naturalism in the philosophical sense (pp. 4, 6).
5. Roy Wood Sellars, *Evolutionary Naturalism* (New York: Russell & Russell, 1922), p. i.
6. Philip Kitcher, 'The Naturalists Return', *Philosophical Review*, 101/1 (1992): 54; Kitcher refers to Descartes, Locke, Leibniz, Hume, Kant, and Mill in this regard. Keil, 'Naturalism', indicates that the term 'naturalism' was already in widespread use by the end of the 19th century; Moore developed his notion of the 'naturalistic fallacy' in *Principia Ethica* in 1903.
7. Andy Clark, *Mindware: An Introduction to the Philosophy of Cognitive Science*, 2nd edn (Oxford: OUP, 2013), p. xi; Fred Dretske, *Naturalizing the Mind* (Cambridge, MA: MIT Press, 1995), 28.
8. Richard Wollheim, 'Representation: The Philosophical Contribution to Psychology', in *The Mind and its Depths* (Cambridge, MA: Harvard University Press, 1993), 159.
9. Sometimes these two aspects are held to be detachable; in what follows, I assume that a robust naturalism is characterized by some version of both principles.
10. Both essays are available in Quine, *Quintessence*, ed. Roger F. Gibson Jr (Cambridge, MA: Harvard University Press, 2008).
11. Kendall Walton, 'Aesthetics: What? Why? And Wherefore?', *Journal of Aesthetics and Art Criticism*, 65/2 (Spring 2007): 151.
12. Walton, 'Aesthetics', 152.
13. Kendall L. Walton, 'Transparent Pictures: On the Nature of Photographic Realism', *Critical Inquiry*, 11/2 (Dec. 1984): 246–77. Walton quotes from Bazin's essay 'The Ontology of the Photographic Image', in *What is Cinema?*, i, ed. and tr. Hugh Gray (Berkeley, CA: University of California Press, 1967), 9–16.
14. Kendall L. Walton, 'Postscripts to "Transparent Pictures"', in *Marvelous Images: On Values and the Arts* (Oxford: OUP, 2008), 111.

15. 'We fix on the particular functions of the unclear expression that make it worth troubling about, and then devise a substitute, clear and couched in terms to our liking, that fills those functions': Willard Van Orman Quine, 'Ontic Decision', §53, in *Word and Object* (Cambridge, MA: MIT Press, 1960), 258–9. See also the discussion of Quinean paraphrase in Frank Jackson, *From Metaphysics to Ethics: A Defence of Conceptual Analysis* (Oxford: Clarendon Press, 1998), 44–5.

16. Kwame Anthony Appiah, *Experiments in Ethics* (Cambridge, MA: Harvard University Press, 2008); Joshua Alexander, *Experimental Philosophy: An Introduction* (Cambridge: Polity, 2012).

17. Thomas Munro, *Towards Science in Aesthetics: Selected Essays* (New York: Liberal Arts Press, 1956); David E. Fenner, 'Modest Aesthetic Naturalism', *Journal of Aesthetics and Art Criticism*, 50/4 (Autumn 1992): 283–9; Douglas Dempster, 'Renaturalizing Aesthetics', *Journal of Aesthetics and Art Criticism*, 51/3 (Summer 1993): 351–61. The BSA was founded in 1960.

18. Dissanayake's first article on this topic appeared in 1980: 'Art as a Human Behavior: Toward an Ethological View of Art', *Journal of Aesthetics and Art Criticism*, 38/4 (Summer 1980): 397–406.

19. Wilfrid Sellars, 'Philosophy and the Scientific Image of Man', in Robert Colodny (ed.), *Frontiers of Science and Philosophy* (Pittsburgh, PA: University of Pittsburgh Press, 1962), 37.

20. Rachel Cooper, *Psychiatry and Philosophy of Science* (Stocksfield: Acumen, 2007), 65–6.

21. Wilfrid Sellars, *Empiricism and the Philosophy of Mind*, ed. Robert Brandom (Cambridge, MA: Harvard University Press, 1997), §40, 81.

22. Edouard Machery, *Doing without Concepts* (Oxford: OUP, 2009), 6.

23. Timothy Williamson, *The Philosophy of Philosophy* (Malden, MA: Blackwell, 2008), argues that (analytic) philosophical practice is out of step with the standard descriptions of it. See also Williamson's essay 'How did we Get Here from There? The Transformation of Analytic Philosophy', *Belgrade Philosophical Annual*, 27 (2014): 7–37.

24. Quine makes reference to 'theory-building' in 'Beginning with Ordinary Things', §1 in *Word and Object*, 1–5.

25. Noël Carroll, *Philosophy of Art: A Contemporary Introduction* (London: Routledge, 1999), 13.

26. Ryle's comment was made in the context of a debate with Maurice Merleau-Ponty, Quine, A. J. Ayer, and other philosophers, recorded in Maurice Merleau-Ponty, *Texts and Dialogues: On Philosophy, Politics, and Culture*, tr. and ed. Hugh Silverman and James Barry (Amherst, NY: Prometheus Press, 1996), 68. Hacker's position is laid out in, among other places, M. R. Bennett and P. M. S. Hacker, *Philosophical Foundations of Neuroscience* (Oxford: Blackwell, 2003), 2. I return to Hacker's views on philosophy and neuroscience later in this chapter, and in Ch. 3.

27. George Dickie, 'Is Psychology Relevant to Aesthetics?', *Philosophical Review*, 71/3 (July 1962): 300.

28. Gregory Currie, 'Aesthetic Explanation', in *Arts and Minds* (Oxford: Clarendon Press, 2004), 243. Currie's view here is echoed by David Davies; see Ch. 3 n. 33.

29. For a body of philosophical work on pornography significantly informed by various kinds of empirical research, as well as the reflections of practitioners, see Hans Maes and Jerrold Levinson (eds), *Art and Pornography: Philosophical Essays* (Oxford: OUP, 2012), and esp. Hans Maes (ed.), *Pornographic Art and the Aesthetics of Pornography* (Basingstoke: Palgrave Macmillan, 2013).

30. Kendall L. Walton, *Mimesis as Make-Believe: On the Foundations of the Representational Arts* (Cambridge, MA: Harvard University Press, 1990), 21.

31. Derek Matravers, *Fiction and Narrative* (Oxford: OUP, 2014).

32. Paul E. Griffiths, *What Emotions Really Are: The Problem of Psychological Categories* (Chicago: University of Chicago Press, 1997), ch. 2, and p. 5.

33. A shift which happened in the West much earlier than is often assumed; Aristotle e.g. argues in favour of the spherical shape of the Earth.

34. Jaegwon Kim, *Physicalism, or Something Near Enough* (Princeton: Princeton University Press, 2005), 168.

35. Locke argues that 'consciousness... is inseparable from thinking, and as it seems to me essential to it: It being impossible for any one to perceive, without perceiving, that he does perceive. When we see, hear, smell, taste, feel, meditate, or will any thing, we know that we do so.' John Locke, *An Essay Concerning Human Understanding*, ed. Peter H. Nidditch (Oxford: OUP, 1975), bk II, ch. XXVII, §9, p. 335.

36. Gregory Currie, 'The Paradox of Caring: Fiction and the Philosophy of Mind', in Mette Hjort and Sue Laver (eds), *Emotion and the Arts* (New York: OUP, 1997), 63.

37. Diana Raffman, *Language, Music, and Mind* (Cambridge, MA: MIT Press, 1993); see also Daniel Levitin, *This is your Brain on Music: Understanding a Human Obsession* (New York: Dutton, 2006), 149–50.

38. M. G. F. Martin, 'Perception, Concepts, and Memory', *Philosophical Review* 101/4 (Oct. 1992), 758–9.

39. Note that neither Raffman, Robinson, nor Nanay use the phrase 'theory construction'. Their arguments nonetheless exemplify the procedure.

40. Jenefer Robinson, *Deeper than Reason: Emotion and its Role in Literature, Music, and Art* (Oxford: Clarendon Press, 2005), ch. 7. Dickie regards Bullough's notion of 'aesthetic distance' as a particularly strong version of the wider family of 'aesthetic attitude' theories: George Dickie, 'The Myth of the Aesthetic Attitude', *American Philosophical Quarterly*, 1/1 (Jan. 1964): 56–65. Emotional coping is also a central pillar of Torben Grodal's 'biocultural' theory of film spectatorship, as laid out in his *Embodied Visions: Evolution, Emotion, Culture, and Film* (Oxford: OUP, 2009).

41. Robinson, *Deeper than Reason*, 227; emphasis in the original.

42. Bence Nanay, *Aesthetics as Philosophy of Perception* (Oxford: OUP, 2016), ch. 2.

43. Nanay, *Aesthetics*, 180–1.

44. Michael Strevens, *Depth: An Account of Scientific Explanation* (Cambridge, MA: Harvard University Press, 2008), 3.

45. Wilhelm Dilthey, *Descriptive Psychology and Historical Understanding*, in *Selected Writings*, ed. and tr. H. P. Rickman (Cambridge: CUP, 1976), 89.

46. Clifford Geertz, *The Interpretation of Cultures* (New York: Basic Books, 1973), 5; for commentary, see Adam Kuper, *Culture: The Anthropologists' Account* (Cambridge, MA: Harvard University Press, 1999), 72, and ch. 3.

47. Bordwell, introducing a free download of his article 'A Case for Cognitivism: Further Reflections', *Iris*, 11 (Summer 1990): 107–12, available with the introduction at <http://www.davidbordwell.net/articles>.

48. Clark, *Mindware*, 178–9.

49. Mitchell S. Green, *Self-Expression* (Oxford: Clarendon Press, 2007), 54, notes that in debates about Grice's 'non-natural meaning', that expression has in general been replaced by the phrase 'speaker meaning', perhaps reflecting the concerns I raise here about the unfortunate implications of the modifier 'non-natural'. Green presents an alternative model of human communication, expression, and meaning displacing intention from centre stage.

50. Paul Grice, 'Meaning', in *Studies in the Way of Words* (Cambridge, MA: Harvard University Press, 1989), 213–23.

51. James R. Hurford, 'The Neural Basis of Predicate-Argument Structure', *Behavorial and Brain Sciences*, 26 (2003): 261–83; James R. Hurford, *The Origins of Meaning* (Oxford: OUP, 2007); Michael Tomasello, *Origins of Human Communication* (Cambridge, MA: MIT Press, 2008). See also the essays collected in Susan Hurley and Matthew Nudds (eds), *Rational Animals?* (Oxford: OUP, 2006); and Peter Carruthers, 'Animal Minds Are Real, (Distinctively) Human Minds Are Not', *American Philosophical Quarterly*, 50/3 (July 2013): 233–48.

52. Michael Tomasello, *The Cultural Origins of Human Communication* (Cambridge, MA: Harvard University Press, 1999), ch. 4; Robert Boyd and Peter J. Richerson, *Not by Genes Alone: How Culture Transformed Human Evolution* (Chicago: University of Chicago Press, 2005); Andrew Whiten, 'The Second Inheritance System of Chimpanzees and Humans', *Nature*, 437 (1 Sept. 2005), box 1, p. 53.

53. Mark Rowlands, *The Philosopher and the Wolf: Lessons from the Wild on Love, Death and Happiness* (London: Granta, 2008).

54. See Dretske, *Naturalizing the Mind*; Ruth Garrett Millikan, *Varieties of Meaning* (Cambridge, MA: MIT Press, 2004); Ruth Garrett Millikan, 'Biosemantics', in Ansgar Beckermann, Brian P. McLaughlin, and Sven Walter (eds), *The Oxford Handbook of Philosophy of Mind* (Oxford: OUP, 2009), 394–406; Carolyn Price, *Functions in Mind: A Theory of Intentional Content* (Oxford: Clarendon Press, 2001); Ronald de Sousa, *Why Think? Evolution and the Rational Mind* (New York: OUP, 2007); Kim Sterelny, *Thought in a Hostile World: The Evolution of Human Cognition* (Malden, MA: Blackwell, 2005). Hurford develops a broadly similar position, from within linguistics, in *The Origins of Meaning*.

55. On the character of theatrical magic as a specific type of aesthetic experience, see Jason Leddington, 'The Experience of Magic', *Journal of Aesthetics and Art Criticism*, 74/3 (Summer 2016): 253–64.

56. Daniel Barratt, '"Twist Blindness": The Role of Primacy, Priming, Schemas, and Reconstructive Memory in a First-Time Viewing of *The Sixth Sense*', in Warren Buckland (ed.), *Puzzle Films: Complex Storytelling in Contemporary Cinema* (Malden, MA: Wiley-Blackwell, 2009), 62–86.

57. See Richard Allen, *Projecting Illusion: Film Spectatorship and the Impression of Reality* (Cambridge: CUP, 1997); my 'Film Spectatorship and the Institution of Fiction', *Journal of Aesthetics and Art Criticism*, 52/1 (Spring 1995): 113–27; and the exchange between the two of us in the *Journal of Aesthetics and Art Criticism*, 56/1 (Winter 1998). Jake Quilty-Dunn seeks to rehabilitate a related position in 'Believing our Eyes: The Role of False Belief in Our Experience of Cinema', *British Journal of Aesthetics*, 55/3 (July 2015): 269–83.

58. Paisley Livingston, *Cinema, Philosophy, Bergman: On Film as Philosophy* (Oxford: OUP, 2009), 102–21.

59. For recent examples, see Livingston, *Cinema, Philosophy, Bergman*; and Gregory Currie, 'Standing in the Last Ditch: On the Communicative Intentions of Fiction Makers', *Journal of Aesthetics and Art Criticism,* 72/4 (2014): 351–63.

60. David Bordwell, *Making Meaning: Inference and Rhetoric in the Interpretation of Cinema* (Cambridge, MA: Harvard University Press, 1989); Dan Sperber, *Explaining Culture: A Naturalistic Approach* (Oxford: Blackwell, 1996). I discuss 'memetics' in my 'Against Nature? Or, Confessions of a Darwinian Modernist', in 'Philosophical Aesthetics and the Sciences of Art', *Royal Institute of Philosophy Supplement,* 75 (Oct. 2014): 151–82.

61. Roger Rothman and Ian Verstegen, 'Arnheim's Lesson: Cubism, Collage, and Gestalt Psychology', *Journal of Aesthetics and Art Criticism,* 65/3 (Summer 2007): 287. Arnheim, E. H. Gombrich, Richard Wollheim, and Julian Hochberg, in their different ways, are staunch advocates of grounding our understanding of depiction in our knowledge of (visual) perception; Nanay's *Aesthetics as Philosophy of Perception* is a recent and very explicit example. Rothman and Verstegen cite Norman Bryson, *Vision and Painting: The Logic of the Gaze* (New Haven: Yale University Press, 1983) as an influential critique of 'perceptualism' (the term itself may be Bryson's). An emphasis on the perceptual foundations of cinema has been evident in cognitive film theory from the outset, notably in the work of Bordwell and Joe Anderson, the latter advancing a theory of film informed by the perceptual psychology of J. J. Gibson. See Joseph D. Anderson, *The Reality of Illusion: An Ecological Approach to Cognitive Film Theory* (Carbondale, IL: Southern Illinois University Press, 1996).

62. On these sonic phenomena, see Shinsuke Shimojo and Ladan Shams, 'Sensory Modalities are Not Separate Modalities: Plasticity and Interactions', *Current Opinion in Neurobiology,* 11/4 (Aug. 2001): 505–9. The sound-induced visual flash illusion is demonstrated at <http://shamslab.psych.ucla.edu/demos>.

63. A high degree of reliability—but not infallible predictability, of course. Noting that 'auditory qualities alone are insufficient to classify a musical work', Ted Gracyk shows how the opening of Steely Dan's 'Ricki Don't Lose That Number' is, in strictly auditory terms, indeterminate between Horace Silver's jazz composition 'Song for My Father', and the Steely Dan song which opens by quoting the bass line from Silver's composition. Nonetheless, the inferences and expectations we form on the basis of such perceptual cues are integral to our aesthetic experience, as much in the case of wrong-footing or other intricate instances as in cases where low-level perceptual cues generate expectations which are fulfilled. See Theodore Gracyk, *Rhythm and Noise: An Aesthetics of Rock* (Durham, NC: Duke University Press, 1996), 1–5 (on Steely Dan), and 66–7 (on XTC's use of rapidly identifiable, characteristic sounds in their twenty-two-second 'History of Rock 'n' Roll').

64. See Kaitlin L. Brunick, James E. Cutting, and Jordan E. DeLong, 'Low-Level Features of Film: What they are and Why we would be Lost without Them', in Arthur P. Shimamura (ed.), *Psychocinematics: Exploring Cognition at the Movies* (New York: OUP, 2013), 133–48; and Valentijn Visch, 'Looking for Genres: The Effect of Film Figure Movement on Genre Recognition' (Ph.D. dissertation, University of Amsterdam, 2007). On the impact of categorization on appreciation, see Kendall L. Walton, 'Categories of Art', *Philosophical Review,* 79/3 (July 1970): 334–67.

65. Dominic McIver Lopes, 'Pictures and the Representational Mind', *The Monist,* 86/4 (Jan. 2003): 645–6.

232 NOTES TO PAGES 38-46

66. Rothman and Verstegen, 'Arnheim's Lesson', 296.
67. I discuss this technique with von Trier in the DVD commentary for *Antichrist* (Zentropa, 2009), at 46:25.
68. David Bordwell and Kristin Thompson, *Film Art: An Introduction*, 10th edn (New York: McGraw-Hill, 2013), 173.
69. David Bordwell, *Narration in the Fiction Film* (Madison: University of Wisconsin Press, 1985), 110.
70. Dominic Lopes, *Understanding Pictures* (Oxford: Clarendon Press, 1996), 147.
71. Richard Wollheim, *Painting as an Art* (London: Thames & Hudson, 1987); 'Representation', 165.
72. Murray Smith, 'Just What is it that Makes Tony Soprano Such an Appealing, Attractive Murderer?', in Ward E. Jones and Samantha Vice (eds), *Ethics at the Cinema* (Oxford: OUP, 2011), 66–90; Margrethe Bruun Vaage, *The Antihero in American Television* (London: Routledge, 2015).
73. Mike Martin, obituary for Brian O'Shaughnessy, *Guardian* 14 July 2010, <http://www.theguardian.com/books/2010/jul/14/brian-oshaughnessy-obituary>. O'Shaughnessy lays out his arguments on the sub-intentional in *The Will: A Dual Aspect Theory*, ii (Cambridge: CUP, 1980), ch. 10. The concept also briefly surfaces in his *Consciousness and the World* (Oxford: Clarendon Press, 2000), 134.
74. Donald Davidson, 'Agency', in *Essays on Actions and Events*, 2nd edn (Oxford: Clarendon Press, 2001), 53.
75. Dominic McIver Lopes, 'Afterword: Photography and the "Picturesque Agent"', in Diarmuid Costello, Margaret Iversen, and Joel Snyder (eds), *Agency and Automatism: Photography as Art since the Sixties, Critical Inquiry*, 38/4 (Summer 2012): 862.
76. Donald Davidson, 'Actions, Reasons, and Causes', in *Essays on Actions and Events*, 3.
77. Michael Baxandall, *Patterns of Intention: On the Historical Explanation of Pictures* (New Haven: Yale University Press, 1985), p. vi.
78. See e.g. the 'The Anthill Chronicles' section of E. O. Wilson, *Anthill* (New York: W. W. Norton, 2010), and the passages detailing the actions of insects on a decaying human body in Jim Crace, *Being Dead* (London: Viking, 1999). Children's literature also features attempts to render animal subjectivity while eschewing or at least minimizing the tendency to anthropomorphization: consider Michelle Paver, *Wolf Brother* (London: Orion Children's Books, 2004), and the other novels in Paver's 'Chronicles of Ancient Darkness' series, for example. Rowlands explores the same territory from a philosophical point of view in his autobiographical essay *The Philosopher and the Wolf*.
79. Locke, *Human Understanding*, bk II, ch. XXVII, §9, p. 335.
80. Tomasello, *Cultural Origins*, ch. 3.
81. Jenefer Robinson, *Deeper than Reason: Emotion and its Role in Literature, Music, and Art* (Oxford: Clarendon Press, 2005), 75–9. On the 'cognitive unconscious', see Carl Plantinga, *Moving Viewers: American Film and the Spectator's Experience* (Berkeley, CA: University of California Press, 2009), 49–50. See also Timothy D. Wilson, *Strangers to Ourselves: Discovering the Adaptive Unconscious* (Cambridge, MA: Belknap Press, 2002).
82. For background to the paragraphs that follow, see Daniel Dennett, 'Philosophy as Naïve Anthropology: Comment on Bennett and Hacker', in Maxwell Bennett, Daniel Dennett, Peter Hacker, John Searle, and Daniel Robinson, *Neuroscience and Philosophy: Brain, Mind, and Language* (New York: Columbia University Press, 2007), 73–95.

83. David Milner and Melvyn A. Goodale, 'Separate Visual Pathways for Perception and Action', *Trends in Neurosciences*, 15/1 (1992): 20–5; Clark, *Mindware*, on Milner and Goodale, 160–3; Pierre Jacob and Marc Jeannerod, *Ways of Seeing: The Scope and Limits of Visual Cognition* (Oxford: OUP, 2003).

84. Clark, *Mindware*, 44.

85. Bennett and Hacker, *Philosophical Foundations*, ch. 3.

86. Bennett and Hacker, *Philosophical Foundations*, 79, 386–8.

87. Bennett and Hacker, *Philosophical Foundations*, 80.

88. Dennett teases out the cognitive work being done by, and the factors motivating and justifying, such metaphors and extensions of psychological predication to (parts of) the brain in his response to Bennett and Hacker, 'Philosophy as Naïve Anthropology', 86–9.

89. Shimojo and Shams, 'Sensory Modalities'; Anderson, *Reality*, ch. 5; Michel Chion, *Audio-Vision: Sound on Screen*, tr. Claudia Gorbman (New York: Columbia University Press, 1994), 69–71.

90. Livingston, *Cinema, Philosophy, Bergman*, 68.

91. Michael Smith, *Ethics and the A Priori* (Cambridge: CUP, 2004), 267–73, 301–3. Smith's coherence constraint bears on the rationality of an action; here I extend the idea to encompass even the realizability of an action. Insufficient coherence among an agent's states will lead to compromised agency and, in the extreme, agential paralysis.

92. Andy Clark, *Natural-Born Cyborgs: Minds, Technologies, and the Future of Human Intelligence* (Oxford: OUP, 2003), 4–5.

93. Flanagan, *Consciousness Reconsidered*, 92.

94. Tomasello, *Cultural Origins*, 37–40.

95. Comment on Tomasello, *Origins*, <https://mitpress.mit.edu/books/origins-human-communication>.

96. Clifford Geertz, 'Thick Description: Toward an Interpretive Theory of Culture', in *The Interpretation of Cultures* (New York: Basic Books, 1973), 6.

97. Gilbert Ryle, 'The Thinking of Thoughts: What is "Le Penseur" Doing?', in *Collected Essays 1929–1968* (London: Routledge, 2009), 496–7.

98. Geertz, 'Thick Description', 6 and 7.

99. Geertz, 'Thick Description', 9.

100. David Lewis, 'Causal Explanation', *Philosophical Papers II* (Oxford: OUP, 1986), 226–8; Lewis provides a more intricate schema than the one presented here, enumerating seven factors that may bear on the quality of an explanation. John Dupré makes his observation in *Human Nature and the Limits of Science* (Oxford: Clarendon Press, 2001), 23. For another defence of the view that explanation comes in degrees, with a particular eye to how this fact plays out for different disciplines, see F. A. Hayek, 'Degrees of Explanation', *British Journal for the Philosophy of Science*, 6/3 (1955): 209–25. An ambitious, recent treatment is advanced by Strevens, *Depth*, in particular pp. 129–37 and 153–4.

101. Robert van Gulick, 'Consciousness, Intrinsic Intentionality, and Self-Understanding Machines', in A. J. Marcel and E. Bisiach (eds), *Consciousness in Contemporary Science* (Oxford: Clarendon Press, 1988), 96, quoted in Daniel C. Dennett, *Consciousness Explained* (Boston: Little, Brown & Co., 1991), 279.

102. Bernard Williams, *Ethics and the Limits of Philosophy* (London: Fontana, 1993). Williams is concerned specifically with ethical concepts, 'such as *treachery* and *promise* and *brutality* and *courage*, which seem to express a union of fact and value' (p. 129).

103. Nick Zangwill, *Metaphysics of Beauty* (Ithaca, NY: Cornell University Press, 2001).
104. Cooper, *Psychiatry and Philosophy of Science*, compares psychiatry, botany, and zoology in this regard, p. 136.
105. Michael Chanan, 'Blinded by Science?' posted 21 June 2011, <http://www.putneydebater. com/blinded-by-science>.
106. George Santayana, 'Dewey's Naturalistic Metaphysics', *Journal of Philosophy*, 22/25 (1925): 674.
107. Both were Presidents of the Society for Psychical Research, founded in 1882; other members included psychologist Edmund Gurney and moral philosopher and economist Henry Sidgwick.
108. Holmes declares this in 'The Sussex Vampire' (1924), in *The Case-Book of Sherlock Holmes* (Oxford: OUP, 2009), 73. There is a further irony here. Holmes's creator, Sir Arthur Conan Doyle, was a dedicated spiritualist, and a member of the Society for Psychical Research who led a mass resignation in 1930, condemning the organization for its insufficiently 'sympathetic' approach to putatively spiritual phenomena.
109. Peter Kivy, 'Mozart's Skull', in *Sounding Off: Eleven Essays in the Philosophy of Music* (Oxford: OUP, 2012), 16–18.
110. See the passage from Walton, 'Aesthetics', 152, already quoted, 23 and n. 14. It is of course true that many philosophers have engaged, to one degree or another, in empirical research; in the contemporary scene, experimental philosophers have made this an article of faith.

Chapter 2 Triangulating Aesthetic Experience

1. The use of average shot lengths as a means of gauging one important aspect of film style was pioneered by Barry Salt, and by David Bordwell and Kristin Thompson. Representative works include Barry Salt, *Film Style and Technology: History and Analysis*, 3rd edn (London: Starword, 2009), and David Bordwell, *The Way Hollywood Tells it* (Berkeley, CA: University of California Press, 2006). More recently the technique has been adopted by, among others, James Cutting, and Yuri Tsivian. On his website Cinemetrics, <http:// www.cinemetrics.lv>, Tsivian writes that 'cinema is the art of timing', noting that control of rhythm in film editing is no less important to cinema than it is through metrical control in poetry. Tsivian's remarks draw our attention to the fact that precise counting and quantification are essential for many musicians, choreographers, dancers and martial artists, poets and filmmakers. That fact alone should give pause to theorists apt to dismiss the relevance of quantitative methods for critical analysis.
2. George Dickie, 'Is Psychology Relevant to Aesthetics?', *Philosophical Review*, 71/3 (July 1962): 297.
3. An entertaining and wide-ranging discussion of this theme can be found in Christopher Chabris and Daniel Simons, *The Invisible Gorilla: And Other Ways our Intuitions Deceive Us* (New York: Crown Publishers, 2010).
4. Owen Flanagan, *Consciousness Reconsidered* (Cambridge, MA: MIT Press, 1992), 11–20.
5. Flanagan, *Consciousness Reconsidered*, 11.
6. This is distinct, of course, from the question of whether there is an ontological hierarchy among the three levels. Here I make the common physicalist assumption that

psychological and phenomenological phenomena emerge from—and are in that sense dependent on—neural phenomena. In that sense there is an ontological hierarchy among the three levels, though it does not follow, on my view, that (say) perception, or the distinct qualia associated with perceiving a particular low-pitched but harmonically complex sound, are any less *real* than the neural activity underlying them. For if we go down that particular reductionist path, we will need to say that neural activity is itself less real than the biochemical domain on which it, in turn, depends. And so on, as low as we can go.

7. Otto Neurath, *Anti-Splenger* (1921), available in translation in *Empiricism and Sociology*, ed. Marie Neurath and Robert S. Cohen (Dordrecht: D. Reidel, 1973), 199. W. V. O. Quine uses the passage as an epigraph in *Word and Object* (Cambridge, MA: MIT Press, 1960), notably commenting: 'The philosopher and the scientist are in the same boat' (§1, p. 3).

8. Wilfrid Sellars, *Empiricism and the Philosophy of Mind*, ed. Robert Brandom (Cambridge, MA: Harvard University Press, 1997), §38, 79.

9. Flanagan, *Consciousness Reconsidered*, 12.

10. Chabris and Simons, *Invisible Gorilla*, 7.

11. Daniel C. Dennett, *Consciousness Explained* (Boston: Little, Brown, & Co., 1991), 53–4.

12. Chabris and Simons, *Invisible Gorilla*, 54–5.

13. I cannot be wrong about my *impression*—if it seems to me the world or my perception of it is thus and so, then so be it. But an impression is, precisely, a diffuse and vague apprehension of something, and impressions can be wrong about what they apprehend. Daniel Dennett puts it this way: 'subjects are unwitting creators of fiction, but to say that they are unwitting is to grant that what they say is, or can be, an account of *exactly how it seems to them*. They tell us *what it is like* to them to solve the problem [etc.] ... but then it follows that what it is like to them is at best an uncertain guide to what is going on in them' (*Consciousness Explained*, 94). See also Eric Schwitzgebel, *Perplexities of Consciousness* (Cambridge, MA: MIT Press, 2011). Schwitzgebel emphasizes the unreliable and incomplete nature of phenomenological evidence.

14. Jesse J. Prinz, *Gut Reactions: A Perceptual Theory of Emotion* (Oxford: OUP, 2004), 240.

15. Leda Cosmides and John Tooby, 'Cognitive Adaptations for Social Exchange', in Jerome H. Barkow, Leda Cosmides, and John Tooby (eds), *The Adapted Mind: Evolutionary Psychology and the Generation of Culture* (New York: OUP, 1992), 163–228.

16. Flanagan, *Consciousness Reconsidered*, 12.

17. Flanagan refers to James Lackner and Merrill F. Garrett, 'Resolving Ambiguity: Effects of Biasing Context in the Unattended Ear', *Cognition*, 1/4 (1972): 359–72.

18. Flanagan, *Consciousness Reconsidered*, 12. Flanagan writes here of an imagined 'complete explanation of the brain framed in the languages of physics, chemistry, and biochemistry'. But I wonder if the brain (let alone the mind) *can* be fully *explained* in these languages alone, because the concepts available within these sciences would not enable us to capture the purposes of the brain (whether or not we conceive of these purposes as simply a matter of biological evolution, or of the cultural extension of brain capacities beyond those for which it evolved). Restricting ourselves to the concepts and language of physics, chemistry, and biochemistry, we would at most be able to forge a complete *description* of the brain and its activities at the level of these sciences. See also Schwitzgebel, *Perplexities of Consciousness*, 98, 114–15.

19. Cf. Fred Dretske, *Naturalizing the Mind* (Cambridge, MA: MIT Press, 1995), 37.

20. Jaegwon Kim, *Physicalism, or Something Near Enough* (Princeton: Princeton University Press, 2005), 168; I refer to this passage in Kim in Ch. 1 n. 34.

21. James Kilner, Wellcome Trust Centre for Neuroimaging, University College London, personal correspondence.

22. See Alison Motluk, 'Read my Mind', *New Scientist*, 169/2275 (27 Jan. 2001): 23.

23. The *Journal of Serendipitous and Unexpected Results* is specifically devoted to such discoveries. If it exists, that is. See also the *Journal of Negative Results* and the *Journal of Negative Results in Biomedicine*, which do exist.

24. One question that arises here, then, is the relationship between triangulation and the various forms of mind–brain identity theory. Flanagan adopts a stance here which is broadly agnostic, suggesting that the 'natural method' must be committed to token physicalism, in the sense that 'each and every mental state is a neural state', but remains neutral on more specific claims about the relationship between the mental and physical (Flanagan, *Consciousness Reconsidered*, 19; see also his earlier *The Science of the Mind* (Cambridge, MA: MIT Press, 1984), 59, for a related exposition). He goes on to suggest that, beyond the broad claim of token physicalism, there might be considerable heterogeneity with respect to the nature of the relationship between the mental and the physical across different domains of cognition: type-identity claims might hold for certain types of perception but not for semantic memory, for example (Flanagan, *Consciousness Reconsidered*, 19–20). Triangulation as a method is designed to be capacious and flexible enough to capture such variety, framed by nonreductive physicalist assumptions. Kim identifies nonreductive physicalism with three doctrines—mind–body supervenience, the physical irreducibility of the mental, and the causal efficaciousness of the mental (*Physicalism*, 33–5). Note that Kim ultimately rejects this conjunction of commitments, and defends a reductive perspective on almost all mental states.

25. Brian O'Shaughnessy, *Consciousness and the World* (Oxford: Clarendon Press, 2003); the passage quoted is from the Oxford Scholarship Online abstract for the volume as a whole, available at <http://www.oxfordscholarship.com>. O'Shaughnessy continues and concludes the abstract: 'So it is that the gap is closed between the mental and physical domains, and the epistemological basis of mind is established.'

26. Paul Churchland, 'Chimerical Colours: Some Phenomenological Predictions from Cognitive Neuroscience', *Neurophilosophy at Work* (Cambridge: CUP, 2007), 161.

27. Churchland, 'Chimerical Colours', 183. Churchland's essay is also available online, and includes an illustration of the Hurvich-Jameson colour spindle as well as various demonstration charts, enabling readers to test out his predictions: <http://web.gc.cuny.edu/cogsci/private/Churchland-chimeric-colors.pdf>.

28. Frank Jackson, 'Epiphenomenal Qualia', *Philosophical Quarterly*, 32/127 (Apr. 1982): 127–36, is the most famous instance; see also Joseph Levine, 'Materialism and Qualia: The Explanatory Gap', *Pacific Philosophical Quarterly* 64 (Oct. 1983): 354–61.

29. On *The Velvet Underground* (1969).

30. Compare e.g. Brakhage's interest in 'hypnagogic' colours, in 'Metaphors on Vision', *Film Culture*, 30 (special issue, Fall 1963), with Churchland's discussion, 'Chimerical Colours', 182.

For an analysis of the attempt to represent phosphenes and other non-veridical visual phenomena in Brakhage's work, see William C. Wees, *Light Moving in Time: Studies in the Visual Aesthetics of Avant-Garde Film* (Berkeley, CA: University of California Press, 1985), chs. 3 and 4.

31. Entoptic phenomena are visual effects whose source lies within the eye; phosphenes are a subtype in which our experience suggests, misleadingly, that light is entering the eye.

32. See William Whewell, *The Philosophy of the Inductive Sciences: Founded upon their History* (London: J. W. Parker, 1840); Edward O. Wilson, *Consilience: The Unity of Knowledge* (London: Little, Brown, & Co., 1998); and Churchland, *Neurophilosophy at Work*, p. viii.

33. See Mark Rollins, 'Neurology and the New Riddle of Pictorial Style', in Elisabeth Schellekens and Peter Goldie (eds), *The Aesthetic Mind: Philosophy and Psychology* (Oxford: OUP, 2011), 391–443, for a particularly systematic example of triangulation, applied to Monet's *Poppy Field Outside of Argentueil* (1873). Rollins shows how our impression of movement and spatial imprecision in the painting arises from a deliberate challenge to our perceptual ability to locate objects in space. That challenge is realized through a deployment of contrasting but equiluminant hues in the foreground and background, which has the effect of defeating the neural system which normally deals with spatial location, leaving our colour processing system to do the job. The 'failure' of our visual system to place objects in the painting precisely leads to the sense of movement, and is, of course, anything but a failure in the aesthetic context.

34. The phrase was coined by Richard Gerrig, *Experiencing Narrative Worlds: On the Psychological Activities of Reading* (New Haven: Yale University Press, 1993), 79–80, and ch. 5.

35. Jerry A. Fodor, *The Modularity of Mind: An Essay on Faculty Psychology* (Cambridge, MA: MIT Press, 1983), 41ff.

36. David Bordwell, 'This is your Brain on Movies, Maybe', *Observations on Film Art*, revised 8 Mar. 2011, <http://www.davidbordwell.net/blog/?p=300>. Bordwell's argument develops ideas from, among others, Ray Jackendoff, Daniel Levitin, and Gerrig himself. The title of Bordwell's essay is inspired by Levitin's *This is your Brain on Music: Understanding a Human Obsession* (London: Atlantic Books, 2007).

37. Theodore Gracyk, *Rhythm and Noise: An Aesthetics of Rock* (Durham, NC: Duke University Press, 1996), 60–1; inner quote from Diana Raffman, *Language, Music, and Mind* (Cambridge, MA: MIT Press, 1993).

38. Bordwell quotes Jackendoff, who argues that music perception depends on 'a number of autonomous units, each working in its own limited domain, with limited access to memory. For under this conception, expectation, suspense, satisfaction, and surprise can occur within the processor: in effect, the processor is always hearing the piece for the first time' (*Consciousness and the Computational Mind* (Cambridge, MA: MIT Press, 1987), 245). Raffman draws on Jackendoff and Lerdahl throughout her study.

39. Flanagan, *Consciousness Reconsidered*, 11.

40. Christine N. Brinckmann, 'Motor Mimicry in Hitchcock', in *Color and Empathy: Essays on Two Aspects of Film* (Amsterdam: Amsterdam University Press, 2014), 135 n. 2.

41. See e.g. Gregory Currie and Ian Ravenscroft, *Recreative Minds: Imagination in Philosophy and Psychology* (Oxford: Clarendon Press, 2002), who date the contemporary debate on simulation to 1986 (50 n. 1).

42. Vittorio Gallese, Christian Keysers, and Giacomo Rizzolatti, 'A Unifying View of the Basis of Social Cognition', *Trends in Cognitive Sciences*, 8/9 (Sept. 2004): 396–403; Giacomo Rizzolatti and Corrado Sinigaglia, *Mirrors in the Brain: How our Minds Share Actions and Emotions*, tr. Frances Anderson (Oxford: OUP, 2006). I should note that research in this area is still at an early stage, and many aspects of the theory and research methodology have been questioned. For a sympathetic but critical overview, see Ilan Dinstein, Cibu Thomas, Marlene Behrmann, and David J. Heeger, 'A Mirror up to Nature', *Current Biology*, 18/1 (8 Jan. 2008): R13–18. For more sceptical perspectives, see Alison Gopnik, 'Cells that Read Minds?', *Slate*, 26 Apr. 2007, <http://www.slate.com/articles/life/brains/2007/04/cells_that_read_minds.single.html>, and Gregory Hickok, *The Myth of Mirror Neurons: The Real Science of Communication and Cognition* (New York: W. W. Norton & Co., 2014).

43. Andy Clark, *Mindware: An Introduction to the Philosophy of Cognitive Science*, 2nd edn (Oxford: OUP, 2013), 105–6.

44. V. S. Ramachandran and Sandra Blakeslee, *Phantoms in the Brain: Human Nature and the Architecture of the Mind* (London: Fourth Estate, 1998).

45. Jeff Hawkins, *On Intelligence* (New York: Henry Holt, 2004), 200.

46. Here I take issue with the philosophical spin that Ramachandran puts on the material under discussion. '*Your own body* is a phantom', he writes, 'one that your brain has temporarily constructed purely for convenience' (emphasis in the original, p. 58); and earlier on the same page he states that 'pain itself is an illusion—constructed entirely in your brain like any other sensory experience'. But the force of the 'phantom' metaphor—and the casting of pain as an 'illusion'—only applies properly to cases where there is a more or less dramatic inconsistency between what is sensed and what is physically the case, as in the classic case of a phantom limb: I still sense an arm even though it has been amputated. The 'convenience' of which Ramachandran writes is, of course, largely a matter of negotiating the physical world, and generally speaking, a rather high degree of veridicality of perception (and neural mapping of the body) is essential for such negotiation. In short, the seed of philosophical idealism is present in the extension of the 'phantom' metaphor from the exceptional to the standard cases of perception, which flies in the face of the multifaceted realism I argue for here. Such idealism is also at variance with much else in Ramachandran's own perspective on the brain, though I will not pursue this point here.

47. Ramachandran and Blakeslee, *Phantoms in the Brain*, 58–62.

48. Not a very compelling proportion, you say? What the results suggest is that susceptibility to impressions of extended bodily selfhood is variable. Some of us are more disposed than others to this experience. And it may be that there are patterns to the dispositional variation, just as there is evidence that women are, on average, more psychologically empathic than men. Just how widespread the phenomenon is, and whether there are patterns of susceptibility within and among populations, is a matter for further empirical research. On gendered patterns of empathy in relation to film, see Mette Kramer, 'The Mating Game in Hollywood Cinema: A Darwinian Approach', *New Review of Film and Television Studies*, 2/2 (Nov. 2004): 137–59.

49. Ramachandran argues that experiments of this sort illustrate 'the single most important principle underlying all of perception—that the mechanisms of perception are mainly involved in extracting statistical correlations from the world to create a model that is temporarily useful' (*Phantoms in the Brain*, 59).

50. Although they do not use the term 'confabulation', the classic account of the phenomenon is Richard E. Nisbett and Timothy DeCamp Wilson, 'Telling More than we Can Know: Verbal Reports on Mental Processes', *Psychological Review*, 84/3 (May 1977): 231–59. See also William Hirstein, *Brain Fiction: Self-Deception and the Riddle of Confabulation* (Cambridge, MA: MIT Press, 2006).
51. Ramachandran and Blakeslee, *Phantoms in the Brain*, 61.
52. Valeria I. Petkova and H. Henrik Ehrsson, 'If I Were You: Perceptual Illusion of Body Swapping', *PloS ONE*, 3/12 (Dec. 2008): 7.
53. Ramachandran and Blakeslee, *Phantoms in the Brain*, 218. A recent study is reported in BBC News, 'Men Suffer from Phantom Pregnancy', 14 June 2007, <http://news.bbc.co.uk/1/hi/6751709.stm?lsm>.
54. On empathy and related effects in the work of Hitchcock, see Murray Smith, *Engaging Characters: Fiction, Emotion, and the Cinema* (Oxford: Clarendon Press, 1995), 95–106, and Ch. 7 here. On the 'scene of empathy', see Carl Plantinga, *Moving Viewers: American Film and the Spectator's Experience* (Berkeley, CA: University of California Press, 2009), 125–8.
55. Adrian M. Owen, Martin R. Coleman, Melanie Boly, Matthew H. Davis, Steven Laureys, and John D. Pickard, 'Detecting Awareness in the Vegetative State', *Science*, 313/5792 (8 Sept. 2006): 1402. Owen's research in this area is documented in *The Mind Reader: Unlocking my Voice*, an episode of the BBC current affairs series *Panorama* broadcast in 2012.
56. Indeed this was evident in the initial two-part schema for the empirical analysis of aesthetic experience set out at the opening of this chapter, comparing specific properties of films (such as duration and aspect ratio) with our experience of those properties. The model of triangulation in effect focuses on and refines one half of this equation, breaking down the mental into the triad of the phenomenal, the psychological, and the neural, while assuming the empirical tractability of the other half of the equation, the work itself.
57. Marco Iacoboni, 'Who Really Won the Super Bowl?', *Edge*, 2 May 2006, <http://edge.org/conversation/who-really-won-the-super-bowl>. Iacoboni is a major figure in mirror neuron research—see his *Mirroring People: The New Science of How we Connect with Others* (New York: Farrar, Straus & Giroux, 2008). I should note that Iacoboni's Super Bowl experiment was not published in a peer-reviewed scientific journal, and he does not present it as a polished, fully fledged piece of research; he rather jokingly refers to it as a piece of 'instant science'. Nevertheless, since the essay was (and remains) posted on a respected website and thus exists in the public domain, and argues for a particular view of the value of neuroscientific evidence, it is fair game for comment. See also the critique of the study in Sally Satel and Scott O. Lilienfeld, *Brainwashed: The Seductive Appeal of Mindless Neuroscience* (New York: Basic Books, 2013).
58. For an analysis of the way in which emotions, in the familiar folk psychological sense, emerge out of a number of component subpersonal processes, see the discussion of the research of psychologist Phoebe Ellsworth in Jenefer Robinson, *Deeper than Reason: Emotion and its Role in Literature, Music, and Art* (Oxford: Clarendon Press, 2005), 76–7.
59. Michael Smith, *Ethics and the A Priori* (Cambridge: CUP, 2004), 267–73, 301–3.
60. Daniel H. Barratt, 'The Paradox of Fiction Revisited: A Cognitive Approach to Understanding (Cinematic) Emotion' (Ph.D. dissertation, University of Kent, 2004), posits a

general theory of film spectatorship integrating low-level subpersonal responses with
higher-level cognitive awareness.

Chapter 3 The Engine of Reason and the Pit of Naturalism

1. Semir Zeki, *Inner Vision: An Exploration of Art and the Brain* (Oxford: OUP, 1999);
   V. S. Ramachandran and William Hirstein, 'The Science of Art: A Neurological Theory of
   Aesthetic Experience', *Journal of Consciousness Studies*, 6/6–7 (1999): 15–51.
2. See e.g. Eric R. Kandel, *The Age of Insight: The Quest to Understand the Unconscious in Art,
   Mind, and Brain, from Vienna 1900 to the Present* (New York: Random House, 2012);
   Anjan Chatterjee, *The Aesthetic Brain: How we Evolved to Desire Beauty and Enjoy Art*
   (New York: OUP, 2014); and for a study emphasizing literature rather than the visual arts,
   G. Gabrielle Starr, *Feeling Beauty: The Neuroscience of Aesthetic Experience* (Cambridge,
   MA: MIT Press, 2013).
3. John R. Searle, 'Twenty-One Years in the Chinese Room', in John Preston and Mark
   Bishop (eds), *Views into the Chinese Room: New Essays on Searle and Artificial Intelligence*
   (Oxford: Clarendon Press, 2002), 69.
4. Uri Hasson, Ohad Landesman, Barbara Knappmeyer, Ignacio Vallines, Nava Rubin, and
   David J. Heeger, 'Neurocinematics: The Neuroscience of Film', *Projections*, 2/1 (Summer
   2008): 1–26; Gal Raz, Yonatan Winetraub, Yael Jacob, Sivan Kinreich, Adi Maron-Katz,
   Galit Shaham, Ilana Podlipsky, Gadi Gilam, Eyal Soreq, and Talma Hendler, 'Portraying
   Emotions at their Unfolding: A Multilayered Approach for Probing Dynamics of Neural
   Networks', *NeuroImage*, 59/2 (16 Jan. 2012): 1448–61; Pia Tikka, Aleksander Väljamäe,
   Aline W. de Borst, Roberto Pugliese, Niklas Ravaja, Mauri Kaipainen, and Tapio Takala,
   'Enactive Cinema Paves Way for Understanding Complex Real-Time Social Interaction in
   Neuroimaging Experiments', *Frontiers in Human Neuroscience*, 6 (1 Nov. 2012): 1–6;
   Katrin Heimann, Maria Alessandra Umilti, Michele Guerra, and Vittorio Gallese, 'Moving
   Mirrors: A High-Density EEG Study Investigating the Effect of Camera Movements on
   Motor Cortex Activation during Action Observation', *Journal of Cognitive Neuroscience*,
   26/9 (Sept. 2014): 2087–101.
5. See e.g. Raymond Bellour, 'Deleuze: The Thinking of the Brain', *Cinema: Journal of
   Philosophy and the Moving Image*, 1 (2010): 81–94, <http://cjpmi.ifilnova.pt/1-contents>.
   See also Jaak Panksepp, 'What is Neuropsychoanalysis? Clinically Relevant Studies of the
   Minded Brain', *Trends in Cognitive Sciences*, 16/1 (Jan. 2012): 6–8.
6. On brain scanning used as a vehicle of audience testing, see Curtis Silver, 'Neurocinema
   Aims to Change the Way Movies are Made', *Wired* (23 Sept. 2009), <http://www.wired.
   com/geekdad/2009/09/neurocinema-aims-to-change-the-way-movies-are-made>; on *Focus
   Pocus*, see Christina DesMarais, 'Video Game Uses Brain to Control Action', *PCWorld*
   (16 Oct. 2011), <http://www.pcworld.com/article/241993/video_game_uses_brain_to_con
   trol_action.html>; on MyndPlay, see Charlie Burton, 'Directed by Brainwave', *Wired*
   (13 Sept. 2011), <http://www.wired.co.uk/magazine/archive/2011/10/play/directed-by-
   brainwave>.
7. Ben Johnson, 'Scientists Turn Brain Activity into Moving Images', *Slate* (24 Sept. 2011),
   <http://slatest.slate.com/posts/2011/09/24/scientists_turn_brain_activity_into_moving_
   images.html>.

8. Jeffrey M. Zacks, *Flicker: Your Brain on Movies* (New York: OUP, 2015), 258. Zacks argues that the idea is not completely farfetched. Certainly such a technology would fit into the history of embellishing the core technology of cinema with devices directly stimulating our senses of smell, touch, and balance, currently visible in the idea of '4D' cinema. Incorporating the sense of taste may be the final frontier. Magnovision, of course, would be able to tickle all these areas.

9. Jerry Fodor, 'Diary', *London Review of Books*, 21/19 (30 Sept. 1999): 68–9, <http://www.lrb. co.uk/v21/n19/jerry-fodor/diary>. In correspondence following the publication of this essay, Fodor remarks on 'the difference between a scientist who has a hypothesis and one who only has a camera'. Jerry Fodor, 'Where's the Carburettor?', *London Review of Books*, 22/1 (6 Jan. 2000): 15, <http://www.lrb.co.uk/v21/n19/jerry-fodor/diary>.

10. David A. Barrett, 'Multiple Realizability, Identity Theory, and the Gradual Reorganization Principle', *British Journal for the Philosophy of Science*, 64/2 (June 2013): 325–46.

11. M. R. Bennett and P. M. S. Hacker, *Philosophical Foundations of Neuroscience* (Oxford: Blackwell, 2003).

12. Marco Iacoboni, 'Who Really Won the Super Bowl?', *Edge* 2 May 2006, <http://edge.org/conversation/who-really-won-the-super-bowl>.

13. Raymond Tallis, *Aping Mankind: Neuromania, Darwinitis, and the Misrepresentation of Humanity* (Durham: Acumen, 2011).

14. Neuroaesthetics is a particular target in Raymond Tallis, 'License My Roving Hands', *Times Literary Supplement*, 5480 (11 Apr. 2008): 13–15, and in *Aping Mankind*, 60–3, 284–306.

15. Raymond Tallis, *Not Saussure: A Critique of Post-Saussurean Literary Theory* (Basingstoke: Macmillan Press, 1988); Raymond Tallis, *In Defence of Realism* (Lincoln, NE: University of Nebraska Press, 1991).

16. Raymond Tallis, *The Kingdom of Infinite Space: A Fantastical Journey around your Head* (London: Atlantic, 2008).

17. *Start the Week*, BBC Radio 4, 21 Apr. 2008. Tallis refers in this passage to another guest on this episode of the show: Daniel Dennett, dean of Darwinian philosophers, and author of *Darwin's Dangerous Idea: Evolution and the Meanings of Life* (New York: Simon & Schuster, 1995), among many other works.

18. Tallis, *The Kingdom*, 288; see also Tallis, *Aping Mankind*, 319.

19. Richard Dawkins, *The Selfish Gene* (Oxford: OUP, 1976). Dawkins's position is rather more sophisticated than this bald summary suggests, in particular because he is at pains to emphasize the ways in which humans transcend genetic pressures. This is an important dimension of his thinking routinely ignored or underplayed by his opponents, including Tallis. I return to Dawkins in Chapter 6.

20. Tallis, *Aping Mankind*, 283.

21. Tallis, *Aping Mankind*, 319.

22. Raymond Tallis, *The Knowing Animal: A Philosophical Inquiry into Knowledge and Truth* (Edinburgh: Edinburgh University Press, 2005).

23. Tallis, *The Kingdom*, 68.

24. Helena Cronin, quoted in Matt Ridley, *The Origins of Virtue* (London: Penguin, 1997), 156; see also Frans de Waal, *Good Natured: The Origins of Right and Wrong in Humans and Other Animals* (Cambridge, MA: Harvard University Press, 1996), 126–7.

25. Mark Rowlands, *The Philosopher and the Wolf: Lessons from the Wild on Love, Death, and Happiness* (London: Granta, 2008).

26. Wilfrid Sellars, *Empiricism and the Philosophy of Mind*, ed. Robert Brandom (Cambridge, MA: Harvard University Press, 1997), §36, 76.

27. See José Luis Bermúdez, *Thinking without Words* (Oxford: OUP, 2003); Susan Hurley, 'Animal Action in the Space of Reasons', *Mind and Language*, 18/3 (June 2003): 231–56.

28. Gerd Gigerenzer and Reinhard Selten (eds), *Bounded Rationality: The Adaptive Toolbox* (Cambridge, MA: MIT Press, 2001). Gigerenzer and his circle of associates refer to 'fast and frugal' heuristics.

29. Jesse J. Prinz, *Gut Reactions: A Perceptual Theory of Emotion* (Oxford: OUP, 2004); Jenefer Robinson, *Deeper than Reason: Emotion and its Role in Literature, Music, and Art* (Oxford: Clarendon Press, 2005).

30. John Hyman, 'Art and Neuroscience', in Roman Frigg and Matthew C. Hunter (eds), *Beyond Mimesis and Convention: Representation in Art and Science* (Dordrecht: Springer, 2010), 245–61.

31. Hyman is, of course, alluding to the American television series *Baywatch* (Michael Berk, Douglas Schwartz, and Gregory J. Bonann, 1989–99), and its icons of exaggerated physical beauty—especially in its female variant, as embodied in the show by Pamela Anderson. Colin McGinn offers the same criticism in a review of Ramachandran's *The Tell-Tale Brain* (New York: W. W. Norton & Co., 2011), which includes a chapter on neuroaesthetics: 'The discussion of art seems largely about another subject entirely—what elicits human attention'. Colin McGinn, 'Can the Brain Explain your Mind?', *New York Review of Books* (24 Mar. 2011), <http://www.nybooks.com/articles/archives/2011/mar/24/can-brain-explain-your-mind>.

32. Vincent Bergeron and Dominic McIver Lopes, 'Aesthetic Theory and Aesthetic Science: Prospects for Integration', in Arthur P. Shimamura and Stephen E. Palmer (eds), *Aesthetic Science: Connecting Minds, Brains, and Experience* (New York: OUP, 2012), 63–79.

33. David Davies, '"This is your Brain on Art": What Can Philosophy of Art Learn from Neuroscience?', in Gregory Currie, Matthew Kieran, and Aaron Meskin (eds), *Aesthetics and the Sciences of Mind* (Oxford: OUP, 2014), 57–74.

34. For more detail, see Ronald C. Simons, *Boo! Culture, Experience, and the Startle Reflex* (Oxford: OUP, 1996), 9–15; and Michael Davis, 'The Mammalian Startle Response', in Robert C. Eaton (ed.), *Neural Mechanisms of Startle Behavior* (New York: Plenum, 1984), 287–351.

35. Juan M. Castellote, Hatice Kumru, Ana Queralt, and Josep Valls-Solé, 'A Startle Speeds up the Execution of Externally Guided Saccades', *Experimental Brain Research*, 177/1 (Feb. 2007): 129–36.

36. Robert Baird, 'The Startle Effect: Implications for Spectator Cognition and Media Theory', *Film Quarterly*, 53/3 (Spring 2000): 12–24.

37. In fact, the onset of the explosion is visible in both the first and second of these three shots. But this is not an instance of true 'overlapping' editing, in the Eisensteinian sense, since the very brief overlap is not consciously perceptible under ordinary viewing conditions. It is nevertheless very likely that the overlap is registered non-consciously, and may play an indirect role in our conscious experience of the action as rapid, disjunctive, and chaotic.

38. Baird, 'Startle Effect', 15.

39. See in particular Tallis, *The Kingdom*.

40. In describing *Ran* as a 'free' adaptation, I mean to indicate that the film borrows many elements from *King Lear* and seems designed to bring Shakespeare's play to mind, but it does not seem intended as a 'faithful' adaptation, in which overall fidelity to the play is a primary goal. See Paisley Livingston, 'On the Appreciation of Cinematic Adaptations', *Projections*, 4/2 (Winter 2010): 104–27. Livingston notes the use of the phrase 'free adaptation' in the credits for *Fellini Satyricon* (Federico Fellini, 1969).

41. Robert Baird, 'Startle and the Film Threat Scene', <http://www.imagesjournal.com/ issue03/features/startle1.htm>.

42. Peter J. Lang, Margaret M. Bradley, and Bruce N. Cuthbert, 'Emotion, Attention, and the Startle Reflex', *Psychological Review*, 97/3 (July 1990): 377; quoted in Baird, 'Startle Effect', 20.

43. Jesse J. Prinz, *Beyond Human Nature: How Culture and Experience Shape our Lives* (London: Penguin, 2012), 286.

44. Simons, *Boo!*, 162. Prinz, *Beyond Nature*, notes that the condition may be a coping mechanism to 'help relieve the stress of conforming to societal norms' (286).

45. Baird, 'Startle Effect', 21. See also Carl Plantinga, *Moving Viewers: American Film and the Spectator's Experience* (Berkeley, CA: University of California Press 2009), 119.

46. Prinz, *Beyond Human Nature*, 285; see also 288. According to Simons, versions of *latah* are scattered not only across various Southeast Asian societies, but 'in a most improbable set of other places around the globe—Siberia, Maine, Yemen, and the Island of Hokkaido, to name a few'. Simons, *Boo!*, p. vii.

47. On the distinction between affective mimicry and contagion, see Ch. 7. In the case of contagion, we lack awareness of and control over not merely the mechanism by which we pick up the emotions of others, but awareness of even the fact that our emotional state derives from or has been triggered by the states of those around us.

48. See David Freedberg and Vittorio Gallese, 'Motion, Emotion and Empathy in Esthetic Experience', *Trends in Cognitive Sciences*, 11/5 (2007): 197–203; Christian Keysers, Jon H. Kaas, and Valeria Gazzola, 'Somatosensation in Social Perception', *Nature Reviews: Neuroscience*, 11/6 (June 2010): 417–28; and Alison Motluk, 'Mirror Neurons Control Erection Response to Porn', *New Scientist* (16 June 2008), <http://www.newscientist.com/ article/dn14147-mirror-neurons-control-erection-response-to-porn.html>.

49. Vittorio Gallese and Michele Guerra, *Lo schermo empatico: Cinema e neuroscienze* (Milan: Raffaello Cortina Editore, 2015).

50. Margrethe Bruun Vaage, 'Seeing is Feeling: Empathy and the Film Spectator' (Ph.D. dissertation, University of Oslo, 2009).

51. Charles Darwin, *The Expression of the Emotions in Man and Animals* (1872), 3rd edn, ed. Paul Ekman (London: HarperCollins, 1998).

52. On this explanatory principle, see the references to Cronin, Ridley, and de Waal in n. 24 of this chapter.

53. Vittorio Gallese, Christian Keysers, and Giacomo Rizzolatti, 'A Unifying View of the Basis of Social Cognition', *Trends in Cognitive Sciences*, 8/9 (Sept. 2004): 397.

54. Marco Iacoboni, 'Within Each Other: Neural Mechanisms for Empathy in the Primate Brain', in Amy Coplan and Peter Goldie (eds), *Empathy: Philosophical and Psychological Perspectives* (Oxford: OUP, 2011), 57.

55. On this theme see Daniel C. Dennett, *Kinds of Minds: The Origins of Consciousness* (London: Phoenix, 1997), particularly ch. 3.

56. See e.g. Shinsuke Shimojo and Ladan Shams, 'Sensory Modalities are Not Separate Modalities: Plasticity and Interactions', *Current Opinion in Neurobiology*, 11/4 (Aug. 2001): 505–9.

57. Andy Clark, *Mindware: An Introduction to the Philosophy of Cognitive Science*, 2nd edn (Oxford: OUP, 2013), 39–40.

58. Yuri Tsivian, 'About Cinemetrics', <http://www.cinemetrics.lv>.

Chapter 4 Papaya, Pomegranates, and Green Tea

1. C. D. Broad, *The Mind and its Place in Nature* (London: Routledge & Kegan Paul, 1925); Gilbert Ryle, *The Concept of Mind* (London: Hutchinson's University Library, 1949); Edmund Husserl, *Cartesian Meditations: An Introduction to Phenomenology*, tr. Dorion Cairns (Dordrecht: Kluwer, 1960).

2. For overviews, see Owen Flanagan, *Consciousness Reconsidered* (Cambridge, MA: MIT Press, 1992), and Rita Carter, *Exploring Consciousness* (Berkeley, CA: University of California Press, 2002).

3. Steven Pinker, 'The Cognitive Revolution', *Harvard Gazette*, 12 Oct. 2011, <http://www.news.harvard.edu/gazette/story/2011/10/the-cognitive-revolution>.

4. Jaegwon Kim, *Physicalism, or Something Near Enough* (Princeton: Princeton University Press, 2005), ch. 6. Kim argues that while it is difficult to see how the intrinsic qualities of qualia can be functionalized, the differences and similarities among qualia can be functionalized. Distinctive colour qualia are one means we have of distinguishing lettuces and tomatoes; but the function of discriminating between objects of these reflectance profiles would be preserved if we experienced tomatoes as green and lettuces as red. Kim thereby stresses the discriminative function of qualia in perception. Another major function of qualia is motivational: the relative pleasantness or unpleasantness of particular qualia will, all other things being equal, propel or brake action. I return to this theme in Chapter 5, in relation to the qualia of emotional states.

5. Bernard J. Baars, *In the Theater of Consciousness: The Workspace of the Mind* (Oxford: OUP, 1997).

6. Vilayanur S. Ramachandran, *The Emerging Mind: The Reith Lectures 2003* (London: Profile Books, 2003), 35–6.

7. Gregory Currie and Ian Ravenscroft, *Recreative Minds: Imagination in Philosophy and Psychology* (Oxford: Clarendon Press, 2002), 198.

8. Daniel C. Dennett, 'Quining Qualia', in A. J. Marcel and E. Bisiach (eds), *Consciousness in Contemporary Science* (New York: OUP, 1992), 71.

9. Currie and Ravenscroft, *Recreative Minds*, 198.

10. Arien Mack and Irwin Rock, *Inattentional Blindness* (Cambridge, MA: MIT Press, 1998); Daniel T. Levin and Daniel J. Simons, 'Failure to Detect Changes to Attended Objects in Motion Pictures', *Psychonomic Bulletin and Review*, 4/4 (Dec. 1997): 501–6; Ronald A. Rensink, J. Kevin O'Regan, and James J. Clark, 'To See or Not to See: The Need for

Attention to Perceive Changes in Scenes', *Psychological Science*, 8/5 (Sept. 1997): 368–73; Christopher Chabris and Daniel Simons, *The Invisible Gorilla: And Other Ways our Intuitions Deceive Us* (New York: Crown Publishers, 2010), ch. 2.

11. The invisible gorilla experiment is described in Chabris and Simons, *The Invisible Gorilla*, ch. 1.

12. On the significance of change blindness for continuity editing, see Tim J. Smith, 'The Attentional Theory of Continuity', *Projections*, 6/1 (June 2012): 1–27.

13. David J. Chalmers, *The Conscious Mind: In Search of a Fundamental Theory* (New York: OUP, 1996), p. xii. See also Andy Clark, *Mindware: An Introduction to the Philosophy of Cognitive Science*, 2nd edn (Oxford: OUP, 2013), appendix II.

14. Ryle, *Concept of Mind*.

15. Chalmers, *Conscious Mind*, p. xi.

16. Colin McGinn, *Consciousness and its Objects* (Oxford: Clarendon Press, 2006).

17. Chalmers, *Conscious Mind*; Galen Strawson, *Consciousness and its Place in Nature: Does Physicalism Entail Panpsychism?* (Exeter: Imprint Academic Press, 2006).

18. Daniel C. Dennett, *Consciousness Explained* (Boston: Little, Brown & Co., 1991).

19. Gerald M. Edelman, *Bright Air, Brilliant Fire: On the Matter of the Mind* (Harmondsworth: Penguin, 1992).

20. I consider the difficulties raised by Kant's Third Antinomy for naturalistic accounts of mind and art from the perspective of evolutionary theory in my 'Against Nature? Or, Confessions of a Darwinian Modernist', in 'Philosophical Aesthetics and the Sciences of Art', *Royal Institute of Philosophy Supplement*, 75 (Oct. 2014), 151–82.

21. Ch. 1 explores the account of 'aesthetic attention' advanced by Bence Nanay in *Aesthetics as Philosophy of Perception* (Oxford: OUP, 2016).

22. Eric Schwitzgebel, *Perplexities of Consciousness* (Cambridge, MA: MIT Press, 2011).

23. Kathryn Kalinak, *Settling the Score: Music and the Classical Hollywood Film* (Madison: University of Wisconsin Press, 1992), 3.

24. Greg M. Smith, *Film Structure and the Emotion System* (New York: CUP, 2003).

25. Karen Renner, 'Repeat Viewings Revisited: Emotion, Memory, and *Memento*', *Film Studies: An International Review*, 8 (2006): 106–15 (special issue, 'Film, Cognition, and Emotion', ed. Daniel Barratt and Jonathan Frome).

26. J. Allan Hobson, *The Dreaming Brain: How the Brain Creates Both the Sense and the Nonsense of Dreams* (New York: Basic Books, 1988); J. Allan Hobson, Edward F. Pace-Schott, and Robert Stickgold, 'Dreaming and the Brain: Toward a Cognitive Neuroscience of Conscious States', *Behavioral and Brain Sciences*, 23/6 (2000): 793–842.

27. See the discussion of naturalistic rehabilitations of aesthetic attention by Jenefer Robinson and Bence Nanay in Chapter 1.

28. Hugo Münsterberg, *The Photoplay: A Psychological Study* (1916), in *Hugo Münsterberg on Film*: The Photoplay: A Psychological Study *and Other Writings*, ed. Alan Langdale (New York: Routledge, 2002).

29. See Frank Cioffi, *Wittgenstein on Freud and Frazer* (Cambridge: CUP, 1998); and Simon Critchley's tribute to Cioffi, 'There is No Theory of Everything', *New York Times* (12 Sept. 2015), <http://www.opinionator.blogs.nytimes.com/2015/09/12/there-is-no-theory-of-everything/?_r=0>.

30. Bruce F. Kawin, *Mindscreen: Bergman, Godard and First-Person Film* (Princeton: Princeton University Press, 1978); David Bordwell, *Narration in the Fiction Film* (Madison: University of Wisconsin Press, 1985), ch. 10.

31. Richard Abel, *French Cinema: The First Wave, 1915–29* (Princeton: Princeton University Press, 1984).

32. András Bálint Kovács, 'Sartre, the Philosophy of Nothingness, and the Modern Melodrama', in Murray Smith and Thomas E. Wartenberg (eds), *Thinking through Cinema: Film as Philosophy* (Malden, MA: Blackwell, 2006), 135–46.

33. Annette Michelson, 'Toward Snow', *Artforum*, 9 (1971): 30–7; see also James Peterson, *Dreams of Chaos, Visions of Order: Understanding the American Avant-Garde Cinema* (Detroit: Wayne State University Press, 1994), ch. 5. Oliver Sacks, 'In the River of Consciousness', *New York Review of Books*, 51/1 (15 Jan. 2004): 41–4, <http://www.nybooks.com/articles/2004/01/15/in-the-river-of-consciousness/>.

34. Gérard Granel, *Le sens du temps et de la perception chez Husserl* (Paris: Gallimard, 1968), 108, quoted and tr. Michelson, 'Toward Snow', 30; Michelson's description of *The Photoplay* appears on p. 37.

35. See also the comparable analysis of Derek Jarman's *Blue* (1993) advanced by Vivian Sobchak in 'Phenomenology', in Paisley Livingston and Carl Plantinga (eds), *The Routledge Companion to Philosophy and Film* (New York: Routledge, 2009), 437.

36. Stephen Mulhall gives this a Heideggerian spin in *On Film*, 3rd edn (London: Routledge, 2015).

37. Murray Smith, 'Film Art, Argument, and Ambiguity', in Smith and Wartenberg, *Thinking through Cinema*, 36–8.

38. Nelson Goodman and Catherine Z. Elgin, *Reconceptions in Philosophy and Other Arts and Sciences* (Indianapolis: Hackett, 1988).

39. Jonathan Cole, *About Face* (Cambridge, MA: MIT Press, 1998); Paul Broks, *Into the Silent Land: Travels in Neuropsychology* (London: Atlantic, 2003); Suzanne Corkin, *Permanent Present Tense* (New York: Allen Lane, 2013); and Jean-Dominique Bauby, *The Diving-Bell and the Butterfly*, tr. Jeremy Leggatt (London: Fourth Estate, 1997). Jonathan Cole writes: 'In addition to these neurophysiological and cognitive neuroscientific experiments, I also believe that to understand what it is like to live with neurological impairment an empathetic, neurophenomenological approach to the lived experience of others is required.' <http://www.cogric.reading.ac.uk/biographies/Cole%20Jonathan.pdf>.

40. A. R. Luria, *The Man with a Shattered World: The History of a Brain Wound* (Cambridge, MA: Harvard University Press, 1987); Oliver Sacks, *The Man Who Mistook his Wife for a Hat* (London: Duckworth, 1985).

41. Frank Jackson, 'Epiphenomenal Qualia', *Philosophical Quarterly*, 32/127 (Apr. 1982): 127–36; see also Peter Ludlow, Yujin Nagasawa, and Daniel Stoljar (eds), *There's Something about Mary: Essays on Phenomenal Consciousness and Frank Jackson's Knowledge Argument* (Cambridge, MA: MIT Press, 2004).

42. Frank Jackson, *From Metaphysics to Ethics: A Defence of Conceptual Analysis* (Oxford: Clarendon Press, 1998).

43. Jackson, 'Postscript on Qualia', in Ludlow et al., *There's Something*, 419.

44. Joseph D. Anderson, *The Reality of Illusion: An Ecological Approach to Cognitive Film Theory* (Carbondale, IL: Southern Illinois University Press, 1996), 22; Brian O'Shaughnessy,

Consciousness and the World (Oxford: Clarendon Press, 2003); the passage quoted is from the Oxford Scholarship Online abstract for the volume as a whole, available at <http://www.oxfordscholarship.com>.

45. Jackson, *From Metaphysics to Ethics*, ch. 4; Frank Jackson, 'Colour for Representationalists', *Erkenntnis* 66 (2007): 169–85. Churchland's investigation of 'chimerical' colours, discussed in Ch. 2, is also directly relevant here. Churchland's argument there suggests that once we have had an experience of colour and understand how the physical account maps onto the experiences with which we are familiar—triangulation at work again—we can then predict colour experiences, including those which we are very unlikely ever to have had, on the basis of physiological knowledge of the visual system.

46. Jesse J. Prinz, *The Emotional Construction of Morals* (New York: OUP, 2007), 40; my emphasis. Cf. Sean Sayers, 'A Note on Emergent Materialism', 1: 'But even if, *per impossibile*, a Laplacean brain did succeed in describing and explaining a human thought or action in purely physical terms, it would not have described and explained it *as* a mental and intentional phenomenon. For the reasons given by Davidson, descriptions using mental concepts are irreducible to purely physical terms. There is a token not a type identity between the mental and the physical.' <https://kent.academia.edu/seansayers/Unpublished-papers>.

47. Marcel Proust, *Remembrance of Things Past* (1913–27), tr. C. K. Scott Moncrieff, M. Kilmartin, and Terence Kilmartin (London: Chatto & Windus, 1981).

48. David Bordwell, *Ozu and the Poetics of Cinema* (Princeton: Princeton University Press, 1988), 370–1.

49. Stan Brakhage, 'Metaphors on Vision', *Film Culture*, 30 (special issue, Fall 1963), 25.

50. Viktor Shklovsky, *Theory of Prose*, tr. Benjamin Sher (Elmwood Park: Dalkey Archive Press, 1991), 5–6.

51. Diana Raffman, *Language, Music, and Mind* (Cambridge, MA: MIT Press, 1993).

Chapter 5 Who's Afraid of Charles Darwin?

1. Brian Boyd, *On the Origin of Stories: Evolution, Cognition, and Fiction* (Cambridge, MA: Harvard University Press, 2009). See also John Tooby and Leda Cosmides, 'Does Beauty Build Adapted Minds? Toward an Evolutionary Theory of Aesthetics, Fiction, and the Arts', *SubStance*, 30/1 and 2 (2001): 6–27.

2. On imagination as 'simulation', see Gregory Currie, *Image and Mind: Film, Philosophy, and Cognitive Science* (Cambridge: CUP, 1995), ch. 5, and Murray Smith, *Engaging Characters: Fiction, Emotion, and the Cinema* (Oxford: Clarendon Press, 1995), ch. 3.

3. Spock (Leonard Nimoy), from the original *Star Trek* series (Gene Roddenberry, 1966–9), is of mixed human and Vulcan ancestry and has trained himself to suppress his emotions; Data (Brent Spiner), a sophisticated android introduced in *Star Trek: The Next Generation* (Gene Roddenberry, Maurice Hurley, Rick Berman, and Michael Piller, 1987–91) possesses no circuitry to allow him to feel emotion, though in some episodes the effects of the addition of an 'emotion chip' on Data are dramatized.

4. Important works arguing in different ways for the rationality of emotions include Ronald de Sousa, *The Rationality of Emotion* (Cambridge, MA: MIT Press, 1987); Patricia

Greenspan, *Emotions and Reasons: An Inquiry into Emotional Justification* (New York: Routledge, 1988); Antonio R. Damasio, *Descartes' Error: Emotion, Reason, and the Human Brain* (New York: G. P. Putnam's Sons, 1994); Peter Goldie, *The Emotions: A Philosophical Exploration* (Oxford: Clarendon Press, 2000); Martha Nussbaum, *Upheavals of Thought: The Intelligence of Emotions* (New York: CUP, 2001); Jesse J. Prinz, *Gut Reactions: A Perceptual Theory of Emotion* (Oxford: OUP, 2004); and Jenefer Robinson, *Deeper than Reason: Emotion and its Role in Literature, Music, and Art* (Oxford: Clarendon Press, 2005). Goldie argues that we need to think in terms of the 'intelligibility' and 'appropriateness' of emotions, as well as (more narrowly) their 'rationality'. Goldie also addresses the complexities arising from the interrelationship between evolution and culture in the domain of emotions. The idea of 'ecological' or 'evolutionary rationality' is drawn from Dylan Evans, *Emotion: The Science of Sentiment* (Oxford: OUP, 2001), who refers to it as 'an enlarged notion of rationality' relative to the narrower conception of rationality favoured by orthodox economists. Evans in turn develops this idea from Gerd Gigerenzer—see e.g. Gerd Gigerenzer and Reinhard Selten (eds), *Bounded Rationality: The Adaptive Toolbox* (Cambridge, MA: MIT Press, 2001).

5. Of course all of these factors are at play within stage performance as well; but the cinema enables a new and special emphasis on facial expression, in particular through the close-up, hence my stress on it here.

6. On syndromes involving the loss of the power of facial expression, see Jonathan Cole, *About Face* (Cambridge, MA: MIT Press, 1998); on the loss of affective orientation due to brain injury and the impact of this loss on decision-making, see Damasio, *Descartes' Error*.

7. David Bordwell, *Poetics of Cinema* (New York: Routledge, 2008), 82. See J. J. Gibson, *The Ecological Approach to Visual Perception* (Boston: Houghton Mifflin, 1979). A Gibsonian perspective on film has been most fully developed by Joseph D. Anderson in his *The Reality of Illusion: An Ecological Approach to Cognitive Film Theory* (Carbondale, IL: Southern Illinois University Press, 1996).

8. Paul Ekman (ed.), *Emotion in the Human Face*, 2nd edn (Cambridge: CUP, 1982), 34–5, and Vicki Bruce and Andy Young, *In the Eye of the Beholder: The Science of Face Perception* (Oxford: OUP, 1998), 191, comment on this issue from the point of view of psychological research.

9. Charles Darwin, *The Expression of the Emotions in Man and Animals*, 3rd edn (London: HarperCollins, 1998), 234; William James, 'What is an Emotion?', *Mind*, 9/34 (Apr. 1884): 190.

10. Accounts of the experiments undertaken by Kuleshov putatively demonstrating the 'effect' vary the details, but the core theoretical claim is constant. A careful overview and re-evaluation of the Kuleshov effect is provided by Stephen Prince and Wayne Hensley, 'The Kuleshov Effect: Recreating the Classic Experiment', *Cinema Journal*, 31/2 (Winter 1992): 59–75. Kuleshov describes the experiments in *Kuleshov on Film*, tr. Ronald Levaco (Berkeley, CA: University of California Press, 1974), 51–5; at one point he claims that montage is capable of imbuing 'a serious face with a changed expression characteristic of [a] playful moment', thus going beyond the claim associated with the Mosjoukine experiment, in which Mosjoukine's expression is neutral. Kuleshov mentions the Mosjoukine experiment specifically on p. 200, though the best-known account of the Mosjoukine experiment is given by V. I. Pudovkin, *Film Technique and Film Acting* (London: Vision

Press, 1954), 168. It should also be noted here that in later years Kuleshov qualified his views, albeit reluctantly, acknowledging to a greater extent the role of the individual shot, and the expressive work of the actor, in the creation of cinematic meaning (*Kuleshov on Film*, 193).

11. Research by Ekman, his colleagues, and sympathetic researchers, is voluminous. See e.g. Ekman, *Emotion in the Human Face*, and Carroll E. Izard, *The Face of Emotion* (New York: Appleton-Century-Crofts, 1971). Important evidence supporting the basic emotion thesis includes the expression and recognition of these emotions in remote and 'visually isolated' societies (one of Ekman's earliest studies took as its subject the South Fore people of Papua New Guinea). There is also evidence that congenitally blind children come to express many of the same facial expressions as those in sighted individuals (see Darwin's references to the case of Laura Bridgman, *Expression of the Emotions*, and Ekman, *Emotion in the Human Face*, 68–9, 152). Proponents of the view that basic emotional expressions are largely learned and culturally determined are hard pressed to explain such phenomena.

12. A nuanced overview of this issue is provided in Bruce and Young, *In the Eye of the Beholder*, 187–204.

13. Darwin discusses the expressions and gestures of anger evident here, *Expression of the Emotions*, 236–8.

14. Errol Morris, 'Abu Ghraib Essays (Photographs Reveal and Conceal)', in *Believing is Seeing: Observations on the Mysteries of Photography* (New York: Penguin Press, 2011), 75–122.

15. According to Pudovkin, 'We chose close-ups which were static and which did not express any feeling at all—quiet close-ups', *Film Technique and Film Acting*, 168. This is particularly noteworthy given that Mosjoukine was associated with (and often criticized for) a highly emotive, 'tear jerking' acting style. It is as if Kuleshov selected him as the most expressive of actors, only then to use a shot unrepresentative of this very quality.

16. Darwin, *Expression of the Emotions*, 278.

17. Note that the analysis I offer here of this sequence from *North by Northwest* modifies the one advanced in my *Engaging Characters*, 159. Similarly, in what follows I elaborate on the analysis of Hitchcock's *Saboteur* laid out in the same work, 103–6.

18. On the notion of 'added value', see Michel Chion, *Audiovision: Sound on Screen*, tr. Claudia Gorbman (New York: Columbia University Press, 1994), ch. 1.

19. *Howard Goodall's 20th Century Greats: Bernard Herrmann* (Howard Goodall and Francis Hanly, 2004). Goodall's discussion of the sequence begins at 31:22.

20. Though I do not follow him here, it is worth noting that Paul Griffiths argues that such higher emotions are sufficiently different from basic emotions that we should dispense with a unified category of emotion and instead recognize three distinct phenomena: basic emotions, socially sustained pretences, and 'higher' cognitive-affective states. Paul E. Griffiths, *What Emotions Really Are: The Problem of Psychological Categories* (Chicago: University of Chicago Press, 1997).

21. On display rules, see Ekman, *Emotion in the Human Face*, 17–19, 151–2; and Keith Oatley and Jennifer M. Jenkins, *Understanding Emotions* (Oxford: Blackwell, 1996), 52–3.

22. Dacher Keltner, *Born to be Good: The Science of a Meaningful Life* (New York: W. W. Norton & Co., 2009), 102. Keltner notes that the 'Duchenne/non-Duchenne distinction is the first big distinction in a taxonomy of different smiles', arguing that the two types of smile have

distinct evolutionary origins. While the social smile evolved 'to facilitate cooperative and affiliative proximity', the Duchenne smile, along with laughter, 'emerged to promote play and levity' (108, 103).

23. See Paul Ekman, *Emotions Revealed: Understanding Faces and Feelings* (London: Weidenfeld & Nicolson, 2003), 206. Keltner makes the comparison with the effect of Botox in *Born to be Good*, p. 105.

24. Michael Z. Newman, 'Characterization as Social Cognition in *Welcome to the Dollhouse*', *Film Studies: An International Review*, 8 (Summer 2006): 61.

25. A dialogue between two related views of emotion is dramatized in Jacob Cartwright and Nick Jordan's essay film *The Emotions of Others* (2015), scripted by Catharine Abell and Joel Smith. The film, funded by the British Society of Aesthetics and produced as part of the AHRC project 'Knowledge of Emotion', is available at <http://british-aesthetics.or g/the-emotions-of-others>.

26. Alan J. Fridlund, *Human Facial Expression: An Evolutionary Perspective* (San Diego, CA: Academic Press, 1994); Ekman, *Emotion in the Human Face*, 17–18.

27. Darwin, *Expression of the Emotions*, 212.

28. Ronald de Sousa, *The Rationality of Emotion*, p. xvi. I explore the role and significance of paradigm scenarios in Ch. 8.

29. Rudolf Arnheim, *Film as Art* (London: Faber & Faber, 1983), 115.

30. Fritz Heider and Marianne Simmel, 'An Experimental Study of Apparent Behavior', *American Journal of Psychology*, 57/2 (Apr. 1944): 243–59.

31. Arvid Kappas, 'What Facial Expressions Can and Cannot Tell us about Emotions', in Mary Katsikitis (ed.), *The Human Face: Measurement and Meaning* (Dordrecht: Kluwer, 2003), 215–34.

32. Newman, 'Characterization as Social Cognition', 60–1.

33. In *Emotions* (New York: Ronald Press Co., 1939), Frederick H. Lund argues that 'fear, horror, disgust [and other emotions] . . . are not descriptive of so many internal or organic states. They are descriptive of objective situations and of accepted modes of handling and dealing with these' (113–14). Quoted in Carl Plantinga, *Moving Viewers: American Film and the Spectator's Experience* (Berkeley, CA: University of California Press, 2009), 82. See also Hermann Schmitz, 'Emotions Outside of the Box: The New Phenomenology of Feelings and Corporeality', tr. Rudolf Owen Müllan and Jan Slaby, *Phenomenology and the Cognitive Sciences*, 10/2 (June 2011): 241–59.

34. See Ekman's 'Afterword' to his edition of Darwin's *Expression of the Emotions*, 363–93. It is worth noting here, however, that Darwin did not ignore cultural variability; his study of emotions is littered with remarks on such variation. This is set against the backdrop of a foundation of evolved, universal emotions—'basic' emotions, in contemporary parlance.

35. Béla Balázs, *Theory of the Film* (New York: Arno Press, 1972), 42.

36. On emotional contagion, see Elaine Hatfield, John T. Cacioppo, and Richard L. Rapson, *Emotional Contagion* (Cambridge: CUP, 1994). For a broader discussion of empathy, and the relationship between this concept and kindred psychological concepts such as 'simulation', motor and affective mimicry, and emotional contagion, see Ch. 7 of the current work as well as my *Engaging Characters*, 95–102. Carl Plantinga provides an important analysis of empathy and facial expression in film in 'The Scene of Empathy and the Human Face on Film', in Carl Plantinga and Greg M. Smith (eds), *Passionate Views: Film, Cognition, and Emotion*

(Baltimore: Johns Hopkins University Press, 1999), 239–55; and Plantinga, *Moving Viewers*, 125–8; see the stills of Chaplin from *City Lights* and Rose from *Titanic* (127 and 170 respectively).

37. Noll Brinckmann stresses the significance of motor rather than affective mimicry in this sequence (and in Hitchcock in general): 'Motor Mimicry in Hitchcock', in Christine N. Brinckmann, *Color and Empathy: Essays on Two Aspects of Film* (Amsterdam: Amsterdam University Press, 2014), 135–44.
38. François Truffaut, *Hitchcock/Truffaut*, rev. edn (New York: Touchstone, 1985), 108.
39. Bill Krohn, *Hitchcock at Work* (London: Phaidon, 2000), 50.
40. Stephen Jay Gould, 'Biological Potentiality vs. Biological Determinism', in *Ever Since Darwin: Reflections in Natural History* (Harmondsworth: Pelican, 1980), 251–9.
41. David Bordwell, *The Films of Carl-Theodor Dreyer* (Berkeley, CA: University of California Press, 1981), 51.
42. Balázs, *Theory of the Film*, 74.
43. Quoted in Paisley Livingston, *Cinema, Philosophy, Bergman: On Film as Philosophy* (Oxford: OUP, 2009), 149.
44. See also my essay 'Against Nature? Or, Confessions of a Darwinian Modernist', in 'Philosophical Aesthetics and the Sciences of Art', *Royal Institute of Philosophy Supplement*, 75 (2014): 151–82, which looks at the case of Bresson in more detail.
45. David Bordwell, *Planet Hong Kong: Popular Cinema and the Art of Entertainment* (Cambridge, MA: Harvard University Press, 2000), 285.
46. For a parallel analysis of the aesthetic transformation of eye behaviour in film, see David Bordwell, 'Who Blinked First?' in *Poetics of Cinema* (New York: Routledge, 2008), 327–35.

Chapter 6 What Difference does it Make?

1. Ludwig Wittgenstein, *Lectures and Conversations on Aesthetics, Psychology and Religious Belief*, compiled from notes taken by Yorick Smythies, Russ Rhees, and James Taylor, ed. Cyril Barrett (Oxford: Blackwell, 1966), 11.
2. George Dickie, 'Is Psychology Relevant to Aesthetics?', *Philosophical Review*, 71/3 (July 1962): 285–302.
3. Gregory Currie, 'Cognitive Film Theory', in *Arts and Minds* (Oxford: Clarendon Press, 2004), 153–72.
4. Antonio R. Damasio, *Descartes' Error: Emotion, Reason, and the Human Brain* (New York: G. P. Putnam's Sons, 1994), ch. 9.
5. J. L. Mackie, *Ethics: Inventing Right and Wrong* (Harmondsworth: Penguin, 1977), 36. See also Rom Harré (ed.), *The Social Construction of Emotions* (Oxford: OUP, 1986), and Greg M. Smith, *Film Structure and the Emotion System* (New York: CUP, 2003), 18, 34–6 for similar formulations on emotion.
6. Charles Darwin, *The Expression of the Emotions in Man and Animals* (1872), 3rd edn, ed. Paul Ekman (London: HarperCollins, 1998), 355.
7. Brent Berlin and Paul Kay, *Basic Colour Terms: Their Universality and Evolution* (Berkeley, CA: University of California Press, 1969).
8. James R. Averill, 'A Constructivist View of Emotion', in Robert Plutchik and Henry Kellerman (eds), *Emotion: Theory, Research, and Experience*, i (New York: Academic Press, 1980),

252 NOTES TO PAGES 156-162

305–39; Catherine A. Lutz, *Unnatural Emotions: Everyday Sentiments on a Micronesian Atoll and their Challenge to Western Theory* (Chicago: University of Chicago Press, 1988).

9. Kim Sterelny, 'Po-Bo Man?', *Studies in History and Philosophy of Biological and Biomedical Sciences*, 35 (2004): 739. See also Paul E. Griffiths, *What Emotions Really Are: The Problem of Psychological Categories* (Chicago: University of Chicago Press, 1997), 15.

10. Steven Pinker, *The Better Angels of our Nature: The Decline of Violence in History and its Causes* (London: Allen Lane, 2011), 611–22.

11. G. W. F. Hegel, *Phenomenology of Spirit*, tr. A. V. Miller, (Oxford: OUP, 1977), 294ff.

12. Elliot Sober, 'Models of Cultural Evolution', in Elliot Sober (ed.), *Conceptual Issues in Evolutionary Biology*, 2nd edn (Cambridge, MA: MIT Press, 1994), 489. David Bordwell distinguishes between a general 'metaculture' and specific cultures in *Figures Traced in Light: On Cinematic Staging* (Berkeley, CA: University of California Press, 2005), 258–65.

13. Richard Dawkins, *The Extended Phenotype: The Long Reach of the Gene* (Oxford: OUP, 1982), 198–9. Dawkins notes that variation is evident between the webs of different individual spiders, so the variation inherent in culture is not a problem for the idea of treating culture as part of the extended phenotype of the human species.

14. Dawkins, *Extended Phenotype*, 292.

15. More technically, the extended phenotype is defined in terms of 'functionally important consequences of gene differences, outside the bodies in which the gene sits'. Dawkins, *Extended Phenotype*, 292.

16. Sober, 'Models of Cultural Evolution', 489.

17. Torben Grodal, *Embodied Visions: Evolution, Emotion, Culture, and Film* (Oxford: OUP, 2009), 36 and 76.

18. Daniel C. Dennett, *Darwin's Dangerous Idea: Evolution and the Meanings of Life* (New York: Simon & Schuster, 1995), 73–80.

19. Dennett, *Darwin's Dangerous Idea*, 75.

20. Donald E. Brown, *Human Universals* (Boston: McGraw Hill, 1991), 156.

21. Dawkins, *Extended Phenotype*, 111, and 109–12 generally.

22. Dawkins, *Extended Phenotype*, 199.

23. Dennett, *Darwin's Dangerous Idea*, 366.

24. 'The genes hold culture on a leash. The leash is very long, but inevitably values will be constrained in accordance with their effects on the human gene pool. The brain is a product of evolution. Human behavior—like the deepest capacities for emotional response which drive and guide it—is the circuitous technique by which human genetic material has been and will be kept intact.' Edward O. Wilson, *On Human Nature* (Cambridge, MA: Harvard University Press, 1978), 167.

25. Stephen Jay Gould, 'Biological Potentiality vs. Biological Determinism', in *Ever since Darwin: Reflections in Natural History* (Harmondsworth: Pelican, 1980), 251.

26. Lutz, *Unnatural Emotions*, 225; Ray Birdwhistell, *Kinesics and Context: Essays on Body Motion Communication* (Philadelphia: University of Pennsylvania Press, 1970), 29–30.

27. Peter Goldie, *The Emotions: A Philosophical Exploration* (Oxford: Clarendon Press, 2000), 100.

28. One of the facts that makes Dawkins controversial, however, is his proposal—these days more often pursued by others and qualified by Dawkins himself—that the dynamics of cultural change might themselves be characterized in (strictly defined) *evolutionary* terms; that cultural change occurs through the selective replication of 'memes', the equivalent of

the gene in the realm of culture. Note, however, that the quotation from the conclusion to *The Selfish Gene* here pertains to both 'the selfish genes of our birth' and 'the selfish memes of our indoctrination', demonstrating that Dawkins is (or at least, at this point in his career, was) neither a biogenetic nor a cultural-memetic determinist. Richard Dawkins, *The Selfish Gene* (Oxford: OUP, 1976), 215.

29. Ernst Mayr, *What Evolution Is* (London: Weidenfeld & Nicolson, 2002), 142–3.

30. Jesse J. Prinz, *Gut Reactions: A Perceptual Theory of Emotion* (Oxford: OUP, 2004).

31. Jenefer Robinson, *Deeper than Reason: Emotion and its Role in Literature, Music, and Art* (Oxford: Clarendon Press, 2005), 41–5. Prinz adopts the 'gut feelings' idiom as a label for his broadly similar theory of emotion: Prinz, *Gut Reactions*.

32. Several theorists converge on the kinship between perception and emotion: Gregory Currie and Ian Ravenscroft, *Recreative Minds: Imagination in Philosophy and Psychology* (Oxford: Clarendon Press, 2002), 191–9; Prinz, *Gut Reactions*, ch. 10; Carl Plantinga, *Moving Viewers: American Film and the Spectator's Experience* (Berkeley, CA: University of California Press, 2009), 56, drawing on Robert C. Roberts, *Emotions: An Essay in Aid of Moral Psychology* (Cambridge: CUP, 2003).

33. Prinz, *Gut Reactions*, 240.

34. Joseph LeDoux, *The Emotional Brain: The Mysterious Underpinnings of Emotional Life* (New York: Simon & Schuster, 1996), 163–5.

35. Smith, *Film Structure*, 39; drawing on Nico H. Frijda, 'Moods, Emotion Episodes, and Emotions', in Michael Lewis and Jeannette M. Haviland (eds), *Handbook of Emotions* (New York: Guilford Press, 1993), 381–403.

36. Robinson, *Deeper than Reason*, 61–75.

37. Martha Nussbaum, *Upheavals of Thought: The Intelligence of Emotions* (New York: CUP, 2001).

38. Darwin's chapter titles include e.g. 'VII Low Spirits, Anxiety, Grief, Dejection, Despair', 'X Hatred and Anger', and 'XII Surprise—Astonishment—Fear—Horror'. Darwin, *Expression of the Emotions*.

39. Paul Ekman, 'All Emotions are Basic', in Paul Ekman and Richard J. Davidson (eds), *The Nature of Emotion: Fundamental Questions* (New York: OUP, 1994), 15–19; and Paul Ekman, *Emotions Revealed: Understanding Faces and Feelings* (London: Weidenfeld & Nicolson, 2003), ch. 9.

40. Michael Z. Newman, 'Characterization as Social Cognition in *Welcome to the Dollhouse*', *Film Studies: An International Review*, 8 (Summer 2006): 61, my emphases.

41. Robinson, *Deeper than Reason*, 81.

42. David Lodge, *Thinks...* (London: Penguin, 2002), 338.

43. Smith, *Film Structure*.

44. Noël Carroll, *A Philosophy of Mass Art* (Oxford: Clarendon Press, 1998). Plantinga, *Moving Viewers*, 82–4, discusses the interplay in Hollywood filmmaking between universal 'paradigm scenarios' of emotion with more culturally specific concerns.

45. Raymond Bellour, 'Deleuze: The Thinking of the Brain', *Cinema: Journal of Philosophy and the Moving Image*, 1 (2010): 92.

46. Roland Barthes, *Mythologies*, tr. Annette Lavers (London: Paladin, 1972).

47. I explore this tendency in 'Against Nature? Or, Confessions of a Darwinian Modernist', in 'Philosophical Aesthetics and the Sciences of Art', *Royal Institute of Philosophy Supplement*, 75 (2014): 151–82.

48. Robinson, *Deeper than Reason*, 199, drawing on Richard S. Lazarus, *Emotion and Adaptation* (New York: OUP, 1991). In Ch. 1 we saw how Robinson draws on Lazarus's notion of emotional coping to provide a naturalistic theory of Edward Bullough's notion of 'aesthetic distance'. In the current context, the notion of coping plays a quite different role, illuminating the behaviour of a fictional character rather than furnishing an explication of the nature of aesthetic attention.

49. Ekman, *Emotions Revealed*, 15.

50. Bertolt Brecht, *Brecht on Theatre*, ed. and tr. John Willett (London: Methuen, 1964); on Manichaean moral structures, see my *Engaging Characters: Fiction, Emotion, and the Cinema* (Oxford: Clarendon Press, 1995), ch. 6.

51. Ekman, *Emotions Revealed*, 197. For further examples, see Peter Goldie, *The Emotions: A Philosophical Exploration* (Oxford: Clarendon Press, 2000), 90–1.

52. Crispin Sartwell, *Six Names of Beauty* (New York: Routledge, 2004) provides a series of interesting and pertinent examples of such acts of translation.

53. The background here is the debate over the Sapir-Whorf hypothesis (named after linguist Edward Sapir and his student Benjamin Lee Whorf), a variety of linguistic determinism which holds that the language we speak profoundly shapes our perception and understanding of the world. The view persists in spite of its multifarious problems. Recent critiques are provided by Steven Pinker, *The Stuff of Thought: Language as a Window into Human Nature* (London: Penguin, 2008), 124–50, and John H. McWhorter, *The Language Hoax: Why the World Looks the Same in Any Language* (New York: OUP, 2014).

54. One theoretical option here is to disaggregate the normally unified concept of culture, in order to highlight the heterogeneity of the elements that we treat as aspects of culture, which may be characterized by very different interactions between genetic and environmental factors. On this possibility, which has been advocated by cultural, cognitive, and bio-anthropologists, see Adam Kuper, *Culture: The Anthropologists' Account* (Cambridge, MA: Harvard University Press, 1999), 245–7; and Andrew Whiten, 'The Second Inheritance System of Chimpanzees and Humans', *Nature*, 437 (1 Sept. 2005): box 1, p. 53.

55. Lutz, *Unnatural Emotions*, 225.

56. Smith, *Film Structure*, 18.

Chapter 7 Empathy, Expansionism, and the Extended Mind

1. Waters makes this remark in *Classic Albums: Dark Side of the Moon* (Matthew Longfellow, 2003), at 6:25.

2. Marco Iacoboni, *Mirroring People: The New Science of How we Connect with Others* (New York: Farrar, Straus & Giroux, 2008), 239–58.

3. Iacoboni, *Mirroring People*, 268.

4. The contrast between central and acentral imagining is from Richard Wollheim, *The Thread of Life* (Cambridge, MA: Harvard University Press, 1984), 74; that between personal and impersonal imagining is from Gregory Currie, *Image and Mind: Film, Philosophy, and Cognitive Science* (Cambridge: CUP, 1995), ch. 6. Although subtle differences may arise from the larger conceptual schemes in which the contrasts are situated, for present purposes, they may be treated as identical. I also follow Wollheim,

Currie, and many others in treating imagination as a form of mental simulation. For an overview, see Alvin Goldman, *Simulating Minds: The Philosophy, Psychology, and Neuroscience of Mindreading* (Oxford: OUP, 2006). For more detail on the connections between Wollheim and Currie on empathy, see my 'Imagining from the Inside', in Richard Allen and Murray Smith (eds), *Film Theory and Philosophy* (Oxford: Clarendon Press, 1997), 412–30.

5. Note the importance of the causal history of the state here: a *parallel* state of mind—as when two people are both shocked by the same event—is not, on this definition, an empathic state of mind.

6. Kendall L. Walton, *Mimesis as Make-Believe: On the Foundations of the Representational Arts* (Cambridge, MA: Harvard University Press, 1990), 28–35. I discuss Walton's views on empathy in 'Imagining from the Inside', 413–14.

7. Susan L. Feagin, *Reading with Feeling: The Aesthetics of Appreciation* (Ithaca, NY: Cornell University Press, 1996), 95.

8. An illuminating discussion of this distinction, and a very thorough review of the pertinence of empathy for film, is provided by Margrethe Bruun Vaage, 'Seeing is Feeling: Empathy and the Film Spectator' (Ph.D. dissertation, University of Oslo, 2009).

9. I provide a fuller account of this process in *Engaging Characters: Fiction, Emotion, and the Cinema* (Oxford: Clarendon Press, 1995), 98–102.

10. Walton, *Mimesis as Make-Believe*, ch. 1.

11. Vittorio Gallese, Christian Keysers, and Giacomo Rizzolatti, 'A Unifying View of the Basis of Social Cognition', *Trends in Cognitive Sciences*, 8/9 (Sept. 2004): 397; Iacoboni, *Mirroring People*, 111; Marco Iacoboni, 'Within Each Other: Neural Mechanisms for Empathy in the Primate Brain', in Amy Coplan and Peter Goldie (eds), *Empathy: Philosophical and Psychological Perspectives* (Oxford: Clarendon Press, 2011), 45–57.

12. Gallese et al., 'A Unifying View', 397 and box 3, p. 401. Those neural structures being (predominantly) the amygdala in the case of fear, and the insula in the case of disgust: box 1, p. 399.

13. Gallese et al., 'A Unifying View', box 3, p. 401. Giacomo Rizzolatti treats affective mirroring as 'a necessary condition for' fully fledged imaginative empathy, while stressing that on its own such mirroring does not amount to empathy. Rizzolatti's perspective on mirror neurons is laid out in full in Giacomo Rizzolatti and Corrado Sinigaglia, *Mirrors in the Brain: How our Minds Share Actions and Emotions*, tr. Frances Anderson (Oxford: OUP, 2008). The quoted phrase appears on p. 190. The account here is also broadly consistent with Karsten R. Stueber, *Rediscovering Empathy: Agency, Folk Psychology, and the Human Sciences* (Cambridge, MA: MIT Press, 2006), who contrasts 'basic empathy' with higher-level 'reenactive empathy'.

14. On the significance of motor mimicry as an aspect of Hitchcock's style, see Christine N. Brinckmann, 'Motor Mimicry in Hitchcock', in *Color and Empathy: Essays on Two Aspects of Film* (Amsterdam: Amsterdam University Press, 2014), 135–44. Alongside this essay, Brinckmann's volume contains a range of illuminating essays on empathy in film, addressing empathy with animals, as well as in documentary, abstract, and other forms of experimental filmmaking.

15. The example does raise a further complication: given that the sequence (and the film as a whole) alternates our attention between two characters with opposing goals, how do we

'manage' conflicting mimickings and imaginings? Can we run, in parallel, two conflicting empathic scenarios in our minds, or does the larger context of our sympathy for Guy entail that the sequence will likely only prompt empathic imagining for him, while our response to Bruno will be 'contained' at the lower level of motor and affective mimicry?

16. Marco Iacoboni, 'Within Each Other', 48.

17. Kendall Walton, 'Aesthetics: What? Why? And Wherefore?', *Journal of Aesthetics and Art Criticism*, 65/2 (Spring 2007): 152–6.

18. Noël Carroll has pursued this line of argument for many years. See e.g. *The Philosophy of Horror; or, Paradoxes of the Heart* (New York: Routledge, 1990), ch. 2; and 'Simulation, Emotions, and Morality', in *Beyond Aesthetics: Philosophical Essays* (New York: CUP, 2001), 306–16. See also Peter Goldie, 'Anti-Empathy', in Coplan and Goldie, *Empathy*, 302–17.

19. Peter Goldie, *The Emotions: A Philosophical Exploration* (Oxford: Clarendon Press, 2000), ch. 7. Currie, *Image and Mind*, presents his notion of empathy/secondary imagining in these terms, 153 and 158.

20. Cf. Smith, *Engaging Characters*, 80, and Goldman, *Simulating Minds*, ch. 7. In the Oxford Scholarship Online abstract for this chapter, available at <http://www.oxfordscholarship.com>, Goldman notes that 'an important stage of simulation for mindreading requires reflection on one's own current states'.

21. 'David Cronenberg Speaks', interview with Sam Thielman, *Variety*, online 21 Sept. 2007, <http://variety.com/2007/film/awards/david-cronenberg-speaks-1117972489>.

22. Dan Flory notes the use of the tagline 'entertainment that challenges your own ability to experience the emotions of others' in the trailer for *No Way Out* (Joseph Mankiewicz, 1950), a formulation that once again points to the idea of empathy. Dan Flory, *Philosophy, Black Film, Film Noir* (University Park, PA: Pennsylvania State University Press, 2008), 31–2.

23. Noël Carroll (in conversation) suggested this way of characterizing the case against empathy. Carroll and I have both pursued an 'error theory' of the notion of 'identification', arguing that all or most of the implications of the concept are conceptually confused or empirically unfounded (see my *Engaging Characters*, and the references to Carroll in n. 18). In effect, Carroll carries over his error theory of identification to empathy, while I take the latter concept to be defensible and to pick out a real phenomenon.

24. Andy Clark and David Chalmers, 'The Extended Mind', *Analysis*, 58/1 (Jan. 1998): 7. Clark elaborates the theory of the extended mind in *Supersizing the Mind: Embodiment, Action, and Cognitive Extension* (New York: OUP, 2008), and in *Mindware: An Introduction to the Philosophy of Cognitive Science*, 2nd edn (Oxford: OUP, 2013), ch. 9.

25. Clark and Chalmers, 'Extended Mind', 8.

26. See Ch. 1, 34.

27. Clark, *Mindware*, box 8.3, p. 177.

28. Stephen M. Kosslyn, 'On the Evolution of Human Motivation: The Role of Social Prosthetic Systems', in Steven Platek, Julian Paul Keenan, and Todd Shackelford (eds), *Evolutionary Cognitive Neuroscience* (Cambridge, MA: MIT Press, 2007), 547.

29. Frederick Adams and Kenneth Aizawa, *The Bounds of Cognition* (Malden, MA: Blackwell, 2008), 11; see also pp. x and 106–32.

30. Clark and Chalmers, 'Extended Mind', 12–13.

31. Clark, response to Fodor, 'Where is my Mind?', *London Review of Books*, 31/6 (26 Mar. 2009): 6, <http://www.lrb.co.uk/v31/n06/letters>.

32. Adams and Aizawa add that (what they regard as) authentic cognition is generally not only non-derived but underpinned by distinctive mechanisms, such as those characterizing short-term memory. Adams and Aizawa, *Bounds of Cognition*, 9–10, chs. 3 and 4. For an instructive exchange on the question of '(non-)derived' content, see the review of Clark's *Supersizing the Mind* by Jerry Fodor, 'Where is my Mind?', *London Review of Books*, 31/3 (12 Feb. 2009): 13–15, <http://www.lrb.co.uk/v31/n03/jerry-fodor/where-is-my-mind>, and Clark's response: *London Review of Books* 31/6 (26 Mar. 2009): 6, <http://www.lrb. co.uk/v31/n06/letters>.

33. The phrase—not the argument—is from Jerry Fodor, 'Diary', *London Review of Books*, 21/19 (30 Sept. 1999): 69, <http://www.lrb.co.uk/v21/n19/jerry-fodor/diary>. Recall here also the study by Petkova and Ehrsson, discussed in Ch. 2, which demonstrates how our normal sense of self-location can be displaced through a combination of visual and tactile cues. See Valeria I. Petkova and H. Henrik Ehrsson, 'If I Were You: Perceptual Illusion of Body Swapping', *PloS ONE*, 3/12 (Dec. 2008): 1–9.

34. Patrick Maynard, *The Engine of Visualization: Thinking through Photography* (Ithaca, NY: Cornell University Press, 1997), 75.

35. F. John Odling-Smee, Kevin N. Laland, and Marcus W. Feldman, *Niche Construction: The Neglected Process in Evolution* (Princeton: Princeton University Press, 2003), 241.

36. Michael Tomasello, *The Cultural Origins of Human Communication* (Cambridge, MA: Harvard University Press, 1999), 81.

37. Tomasello, *Cultural Origins*, 5.

38. Kim Sterelny, *Thought in a Hostile World: The Evolution of Human Cognition* (Malden, MA: Blackwell, 2005), ch. 8.

39. Brian Boyd, *On the Origin of Stories: Evolution, Cognition, and Fiction* (Cambridge, MA: Harvard University Press, 2009).

40. Iacoboni, *Mirroring People*, 265. Iacoboni also states that 'The mirror neuron system seems to project internally ... other people onto our own brains' (p. 260). In his contribution to Coplan and Goldie, *Empathy*, he writes: 'We empathize effortlessly and automatically with each other because evolution has selected neural systems that blend self and other's actions, intentions, and emotions ... Our neurobiology ... puts us "within each other"' (p. 57).

41. Dominic McIver Lopes, 'The Empathic Eye', in Coplan and Goldie, *Empathy*, 131. Of course, it remains true in this example that, in theory, a non-empathic process of inference—of the sort associated with 'theory of mind'—would be sufficient to arrive at the conclusion that Amy is alarmed by some change in the environment. Here I simply assume that mimicry, or some such process, is in fact the characteristic way in which we make such inferences, in order to focus on how such a process would cohere with the theory of the extended mind.

42. Steven Pinker, *How the Mind Works* (London: Penguin, 1999), 543.

43. Note also that Pinker likens this process to *case-based reasoning* in AI. One might also connect the role of gossip and fiction in building up such a catalogue of 'cases' with a particularist view of moral psychology and reasoning: the making of moral judgements is so complex that it cannot be based (at least not entirely) on the application of abstract moral principles, but must work via analogy with, or through, the database of cases. The

complex domain of moral deliberation and action is a central part of the broader complexity of human interaction and conflict described by Pinker.

44. Walton, *Mimesis as Make-Believe*.

45. 'Instructive' is the word Zunshine uses: Lisa Zunshine, *Why we Read Fiction: Theory of Mind and the Novel* (Columbia, OH: Ohio State University Press, 2006), 178. Hogan's remarks are made in Patrick C. Hogan, *Cognitive Science, Literature, and the Arts: A Guide for Humanists* (London: Routledge, 2003), 211-12.

46. Truman Capote, *In Cold Blood* (London: Penguin, 2000), 28.

47. See e.g. Keith Oatley and Jennifer M. Jenkins, *Understanding Emotions* (Oxford: Blackwell, 1996), 96, 105-6.

48. Rachel Cooper, *Psychiatry and Philosophy of Science* (Stocksfield: Acumen, 2007), 74-5. Cooper notes the tactics used by therapists and paramedics to *avoid* empathizing with traumatized patients. She also notes that even those who have had traumatic experiences usually find it difficult to empathize with others finding themselves in similar circumstances, suggesting that the second factor (lack of imaginative will and ability) may be more significant than first factor (the extremity of such situations and their remoteness from ordinary experience).

49. Patrick Maynard describes drawing as 'a way of thinking for most of us [as pre-adolescent children], for working out, observing, imagining, stating; and, for most, the fossil that remains is a doodle on a telephone pad'. 'Drawing Distinctions I: The First Projects', *Philosophical Topics*, 25/1 (Spring 1997): 231.

50. Dominic McIver Lopes, 'Pictures and the Representational Mind', *The Monist*, 86/4 (2003): 645-6. The first and second proposals here correspond, respectively, with the problems of 'carryover' and 'difference' discussed in Lopes, 'The Empathic Eye', 119; Lopes also speaks here of pictures as 'perceptual prostheses' (p. 133). On this theme, see also Lopes's *Understanding Pictures* (Oxford: Clarendon Press, 1996).

51. The link between the everyday functioning of emotion and its operation in relation to fictional entities is also made by Jenefer Robinson in her theory of emotion, explored in the present work in Ch. 6: *Deeper than Reason: Emotion and its Role in Literature, Music, and Art* (Oxford: Clarendon Press, 2005), 130.

52. Lopes, 'Pictures', 645.

53. Paul Bloom, *How Pleasure Works: The New Science of Why we Like What we Like* (London: Bodley Head, 2010), 166; Colin Radford, 'How can we be Moved by the Fate of Anna Karenina?', *Proceedings of the Aristotelian Society*, 49 (1975), 77. This assumption is also present in Currie's simulation theory of fiction; or at least, something like this is suggested by him in 'The Capacities that Enable us to Produce and Consume Art', in Matthew Kieran and Dominic McIver Lopes (eds), *Imagination, Philosophy, and the Arts* (New York: Routledge, 2003), 294, where he states: 'Imaginative counterparts of beliefs and desires will have these capacities to mimic beliefs and desires only in certain circumstances and even then only approximately.'

54. Carl Plantinga, 'The Scene of Empathy and the Human Face on Film', in Carl Plantinga and Greg M. Smith (eds), *Passionate Views: Film, Cognition, and Emotion* (Baltimore: Johns Hopkins University Press, 1999), 239-55, and Carl Plantinga, *Moving Viewers: American Film and the Spectator's Experience* (Berkeley, CA: University of California Press, 2009), 125-8.

55. Currie, 'The Capacities', 295. Currie is responding to, among others, Matthew Kieran, 'In Search of a Narrative', in Kieran and Lopes, *Imagination*, 69-87.

56. Currie, *Image and Mind*, 152–5.
57. Feagin, *Reading with Feeling*, 95.
58. Jesse J. Prinz, *Gut Reactions: A Perceptual Theory of Emotion* (Oxford: OUP, 2004), 201–5, argues in favour of the cogency and existence of unconscious emotions, drawing parallels with both unconscious perception and unconscious pain. Paul E. Griffiths, *What Emotions Really Are: The Problem of Psychological Categories* (Chicago: University of Chicago Press, 1997), 149–55, provides a complementary discussion of our lack of conscious access to the causes and cognitive mechanisms underlying some emotions.
59. Clark, *Mindware*, 266. See also the quote from Marvin Minsky, in Clark, *Mindware*, 44; and Daniel C. Dennett, *Consciousness Explained* (Boston: Little, Brown & Co., 1991), ch. 5, where Dennett lays out his conception of the mind as a composite of 'multiple drafts'.
60. Currie, 'The Capacities', 297.

Chapter 8 Feeling Prufish

1. The phrase 'garden-variety' derives from Noël Carroll, 'Film, Emotion, and Genre', in *Engaging the Moving Image* (New Haven: Yale University Press, 2003), 60–1.
2. In fact, the sense in which some emotions are 'basic', and others less so, is more complex and more controversial than I imply here. See Paul Ekman, 'All Emotions are Basic', in Paul Ekman and Richard J. Davidson (eds), *The Nature of Emotion: Fundamental Questions* (Oxford: OUP, 1994), 15–19; Jesse Prinz, 'Which Emotions are Basic?', in Dylan Evans and Pierre Cruse (eds), *Emotion, Evolution, and Rationality* (Oxford: OUP, 2004), 69–87; and Jesse J. Prinz, *Gut Reactions: A Perceptual Theory of Emotion* (Oxford: OUP, 2004), ch. 4.
3. De Sousa, *Rationality*, p. xvi, quoted in Carl Plantinga, *Moving Viewers: American Film and the Spectator's Experience* (Berkeley, CA: University of California Press, 2009), 80; see also the quote from Frederick Lund on p. 82. Plantinga draws on the notion of paradigm scenarios in order to emphasize the importance of 'garden-variety' emotions, at least with respect to Hollywood filmmaking: 'Most often, movies are made up, at least in part, of paradigm scenarios that correspond to primary emotions and to common adaptive behaviors...These are often scenarios of coupling/mating, integration into the social group, and/or survival in the face of threat' (p. 83).
4. I draw this example from Paul Ekman, *Emotions Revealed: Understanding Faces and Feelings* (London: Weidenfeld & Nicolson, 2003), 82–4. Without using the phrase, Ekman often introduces his discussions of particular emotions (or emotion families) via paradigm scenarios, in which paradigmatic emotion expressions are manifest.
5. De Sousa, *Rationality*, 184.
6. De Sousa (*Rationality*, 182) stresses the role of literature in 'refining' and 'supplementing' our repertoire of paradigm scenarios, in line with his emphasis on language and the acquisition of a *vocabulary* of emotion terms. However, it is surely both plausible and important to think about the full range of representational media as vehicles for paradigm scenarios and the acquisition of knowledge about emotion—a theme I develop more fully in this chapter.
7. Plantinga, *Moving Viewers*, 140–68.
8. The converse may also be true: we cannot properly apprehend a generic set of elements without specific placeholders instantiating these elements. For example, in order to grasp the idea that a Western will typically feature a certain type of landscape, an actual or imagined token—that is, a particular instance—of that landscape may be necessary. If this

is correct, then we might talk more generally of the *interdependence* of the generic and the particular, not only of the dependence of the particular on the generic, although I restrict myself to this latter phenomenon here.

9. Quoted in Paisley Livingston, *Cinema, Bergman, Philosophy: On Film as Philosophy* (Oxford: OUP, 2009), 41.

10. John Benson, 'Emotion and Expression', *Philosophical Review*, 76/3 (July 1967): 338–9.

11. Benson, 'Emotion', 336.

12. Benson, 'Emotion', 339.

13. William James, *The Principles of Psychology*, ii (New York: Dover Publications, 1950), 448.

14. Ekman, *Emotions Revealed*, 70.

15. Ekman, *Emotions Revealed*, 186.

16. Christopher Grau, '*American History X*, Cinematic Manipulation, and Moral Conversion', in 'Film and the Emotions', *Midwest Studies in Philosophy* 34 (2010): 52–76. Plantinga discusses instances of shame and guilt in a similar way, focusing on the works of Hitchcock, *Moving Viewers*, 159–66. Margrethe Bruun Vaage analyses the emotional structure of contemporary antiheroic TV series in terms of a similar dynamic between underpinning sympathy 'checked' by periodic moral revulsion: *The Antihero in American Television* (London: Routledge, 2015), 25–6, 109–10.

17. See the discussion of the 'leakage' of emotional expressions in Ch. 6, 170 and n. 49.

18. Noël Carroll, *The Philosophy of Horror; or, Paradoxes of the Heart* (New York: Routledge, 1990), 178–95.

19. Gary Iseminger, 'How Strange a Sadness?', *Journal of Aesthetics and Art Criticism*, 42/1 (1983): 81–2. Carroll introduces Iseminger's distinction in *Philosophy of Horror*, 191. My intervention in the debate appears in Murray Smith, '(A)moral Monstrosity', in Michael Grant (ed.), *The Films of David Cronenberg* (Trowbridge: Flicks Books, 2000), 69–83.

20. The context of art, then, sheds some light on 'odd couple' combinations of emotions. In general it appears that once we allow for second-order emotional experience—metaemotions in everyday life, 'art' emotions—no combination of emotions seems to be impossible, no matter how unlikely on the face of it. As a further example, consider A. O. Scott's attribution of a mood of 'happy agony' or 'exuberant melancholy' to Pedro Almodóvar's *Los abrazos rotos/Broken Embraces*, New York Times (20 Nov. 2009), C14, <http:movies.nytimes.com/2009/11/20movies/20broken.html>. Carroll discusses art emotions in *Philosophy of Horror*, ch. 1.

21. Jenefer Robinson, *Deeper than Reason: Emotion and its Role in Literature, Music, and Art* (Oxford: Clarendon Press, 2005), 80.

22. De Sousa, *Rationality*, 184.

23. It's worth noting that such appraisals are 'non-cognitive' for Robinson because of their place within our neural and cognitive architecture—they are implemented through neural pathways enabling a rapid but coarse response, in contrast to the cortex-implemented cognitive monitoring which follows the initial appraisal. These appraisals are still representational, however; they are, no matter how coarse, responses to 'outer' or 'inner' objects (events in the environment, or thoughts). Importantly, they are not 'non-cognitive' in the sense understood in metaethical debates regarding emotivism, where 'non-cognitive' denotes an understanding of moral states as purely subjective states. In a similar spirit, Jesse Prinz

denies that emotions are 'cognitive in any sense', while maintaining (like Robinson) that emotions are nevertheless representational states. Prinz, *Gut Reactions*, 69, 82–3.

24. Plantinga, *Moving Viewers*, 131.
25. Robinson, *Deeper than Reason*, 85.
26. Robinson, *Deeper than Reason*, 161.
27. Robinson draws on Patricia S. Greenspan, *Emotions and Reasons: An Inquiry into Emotional Justification* (New York: Routledge, 1988), 431, n. 5, in underlining this point. See also Murray Smith, *Engaging Characters: Fiction, Emotion, and the Cinema* (Oxford: Clarendon Press, 1995), 60–1. Tamar Szabó Gendler has developed the fullest account of primitive belief-like states, through the notion of 'aliefs'. See her *Intuition, Imagination, and Philosophical Methodology* (Oxford: OUP, 2010), chs. 13 and 14.
28. Paul Churchland, in 'What Happens to Reliabilism When it is Liberated from the Propositional Attitudes?', in *Neurophilosophy at Work* (Cambridge: CUP, 2007), 91.
29. Churchland, 'What Happens', 91–2.
30. Churchland stresses the conceptual and representational capacities possessed by non-human animals, and by humans who have lost most or all of their linguistic abilities: such 'global aphasics...can still play a game of chess, cook a dinner, appreciate an unfolding football game, drive a car across the state, or shop for the weekend groceries (although the shopping list must be iconic). Such people retain a rich conceptual framework, a rich appreciation of both natural and functional kinds' ('What Happens', 93). The limits of my language do *not* mean the limits of my world.
31. Dominic McIver Lopes, 'The Empathic Eye', in Amy Coplan and Peter Goldie (eds), *Empathy: Philosophical and Psychological Perspectives* (Oxford: Clarendon Press, 2011), 132.
32. Jane Pollard, speaking in *The Making of 20,000 Days on Earth*, available on the Blu-ray disc of the feature (Channel 4 DVD, 2014).
33. Ward E. Jones, 'Philosophy and the Ethical Significance of Spectatorship', in Ward E. Jones and Samantha Vice (eds), *Ethics at the Cinema* (Oxford: OUP, 2011), 5.
34. Robinson, *Deeper than Reason*, 79.
35. Cleanth Brooks, 'The Heresy of Paraphrase', in *The Well Wrought Urn: Studies in the Structure of Poetry* (London: Methuen, 1968), 192–213.
36. Andy Clark, *Mindware: An Introduction to the Philosophy of Cognitive Science*, 2nd edn (Oxford: OUP, 2013), 172.
37. Diana Raffman, *Language, Music, and Mind* (Cambridge, MA: MIT Press, 1993), esp. chs. 5 and 7. Raffman's argument is very specifically directed at musical cognition and experience. My aim here is to demonstrate that in certain respects her thesis generalizes to other art forms and types of cognition.
38. James, *Principles of Psychology*, ii. 448.
39. Raffman, *Language, Music, and Mind*, 136.
40. Robinson, *Deeper than Reason*, 159.
41. But see Ch. 6 on some reservations regarding the idea of homogeneous, integrated cultures possessed of distinctive themes.
42. See Ch. 6, n. 28. I consider memetics and other models of cultural evolution at greater length in 'Against Nature? Or, Confessions of a Darwinian Modernist', in 'Philosophical Aesthetics and the Sciences of Art', *Royal Institute of Philosophy Supplement*, 75 (Oct. 2014): 151–82. I defend the idea that, whatever the problems with these current models, we

262 NOTES TO PAGES 214–223

need to make space for some notion of cultural evolution in our theories of culture and human behaviour.

43. David Lewis, 'Postscripts to "Truth in Fiction"', in *Philosophical Papers*, i (New York: OUP, 1983), 279.

44. A. O. Scott, 'Almodóvar's Happy Agony'.

45. *The Architecture of the International*, 1:38; available as one of the special features on the DVD of *The International* (Sony Pictures Home Entertainment, 2009).

46. Robinson, *Deeper than Reason*, 159; see also 166. Martha Nussbaum, *Love's Knowledge: Essays on Philosophy and Literature* (New York: OUP, 1990) also puts an emphasis on the role of particularity in art, e.g. p. 3.

47. Organisation Européenne pour la Recherche Nucléaire; originally Conseil Européen pour la Recherche Nucléaire—hence CERN—based in Geneva, Switzerland.

48. Robinson, *Deeper than Reason*, 99.

Conclusion

1. James, *Principles of Psychology*, ii, 448–9.

2. Danto makes this remark in Hans Maes (ed.), *Conversations on Art and Aesthetics* (Oxford: OUP, forthcoming 2017). Arthur Danto, *Unnatural Wonders: Essays from the Gap between Art and Life* (New York: Columbia University Press, 2005).

3. Frank Cioffi, *Wittgenstein on Freud and Frazer* (Cambridge: CUP, 1998), 301–4 and 79. See also Simon Critchley's tribute to Cioffi, 'There is No Theory of Everything', *New York Times* (12 Sept. 2015), <http://opinionator.blogs.nytimes.com/2015/09/12/there-is-no-theory-of-everything/?_r=0>.

4. Philip Kitcher, 'Seeing is Unbelieving', review of Alex Rosenberg, *The Atheist's Guide to Reality* (2011), *New York Times* (25 Mar. 2012): BR31, <http://www.nytimes.com/2012/03/25/books/review/alex-rosenbergs-the-atheists-guide-to-reality.html>.

5. Sellars introduces the distinction in 'Philosophy and the Scientific Image of Man', in Robert Colodny (ed.), *Frontiers of Science and Philosophy* (Pittsburgh, PA: University of Pittsburgh Press, 1962), 35–78; the 'logical space of reasons' first surfaces in Wilfrid Sellars, *Empiricism and the Philosophy of Mind*, ed. Robert Brandom (Cambridge, MA: Harvard University Press, 1997), §36, 76.

6. Sellars, 'Philosophy', 372 and 377.

7. Brian O'Shaughnessy, *Consciousness and the World* (Oxford: Clarendon Press, 2003); the passage quoted is from the Oxford Scholarship Online abstract for the volume as a whole, available at <www.oxfordscholarship.com>. As we saw in Ch. 2, O'Shaughnessy concludes the abstract: 'So it is that the gap is closed between the mental and physical domains, and the epistemological basis of mind is established.'

8. Kim Sterelny, *Thought in a Hostile World: The Evolution of Human Cognition* (Malden, MA: Blackwell, 2005); Daniel C. Dennett, *Kinds of Minds: The Origins of Consciousness* (London: Phoenix, 1997).

9. Kendall L. Walton, 'Transparent Pictures: On the Nature of Photographic Realism', *Critical Inquiry*, 11/2 (Dec. 1984): 271.

10. Jerry Fodor, 'Where is my Mind?', review of Andy Clark, *Supersizing the Mind: Embodiment, Action, and Cognitive Extension*, *London Review of Books*, 31/3 (12 Feb. 2009): 15.

Bibliography

Abel, Richard, *French Cinema: The First Wave, 1915–29* (Princeton: Princeton University Press, 1984).

Adams, Frederick, and Kenneth Aizawa, *The Bounds of Cognition* (Malden, MA: Blackwell, 2008).

Alexander, Joshua, *Experimental Philosophy: An Introduction* (Cambridge: Polity, 2012).

Allen, Richard, *Projecting Illusion: Film Spectatorship and the Impression of Reality* (Cambridge: Cambridge University Press, 1997).

Allen, Richard, 'Film Spectatorship: A Reply to Murray Smith', *Journal of Aesthetics and Art Criticism* 56/1 (1998): 61–3. doi:10.2307/431951.

Anderson, Joseph D., *The Reality of Illusion: An Ecological Approach to Cognitive Film Theory* (Carbondale, IL: Southern Illinois University Press, 1996).

Appiah, Kwame Anthony, *Experiments in Ethics* (Cambridge, MA: Harvard University Press, 2008).

Arnheim, Rudolf, *Film as Art* (London: Faber & Faber, 1983).

Averill, James R., 'A Constructivist View of Emotion', in Robert Plutchik and Henry Kellerman (eds), *Emotion: Theory, Research, and Experience*, i (New York: Academic Press, 1980), 305–39.

Baars, Bernard J., *In the Theater of Consciousness: The Workspace of the Mind* (Oxford: Oxford University Press, 1997).

Baird, Robert, 'Startle and the Film Threat Scene', *Images: A Journal of Film and Popular Culture*, 3 (Mar. 1997). <http://www.imagesjournal.com/issue03/features/startle1.htm>.

Baird, Robert, 'The Startle Effect: Implications for Spectator Cognition and Media Theory', *Film Quarterly*, 53/3 (Spring 2000): 12–24. doi:10.2307/1213732.

Balázs, Béla, *Theory of the Film* (New York: Arno Press, 1972).

Barratt, Daniel H., 'The Paradox of Fiction Revisited: A Cognitive Approach to Understanding (Cinematic) Emotion' (Ph.D. dissertation, University of Kent, 2004).

Barratt, Daniel, '"Twist Blindness": The Role of Primacy, Priming, Schemas, and Reconstructive Memory in a First-Time Viewing of *The Sixth Sense*', in Warren Buckland (ed.), *Puzzle Films: Complex Storytelling in Contemporary Cinema* (Malden, MA: Wiley-Blackwell, 2009), 62–86.

Barrett, David A., 'Multiple Realizability, Identity Theory, and the Gradual Reorganization Principle'. *British Journal for the Philosophy of Science*, 64/2 (June 2013): 325–46. doi:10.1093/bjps/axs011.

Barthes, Roland, *Mythologies*, tr. Annette Lavers (London: Paladin, 1972).

Bauby, Jean-Dominique, *The Diving-Bell and the Butterfly*, tr. Jeremy Leggatt (London: Fourth Estate, 1997).

Baxandall, Michael, *Patterns of Intention: On the Historical Explanation of Pictures* (New Haven: Yale University Press, 1985).

Bazin, André, 'The Ontology of the Photographic Image', in *What is Cinema?*, i, ed. and tr. Hugh Gray (Berkeley, CA: University of California Press, 1967), 9–16.

BBC News, 'Men Suffer from Phantom Pregnancy', 14 June 2007. <http://news.bbc.co.uk/1/hi/6751709.stm?lsm>.

Bellour, Raymond, 'Deleuze: The Thinking of the Brain', *Cinema: Journal of Philosophy and the Moving Image*, 1 (2010), 81–94. <http://cjpmi.ifilnova.pt/1-contents>.

Bennett, M. R., and P. M. S. Hacker, *Philosophical Foundations of Neuroscience* (Oxford: Blackwell, 2003).

Benson, John, 'Emotion and Expression', *Philosophical Review*, 76/3 (July 1967): 335–57. doi:10.2307/2183623.

Bergeron, Vincent, and Dominic McIver Lopes, 'Aesthetic Theory and Aesthetic Science: Prospects for Integration', in Arthur P. Shimamura and Stephen E. Palmer (eds), *Aesthetic Science: Connecting Minds, Brains, and Experience* (New York: Oxford University Press, 2012), 63–79.

Berlin, Brent, and Paul Kay, *Basic Colour Terms: Their Universality and Evolution* (Berkeley, CA: University of California Press, 1969).

Bermúdez, José Luis, *Thinking Without Words* (Oxford: Oxford University Press, 2003).

Birdwhistell, Ray, *Kinesics and Context: Essays on Body Motion Communication* (Philadelphia: University of Pennsylvania Press, 1970).

Bordwell, David, *The Films of Carl-Theodor Dreyer* (Berkeley, CA: University of California Press, 1981).

Bordwell, David, *Narration in the Fiction Film* (Madison: University of Wisconsin Press, 1985).

Bordwell, David, *Ozu and the Poetics of Cinema* (Princeton: Princeton University Press, 1988).

Bordwell, David, *Making Meaning: Inference and Rhetoric in the Interpretation of Cinema* (Cambridge, MA: Harvard University Press, 1989).

Bordwell, David, 'A Case for Cognitivism: Further Reflections', *Iris*, 11 (Summer 1990): 107–12. <http://www.davidbordwell.net/articles>.

Bordwell, David, *Planet Hong Kong: Popular Cinema and the Art of Entertainment* (Cambridge, MA: Harvard University Press, 2000).

Bordwell, David, *Figures Traced in Light: On Cinematic Staging* (Berkeley, CA: University of California Press, 2005).

Bordwell, David, *The Way Hollywood Tells it* (Berkeley, CA: University of California Press, 2006).

Bordwell, David, *Poetics of Cinema* (New York: Routledge, 2008).

Bordwell, David, 'This is your Brain on Movies, Maybe', *Observations on film art* blog, 8 Mar. 2011. <http://www.davidbordwell.net/blog/?p=300>.

Bordwell, David, and Kristin Thompson, *Film Art: An Introduction*, 10th edn (New York: McGraw-Hill, 2013).

Boyd, Brian, *On the Origin of Stories: Evolution, Cognition, and Fiction* (Cambridge, MA: Harvard University Press, 2009).

Boyd, Robert, and Peter J. Richerson, *Not by Genes Alone: How Culture Transformed Human Evolution* (Chicago: University of Chicago Press, 2005).

Brakhage, Stan, 'Metaphors on Vision', *Film Culture*, 30 (special issue, Fall 1963).

Brecht, Bertolt, *Brecht on Theatre*, ed. and tr. John Willett (London: Methuen, 1964).

Brinckmann, Christine Noll, 'Motor Mimicry in Hitchcock', in Christine N. Brinckmann (ed.), *Color and Empathy: Essays on Two Aspects of Film* (Amsterdam: Amsterdam University Press, 2014), 135–44.

Broad, C. D., *The Mind and its Place in Nature* (London: Routledge & Kegan Paul, 1925).

Broks, Paul, *Into the Silent Land: Travels in Neuropsychology* (London: Atlantic, 2003).

Brooks, Cleanth, 'The Heresy of Paraphrase', in *The Well Wrought Urn: Studies in the Structure of Poetry* (London: Methuen, 1968), 192–213.

Brown, Donald E., *Human Universals* (Boston: McGraw Hill, 1991).

Bruce Vicki, and Andy Young, *In the Eye of the Beholder: The Science of Face Perception* (Oxford: Oxford University Press, 1998).

Brunick, Kaitlin L., James E. Cutting, and Jordan E. DeLong, 'Low-Level Features of Film: What They Are and Why We Would Be Lost Without Them', in Arthur P. Shimamura (ed.), *Psychocinematics: Exploring Cognition at the Movies* (New York: Oxford University Press, 2013), 133–48. doi:10.1093/acprof:oso/9780199862139.003.0007.

Bryson, Norman, *Vision and Painting: The Logic of the Gaze* (New Haven: Yale University Press, 1983).

Burton, Charlie, 'Directed by Brainwave', *Wired*, 13 Sept. 2011. <http://www.wired.co.uk/magazine/archive/2011/10/play/directed-by-brainwave>.

Capote, Truman, *In Cold Blood* (London: Penguin, 2000).

Carroll, Noël, *The Philosophy of Horror; or, Paradoxes of the Heart* (New York: Routledge, 1990).

Carroll, Noël, *A Philosophy of Mass Art* (Oxford: Clarendon Press, 1998).

Carroll, Noël, *Philosophy of Art: A Contemporary Introduction* (London: Routledge, 1999).

Carroll, Noël, *Beyond Aesthetics: Philosophical Essays* (New York: Cambridge University Press, 2001).

Carroll, Noël, 'Film, Emotion, and Genre', in *Engaging the Moving Image* (New Haven: Yale University Press, 2003), 59–87.

Carruthers, Peter, 'Animal Minds are Real, (Distinctively) Human Minds are Not', *American Philosophical Quarterly*, 50/3 (July 2013): 233–48.

Carter, Rita, *Exploring Consciousness* (Berkeley, CA: University of California Press, 2002).

Castellote, Juan M., Hatice Kumru, Ana Queralt, and Josep Valls-Solé, 'A Startle Speeds up the Execution of Externally Guided Saccades', *Experimental Brain Research*, 177/1 (Feb. 2007): 129–36. doi:10.1007/s00221-006-0659-4.

Chabris, Christopher, and Daniel Simons, *The Invisible Gorilla: And Other Ways our Intuitions Deceive Us* (New York: Crown Publishers, 2010).

Chalmers, David J., *The Conscious Mind: In Search of a Fundamental Theory* (New York: Oxford University Press, 1996).

Chanan, Michael, 'Blinded by Science?', *Putney Debater* blog, 21 June 2011. <http://www.putneydebater.com/blinded-by-science>.

Chatterjee, Anjan, *The Aesthetic Brain: How we Evolved to Desire Beauty and Enjoy Art* (New York: Oxford University Press, 2014).

Chion, Michel, *Audio-Vision: Sound on Screen*, tr. Claudia Gorbman (New York: Columbia University Press, 1994).

Churchland, Patricia S., *Neurophilosophy: Towards a Unified Science of the Mind-Brain* (Cambridge, MA: MIT Press, 1996).

Churchland, Paul M., 'Eliminative Materialism and the Propositional Attitudes', *Journal of Philosophy*, 78/2 (Feb. 1981): 67–90. doi:10.2307/2025900.

Churchland, Paul, 'Chimerical Colours: Some Phenomenological Predictions from Cognitive Neuroscience', in *Neurophilosophy at Work* (Cambridge: Cambridge University Press, 2007), 161–97. <http://web.gc.cuny.edu/cogsci/private/Churchland-chimeric-colors.pdf>.

Churchland, Paul, 'What Happens to Reliabilism When it is Liberated from the Propositional Attitudes?', in *Neurophilosophy at Work* (Cambridge: Cambridge University Press, 2007), 88–112.

Cioffi, Frank, *Wittgenstein on Freud and Frazer* (Cambridge: Cambridge University Press, 1998).

Clark, Andy, *Natural-Born Cyborgs: Minds, Technologies, and the Future of Human Intelligence* (Oxford: Oxford University Press, 2003).

Clark, Andy, *Supersizing the Mind: Embodiment, Action, and Cognitive Extension* (New York: Oxford University Press, 2008).

Clark, Andy, response to Jerry Fodor, 'Where is my Mind?', *London Review of Books*, 31/6 (26 Mar. 2009): 6. <http://www.lrb.co.uk/v31/n06/letters>.

Clark, Andy, *Mindware: An Introduction to the Philosophy of Cognitive Science*, 2nd edn (Oxford: Oxford University Press, 2013).

Clark, Andy, and David Chalmers, 'The Extended Mind', *Analysis*, 58/1 (Jan. 1998): 7–19. doi:10.1093/analys/58.1.7.

Cole, Jonathan, *About Face* (Cambridge, MA: MIT Press, 1998).

Cooper, Rachel, *Psychiatry and Philosophy of Science* (Stocksfield: Acumen, 2007).

Corkin, Suzanne, *Permanent Present Tense* (New York: Allen Lane, 2013).

Crace, Jim, *Being Dead* (London: Viking, 1999).

Critchley, Simon, 'There is No Theory of Everything', *New York Times*, 12 Sept. 2015. <http://opinionator.blogs.nytimes.com/2015/09/12/there-is-no-theory-of-everything/?_r=0>.

Currie, Gregory, *Image and Mind: Film, Philosophy, and Cognitive Science* (Cambridge: Cambridge University Press, 1995).

Currie, Gregory, 'The Paradox of Caring: Fiction and the Philosophy of Mind', in Mette Hjort and Sue Laver (eds), *Emotion and the Arts* (New York: Oxford University Press, 1997), 63–77.

Currie, Gregory, 'The Capacities that Enable us to Produce and Consume Art', in Matthew Kieran and Dominic McIver Lopes (eds), *Imagination, Philosophy, and the Arts* (New York: Routledge, 2003), 293–303.

Currie, Gregory, *Arts and Minds* (Oxford: Clarendon Press, 2004).

Currie, Gregory, 'Standing in the Last Ditch: On the Communicative Intentions of Fiction Makers', *Journal of Aesthetics and Art Criticism*, 72/4 (2014): 351–63. doi:10.1111/jaac.12109.

Currie, Gregory, and Ian Ravenscroft, *Recreative Minds: Imagination in Philosophy and Psychology* (Oxford: Clarendon Press, 2002).

Damasio, Antonio R., *Descartes' Error: Emotion, Reason, and the Human Brain* (New York: G. P. Putnam's Sons, 1994).

Danto, Arthur C., *The Transfiguration of the Commonplace: A Philosophy of Art* (Cambridge, MA: Harvard University Press, 1981).

Danto, Arthur C., 'Christian Boltanksi', in *Encounters and Reflection: Art in the Historical Present* (New York: Noonday Press, 1991), 257–63.

Danto, Arthur, *Unnatural Wonders: Essays from the Gap between Art and Life* (New York: Columbia University Press, 2005).

Darwin, Charles, *Charles Darwin's Notebooks, 1836–1844: Geology, Transmutation of Species, Metaphysical Enquiries*, ed. Paul H. Barrett, Peter J. Gautrey, Sandra Herbert, David Kohn, and Sydney Smith (Cambridge: Cambridge University Press, 1987).

Darwin, Charles, *The Expression of the Emotions in Man and Animals*, 3rd edn, ed. Paul Ekman (London: HarperCollins, 1998).

Davidson, Donald, 'Actions, Reasons, and Causes', in *Essays on Actions and Events*, 2nd edn (Oxford: Clarendon Press, 2001), 3–19.

Davidson, Donald, 'Agency', in *Essays on Actions and Events*, 2nd edn (Oxford: Clarendon Press, 2001), 43–62.

Davies, David, '"This is your Brain on Art": What Can Philosophy of Art Learn from Neuroscience?', in Gregory Currie, Matthew Kieran, Aaron Meskin, and Jon Robson (eds), *Aesthetics and the Sciences of Mind* (Oxford: Oxford University Press, 2014), 57–74.

Davis, Michael, 'The Mammalian Startle Response', in Robert C. Eaton (ed.), *Neural Mechanisms of Startle Behavior* (New York: Plenum, 1984), 287–351.

Dawkins, Richard, *The Selfish Gene* (Oxford: Oxford University Press, 1976).

Dawkins, Richard, *The Extended Phenotype: The Long Reach of the Gene* (Oxford: Oxford University Press, 1982).

Dempster, Douglas, 'Renaturalizing Aesthetics', *Journal of Aesthetics and Art Criticism*, 51/3 (Summer 1993): 351–61. doi:10.2307/431508.

Dennett, Daniel C., *Consciousness Explained* (Boston: Little, Brown & Co., 1991).

Dennett, Daniel C., 'Quining Qualia', in A. J. Marcel and E. Bisiach (eds), *Consciousness in Contemporary Science* (New York: Oxford University Press, 1992), 42–77. doi:10.1093/acprof:oso/9780198522379.003.0003.

Dennett, Daniel, *Darwin's Dangerous Idea: Evolution and the Meanings of Life* (New York: Simon & Schuster, 1995).

Dennett, Daniel C., *Kinds of Minds: The Origins of Consciousness* (London: Phoenix, 1997).

Dennett, Daniel, 'Philosophy as Naïve Anthropology: Comment on Bennett and Hacker', in Maxwell Bennett, Daniel Dennett, Peter Hacker, John Searle, and Daniel Robinson (eds), *Neuroscience and Philosophy: Brain, Mind, and Language* (New York: Columbia University Press, 2007), 73–95.

Descartes, René, 'Second Meditation', in *Discourse on Method and the Meditations*, tr. and introd. by F. E. Sutcliffe (Cambridge: Cambridge University Press, 1996), 102–12.

DesMarais, Christina, 'Video Game Uses Brain to Control Action', *PCWorld*, 16 October 2011. <http://www.pcworld.com/article/241993/video_game_uses_brain_to_control_action.html>.

de Sousa, Ronald, *The Rationality of Emotion* (Cambridge, MA: MIT Press, 1987).

de Sousa, Ronald, *Why Think? Evolution and the Rational Mind* (New York: Oxford University Press, 2007).

de Waal, Frans, *Good Natured: The Origins of Right and Wrong in Humans and Other Animals* (Cambridge, MA: Harvard University Press, 1996).

Dickie, George, 'Is Psychology Relevant to Aesthetics?', *Philosophical Review*, 71/3 (July 1962): 285–302.

Dickie, George, 'The Myth of the Aesthetic Attitude', *American Philosophical Quarterly*, 1/1 (Jan. 1964): 56–65. <http://www.jstor.org/stable/20009119>.

Dilthey, Wilhelm, 'Descriptive Psychology and Historical Understanding', in *Selected Writings*, ed. and tr. H. P. Rickman (Cambridge: Cambridge University Press, 1976), 87–97.

Dilthey, Wilhelm, *Introduction to the Human Sciences: An Attempt to Lay a Foundation for the Study of Society and History*, tr. Ramon J. Betanzos (Detroit: Wayne State University Press, 1988).

Dinstein, Ilan, Cibu Thomas, Marlene Behrmann, and David J. Heeger, 'A Mirror up to Nature', *Current Biology*, 18/1 (8 Jan. 2008): R13–R18. doi:org/10.1016/j.cub.2007.11.004.

Dissanayake, Ellen, 'Art as a Human Behavior: Toward an Ethological View of Art', *Journal of Aesthetics and Art Criticism*, 38/4 (Summer 1980): 397–406. doi:10.2307/430321.

Doyle, Arthur Conan, 'The Sussex Vampire', in *The Case-Book of Sherlock Holmes* (Oxford: OUP, 2009), 72–88.

Dretske, Fred, *Naturalizing the Mind* (Cambridge, MA: MIT Press, 1995).

Dupré, John, *Human Nature and the Limits of Science* (Oxford: Clarendon Press, 2001).

Edelman, Gerald M., *Bright Air, Brilliant Fire: On the Matter of the Mind* (Harmondsworth: Penguin, 1992).

Ekman, Paul, ed., *Emotion in the Human Face*, 2nd edn (Cambridge: Cambridge University Press, 1982).

Ekman, Paul, 'All Emotions are Basic', in Paul Ekman and Richard J. Davidson (eds), *The Nature of Emotion: Fundamental Questions* (New York: Oxford University Press, 1994), 15–19.

Ekman, Paul, *Emotions Revealed: Understanding Faces and Feelings* (London: Weidenfeld & Nicolson, 2003).

Evans, Dylan, *Emotion: The Science of Sentiment* (Oxford: Oxford University Press, 2001).

Feagin, Susan L., *Reading with Feeling: The Aesthetics of Appreciation* (Ithaca, NY: Cornell University Press, 1996).

Feldman, Richard, 'Naturalized Epistemology', *Stanford Encyclopedia of Philosophy*, 5 July 2001. <http://plato.stanford.edu/entries/epistemology-naturalized>.

Fenner, David E., 'Modest Aesthetic Naturalism', *Journal of Aesthetics and Art Criticism*, 50/4 (Autumn 1992): 283–9. doi:10.2307/431400.

Flanagan, Owen, *The Science of the Mind* (Cambridge, MA: MIT Press, 1984).

Flanagan, Owen, *Consciousness Reconsidered* (Cambridge, MA: MIT Press, 1992).

Flory, Dan, *Philosophy, Black Film, Film Noir* (University Park, PA: Pennsylvania State University Press, 2008).

Fodor, Jerry A., *The Modularity of Mind: An Essay on Faculty Psychology* (Cambridge, MA, MIT Press, 1983).

Fodor, Jerry, 'Diary', *London Review of Books*, 21/19 (30 Sept. 1999): 68–9. <http://www.lrb.co.uk/v21/n19/jerry-fodor/diary>.

Fodor, Jerry, 'Where's the Carburettor?', *London Review of Books*, 22/1 (6 Jan. 2000): 5. <http://www.lrb.co.uk/v22/n01/letters#letter35>.

Fodor, Jerry, 'Where is my Mind?', *London Review of Books*, 31/3 (12 Feb. 2009): 13–15. <http://www.lrb.co.uk/v31/n03/jerry-fodor/where-is-my-mind>.

Freedberg, David, and Vittorio Gallese, 'Motion, Emotion and Empathy in Esthetic Experience', *Trends in Cognitive Sciences*, 11/5 (2007): 197–203. doi:10.1016/j.tics.2007.02.003.

Freeman, Derek, *Dilthey's Dream: Essays on Human Nature and Culture* (Canberra: Pandanus Books, 2001).

Fridlund, Alan J., *Human Facial Expression: An Evolutionary Perspective* (San Diego, CA: Academic Press, 1994).

Frijda, Nico H., 'Moods, Emotion Episodes, and Emotions', in Michael Lewis and Jeannette M. Haviland (eds), *Handbook of Emotions* (New York: Guilford Press, 1993), 381–403.

Gallese, Vittorio, and Michele Guerra, *Lo schermo empatico: Cinema e neuroscienze* (Milan: Raffaello Cortina Editore, 2015).

Gallese, Vittorio, Christian Keysers, and Giacomo Rizzolatti, 'A Unifying View of the Basis of Social Cognition', *Trends in Cognitive Sciences*, 8/9 (Sept. 2004): 396–403. doi:10.1016/j.tics.2004.07.002.

Geertz, Clifford, *The Interpretation of Cultures* (New York: Basic Books, 1973).

Gendler, Tamar Szabó, *Intuition, Imagination, and Philosophical Methodology* (Oxford: Oxford University Press, 2010).

Gerrig, Richard, *Experiencing Narrative Worlds: On the Psychological Activities of Reading* (New Haven: Yale University Press, 1993).

Gibson, J. J., *The Ecological Approach to Visual Perception* (Boston: Houghton Mifflin, 1979).

Gigerenzer, Gerd, and Reinhard Selten, eds, *Bounded Rationality: The Adaptive Toolbox* (Cambridge, MA: MIT Press, 2001).

Goldie, Peter, *The Emotions: A Philosophical Exploration* (Oxford: Clarendon Press, 2000).

Goldie, Peter, 'Anti-Empathy', in Amy Coplan and Peter Goldie (eds), *Empathy: Philosophical and Psychological Perspectives* (Oxford: Oxford University Press, 2011), 302–17.

Goldman, Alvin, *Simulating Minds: The Philosophy, Psychology, and Neuroscience of Mindreading* (Oxford: Oxford University Press, 2006).

Goodman, Nelson, and Catherine Z. Elgin, *Reconceptions in Philosophy and Other Arts and Sciences* (Indianapolis: Hackett, 1988).

Gopnik, Alison, 'Cells that Read Minds?', *Slate* (26 Apr. 2007). <http://www.slate.com/articles/life/brains/2007/04/cells_that_read_minds.single.html>.

Gould, Stephen Jay, 'Biological Potentiality versus Biological Determinism', in *Ever Since Darwin: Reflections in Natural History* (Harmondsworth: Pelican, 1980), 251–9.

Gracyk, Theodore, *Rhythm and Noise: An Aesthetics of Rock* (Durham, NC: Duke University Press, 1996).

Granel, Gérard, *Le sens du temps et de la perception chez Husserl* (Paris: Gallimard, 1968).

Grau, Christopher, '*American History X*, Cinematic Manipulation, and Moral Conversion', in 'Film and the Emotions', *Midwest Studies in Philosophy*, 34 (2010): 52–76. doi:10.1111/j.1475-4975.2010.00210.x.

Green, Mitchell S., *Self-Expression* (Oxford: Clarendon Press, 2007).

Greenspan, Patricia, *Emotions and Reasons: An Inquiry into Emotional Justification* (New York: Routledge, 1988).

Grice, Paul, 'Meaning', in *Studies in the Way of Words* (Cambridge, MA: Harvard University Press, 1989), 213–23.

Griffiths, Paul E., *What Emotions Really Are: The Problem of Psychological Categories* (Chicago: University of Chicago Press, 1997).

Grodal, Torben, *Embodied Visions: Evolution, Emotion, Culture, and Film* (Oxford: Oxford University Press, 2009).

Harré, Rom, ed., *The Social Construction of Emotions* (Oxford: Oxford University Press, 1986).

Hasson, Uri, Ohad Landesman, Barbara Knappmeyer, Ignacio Vallines, Nava Rubin, and David J. Heeger, 'Neurocinematics: The Neuroscience of Film', *Projections*, 2/1 (Summer 2008): 1–26. doi:10:3167/proj.2008.020102.

Hawkins, Jeff, *On Intelligence* (New York: Henry Holt, 2004).

Hatfield, Elaine, John T. Cacioppo, and Richard L. Rapson, *Emotional Contagion* (Cambridge: Cambridge University Press, 1994).

Hayek, F. A., 'Degrees of Explanation', *British Journal for the Philosophy of Science*, 6/3 (1955): 209–25. doi:10.1093/bjps/VI.23.209.

Hegel, G. W. F., *Phenomenology of Spirit*, tr. A. V. Miller (Oxford: Oxford University Press, 1977).

Heider, Fritz, and Marianne Simmel, 'An Experimental Study of Apparent Behavior', *American Journal of Psychology*, 57/2 (Apr. 1944): 243–59.

Heimann, Katrin, Maria Alessandra Umilti, Michele Guerra, and Vittorio Gallese, 'Moving Mirrors: A High-Density EEG Study Investigating the Effect of Camera Movements on Motor Cortex Activation during Action Observation', *Journal of Cognitive Neuroscience*, 26/9 (Sept. 2014): 2087–101. doi:10.1162/jocn_a_00602.

Hickok, Gregory, *The Myth of Mirror Neurons: The Real Science of Communication and Cognition* (New York: W. W. Norton & Co., 2014).

Hirstein, William, *Brain Fiction: Self-Deception and the Riddle of Confabulation* (Cambridge, MA: MIT Press, 2006).

Hobson, J. Allan, *The Dreaming Brain: How the Brain Creates Both the Sense and the Nonsense of Dreams* (New York: Basic Books, 1988).

Hobson, J. Allan, Edward F. Pace-Schott, and Robert Stickgold, 'Dreaming and the Brain: Toward a Cognitive Neuroscience of Conscious States', *Behavioral and Brain Sciences*, 23/6 (2000): 793–842.

Hogan, Patrick C., *Cognitive Science, Literature, and the Arts: A Guide for Humanists* (London: Routledge, 2003).

Hornby, Nick, *Fever Pitch: A Fan's Life* (London: Victor Gollancz, 1992).

Hurford, James R., 'The Neural Basis of Predicate-Argument Structure', *Behavorial and Brain Sciences*, 26/3 (2003): 261–83. doi:10.1017/S0140525X03000074.

Hurford, James R., *The Origins of Meaning* (Oxford: Oxford University Press, 2007).

Hurley, Susan, 'Animal Action in the Space of Reasons', *Mind and Language*, 18/3 (June 2003): 231–56.

Hurley, Susan, and Matthew Nudds, eds, *Rational Animals?* (Oxford: Oxford University Press, 2006).

Husserl, Edmund, *Cartesian Meditations: An Introduction to Phenomenology*, tr. Dorion Cairns (Dordrecht: Kluwer, 1960).

Hyman, John, 'Art and Neuroscience', in Roman Frigg and Matthew C. Hunter (eds), *Beyond Mimesis and Convention: Representation in Art and Science* (Dordrecht: Springer, 2010), 245–61.

Iacoboni, Marco, 'Who Really Won the Super Bowl?', *Edge*, 2 May 2006. <http://edge.org/conversation/who-really-won-the-super-bowl>.

Iacoboni, Marco, *Mirroring People: The New Science of How we Connect with Others* (New York: Farrar, Straus & Giroux, 2008).

Iacoboni, Marco, 'Within Each Other: Neural Mechanisms for Empathy in the Primate Brain', in Amy Coplan and Peter Goldie (eds), *Empathy: Philosophical and Psychological Perspectives* (Oxford: Oxford University Press, 2011), 45–57.

Irvin, Sherri, 'Is Aesthetic Experience Possible?', in Gregory Currie, Matthew Kieran, Aaron Meskin, and Jon Robson (eds), *Aesthetics and the Sciences of Mind* (Oxford: Oxford University Press, 2014), 37–56. doi:10.1093/acprof:oso/9780199669639.001.0001.

Iseminger, Gary, 'How Strange a Sadness?', *Journal of Aesthetics and Art Criticism*, 42/1 (1983): 81–2. doi:10.2307/429949.

Izard, Carroll E., *The Face of Emotion* (New York: Appleton-Century-Crofts, 1971).

Jackendoff, Ray, *Consciousness and the Computational Mind* (Cambridge, MA: MIT Press, 1987).

Jackson, Frank, 'Epiphenomenal Qualia', *Philosophical Quarterly*, 32/127 (Apr. 1982): 127–36. doi:10.2307/2960077.

Jackson, Frank, *From Metaphysics to Ethics: A Defence of Conceptual Analysis* (Oxford: Clarendon Press, 1998).

Jackson, Frank, 'Postscript on Qualia', in Peter Ludlow, Yujin Nagasawa, and Daniel Stoljar (eds), *There's Something about Mary: Essays on Phenomenal Consciousness and Frank Jackson's Knowledge Argument* (Cambridge, MA: MIT Press, 2004), 417–20.

Jackson, Frank, 'Colour for Representationalists', *Erkenntnis*, 66 (2007): 169–85. doi:10.1007/s10670-006-9031-0.

Jacob, Pierre, and Marc Jeannerod, *Ways of Seeing: The Scope and Limits of Visual Cognition* (Oxford: Oxford University Press, 2003).

James, William, 'What is an Emotion?', *Mind*, 9/34 (Apr. 1884): 188–205. doi:10.1093/mind/os-IX.34.188.

James, William, *The Principles of Psychology*, i (New York: Dover Publications, 1950).

James, William, *The Principles of Psychology*, ii (New York: Dover Publications, 1950).

Johnson, Ben, 'Scientists Turn Brain Activity into Moving Images', *Slate*, 24 Sept. 2011. <http://slatest.slate.com/posts/2011/09/24/scientists_turn_brain_activity_into_moving_images.html>.

Jones, Ward E., 'Philosophy and the Ethical Significance of Spectatorship', in Ward E. Jones and Samantha Vice (eds), *Ethics at the Cinema* (Oxford: Oxford University Press, 2011), 1–19.

Kalinak, Kathryn, *Settling the Score: Music and the Classical Hollywood Film* (Madison: University of Wisconsin Press, 1992).

Kandel, Eric R., *The Age of Insight: The Quest to Understand the Unconscious in Art, Mind, and Brain, from Vienna 1900 to the Present* (New York: Random House, 2012).

Kant, Immanuel, *Critique of Pure Reason*, tr. Norman Kemp Smith (Houndmills: Palgrave, 1929).

Kant, Immanuel, *The Critique of Judgement*, tr. James Creed Meredith (Oxford: Clarendon Press, 1952).

Kappas, Arvid, 'What Facial Expressions Can and Cannot Tell us about Emotions', in Mary Katsikitis (ed.), *The Human Face: Measurement and Meaning* (Dordrecht: Kluwer Academic Publishers, 2003), 215–34.

Kawin, Bruce F., *Mindscreen: Bergman, Godard and First-Person Film* (Princeton: Princeton University Press, 1978).

Keil, Geert, 'Naturalism', in Dermot Moran (ed.), *The Routledge Companion to Twentieth Century Philosophy* (London: Routledge, 2010), 254–307.

Keltner, Dacher, *Born to be Good: The Science of a Meaningful Life* (New York: W. W. Norton & Co., 2009).

Keysers, Christian, Jon H. Kaas, and Valeria Gazzola, 'Somatosensation in Social Perception', *Nature Reviews: Neuroscience*, 11/6 (June 2010): 417–28. doi:10.1038/nrn2833.

Kieran, Matthew, 'In Search of a Narrative', in Matthew Kieran and Dominic McIver Lopes (eds), *Imagination, Philosophy, and the Arts* (New York: Routledge, 2003), 69–87.

Kim, Jaegwon, *Physicalism, or Something Near Enough* (Princeton: Princeton University Press, 2005).

Kitcher, Philip, 'The Naturalists Return', *Philosophical Review*, 101/1 (1992): 53–114. doi:10.2307/2185044.

Kitcher, Philip, 'Seeing is Unbelieving', review of Alex Rosenberg, *The Atheist's Guide to Reality* (2011), *New York Times* (25 Mar. 2012): BR31. <http:www.nytimes.com/2012/03/25books/review/alex-rosenbergstheatheistsguide-to-reality.html>.

Kivy, Peter, 'Mozart's Skull', in *Sounding Off: Eleven Essays in the Philosophy of Music* (Oxford: Oxford University Press, 2012), 3–22.

Kosslyn, Stephen M., 'On the Evolution of Human Motivation: The Role of Social Prosthetic Systems', in Steven Platek, Julian Paul Keenan, and Todd Shackelford (eds), *Evolutionary Cognitive Neuroscience* (Cambridge, MA: MIT Press, 2007), 541–54.

Kovács, András Bálint, 'Sartre, the Philosophy of Nothingness, and the Modern Melodrama', in Murray Smith and Thomas E. Wartenberg (eds), *Thinking through Cinema: Film as Philosophy* (Malden, MA: Blackwell, 2006), 135–46.

Kramer, Mette, 'The Mating Game in Hollywood Cinema: A Darwinian Approach', *New Review of Film and Television Studies*, 2/2 (Nov. 2004): 137–59. doi:10.1080/1740030042000276626.

Krohn, Bill, *Hitchcock at Work* (London: Phaidon, 2000).

Kuleshov, Lev, *Kuleshov on Film*, tr. Ronald Levaco (Berkeley, CA: University of California Press, 1974).

Kuper, Adam, *Culture: The Anthropologists' Account* (Cambridge, MA: Harvard University Press, 1999).

Lackner, James, and Merrill F. Garrett, 'Resolving Ambiguity: Effects of Biasing Context in the Unattended Ear', *Cognition*, 1/4 (1972): 359–72. doi:10.1016/0010-0277(72)90002-9.

Lang, Peter J., Margaret M. Bradley, and Bruce N. Cuthbert, 'Emotion, Attention, and the Startle Reflex', *Psychological Review*, 97/3 (July 1990): 377–95. doi:10.1037/0033-295X.97.3.377.

Lazarus, Richard S., *Emotion and Adaptation* (New York: Oxford University Press, 1991).

Leavis, F. R., *Two Cultures? The Significance of C. P. Snow* (Cambridge: Cambridge University Press, 2013).

Leddington, Jason, 'The Experience of Magic', *Journal of Aesthetics and Art Criticism*, 74/3 (Summer 2016): 253–64. doi:10.1111/jaac.12290.

LeDoux, Joseph, *The Emotional Brain: The Mysterious Underpinnings of Emotional Life* (New York: Simon & Schuster, 1996).

Levin, Daniel T., and Daniel J. Simons, 'Failure to Detect Changes to Attended Objects in Motion Pictures', *Psychonomic Bulletin and Review*, 4/4 (Dec. 1997): 501–6. doi:10.3758/BF03214339.

Levine, Joseph, 'Materialism and Qualia: The Explanatory Gap', *Pacific Philosophical Quarterly*, 64 (Oct. 1983): 354–61.

Levitin, Daniel, *This is your Brain on Music: Understanding a Human Obsession* (New York: Dutton, 2006).

Lewis, David, 'Postscripts to "Truth in Fiction"', in *Philosophical Papers*, i (New York: Oxford University Press, 1983), 276–9.

Lewis, David, 'Causal Explanation', in *Philosophical Papers*, ii (Oxford: Oxford University Press, 1986), 214–40.

Livingston, Paisley, *Cinema, Philosophy, Bergman: On Film as Philosophy* (Oxford: Oxford University Press, 2009).

Livingston, Paisley, 'On the Appreciation of Cinematic Adaptations', *Projections*, 4/2 (Winter 2010): 104–27. doi:10.3167/proj.2010.040207.

Locke, John, *An Essay Concerning Human Understanding*, ed. Peter H. Nidditch (Oxford: Oxford University Press, 1975).

Lodge, David, *Thinks...* (London: Penguin, 2002).

Lopes, Dominic, *Understanding Pictures* (Oxford: Clarendon Press, 1996).

Lopes, Dominic McIver, 'Pictures and the Representational Mind', *The Monist*, 86/4 (Jan. 2003): 645–6. doi:10.5840/monist200386432.

Lopes, Dominic McIver, 'The Empathic Eye', in Amy Coplan and Peter Goldie(eds), *Empathy: Philosophical and Psychological Perspectives* (Oxford: Oxford University Press, 2011), 118–33.

Lopes, Dominic McIver, 'Afterword: Photography and the "Picturesque Agent"', *Critical Inquiry*, 38/4 (Summer 2012): 855–69. doi:10.1086/667427.

Ludlow, Peter, Yujin Nagasawa, and Daniel Stoljar, eds, *There's Something about Mary: Essays on Phenomenal Consciousness and Frank Jackson's Knowledge Argument* (Cambridge, MA: MIT Press, 2004).

Luria, A. R., *The Man with a Shattered World: The History of a Brain Wound* (Cambridge, MA: Harvard University Press, 1987).

Lutz, Catherine A., *Unnatural Emotions: Everyday Sentiments on a Micronesian Atoll and their Challenge to Western Theory* (Chicago: University of Chicago Press, 1988).

Macarthur, David, review of Jack Ritchie, *Understanding Naturalism* (2008), *Notre Dame Philosophical Reviews*, 10 Nov. 2009. <https://ndpr.nd.edu/news/24219-understanding-naturalism>.

McGinn, Colin, 'Can the Brain Explain your Mind?', *New York Review of Books*, 24 Mar. 2011. <http://www.nybooks.com/articles/archives/2011/mar/24/can-brain-explain-your-mind>.

McGinn, Colin, 'Storm Over the Brain', *New York Review of Books*, 24 Apr. 2014. <http://www.nybooks.com/articles/2014/04/24/storm-over-the-brain>.

Machery, Edouard, *Doing without Concepts* (Oxford: Oxford University Press, 2009).

Mack, Arien, and Irwin Rock, *Inattentional Blindness* (Cambridge, MA: MIT Press, 1998).

Mackie, J. L., *Ethics: Inventing Right and Wrong* (Harmondsworth: Penguin, 1977).

McWhorter, John H., *The Language Hoax: Why the World Looks the Same in Any Language* (New York: Oxford University Press, 2014).

Maes, Hans, ed., *Pornographic Art and the Aesthetics of Pornography* (Basingstoke: Palgrave Macmillan, 2013).

Maes, Hans, ed., *Conversations on Art and Aesthetics* (Oxford: Oxford University Press, forthcoming 2017).

Maes, Hans, and Jerrold Levinson, eds, *Art and Pornography: Philosophical Essays* (Oxford: Oxford University Press, 2012).

Marcus, Gary, *Kluge: The Haphazard Construction of the Human Mind* (London: Faber, 2008).

Martin, M. G. F., 'Perception, Concepts, and Memory', *Philosophical Review* 101/4 (Oct. 1992), 758–9.

Martin, Mike, 'Brian O'Shaughnessy Obituary', *Guardian*, 14 July 2010. <http://www.theguardian.com/books/2010/jul/14/brian-oshaughnessy-obituary>.

Maynard, Patrick, 'Drawing Distinctions I: The First Projects', *Philosophical Topics*, 25/1 (Spring 1997): 231–53.

Maynard, Patrick, *The Engine of Visualization: Thinking through Photography* (Ithaca, NY: Cornell University Press, 1997).

Mayr, Ernst, *What Evolution Is* (London: Weidenfeld & Nicolson, 2002).

Merleau-Ponty, Maurice, *Texts and Dialogues: On Philosophy, Politics, and Culture*, tr. and ed. Hugh Silverman and James Barry (Amherst, NY: Prometheus Press, 1996).

Michelson, Annette, 'Toward Snow', *Artforum*, 9 (1971): 30–7.

Millikan, Ruth Garrett, *Varieties of Meaning* (Cambridge, MA: MIT Press, 2004).

Millikan, Ruth Garrett, 'Biosemantics', in Brian P. McLaughlin, Ansgar Beckermann, and Sven Walter (eds), *The Oxford Handbook of Philosophy of Mind* (Oxford: Oxford University Press, 2009), 394–406.

Milner, David, and Melvyn A. Goodale, 'Separate Visual Pathways for Perception and Action', *Trends in Neurosciences*, 15/1 (1992): 20–5. doi:10.1016/0166-2236(92)90344-8.

Morris, Errol, 'Abu Ghraib Essays (Photographs Reveal and Conceal)', *Believing is Seeing: Observations on the Mysteries of Photography* (New York: Penguin Press, 2011), 75–122.

Motluk, Alison, 'Read My Mind', *New Scientist*, 169/2275 (27 Jan. 2001): 22.

Motluk, Alison, 'Mirror Neurons Control Erection Response to Porn', *New Scientist*, 16 June 2008. <http://www.newscientist.com/article/dn14147-mirror-neurons-control-erection-response-to-porn.html>.

Mulhall, Stephen, *On Film*, 3rd edn (London: Routledge, 2015).

Munro, Thomas, *Towards Science in Aesthetics: Selected Essays* (New York: Liberal Arts Press, 1956).

Münsterberg, Hugo, *The Photoplay: A Psychological Study* (1916), in *Hugo Münsterberg on Film: The Photoplay: A Psychological Study and Other Writings*, ed. Alan Langdale (New York: Routledge, 2002), 45–163.

Nanay, Bence, *Aesthetics as Philosophy of Perception* (Oxford: Oxford University Press, 2016).

Neurath, Otto, 'Anti-Splenger', in Marie Neurath and Robert S. Cohen (eds), *Empiricism and Sociology* (Dordrecht: D. Reidel, 1973), 158–213.

Newman, Michael Z., 'Characterization as Social Cognition in *Welcome to the Dollhouse*', *Film Studies: An International Review*, 8 (Summer 2006): 53–67.

Nisbett, Richard E., and Timothy DeCamp Wilson, 'Telling More than we Can Know: Verbal Reports on Mental Processes', *Psychological Review*, 84/3 (May 1977): 231–59. doi:10.1037/0033-295X.84.3.231.

Nussbaum, Martha, *Love's Knowledge: Essays on Philosophy and Literature* (New York: Oxford University Press, 1990).

Nussbaum, Martha, *Upheavals of Thought: The Intelligence of Emotions* (New York: Cambridge University Press, 2001).

O'Shaughnessy, Brian, *The Will: A Dual Aspect Theory*, ii (Cambridge: Cambridge University Press, 1980).

O'Shaughnessy, Brian, *Consciousness and the World* (Oxford: Clarendon Press, 2000).

Oatley, Keith, and Jennifer M. Jenkins, *Understanding Emotions* (Oxford: Blackwell, 1996).

Odling-Smee, F. John, Kevin N. Laland, and Marcus W. Feldman, *Niche Construction: The Neglected Process in Evolution* (Princeton: Princeton University Press, 2003).

Ortolano, Guy, *The Two Cultures Controversy: Science, Literature and Cultural Politics in Postwar Britain* (Cambridge: Cambridge University Press, 2009).

Owen, Adrian M., Martin R. Coleman, Melanie Boly, Matthew H. Davis, Steven Laureys, and John D. Pickard, 'Detecting Awareness in the Vegetative State', *Science*, 313/5792 (8 Sept. 2006): 1402. doi:10.1126/science.1130197.

Panksepp, Jaak, 'What is Neuropsychoanalysis? Clinically Relevant Studies of the Minded Brain', *Trends in Cognitive Sciences*, 16/1 (Jan. 2012): 6–8. doi:10.1016/j.tics.2011.11.005.

Paver, Michelle, *Wolf Brother* (London: Orion Children's Books, 2004).

Peterson, James, *Dreams of Chaos, Visions of Order: Understanding the American Avant-Garde Cinema* (Detroit: Wayne State University Press, 1994).

Petkova, Valeria I., and H. Henrik Ehrsson, 'If I Were You: Perceptual Illusion of Body Swapping', *PloS ONE,* 3/12 (Dec. 2008): 1–9. doi:10.1371/journal.pone.0003832.

Pinkard, Terry, *Hegel's Naturalism: Mind, Nature, and the Final Ends of Life* (New York: Oxford University Press, 2012).

Pinker, Steven, *How the Mind Works* (London: Penguin, 1999).

Pinker, Steven, *The Stuff of Thought: Language as a Window into Human Nature* (London: Penguin, 2008).

Pinker, Steven, 'The Cognitive Revolution', *Harvard Gazette,* 12 Oct. 2011. <http://news.harvard.edu/gazette/story/2011/10/the-cognitive-revolution>.

Pinker, Steven, 'Science is Not your Enemy', *New Republic,* 6 Aug. 2013. <http://www.newrepublic.com//article/114127/science-not-enemy-humanities>.

Plantinga, Carl, 'The Scene of Empathy and the Human Face on Film', in Carl Plantinga and Greg M. Smith (eds), *Passionate Views: Film, Cognition, and Emotion* (Baltimore: Johns Hopkins University Press, 1999), 239–55.

Plantinga, Carl, *Moving Viewers: American Film and the Spectator's Experience* (Berkeley, CA: University of California Press, 2009).

Price, Carolyn, *Functions in Mind: A Theory of Intentional Content* (Oxford: Clarendon Press, 2001).

Prince, Stephen, and Wayne Hensley, 'The Kuleshov Effect: Recreating the Classic Experiment', *Cinema Journal,* 31/2 (Winter 1992): 59–75.

Prinz, Jesse J., *Gut Reactions: A Perceptual Theory of Emotion* (Oxford: Oxford University Press, 2004).

Prinz, Jesse, 'Which Emotions are Basic?', in Dylan Evans and Pierre Cruse (eds), *Emotion, Evolution, and Rationality* (Oxford: Oxford University Press, 2004), 69–87.

Prinz, Jesse J., *The Emotional Construction of Morals* (New York: Oxford University Press, 2007).

Prinz, Jesse J., *Beyond Human Nature: How Culture and Experience Shape our Lives* (London: Penguin, 2012).

Proust, Marcel, *Remembrance of Things Past* [1913–27], tr. C. K. Scott Moncrieff, M. Kilmartin, and Terence Kilmartin (London: Chatto & Windus, 1981).

Pudovkin, V. I., *Film Technique and Film Acting* (London: Vision Press, 1954).

Quilty-Dunn, Jake, 'Believing our Eyes: The Role of False Belief in our Experience of Cinema', *British Journal of Aesthetics,* 55/3 (July 2015): 269–83. doi:10.1093/aesthj/ayv016.

Quine, Willard Van Orman, *Word and Object* (Cambridge, MA: MIT Press, 1960).

Quine, W. V. *Quintessence,* ed. Roger F. Gibson Jr (Cambridge, MA: Harvard University Press, 2008).

Raffman, Diana, *Language, Music, and Mind* (Cambridge, MA: MIT Press, 1993).

Ramachandran, Vilayanur S., *The Emerging Mind: The Reith Lectures 2003* (London: Profile Books, 2003).

Ramachandran, V. S., *The Tell-Tale Brain* (New York: W. W. Norton & Co., 2011).

Ramachandran, V. S., and Sandra Blakeslee, *Phantoms in the Brain: Human Nature and the Architecture of the Mind* (London: Fourth Estate, 1998).

Ramachandran, V. S., and William Hirstein, 'The Science of Art: A Neurological Theory of Aesthetic Experience', *Journal of Consciousness Studies,* 6/6–7 (1999): 15–51.

Raz, Gal, Yonatan Winetraub, Yael Jacob, Sivan Kinreich, Adi Maron-Katz, Galit Shaham, Ilana Podlipsky, Gadi Gilam, Eyal Soreq, and Talma Hendler, 'Portraying Emotions at their

Unfolding: A Multilayered Approach for Probing Dynamics of Neural Networks', *Neuro-Image*, 59/2 (16 Jan. 2012): 1448–61. doi:10.1016/j.neuroimage.2011.12.084.

Renner, Karen, 'Repeat Viewings Revisited: Emotion, Memory, and *Memento*', *Film Studies: An International Review*, 8 (2006): 106–15.

Rensink, Ronald A., J. Kevin O'Regan, and James J. Clark, 'To See or Not to See: The Need for Attention to Perceive Changes in Scenes', *Psychological Science*, 8/5 (Sept. 1997): 368–73. doi:10.1111/j.1467-9280.1997.tb00427.x.

Ridley, Matt, *The Origins of Virtue* (London: Penguin, 1997).

Rizzolatti, Giacomo, and Corrado Sinigaglia, *Mirrors in the Brain: How our Minds Share Actions and Emotions*, tr. Frances Anderson (Oxford: Oxford University Press, 2006).

Roberts, Robert C., *Emotions: An Essay in Aid of Moral Psychology* (Cambridge: Cambridge University Press, 2003).

Robinson, Jenefer, *Deeper than Reason: Emotion and its Role in Literature, Music, and Art* (Oxford: Clarendon Press, 2005).

Rollins, Mark, 'Neurology and the New Riddle of Pictorial Style', in Elisabeth Schellekens and Peter Goldie (eds), *The Aesthetic Mind: Philosophy and Psychology* (Oxford: Oxford University Press, 2011), 391–413.

Rosenberg, Alex, *The Atheist's Guide to Reality: Enjoying Life without Illusions* (New York: W. W. Norton & Co., 2012).

Rothman, Roger, and Ian Verstegen, 'Arnheim's Lesson: Cubism, Collage, and Gestalt Psychology', *Journal of Aesthetics and Art Criticism*, 65/3 (Summer 2007): 287–98. doi:10.1111/j.1540-594X.2007.00259.x.

Rowlands, Mark, *The Philosopher and the Wolf: Lessons from the Wild on Love, Death and Happiness* (London: Granta, 2008).

Ryle, Gilbert, *The Concept of Mind* (London: Hutchinson's University Library, 1949).

Ryle, Gilbert, 'The Thinking of Thoughts: What is "Le Penseur" Doing?', in *Collected Essays 1929–1968* (London: Routledge, 2009), 494–509.

Sacks, Oliver, *The Man Who Mistook his Wife for a Hat* (London: Duckworth, 1985).

Sacks, Oliver, 'In the River of Consciousness', *New York Review of Books*, 51/1 (15 Jan. 2004), 41–4. <http://www.nybooks.com/articles/2004/01/15/in-the-river-of-consciousness/>.

Salt, Barry, *Film Style and Technology: History and Analysis*, 3rd edn (London: Starword, 2009).

Santayana, George, 'Dewey's Naturalistic Metaphysics', *Journal of Philosophy*, 22/25 (1925): 673–88. doi:10.2307/2013919.

Sartwell, Crispin, *Six Names of Beauty* (New York: Routledge, 2004).

Satel, Sally, and Scott O. Lilienfeld, *Brainwashed: The Seductive Appeal of Mindless Neuroscience* (New York: Basic Books, 2013).

Sayers, Sean, 'A Note on Emergent Materialism', unpublished paper. <https://kent.academia.edu/seansayers/Unpublished-papers>.

Schwitzgebel, Eric, *Perplexities of Consciousness* (Cambridge, MA: MIT Press, 2011).

Schmitz, Hermann, 'Emotions Outside of the Box: The New Phenomenology of Feelings and Corporeality', tr. Rudolf Owen Müllan and Jan Slaby, *Phenomenology and the Cognitive Sciences*, 10/2 (June 2011): 241–59. doi:10.1007/s11097-011-9195-1.

Scott, A. O., 'Almodóvar's Happy Agony, Swirling amid Jealousy and Revenge', *New York Times*, 20 Nov. 2009, C14. <http://movies.nytimes.com/2009/11/20/movies/20broken.html>.

Searle, John R., 'Twenty-One Years in the Chinese Room', in John Preston and Mark Bishop (eds), *Views into the Chinese Room: New Essays on Searle and Artificial Intelligence* (Oxford: Clarendon Press, 2002), 51–69.

Seeley, William, 'What is the Cognitive Neuroscience of Art . . . And Why Should We Care?', *ASA Newsletter*, 31/2 (Summer 2011): 1–4.

Sellars, Roy Wood, *Evolutionary Naturalism* (New York: Russell & Russell, 1922).

Sellars, Wilfrid, 'Philosophy and the Scientific Image of Man', in Robert Colodny (ed.), *Frontiers of Science and Philosophy* (Pittsburgh, PA: University of Pittsburgh Press, 1962), 35–78.

Sellars, Wilfrid, *Empiricism and the Philosophy of Mind*, ed. Robert Brandom (Cambridge, MA: Harvard University Press, 1997).

Shimojo, Shinsuke, and Ladan Shams, 'Sensory Modalities are Not Separate Modalities: Plasticity and Interactions', *Current Opinion in Neurobiology*, 11/4 (Aug. 2001): 505–9. doi:10.1016/S0959-4388(00)00241-5.

Shklovsky, Viktor, *Theory of Prose*, tr. Benjamin Sher (Elmwood Park: Dalkey Archive Press, 1991).

Silver, Curtis, 'Neurocinema Aims to Change the Way Movies are Made', *Wired*, 23 Sept. 2009. <http://www.wired.com/geekdad/2009/09/neurocinema-aims-to-change-the-way-movies-are-made>.

Simons, Ronald C., *Boo! Culture, Experience, and the Startle Reflex* (Oxford: Oxford University Press, 1996).

Sinnerbrink, Robert, *New Philosophies of Film* (London: Continuum, 2011).

Smith, Greg M., *Film Structure and the Emotion System* (New York: Cambridge University Press, 2003).

Smith, Michael, *Ethics and the A Priori: Selected Essays on Moral Psychology and Meta-Ethics* (Cambridge: Cambridge University Press, 2004).

Smith, Murray, *Engaging Characters: Fiction, Emotion, and the Cinema* (Oxford: Clarendon Press, 1995).

Smith, Murray, 'Film Spectatorship and the Institution of Fiction', *Journal of Aesthetics and Art Criticism*, 53/1 (1995): 113–27. doi:10.2307/431540.

Smith, Murray, 'Imagining from the Inside', in Richard Allen and Murray Smith (eds), *Film Theory and Philosophy* (Oxford: Clarendon Press, 1997), 412–30.

Smith, Murray, 'Regarding Film Spectatorship: A Reply to Richard Allen', *Journal of Aesthetics and Art Criticism*, 56/1 (1998): 63–5. doi:10.2307/431952.

Smith, Murray, '(A)moral Monstrosity', in Michael Grant (ed.), *The Films of David Cronenberg* (Trowbridge: Flicks Books, 2000), 69–83.

Smith, Murray, 'Film Art, Argument, and Ambiguity', in Murray Smith and Thomas E. Wartenberg (eds), *Thinking through Cinema* (Malden, MA: Blackwell, 2006), 33–41.

Smith, Murray, 'Just What is it that Makes Tony Soprano Such an Appealing, Attractive Murderer?', in Ward E. Jones and Samantha Vice (eds), *Ethics at the Cinema* (Oxford: Oxford University Press, 2011), 66–90.

Smith, Murray, 'Against Nature? Or, Confessions of a Darwinian Modernist', in 'Philosophical Aesthetics and the Sciences of Art', *Royal Institute of Philosophy Supplement*, 75 (Oct. 2014): 151–82. doi:10.1017/S1358246114000174.

Smith, Tim J., 'The Attentional Theory of Continuity', *Projections*, 6/1 (June 2012): 1–27. doi: 10.3167/proj.2012.060102.

Snow, C. P., 'The Two Cultures', *New Statesman,* 6 Oct. 1956, 413–14. <http://www. newstatesman.com/cultural-capital/2013/01/c-p-snow-two-cultures>.

Snow, C. P., *The Two Cultures* (Cambridge: Cambridge University Press, 1998).

Sobchak, Vivian, 'Phenomenology', in Paisley Livingston and Carl Plantinga (eds), *The Routledge Companion to Philosophy and Film* (New York: Routledge, 2009), 435–45.

Sober, Elliot, 'Models of Cultural Evolution', in Elliot Sober (ed.), *Conceptual Issues in Evolutionary Biology,* 2nd edn (Cambridge, MA: MIT Press, 1994), 489.

Sperber, Dan, *Explaining Culture: A Naturalistic Approach* (Oxford: Blackwell, 1996).

Sperber, Dan, 'Comment on Michael Tomasello, *Origins of Human Communication'* (2008), <https://mitpress.mit.edu/books/origins-human-communication>.

Starr, G. Gabrielle, *Feeling Beauty: The Neuroscience of Aesthetic Experience* (Cambridge, MA: MIT Press, 2013).

Sterelny, Kim, *Thought in a Hostile World: The Evolution of Human Cognition* (Malden, MA: Blackwell, 2005).

Strawson, Galen, *Consciousness and its Place in Nature: Does Physicalism Entail Panpsychism?* (Exeter: Imprint Academic Press, 2006).

Strevens, Michael, *Depth: An Account of Scientific Explanation* (Cambridge, MA: Harvard University Press, 2008).

Stueber, Karsten R., *Rediscovering Empathy: Agency, Folk Psychology, and the Human Sciences* (Cambridge, MA: MIT Press, 2006).

Tallis, Raymond, *Not Saussure: A Critique of Post-Saussurean Literary Theory* (Basingstoke: Macmillan Press, 1988).

Tallis, Raymond, *In Defence of Realism* (Lincoln, NE: University of Nebraska Press, 1991).

Tallis, Raymond, *The Knowing Animal: A Philosophical Inquiry into Knowledge and Truth* (Edinburgh: Edinburgh University Press, 2005).

Tallis, Raymond, *The Kingdom of Infinite Space: A Fantastical Journey around your Head* (London: Atlantic, 2008).

Tallis, Raymond, 'License My Roving Hands', *Times Literary Supplement,* 5480 (11 Apr. 2008): 13–15.

Tallis, Raymond, *Aping Mankind: Neuromania, Darwinitis, and the Misrepresentation of Humanity* (Durham: Acumen, 2011).

Thielman, Sam, 'David Cronenberg Speaks', *Variety,* 21 Sept. 2007. <http://variety.com/2007/film/awards/david-cronenberg-speaks-1117972489>.

Tomasello, Michael, *The Cultural Origins of Human Communication* (Cambridge, MA: Harvard University Press, 1999).

Tomasello, Michael, *Origins of Human Communication* (Cambridge, MA: MIT Press, 2008).

Tooby, John, and Leda Cosmides, 'Does Beauty Build Adapted Minds? Toward an Evolutionary Theory of Aesthetics, Fiction, and the Arts', *SubStance,* 30/1–2 (2001): 6–27.

Truffaut, François, *Hitchcock/Truffaut,* rev. edn (New York: Touchstone, 1985).

Tsivian, Yuri, 'About Cinemetrics', <http://www.cinemetrics.lv>.

Vaage, Margrethe Bruun, 'Seeing is Feeling: Empathy and the Film Spectator' (Ph.D. dissertation, University of Oslo, 2009).

Vaage, Margrethe Bruun, *The Antihero in American Television* (London: Routledge, 2015).

van Gulick, Robert, 'Consciousness, Intrinsic Intentionality, and Self-Understanding Machines', in A. J. Marcel and E. Bisiach (eds), *Consciousness in Contemporary Science* (New York: Oxford University Press, 1988), 78–100.

Visch, Valentijn, 'Looking for Genres: The Effect of Film Figure Movement on Genre Recognition' (Ph.D. dissertation, University of Amsterdam, 2007).

Walton, Kendall L., 'Categories of Art', *Philosophical Review*, 79/3 (July 1970): 334–67. doi:10.2307/2183933.

Walton, Kendall L., 'Transparent Pictures: On the Nature of Photographic Realism', *Critical Inquiry*, 11/2 (Dec. 1984): 246–77. <http://www.jstor.org/stable/1343394>.

Walton, Kendall L., *Mimesis as Make-Believe: On the Foundations of the Representational Arts* (Cambridge, MA: Harvard University Press, 1990).

Walton, Kendall, 'Aesthetics: What? Why? And Wherefore?', *Journal of Aesthetics and Art Criticism*, 65/2 (Spring 2007): 147–61. doi:10.1111/j.1540-594X.2007.00246.x.

Walton, Kendall L., 'Postscripts to "Transparent Pictures"', in *Marvelous Images: On Values and the Arts* (Oxford: Oxford University Press, 2008), 110–16.

Wees, William C., *Light Moving in Time: Studies in the Visual Aesthetics of Avant-Garde Film* (Berkeley, CA: University of California Press, 1985).

Wheeler, Tom, *The Stratocaster Chronicles* (Milwaukee: Hal Leonard, 2004).

Whewell, William, *The Philosophy of the Inductive Sciences: Founded upon their History* (London: J. W. Parker, 1840).

Whiten, Andrew, 'The Second Inheritance System of Chimpanzees and Humans', *Nature*, 437 (1 Sept. 2005): 52–5. doi:10.1038/nature04023.

Williams, Bernard, *Ethics and the Limits of Philosophy* (London: Fontana, 1993).

Williamson, Timothy, *The Philosophy of Philosophy* (Malden, MA: Blackwell, 2008).

Williamson, Timothy, 'How did we Get Here from There? The Transformation of Analytic Philosophy', *Belgrade Philosophical Annual*, 27 (2014): 7–37. <http://www.f.bg.ac.rs/bpa/pdf/BPA-27-2014-Timothy-Williamson.pdf>.

Wilson, Edward O., *On Human Nature* (Cambridge, MA: Harvard University Press, 1978).

Wilson, Edward O., *Consilience: The Unity of Knowledge* (London: Little, Brown, & Co., 1998).

Wilson, E. O., *Anthill* (New York: W. W. Norton & Co., 2010).

Wilson, Timothy D., *Strangers to Ourselves: Discovering the Adaptive Unconscious* (Cambridge, MA: Belknap Press, 2002).

Wittgenstein, Ludwig, *Lectures and Conversations on Aesthetics, Psychology and Religious Belief*, ed. Cyril Barrett (Oxford: Blackwell, 1966).

Wolf, William, 'Face to Face with Ingmar Bergman', *New York Magazine*, 13/42 (27 Oct. 1980): 33–8.

Wollheim, Richard, *The Thread of Life* (Cambridge, MA: Harvard University Press, 1984).

Wollheim, Richard, *Painting as an Art* (London: Thames & Hudson, 1987).

Wollheim, Richard, 'Representation: The Philosophical Contribution to Psychology', in *The Mind and its Depths* (Cambridge, MA: Harvard University Press, 1993), 159–70.

Zangwill, Nick, *Metaphysics of Beauty* (Ithaca, NY: Cornell University Press, 2001).

Zeki, Semir, *Inner Vision: An Exploration of Art and the Brain* (Oxford: Oxford University Press, 1999).

Zunshine, Lisa, *Why We Read Fiction: Theory of Mind and the Novel* (Columbia, OH: Ohio State University Press, 2006).

Index

Page numbers in italics denote figures. Foreign films are alphabetized under their English titles.

Churchland, Patricia S. 2, 226 n.9
Churchland, Paul 2, 65–8, 73, 206, 207, 226 n.9, 236 nn.26,27,30, 237 n.32, 247 n.45, 261 nn.28,29,30
Cioffi, Frank 114, 220, 245 n.29, 262 n.3
Clark, Andy 22, 33–4, 73, 104, 185, 186, 188, 195, 210, 227 n.7, 229 n.48, 233 nn.83,84,92, 238 n.43, 244 n.57, 245 n.13, 256 nn.24,25,27,30, 257 nn.31,32, 259 n.59, 261 n.36, 262 n.10
The Clock (Christian Marclay, 2001) 143
Cochran, Robert 131; *see also 24*
cognitive aesthetics (including cognitivism, art history) 154, 155
cognitive architecture 30–1, 49, 103–4, 155, 260 n.23; *see also* bottom-up; *see also* top-down
  modularity of the mind 62
  parallel mental processing 198
  see also information encapsulation
cognitive film theory 14, 23, 33, 84, 153, 231 n.61, 246 n.44, 248 n.7, 251 n.3
cognitive impenetrability 163
cognitive neuroscience 83
cognitive psychology 106–7, 154; *see also* levels of analysis – psychological/functional/ informational
cognitive science 83, 84, 88, 185
Cole, Jonathan 117, 246 n.39
Collini, Stefan 225 n.2, 226 n.13
Sayat Nova/The Colour of Pomegranates (Sergei Parajanov, 1968) 120
combat film 200
comedy 200, 212
  gross-out comedy 200, 203
composition 109, 149
  tableaux 147
  split-screen effect 131
Conan Doyle, Arthur 234 n.108
  Sherlock Holmes 55, 234 n.108
conceptual analysis 9, 26–9; *see also* explanation – theory construction; *see also* explanation – thick explanation
conceptual art 6–7
confabulation 81, 239 n.50
Conrad, Tony 67
consciousness 10, 12, 57, 63–4, 65, 68, 79, 82, 91, 97, 99, 106–23, 165, 179, 185, 197, 206, 222, 239 n.55, 242 n.37, 244 nn.55,2,5,8, 245 nn.13,15,16,17,18,22, 26, 259 n.57
  dreaming 113, 114, 245 n.26
  function of 107–10
  hard problem of 59–60, 110
  perceptual/primary consciousness 111
  representation in films 12, 114–16

self-consciousness 12, 111, 115, 156
unconscious processing (including cognitive or adaptive unconscious) 12, 101, 106–7, 113, 114 , 242 n.37, 259 n.57
Cooper, Rachel 191, 228 n.20, 234 n.104, 258 n.48
Corkin, Suzanne 117, 246 n.39
Cosmides, Leda 235 n.15, 247 n.1
Cox, Billy xii, 177
Crace, Jim 232 n.78
Craven, Wes 216
Crichton, Michael 141
crime film 211
Critchley, Simon 245 n.29, 262 n.3
criticism 17, 53, 58, 69, 122–3, 177, 212, 214–17, 219–21
criticisms of naturalism 85–92, 103
  Darwinitis 87, 241 n.13
  neural behaviourism 11, 79, 80–1
  neurofundamentalism 15–16
  neuromania 86, 87, 241 n.13
Cronenberg, David 114, 184, 194, 256 n.21, 260 n.19
Cronin, Helena 90, 99, 241 n.24, 243 n.52
Cubism 38, 42
culture 15, 33, 37, 50, 51, 91, 98, 127, 136, 141, 149, 152, 155–62, 166, 172, 202, 205, 208, 217, 254 n.54, 261 nn.41,42
  and biology, interaction between 155–62, 164, 214, 247 n.4, 252 n.24; *see also* evolutionary theory – extended phenotype; *see also* bioculturalism
cross-cultural comparison, method of 9, 13–14, 135, 141
cultural elaboration 4, 10, 33, 98, 129, 149, 151, 158, 161, 164, 235 n.18
cultural evolution 159, 252 nn.12,28, 261 n.42
culturalism 10, 15, 101, 155–7, 160–1, 166, 172–3, 175–6; *see also* human nature; *see also* scientism; *see also* explanation; *see also* naturalism; *see also* emotion – as cultural construction
cultural learning 158, 187
cultural particularity/variation 4, 9, 14, 26, 83, 98, 134, 135–7, 139–41, 144–5, 155, 157–8, 160–1, 164, 166, 172–6, 205, 208, 250 n.34, 252 n.13, 253 n.44; *see also* emotion – as cultural construction
cultural universality 4, 9, 14, 83, 135–6, 141, 144–5, 149, 151–2, 155, 158, 160–1, 166, 174–6, 250 n.34, 251 n.7, 253 n.44
  metaculture and specific cultures, distinction between 157, 252 n.12
The Curious Incident of the Dog in the Night-Time (Mark Haddon, 2003) 62
Currie, Gregory 27, 29, 36, 108, 109, 153, 193, 228 n.28, 229 n.36, 231 n.59, 237 n.41, 244 n.7, 247 n.2, 251 n.3, 253 n.32, 254 n.4, 256 n.19, 258 n.53, 259 n.60